MW00426670

LAW PROFESSORS

THREE CENTURIES OF SHAPING AMERICAN LAW

■ ■ ■

Stephen B. Presser

Raoul Berger Professor of Legal History Emeritus
Northwestern Pritzker School of Law
Professor of Strategy
Kellogg School of Management
Northwestern University

WEST
ACADEMIC
PUBLISHING

© 2017 LEG, Inc. d/b/a West Academic
    444 Cedar Street, Suite 700
    St. Paul, MN 55101
    1-877-888-1330

West, West Academic Publishing, and West Academic are trademarks of West Publishing Corporation, used under license.

Printed in the United States of America

ISBN: 978-1-63459-045-7

To Susan Graff

PREFACE

This book is a love letter to the teaching of law. It is a biographical examination of American (and two English) law professors, but its purpose is to illuminate what holds American society together, and to further the understanding of shared American values, in an age when those values are more at risk than at any time for the last sixty years. One way of understanding the current American political turmoil is to see it as a struggle over the manner in which the law ought to be understood and administered, a struggle as old, really as our republic itself. Our two major political parties now understand the rule of law very differently, and these two approaches to the law and to the American Constitution provide consistent threads to the analysis offered here. Anyone seeking to understand American law, the Constitution, or American legal education must come to grips with this basic disagreement about law and legal institutions. One view of the law, one reaching all the way back to Plato, if not before, is that it is a reflection of divine order, but another (also offered by Plato) is that the law is nothing but the will of the powerful in society. Put slightly differently, from the beginning of American history some, like Jefferson, believed that the principles of the law were dictated by nature and by nature's God, while others, like the Jacksonian lawyer, Robert Rantoul, thought the law ought simply to be whatever the American people wanted. Many different dualities have captured this fundamental difference in legal and Constitutional perspective, including the divide between natural lawyers and positivists, that between common lawyers and codifiers, that between advocates of Constitutional original understanding and a Living Constitution, and that between the economic analysts of law and Critical Legal Studies.

The continuing academic, political, Constitutional, and social disagreement about the nature of American law, as well as our simultaneous commitment to the irreconcilable competing American values of democracy, equality, economic progress, individualism and altruism, are the twin dynamics that are explored here in the course of an examination of law professors from Blackstone to Barack Obama. Since John Adams wrote it into the Massachusetts Constitution of 1780, it has been our national aspiration to have "a government of laws, and not of men." This book is the story of how one group of men and women, the law professors, tried, and are still trying, to realize that American ideal.

STEPHEN B. PRESSER

August 2016
Asheville, N.C.

ACKNOWLEDGMENTS

This book would not be appearing were it not for the faith in me and the extraordinary encouragement shown by my editors at West, with whom I have had a relationship since 1980. West Academic's current daring and fearless Editor-in-Chief, Louis Higgins, made the decision to accept the proposal for the book when it was little more than an idea, and an idea rather different from the usual law school casebook. He and his colleagues are the kind of publishers every author dreams of. West Academic's Acquisitions Editor, Bonnie Karlen, has cheerfully worked with me shaping the book and overseeing the collection of the pictures, Greg Olson, West Academic's Manager of Editorial Production, has been in charge of the overall editing of the book, aided by Laura Holle, Lead Publication Specialist, and Michele Bassett, Senior Publication Specialist, my scrupulous and devoted copy editor, who has accommodated my eccentricities, including, for example, my desire to have sequentially numbered footnotes for the whole volume. I'm also grateful to Carol Logie, Senior Layout Designer, for her elegant conception of how the book should look.

Northwestern's Pritzker School of Law has always furnished me with superb research assistants, and one of the best I have ever had, Jeffrey Bingham, did the spadework on all of the subjects here treated, and taught me new cyber technologies in the process. Similar aid was provided by Marco Minichiello, Arnav Dutt, and Aaron Washco. My indefatigable faculty assistant, Timothy Jacobs, was, as usual, indispensable in providing all kinds of logistical support and companionship during the three years the book went from conception to execution. Northwestern's current Dean, Daniel Rodriguez, eased my transition to emeritus status and provided me with extraordinary support, as did his predecessors David Van

Zandt, and Robert Bennett. The friendship and mentoring of David S. Ruder, Dean when I joined Northwestern, whom I served as Associate Dean, and who, really, taught me more than anyone else, what it means to be a law professor, has been an essential foundation for my teaching and research. Something similar might be said of the many hundreds of students both at the School of Law and at Kellogg, from whom I have probably learned more than I have taught.

Some of the analysis in this book was formulated in the course of pieces I wrote for *Chronicles: A Magazine of American Culture* (which I have the privilege of serving as legal affairs editor), and reviews that I wrote for the *University Bookman.* Tom Fleming brought me to *Chronicles*, and I've continued to work happily and productively with Chilton Williamson, Aaron Wolfe, and Scott Richert there. I've been similarly lucky in my relationship with Gerald Russello, at the *University Bookman.* Those five have helped me understand and articulate a paleo-conservative approach to American common and Constitutional law, which has informed the treatments in this book.

I've always thought that Alice got it right when she regarded a book without pictures as useless, and hence the portraits which grace each chapter here. Many people were generous in helping to secure and provide permissions for those pictures, including Lesley Schoenfeld and Lorin Granger from the Harvard Law School, Janet Conroy at the Yale Law School, Elizabeth Schmalz and Patricia Williams at the Columbia Law School, Claire Stamler-Goody at the University of Chicago, Shelley Rodgers at the University of Michigan, Andrew Park at Duke University, and Caroline Reppert and Steve Petaway, at the United States Supreme Court. Thanks also to Mary Ann Glendon and Tanit Sakakini, Patricia Goldrick and Richard Posner, Matt

Cournoyer from the Senate Office of Elizabeth Warren, Peter Gabel and Katherine Voutyras, and Mark Tushnet.

Four people took on the difficult task of reading the entire manuscript and offering helpful comments, my sister (and valued reading partner) Pamela Presser, my wonderful wife, Susan Graff (to whom this book is dedicated), my beloved friend and sometime collaborator, Gary McDowell, and David Dorsen, who also shared with me his manuscript on his insightful book on Antonin Scalia. Thanks also to Lincoln Caplan for his help and encouragement over the years, Henry and Leigh Bienen, valued colleagues and friends, and one profiled subject here who wishes to remain anonymous, but who considerably improved one chapter.

My own formidable law professors, especially Jack Dawson, James Chadbourn, Vern Countryman, Samuel Thorne, Lon Fuller, Roger Fisher, Louis Loss, Morton Horwitz, Benjamin Kaplan, and Stephen Breyer provided a standard against which I was able to measure the professors treated here. I could also single out each of my other colleagues from Northwestern (and before that Rutgers-Camden and the University of Virginia) whose examples showed me how to teach and understand law, but that might unduly increase the length of these acknowledgements. Finally, my four children, David, Elisabeth, Joseph, and Eastman, in their own inspired diverse endeavors, and in their teasing affection, reminded me, like Candide, of the primacy of tending one's own garden. As is traditional (and I am nothing if not a traditionalist) anything good, insightful, useful, or informative in these pages is to be credited to those here acknowledged, and for anything unduly provocative, wrong, misinformed, or slipshod, especially those things I was advised against, I bear the sole responsibility.

TABLE OF CONTENTS

LAW
PROFESSORS
THREE CENTURIES OF
SHAPING AMERICAN LAW

INTRODUCTION

■ ■ ■

In an extraordinarily frank political memoir revealing his frustrations with his recent service in the federal government presided over by Barack Obama, Leon Panetta, longtime member of Congress, former White House Chief of Staff, former CIA director, and former Secretary of Defense, said of Mr. Obama, that "his most conspicuous weakness [was] a frustrating reticence to engage his opponents and rally support for his cause." Elaborating, Panetta explained, "That is not a failing of ideas or of intellect," but still "[Mr. Obama] does, however, sometimes lack fire." Then came Panetta's most cutting and much-quoted observation, *"Too often, in my view, the president relies on the logic of a law professor rather than the passion of a leader."*[1]

What was it about this sentence that had such resonance for the national commentariat? The implication is that being like a law professor is something that leaders ought scrupulously to avoid. What exactly constitutes wrongful reliance on the "logic of a law professor?" Explaining Mr. Panetta's view, Chris Cizilla, columnist for the Washington Post, stated that "There is a sense that Obama believes that simply proposing his argument is enough to carry the day."[2] To similar effect, Leslie Gelb,

---

[1]   Leon Panetta with Jim Newton, Worthy Fights: A Memoir of Leadership in War and Peace 442 (Penguin Press, 2014) (Emphasis supplied).

[2]   Chris Cizilla, "Leon Panetta boiled down Democrats' criticism of Barack Obama to one sentence," Washington Post, October 7, 2014, available at http://www.washingtonpost.com/blogs/the-fix/wp/2014/10/07/leon-panetta-boiled-down-democrats-criticism-of-barack-obama-to-one-sentence/ (accessed October 24, 2014).

another pundit, suggested that President Obama was "first rate as an intellectual thinker [sic] but he thinks about problems as an intellectual and not as a policy maker and a leader."[3]

What does this mean? When might it be wrong to be "an intellectual thinker" rather than a policy maker or leader? What sort of a person is the law professor? One intriguing description was that offered by the brilliant radical law professor Duncan Kennedy, when he was a Yale Law Student:

> One of the first and most lasting impressions that many students have of the Law School is that the teachers are either astoundingly intellectually self-confident or just plain *smug*. Many of them seem to their students to be preening themselves before their classes. In most cases, each gesture seems to say: "I am brilliant. I am famous in the only community that matters. I am doing the most difficult and most desirable thing in the world, and doing it well. I am being a Law Professor."[4]

How did we Americans reach the point where there is a public perception that law professors may be habitually deluding themselves, or, indeed, the point where it can be argued that that is what law professors *do*? What has brought us to the view that there is something self-mesmerizing and debilitating in legal pedagogy? Indeed, how can it be that for what is surely one of the most

---

[3]   Leslie H. Gelb, Survival at Stake: This is Obama's Last Foreign Policy Chance, The Daily Beast, January 14, 2015, http://www.thedailybeast.com/articles/2015/01/13/this-is-obama-s-last-foreign-policy-chance.html (accessed January 14, 2015).

[4]   Duncan Kennedy, How the Law School Fails: A Polemic, 1 Yale L. Rev. of Law and Social Action 71 (1970), available on the web at http://digital commons.law.yale.edu/yrlsa/vol1/iss1/7 (accessed 1/10/15). For more on Kennedy see especially Chapter 14, *infra*.

important professions in modern American society we prepare students for legal practice by exposing them to people who have self-consciously chosen to avoid (and, quite possibly are unfit for) that practice itself? As Scott Turow, the author of the most penetrating review of the first year of legal education,[5] put it, "Doctors are trained by practicing doctors. Lawyers are still trained initially by those who'd rather not do what most of their students will undertake for decades."[6] It does appear that law professors train their students to acquire something called "the legal mind," but it is not clear that particular mindset is particularly useful in practice, and it is extraordinarily mysterious. Thus, Henry Friendly, who had one of the best records ever at Harvard Law School, declared that "The legal mind is an inquiring mind. It does not accept; it asks. Its favorite word is 'why.' . . . It is analytical; it picks a problem apart so that the components can be seen and judged. It is selective; it rejects characteristics that are not significant and focuses on those that are. . . . It is a classifying mind; it finds significant differences between cases that superficially seem similar and significant similarities between cases that at first seem different."[7]

Worse, it now appears that what Law Professors do does not even have much of an influence on the judges who administer the law itself. As the author of a survey of the publications by Law Professors observed in 2012, "Some things that are big in the legal academy are considered irrelevant or crackpot by judges. . . . There's a feeling that law schools have become very theoretical and perhaps out

---

[5] For more on the first year law school experience, see Chapter 13, *infra*.

[6] Scott Turow, One L: The Turbulent True Story of a First Year at Harvard Law School 285 (Penguin Books, 2010 reissue with a new afterward).

[7] Quoted by Friendly's biographer, David M. Dorsen, Henry Friendly: Greatest Judge of His Era 22–23 (Harvard, 2012).

of touch with whatever goes on in the courts."[8] Surely this is a curious situation. What accounts for it?

At this point in the history of this nation, then, there is apparently a public perception of the American law professor, as unrealistic, out-of-touch, and quite possibly irrelevant. How did this come to be? Is it accurate? From time to time, American legal scholars have published books or articles describing American legal education, but, curiously, there has been very little monographic work on the teachers of the law, and, as far as I know, no single book treating law professors in general, much less a comparative treatment of the biographies of the most important American law professors. That is the effort put forward here. What prompts this book, then, (besides the absence of any such volume) is the realization (after my four decades of teaching in the legal academy) that what the profession of law teachers has become is, at least in part, responsible for what many, like Secretary Panetta, have seen as a deficiency in law professors. I write also out of a belief that there is now a crisis in legal education, and, even more alarming, a broader crisis in the law itself. For decades, at least, critics of American law schools have wondered whether the kind of analysis that goes on in most law school classes really prepares students for the practice of law.

---

[8]   Joe Palazzolo, "The Most Cited Law Review Articles of All Time," The Wall Street Journal, Law Blog, June 1, 2012, http://blogs.wsj.com/law/2012/06/01/the-most-cited-law-review-articles-of-all-time/ (accessed March 13, 2015) (Quoting Fred Shapiro, "an associate librarian at Yale Law School, who recently finished his third study on the most-cited law review articles of all time, with co-author Michelle Pearse, a Harvard librarian." That study is Fred R. Shapiro & Michelle Pearse, The Most-Cited Law Review Articles of All Time, 110 Mich. L. Rev. 1483 (2012)). It is a nice question whether most law professors, once they receive tenure, actually do much scholarly publishing at all. For two empirical studies suggesting that they do not, see Philip F. Postlewaite, Life After Tenure: Where Have All the Articles Gone?, 48 J.Legal Educ. 558 (1998), and Philip F. Postlewaite, On Writing and Publishing: Publish or Perish: The Paradox, 50 J. Legal Educ. 157 (2000).

There has been an increased perception, in short, that "the logic of a law professor" may somehow be illogical, and detrimental rather than helpful to the development of American law.

The cost of an American legal education has dramatically increased in the last two decades, and many now question the wisdom of the third year in American law schools (President Obama himself recently added his voice to this chorus).[9] More troubling, pundits on the left and right now regularly bemoan that all three branches of our government—legislative, executive, and judicial—appear routinely to ignore the dictates of the Constitution, and indeed, the requirements of the rule of law itself. Has the work of American law professors led to this current situation of lack of faith in legal education and mistrust of those charged with administering the law?[10] Is the fact that the current American President is himself a former law professor an important element in what has happened? The answer to both these questions, it appears, is "Yes," and this study of those who have taught American law is an attempt to determine how we have arrived at such a disconcerting place for American law and legal institutions; how it is that the ancient ideal that ours is a government of laws, not of men, is now so seriously threatened, and how it is that "the logic of a law professor" can be the object of lamentation if not ridicule.

---

[9] See, e.g., Dylan Matthews, "Obama thinks law school should be two years. The British think it should be one," Washington Post, August 27, 2013, available at http://www.washingtonpost.com/blogs/wonkblog/wp/2013/08/27/obama-thinks-law-school-should-be-two-years-the-british-think-it-should-be-one/ (accessed October 24, 2014).

[10] For a powerful argument that this is the case see Robert F. Nagel, Unrestrained: Judicial Excess and the Mind of the American Lawyer (Transaction Publishers, 2008).

In this review of the careers of several law professors, ranging from the first modern models, in the late eighteenth century, to the current President of the United States, what I am seeking to do is first, to suggest what our law and legal institutions were created to accomplish, and second, to show how far we have strayed, in the beginning of the twenty-first century, from that original conception. In the course of this analysis I hope to explore the nature of the American legal system, to make a few observations about how it differs from that of other nations, to suggest some of the most important controversies about the law in the last two centuries, and, in particular, to examine how a particular group of persons—American law professors—have had a profound effect on American law and American life. In no other nation are teachers of law (or indeed judges) venerated in the same manner as they are in ours, and I want to explore how and why this came to be.

This book is aimed at the general American public, because my thesis has to do with issues of concern to all Americans, but I hope that this volume will also serve as an introduction to the law for prospective lawyers, both for undergraduates in history, political science, or legal studies and for beginning students in J.D. or LLM programs, and also for the many researchers in other departments of the University who find themselves thinking and writing about American law.

The American legal academy, as it often has, is going through a period of quandary and self-doubt. As already suggested, it has routinely been attacked by non-lawyers and by judges for failing adequately to prepare lawyers for legal practice. For example, United States Court of Appeals judge Harry T. Edwards famously complained more than two decades ago that "[Many law schools—especially the so-called 'elite' ones—have abandoned their proper place, by emphasizing abstract theory at the expense of practical scholarship and pedagogy."[11] Since Judge Edwards wrote, the trends he observed, have, for the most part, accelerated. The Chief Justice of the United States, John Roberts, like all of his brethren on the Court at this writing[12] a graduate of an "elite" Law School (in his case Harvard), declared that the sort of things law professors now publish in the law reviews is of limited to no value for those actually dealing with the law. "Pick up a copy of any law review that you see and the first article is likely to be, you know, the influence of Immanuel Kant on evidentiary approaches in 18th-century Bulgaria, or something, which I'm sure was of great interest to the academic that wrote it, but isn't of much help to the bar."[13] There are still some critics of law school who

---

[11] Harry T. Edwards, The Growing Disjunction Between Legal Education and the Legal Profession, 91 Mich. L. Rev. 34 (1992–1993).

[12] February 2016, following the death of Justice Scalia (a graduate of Harvard Law School). Of the other Justices, Anthony Kennedy graduated from Harvard Law School, Clarence Thomas graduated from Yale Law School, Ruth Bader Ginsberg began at Harvard Law School and transferred to Columbia, Stephen Breyer is a graduate of Harvard Law School, Samuel Alito is a graduate of Yale, as is Sonya Sotomayor, and Elena Kagan is a graduate of Harvard Law School (and a former Dean there).

[13] Chief Justice John G. Roberts, Jr., Interview at Fourth Circuit Court of Appeals Annual Conference, www.c-span.org/video/?300203–1/conversation -chief-justice-roberts (June 25, 2011)). The Chief Justice's remark prompted a tongue in cheek study of the influence of Immanuel Kant on Evidentiary Approaches in 18th Century Bulgaria, Orin S. Kerr, The Influence of Immanuel Kant on Evidentiary Approaches in 18th-Century Bulgaria, 18 GREEN BAG 2d 251 (2015) (Quite properly concluding that there was no such influence). For a spirited ju-jitsu attack on the Chief Justice's views on this point, see David Pozen, "The Influence of Juridical Cant on Edificatory Approaches in 21st-Century America," 19 Green Bag 2d 111–112 (2015) ("Thousands of federal court rulings are published (or not[footnote omitted]) and then never cited by a single academic paper. All of which raises a serious concern: Are judicial opinions becoming irrelevant?") See also the recent pungent observation by Chapman University Professor Ronald Rotunda, along the same lines, "Let us be blunt: Reading about law is not often fun." Ronald Rotunda, Book Review [of F.H. Buckley, The Once and Future King: The Rise of Crown Government in America (Encounter Books, 2014)], 65 J.Leg. Educ. 434, 438 (2015).

simply lament the fact that we are turning out too many lawyers, when what we need is more scientists, engineers, doctors, and, perhaps, artists.[14] There is some validity to these complaints, but I want to help mount at least a partial defense of legal education, and to explore a time when law professors, in fact, thought of themselves as scientists, social engineers, and, if not artists, then certainly literary stylists devoted to the general service of their fellow citizens, and to the betterment of their societies.

No one ever believed that law professors could cure all the problems of the polity, and no one could mistake them for doctors (and, indeed, until recently most of them had no PhD's, unlike the tradition in some parts of the Continent), but this monograph is undertaken in the belief that there are some things that American law professors have done that might, if remembered and resurrected, still help ameliorate some of the shortcomings of our politics, and maybe even of our culture. If there is a current disparagement of the law and law professors (and there undoubtedly is), I will argue, it is because the law professoriat, has, to an unhealthy extent, forgotten some of the lessons about the law that law professors once understood. Our eighteenth- and nineteenth-century forbears, in particular, understood that societal order required law, law required morality, and morality required religion. These are not widely shared notions now, and, as will be demonstrated, there is now a prevalent feeling, in many parts of the legal academy, that these old notions led to an oppressive, patriarchal system that was hostile to women, minorities, and the powerless. But as we have moved away from the pieties and certainties of the last two

---

[14]   On the myriad effects of too many lawyers and too much law on American society, see, e.g., Philip K. Howard, Life Without Lawyers: Liberating Americans from Too Much Law (W.W. Norton & Co., 2009).

centuries, perhaps something noble has been lost. I want to explore if it's possible that some of that nobility, some of that virtue, can be restored, and with that restoration might come a resurgence of faith in law professors, if not the law itself.

While there has not yet been a book precisely like this one, the model of comparatively short biographical essays is an ancient one. It certainly goes all the way back to *Plutarch's Lives*,[15] if not before, and more recent models include Joseph Epstein's wonderful essays he edited called *Literary Genius: 25 Classic Writers Who Define English & American Literature* (2007),[16] or, before that, Aubrey's *Brief Lives*,[17] and Lytton Strachey's *Eminent Victorians*.[18] The last treated but a few individuals, but here we will examine a number closer to that Epstein did. I have chosen twenty-two individual law professors (two fictional and twenty actual human beings), and included one chapter treating several professors who belong to one school of legal thought, Critical Legal Studies. I have tried to choose a representative number of professors, although I cannot claim to have picked a list that everyone would agree are the very best choices (and those in the legal academy, I am sure, will find glaring omissions). Still there are enough treated here to give what I believe to be a reasonably accurate survey of what law teaching has been like, especially in the twentieth and twenty-first century, in this

---

[15] See, e.g., Plutarch's Lives, Complete and Unabridged in One Volume (Random House, 1975, Arthur Hugh Clough (Editor), John Dryden (Translator). Plutarch was apparently writing in the first century CE, the first printed edition of his book appeared in the sixteenth century).

[16] Joseph Epstein, Literary Genius: 25 Classic Writers Who Define English & American Literature (Paul Dry Books, 2007).

[17] See, e.g., John Aubrey, Brief Lives (Penguin Classics, 2000) (Originally written in the late seventeenth century).

[18] Lytton Strachey, Eminent Victorians (SMK Books, 2009) (Originally published 1918).

country, though we begin with an English jurist and professor.

CHAPTER 1

THE ENGLISH COMMON LAW BACKGROUND OF AMERICAN LAW

EIGHTEENTH CENTURY

Sir William Blackstone
(Oxford)

■ ■ ■

Sir William Blackstone (1723–1780)
Bust by Marius Azzi, Library of Congress Prints and Photographs Division.

Sir William Blackstone, the inaugural Vinerian Professor of law at Oxford (1758–1766), is the first of the great modern law professors. He was the first teacher to occupy a chair at a great University devoted to the study of the English common law, that sprawling body of customs, statutes, and cases, yielding governing principles that served, in effect, as the Constitution for England. He was also "the first law professor to serve as a judge on a common law court," as a puisne (associate) judge on both the English

Court of Common Pleas, and, for a time on the Court of King's Bench.[19] As he explained in his monumental four volume *Commentaries on the Laws of England* (1765–1769), Blackstone believed that the English common law could be reduced to a clear system, that the English common law was based on the law of nature and nature's God, that there were objective answers to legal questions, and that the job of a judge was simply to follow the law as previously laid down.

In an era when a successful candidate for the Presidency of the United States can declare, when seeking the office, that his test for appointing Justices to the United States Supreme Court will be whether they know what life is like for a member of a minority or a single mother,[20] and when, after that candidate won the office, one of his appointments to the Supreme Court earlier declared her assumption that "a wise Latina" would do a better job than a white male at rendering judicial decisions,[21] it is bracing, to say the least, to encounter a very different view of law, a view in which "The job of a judge was to find . . . existing law and make it known," and in which "Judges were, in

---

[19] Emily Kadens, Justice Blackstone's Common Law Orthodoxy, 103 N.U.L.R. 1553, 1554, 1575 (2009). For the early operation of the English common law, see, e.g., Thomas Lund, The Creation of the Common Law: The Medieval Year Books Deciphered (The Lawbook Exchange, Ltd., 2015).

[20] As Barack Obama remarked, in a speech given on July 17, 2007, before the Planned Parenthood Action Fund, "[W]e need somebody who's got the heart—the empathy—to recognize what it's like to be a young teenage mom. The empathy to understand what it's like to be poor or African-American or gay or disabled or old—and that's the criteria by which I'll be selecting my judges." Text of speech available at https://sites.google.com/site/lauraetch/barackobamabeforeplannedparenthoodaction (accessed October 25, 2014).

[21] "I would hope that a wise Latina woman with the richness of her experiences would more often than not reach a better conclusion than a white male who hasn't lived that life," said the then Court of Appeals judge, Sonya Sotomayor, at a 2001 Lecture at the University of California, Berkeley. See, e.g., Charlie Savage, "A Judge's View of Judging in On the Record," New York Times, May 14, 2009, available at http://www.nytimes.com/2009/05/15/us/15judge.html?_r=0 (accessed October 25, 2014).

theory, mere mouthpieces, 'despositor[ies] of the laws' who expressed the law but did not themselves make it."[22] For Blackstone, the notion that a judge should determine the law based on his or her personal experience or values would have been anathema or incomprehensible, because Blackstone believed that it was not the task of the judge to refashion legal rules to arrive at a just result, indeed, as he put it, it would be far better to have "law without equity . . . than equity without law."[23] By this Blackstone meant that it would be better for society to live by fixed and predictable rules than to be governed by the idiosyncratic concepts of justice of individual judges.

In the United States in the twenty-first century, however, we live in an era of a "living constitution," when the President and much of the legal academy, and occasionally a majority of the United States Supreme Court, think it is the job of that Court to remake the document to meet the needs of the times,[24] and, in particular the needs

---

[22]   Kadens, *supra* note 19, at 155, quoting William Blackstone, 1 Commentaries on the Laws of England 69 (Oxford, 1765–1769).

[23]   1 Blackstone's Commentaries, *supra* note 22, at 62. ("[T]he liberty of considering all cases in an equitable light must not be indulged too far, lest thereby we destroy all laws, and leave the decision of every question entirely in the breast of the judge. And law, without equity, tho' hard and disagreeable, is much more desirable for the public good, than equity without law; which would make every judge a legislator, and introduce most infinite confusion; as there would then be almost as many different rules of action laid down in our courts, as there are differences of capacity and sentiment in the human mind.")

[24]   For the latest prominent example see Obergefell v. Hodges, 576 U.S. ___ (2015), where, in a majority opinion for the United States Supreme Court, Justice Kennedy (writing for himself and Justices Breyer, Ginsburg, Sotomayor and Kagan) declared that marriage had come to have a status in modern American society where it violated the Fourteenth Amendment's equal protection and due process clauses to deny gay couples the right to marry. Four Justices (Roberts, Scalia, Thomas and Alito) dissented, essentially on the grounds that legally sanctioned gay marriage would have been inconceivable to the framers of the Fourteenth Amendment, especially since marriage had historically been the province of state, and not federal law, and that it was not the job of the Court to fashion a new Constitutional law of marriage, but rather marriage law formulation was the job of the people of the states and their legislatures.

of the formerly unpowerful. For Blackstone, nevertheless, the primary virtue of the law was not its flexibility, but rather was its static quality, its certainty and its predictability,[25] and when all was said and done, its enduring common sense and, indeed, its accordance with gospel morality. More, for Blackstone "law was a science, which in the parlance of the time meant that it could be turned into a system."[26] When these features of the common law were taken into account, as far as Blackstone was concerned, the common law did incorporate features of justice and fairness, and did about as well as any governing system administered by humans possibly could.

In any event, these Blackstonian ideals—the systemic nature of law, its divine origin, its moral superiority and moral clarity, and its notion that precedent should govern— were adopted early into American law, and it is to Blackstone, or more particularly, to Blackstone's scholarship in his *Commentaries*, that we owe nearly all the basic organization of the law as it is still being taught to first-year students in American law schools. As Daniel Boorstin famously put it, "In the history of American Institutions, no other book—except the Bible—has played so great a role as Blackstone's *Commentaries on the Laws of England*."[27] "[T]he *Commentaries* were accorded near reverential status by both bar and bench in the United States when it came to learning the law"[28] during the nineteenth century, and their influence is still operative.[29]

---

[25]   As Emily Kadens observes, "Blackstone's opinions suggest he thought that the law was a system of well-defined rules in which each problem had one and only one answer." Kadens, *supra* note 19, at 1575.

[26]   Kadens, *supra* note 19, at 1559.

[27]   Daniel J. Boorstin, The Mysterious Science of the Law: An Essay on Blackstone's Commentaries . . . iii (Peter Smith ed., 1973).

[28]   Christopher Tomlins, Adelaide's Blackstone, 36 Adelaide Law Review 599, 607 (2015).

[29]   It must be of some significance as well that in a book that collects essays by the late Wellesley legal historian, Kathryn Preyer, on the reception

Blackstone divided the law into public and private, for example, laying the basis for the distinction between great swathes of legal doctrines, and for differentiating between issues of Constitutional and Criminal Law on the one hand, and the basic organization of the everyday fields of law, Property, Contracts, Torts, Business Organizations, and what we now refer to as personal and civil rights on the other. One of the canniest American expositors of Blackstone, Daniel Boorstin, likened Blackstone's view of the law to the laying out of a great and symmetrical English garden.[30]

English gardens are marvels of artificiality, but for Blackstone the essence of the common law, that body of precedents that dictated the rules that courts applied, was that it was a reflection of divine order. The source of the English common law was the dictates of the Almighty, and the legitimacy of the common law lay in its divine origin. In his youth, at least, Blackstone had a "fervent" commitment to "establishment Anglicanism."[31] In the *Commentaries*, " 'that beautifully balanced construct, the English constitution' stood in for God."[32]

---

of the key English common law institutions and ideas into late eighteenth- and early nineteenth-century America, but that has almost no mention of Blackstone himself or his treatise, the title given is *Blackstone in America: Selected Essays of Kathryn Preyer* (Mary Sarah Bilder, Maeva Marcus, and R.Kent Newmyer, eds. 2014). The significance would seem to be that Blackstone is synonymous with the common law itself. See *id.*, at vii ("Blackstone in America explores the creative process of transplantation—the way in which American legislators and judges refashioned the English common-law inheritance to fit the republican political culture of the new nation.") Ms. Preyer herself contemplated that title for a collection of her essays which was never published during her lifetime. *Id.*, at viii.

[30]   See generally, Daniel J. Boorstin, The Mysterious Science of the Law: An Essay on Blackstone's Commentaries (University of Chicago Press, 1996).

[31]   Tomlins, *supra* note 28, at 603.

[32]   *Id.*, quoting Ian Doolittle, William Blackstone: A Biography 104 (2001).

Blackstone's clear assumption was that the purportedly divine origin of the common law ought to guarantee obedience and deference to it on the part of judges, lawyers, and the English people themselves. It was impossible for him to imagine or to sympathize with a systemic criticism of what he regarded as the perfection of ethics and human reason which he believed the common law revealed. "For Blackstone, the common law was identical with the 'universal-law of society,' as also with the 'law of nations[.]' "[33] As a recent commentary on Blackstone put it, "Blackstone was convinced that English law was 'founded upon principles that are permanent, uniform, and universal; and always conformable to the dictates of truth and justice, the feelings of humanity, and the indelible rights of mankind.' "[34] Accordingly, while American law in the twentieth and twenty-first centuries, according to some of the law professors we will soon examine, is a morass of conflicting rules and principles, for Blackstone there were single, authoritative, venerable, divinely-sanctioned and objective solutions for legal problems.

Blackstone's views became the basis of the American common law of the nineteenth century. It is now a truism that "for many early American lawyers, Blackstone was the Common Law, because, for one thing, they often had no other book."[35] It also appears that those who framed the American Constitution had copies of Blackstone's *Commentaries* at hand, and that "especially in the early hours of American constitutionalism," the *Commentaries* often served "as a benchmark source by reference to which

---

[33]   Horst Dippel, Blackstone's Commentaries and the Origins of Modern Constitutionalism, Chapter 9 in Wilfrid Prest, ed., Re-Interpreting Blackstone's Commentaries: A Seminal Text in National and International Contexts 212 (Hart Publishing, 2014).

[34]   *Id.*, at 213, quoting 4 *Commentaries* 3.

[35]   *Id.*, at 200 quoting Max Radin.

debaters defined their own position."[36] Blackstone should be recognized as an important basis for the veneration of trial by jury in early republican America,[37] for the preservation of the writ of habeas corpus,[38] and, in general, for what he contributed to emerging American ideas about the purpose of society being to secure individuals "in the enjoyment of those absolute rights, which were vested in them by the immutable laws of nature,"[39] and, indeed, for his contribution to the basic American notions of "political rights, limited government and sovereignty, so fundamental to a federal structure[,]"[40] as well as the conception of judicial independence, though not the conception of modern judicial review.[41]

Still, Blackstone's notion of a divinely-inspired and objectively valid system of legal rules has come under ferocious attack in the last two centuries, as, indeed, it did at the time of the publication of his classic four-volume *Commentaries* on English law. There have been several books on Blackstone, most notably the splendid recent biography by Wilfrid Prest,[42] and, clearly, Blackstone's books and his lectures were aimed at the emerging late eighteenth-century aristocracy who studied at Oxford and who needed themselves to administer the law to the tenants of their landed estates, but what Blackstone said and wrote had an impact far greater than that. Through the American judges and lawyers who followed him (most notably Joseph Story[43] and James Kent), it could be said that Blackstone

---

[36]   *Id.*, at 201.

[37]   *Id.*, at 202.

[38]   *Id.*, at 203.

[39]   *Id.*, at 206, quoting I *Commentaries* 124.

[40]   *Id.*, at 203.

[41]   *Id.*, at 210–211.

[42]   Wilfrid Prest, William Blackstone: Law and Letters in the Eighteenth Century (Oxford University Press, 2012). See also Boorstin, *supra* note 30.

[43]   See Chapter 3, *infra*.

was indispensable in creating a model for the rule of law itself in America.

When Blackstone prepared the lectures he gave at Oxford (which became the basis for his four-volume *Commentaries*) he realized that he was embarked on a notable departure in University education. Prior to Blackstone's appointment to the Vinerian Chair at Oxford, the young gentlemen at the University had been able to study Roman law and the Civil law (the law applied on the Continent), but Blackstone decided that the time had come to educate the men at Oxford in the law of their own country, as it was applied in their courts by English lawyers and judges. His notion was that English gentlemen, who would likely serve as Justices of the Peace, jurors, or litigants, were woefully ignorant of the rules that it was their duty to administer.[44]

Equally surprising, Blackstone noted, was the fact that the English Common Law—the widely accepted rules of decisions for courts in England—was largely unknown

---

[44] For some deep skepticism about whether Blackstone's work, which was, after all, "a text designed to help gentlemen understand an important part of their society and fit them for a role in life that might require them to serve as unpaid officers of the law," should be taken as "an immemorial monument to the legal culture of the Atlantic world at the moment of the American founding" see Ruth Paley, "Modern Blackstone: The King's Two Bodies, the Supreme Court and the Present," in Wilfrid Prest (ed.), Reinterpreting Blackstone's Commentaries, *supra* note 33, at 188. For another take on this see, e.g., John Henry Schlegal, Notes Toward An Intimate, Opinionated, and Affectionate History of the Conference on Critical Legal Studies, 36 Stan.L.Rev. 391, 403 (1984) ("At least since Blackstone, and I suspect long before, the central job of legal education has been to justify existing rules of law to the nascent members of the legal elite.") Emily Kadens kindly shared with me some of her research on Blackstone, and among the things she discovered was that he had a certain humility about the task he was undertaking. "For the present," he wrote, "I shall think myself happy if this first rude essay shall give any gentleman who may hereafter be called to the service of the public, a tolerable opinion of the wisdom of our civil polity, and a desire to be better acquainted with the laws and constitution of his country." Notes from Blackstone's first year of lectures, 1753–1754, Somerset Record Office DD/WY/1183 bk. 4, f.161.

among the laity, and had never before been a subject for University education. There were institutions that trained English lawyers, of course, most notably the Inns of Court and the Inns of Chancery, located in London, where those who awaited a call to the bar could apprentice to lawyers, could mix with other students of the law, and could debate and moot legal topics. Blackstone understood, however, that a purely professionally-focused approach to the law risked being deficient in some essential qualities of a lawyer, most notably a sense of the values that undergirded the law, what he called, in striking language, the "spirit of the laws," and the "natural foundations of justice."[45] These could best be transmitted, he argued, in a series of lectures such as the ones he gave to Oxford undergraduates, a fifty-lecture course lasting one year.

Those lectures, originally delivered in the academic year 1753–54, and later published over a four year period from 1765 to 1769,[46] became his *Commentaries on the Laws of England*, certainly the most influential modern books on the law ever published, and a statement of jurisprudence rarely equaled in human history. Thomas Jefferson thought Blackstone a "Tory," and seemed to take extra pains to disparage what he perceived as the conservative character of Blackstone's thought.[47] Recent scholarship on Blackstone, however, has championed his standing as an important Enlightenment thinker, one as committed to

---

[45]   1 Blackstone, Commentaries, *supra* note 22, at 32.

[46]   See generally Wilfrid Prest, Blackstone and Biography, in Wilfrid Prest, ed., Blackstone and His Commentaries: Biography, Law, History 9 (Hart Publishing, 2009) for the dates of the delivery of the lectures, and for the suggestion that as the books were published they were revised, and were also revised in subsequent editions. As Prest put it, "Blackstone was the sort of writer who found it very difficult to refrain from tinkering with his text." *Id.*

[47]   The classic reading of Jefferson's views on Blackstone is Julian S. Waterman, "Thomas Jefferson and Blackstone's Commentaries," 27 Illinois Law Review 629 (1933), reprinted in an excellent collection edited by David Flaherty, Essays in the History of Early American Law (University of North Carolina Press, 1969).

liberty as he was to order. Indeed, if Jefferson is most famous for his felicitous suggestion that American government ought to be committed to "the pursuit of happiness," perhaps he insufficiently appreciated Blackstone's own acknowledgment that the purpose of law generally was the promotion of human "happiness," in accordance with the same dictates of a Creator whom Jefferson himself acknowledged in the Declaration.[48]

The deep religious foundation in Blackstone may have offended the Deist Jefferson, but there was, at least, a coherence to Blackstone's linking the law of God to the law of man. Law, for Blackstone, began with the design of a Creator, whose rules for humankind could be accessed through Scripture. The way in which men ought to relate to each other was the subject of bodies of doctrine, referred to also by Jefferson, in the Declaration, as the "law of nature," the "law of God," and also by ancient customs observed by civilized societies that went by the name of "the law of nations."

Blackstone's primary subject, however, one subordinate to these other venerable bodies of law, was "municipal law," the law of the supreme power in the state, for him the "English Common Law." The "common law," as already indicated, consisted of the decisions of the English courts, the customs of the realm, and the statutes of Parliament. These sources were not the only things important to Blackstone, however, and his claims for English legal institutions and the superiority of those institutions over other human creations were based on more than the ancient and modern records of the law, which revealed these customs, statutes, and decisions. For

---

[48] For the striking manner in which Blackstone anticipates the language in the Declaration of Independence regarding the plan of the Creator for the happiness of mankind, see 1 Blackstone, Commentaries, *supra* note 22, at 40–41.

Blackstone the most impressive achievement of England may have been what has often been referred to as the "perfection" of its Constitution. This was what was achieved in the "Glorious Revolution" of 1688 (when the Catholic monarch, James II, had been removed from the throne and replaced by the Protestants William and Mary, as a result of machinations, in particular, by the great Protestant members of the House of Lords).

For Blackstone, what the British achieved in 1688 was nothing short of the goal that the great Greek and Roman political philosophers had sought—a "balanced" government, which integrated the "one," the "few," and the "many," which sought to incorporate into the government the benefits of monarchy, aristocracy, and democracy.[49] The ancients, according to this set of notions, had appreciated that the benefit of monarchy was that the single executive could act with energy and dispatch, and that such unitary command was crucial, especially in times of war. The defect of monarchy, as the Greeks and Romans understood, of course, was that it could degenerate into tyranny, and untrammeled power in the hands of one person could turn oppressive. Rule by aristocracy had the benefit of allowing the most talented to assume the levers of power in society, to employ the wisdom that they had cultivated as a result of the learning that was encouraged for their class and made possible by the wealth that gave them the leisure for study, for example in England's two great universities. But aristocrats, over the course of history, had a tendency to subrogate the interests of the realm to their own, and aristocracy, history had demonstrated, degenerated into oligarchy or plutocracy. Democracy had the advantage of capturing, so the ancient learning went, the honesty and the morals of the people, but democracies, unfortunately, had a

---

[49]   For Blackstone's summary of the achievement of the "Revolution" of 1688, see, e.g., 1 Commentaries, *supra* note 22, at 322–325.

tendency to decay into anarchy and chaos, as the unhappy proclivity of individual people to pursue their own selfish ends inevitably manifested itself.

So how, then, to get the advantages of each form of government, without the disadvantages? The answer was what we moderns call "checks and balances," or, more simply combining the three—monarchy, aristocracy, and people—in one sovereign entity. This is what the British accomplished, according to Blackstone, in 1688. Before that time the monarchy had claimed the ascendency, but that, of course risked tyranny, which many thought occurred in the early seventeenth century with the Stuarts and their theory of the divine right of kings, which theory put into practice brooked no interference from the aristocracy or people. With the establishment of William and Mary on the throne in 1688, however, through, in effect, a Parliamentary grant of legitimacy, the locus of sovereignty in Britain altered. Now, instead of the King as sole sovereign, sovereignty was vested in "The King in Parliament," which meant that no law could now be passed without the consent of the three elements of Parliament—the monarch, the House of Lords, and the House of Commons. With this change, the three classic elements (monarchy, aristocracy, and people) were combined into one, and, since the consent of each was required for a measure to become law, each would restrain the excesses of the other.[50] Indeed, Blackstone appears to have believed that "the gentry and the nobility 'representing their country in parliament'" would serve as a constitutional check on power:

> They are the guardians of the English constitution: the makers, repealers, and interpreters of the English laws; delegated to watch, to check, and to avert every dangerous

[50] For this Blackstonian view of checks and balances in Parliament see generally 1 Commentaries, *supra* note 22, at 154–155, 240.

innovation, to propose, to adopt, and to cherish any solid and well-weighed improvement; bound by every tie of nature, of honour, and of religion, to transmit that constitution and those laws to their posterity, amended if possible, at least without any derogation.[51]

Some things in Blackstone, such as this dependence on the hereditary monarchy, hereditary aristocracy, and landed gentry may have fit the needs of the times in eighteenth-century England, but there were clear things in his description of the common law that would in time rankle Americans, and, indeed, things that upset contemporary English writers, most notably the great English Utilitarian, Jeremy Bentham. Bentham accused Blackstone of mystifying the English Common Law in order to conceal the crass manner in which it protected the interests of the wealthy and powerful in English society. It is undeniable that Blackstone's idealized view of the common law has within it at least an element of being too good to be true. As one recent scholar put it, "there are aspects of 'everything is as it should be' [in] Blackstone's heady but complacent vision both of the steady workings through of the law through English history [and] of the 'Glory' of the present establishment" which may owe more to the tradition of British poetic culture than to legal realties.[52]

Bentham, once Blackstone's student, came to attack him not only as a legal theorist, but as a man. As Blackstone's leading contemporary biographer put it, for Bentham, "the logical confusion and moral complacency which he detected in Blackstone's *Commentaries* were

---

[51]   Dippel, *supra* note 33, at 208, quoting 1 Commentaries 9.

[52]   Michael Meehan, "Blackstone's Commentaries: England's Legal Georgic?," Chapter 3 in Wilfrid Prest, ed., Re-Interpreting Blackstone's Commentaries: A Seminal Text in National and International Contexts 59, 60 (Bloomsbury Publishing, 2014).

directly linked to their author's failings of character and intellect."[53] Bentham's analysis of Blackstone, could, however be dismissed as "an essentially flat and stylized two-dimensional portrait" of a purported "obscurantist conservative."[54] Even so, Bentham remained Blackstone's "most committed, ferocious and influential" critic, "who never wavered from his famous initial condemnation of the *Commentaries* as fundamentally flawed by an 'antipathy to reformation', of which (as he claimed) their author was 'a determined and persevering enemy.' "[55] Wilfrid Prest, Blackstone's modern biographer, believes that Bentham essentially got it wrong, and that Blackstone actually was engaged in a number of "reformist endeavors."[56]

While Bentham may have been incorrect that Blackstone was simply a "purblind defender of the unreformed common law,"[57] it is nonetheless true that much if not most of the system of law Blackstone limned *was* a conservative one. Blackstonian Property law protected the interests of large landowners, the aristocratic body from which the House of Lords, the House of Commons, and the students at the Universities were drawn. Remedies were given by that common law for any injury done to property, and to penalize anyone who interfered with the natural flow of existing watercourses, or, indeed,

---

[53] Wilfrid Prest, "Blackstone and Biography," Chapter 1 in Prest, ed., Blackstone and His Commentaries: Biography, Law, History, *supra* note 46, at 6.

[54] *Ibid.*

[55] *Id.*, at 10, citing Bentham, A Fragment on Government 4 (Cambridge University Press, ed. R. Harrison, 1988).

[56] *Ibid.*

[57] *Ibid.* Prest suggests that among Blackstone's efforts at reform were seeking to use merit rather than birth as criterion for selection of All Souls College fellows, the "rescue and rehabilitation" of Oxford's "printing and publishing arm," the efforts at creating "rehabilitative confinement" in the prison system ("as a humane penal alternative to execution, flogging or transportation") and, indeed, the efforts to systematize the common law in the *Commentaries* themselves. *Id.*, at 10–11.

anyone who interfered with the profitable operation of an existing market or ferry.

Blackstone also clearly believed that the common law was correct to deprive women of basic legal rights, and to subsume the legal being of the wife in her husband. According to the Blackstonian common law, for example, a wife had no power to enter into contracts on her own, nor did she control any property she brought into the marriage. She was clearly a subordinate, subject to the direction and, perhaps, to the physical chastisement of her husband. In other intriguing aspects of family law in the Blackstonian world only God could make an heir, and while it was possible on the Continent, adoption was not permitted by the common law of England.

Blackstone's was an essentially conservative defense of Parliament and of the English common law generally, and it is probably fair, as Herbert Hovenkamp did in his recent magisterial book on Neoclassical Legal Thought, to link Blackstone with Adam Smith. "Adam Smith's 'invisible hand' of the market," Hovenkamp writes, "which made order out of the chaos of individual trading, also guided the common law. Smith and William Blackstone, whose seminal works were written only a decade apart, shared a common vision about how society and markets work. These ideas led to a powerful bias in favor of common law rules and against legislation."[58] Among other things, for Blackstone, this conservative perspective meant that Blackstone was content to recognize the indispensable nature of an hereditary monarch and an hereditary aristocracy. These two were, however, unappealing to the Americans after 1776, and this meant that Americans had to put together a

---

[58] Herbert Hovenkamp, The Opening of American Law: Neoclassical Legal Thought 1870–1970 1–2 (Oxford, 2015). For Blackstone's views on property, markets, and family law, summarized in the preceding paragraphs, see, e.g., Stephen B. Presser & Jamil S. Zainaldin, Law and Jurisprudence in American History 342–348, 689–697 (West Publishing, 8th ed. 2013).

government that would seek to emulate England's in achieving a "balanced" constitution, but would, nevertheless, manage to dispense with the now odious monarch and aristocrats. The abandonment of the patriarchal family law limned by Blackstone would not occur in America for two more centuries, but the American break with Parliament and the King happened only about a decade after Blackstone wrote. This meant that Americans had to articulate a solution to achieve a balanced Constitution based only on the sovereignty of the American people.

Supporting the American solution was not only the job of American politicians such as Hamilton, Madison, and Jay who, in the most famous American work of sustained political theory, laid out an argument supporting popular sovereignty in The Federalist,[59] but was also the task for American law professors, and perhaps the first sustained effort at such an undertaking was that of James Wilson.[60] Wilson believed that Blackstone could not be relied upon because he was, after all, "an antirepublican lawyer,"[61] and, for Blackstone, when the British Parliament acted it did so with absolute and uncontrolled power. This was unacceptable for Americans, Wilson urged, and it was necessary for Americans to work out their own theory of a limited Constitution, based on something other than the incorporation of monarchy, aristocracy, and the people in

---

[59] See, e.g., Alexander Hamilton, James Madison, and John Jay, The Federalist (Jacob E. Cooke, ed., The Wesleyan University Press, 1961) (Essays originally published 1787–1788, in New York, arguing for the ratification of the 1787 Constitution of the United States).

[60] For Wilson's early effort at challenging Blackstone's defense of parliamentary sovereignty with an assertion of the sole legitimacy of law as based on the consent of the people see Wilson's 1774 Pamphlet, Considerations on the Nature and Extent of the Legislative Authority of the British Parliament. For an analysis of this document, see, e.g., Aaron T. Knapp, Law's Revolutionary: James Wilson and the Birth of American Jurisprudence, 29 J. L. & Politics 189, 199–200 (2014).

[61] Dippel, *supra* note 33, at 204.

the government. As Wilson put it, "The idea of a constitution, limiting and superintending the operations of legislative authority, seems not to have been accurately understood in Britain."[62] In particular, what was needed in the newly-republican America was "all the advantages of checks and balances, without the danger which may arise from a superior and independent order of men."[63] How then, to come up with an American alternative to Blackstone?

---

[62] Dippel, *supra* note 33, at 204, quoting R.G. McCloskey (ed.), The Works of James Wilson (Cambridge MA, 1967) vol. 1, 79.

[63] Dippel, *supra* note 33, at 209–210, quoting the words of Noah Webster published in 1787.

CHAPTER 2

THE COMMON LAW AND POPULAR SOVEREIGNTY

LATE EIGHTEENTH CENTURY

James Wilson
(University of Pennsylvania)

■ ■ ■

Justice James Wilson (1742–1798)
Portrait by Robert S. Susan, after Leopold G. Seyffert,
after Max Rosenthal, circa 1936, Supreme Court official portrait.
Collection of the Supreme Court of the United States.

James Wilson's law lectures at the College of Philadelphia (later the University of Pennsylvania) in the 1790's were crucial in training an early generation of American lawyers in the nature of law and the nature of Constitutional government.[64] These law lectures limn a

---

[64] These lectures are referred to by legal historian Stephen Conrad as the one "extensive patristic contribution to early American legal theory," by a "leading framer." Stephen A. Conrad, James Wilson's "Assimilation of the Common-Law Mind," 84 Nw.U.L.Rev.186, 194 (1989).

theory of Constitutional government "comparable in sophistication to those of Madison, Jefferson, or Hamilton."[65] Wilson, who is often regarded as second only to Madison as a seminal influence at the Constitutional Convention,[66] "was widely regarded by his illustrious American contemporaries as the outstanding legal scholar in the new nation,"[67] and "as the Revolutionary war drew to a close and the new nation took shape . . . [Wilson] grew to be recognized as the best lawyer in the country."[68] Appointed by George Washington as an Associate Justice of the United States Supreme Court, Wilson was one of the most important early Justices, and, indeed, delivered some of his law lectures while still gracing the bench.[69]

Wilson's life, which ended unexpectedly and tragically in penury and disgrace,[70] owing principally to what has

---

[65] William Ewald, James Wilson and the Drafting of the Constitution, 10 U.Pa.J.Const.L. 901 (2008).

[66] See, e.g., id., at 901, where it is noted that Wilson is "generally acknowledged to have been one of [the Constitution's] principal architects, second in important only to Madison." "Scholars interested in the topic have regarded Wilson as the most influential man at the Convention beside Madison," Aaron T. Knapp, Law's Revolutionary: James Wilson and the Birth of American Jurisprudence, 29 J. L. & Politics 189, 207 (2014). Knapp himself is not quite as sure about this, although he notes that Wilson did have a substantial influence on the Convention. Ibid. Knapp's piece, one of the best analysis of Wilson's Constitutional thought, argues that while his critics thought he was too much of an aristocrat, they failed to appreciate the essentially democratic character of Wilson's Law Lectures and his jurisprudence following the adoption of the Constitution.

[67] See Conrad, supra note 64, at 194.

[68] Nicholas Pedersen, The Lost Founder: James Wilson in American Memory, 22 Yale J.L. & Human. 257, 258 (2010).

[69] Knapp, supra note 66, at 252. As explained in the next chapter, our next law professor, Joseph Story, was, while a Harvard law professor, simultaneously an Associate Justice of the United States Supreme Court.

[70] Wilson's sad end is nicely summarized by Knapp, supra note 66, at 283, "Over the course of the 1790s, he found himself increasingly struggling to pay bills, even as he scrambled to secure additional loans to make more investments. A financial panic at the beginning of 1797 left a number of prominent men, including Robert Morris, devastated and hit Wilson especially

been described as his "pathological" tendency to engage in land speculation,[71] is now all but ignored in American law schools. It has been suggested, however, that "relative to the magnitude of his accomplishments [Wilson] has a good claim to be the most neglected of the major American founders."[72] He signed the Declaration of Independence, he was an early foe of slavery,[73] he was an advocate of the expansion of the franchise, and his was even an early voice for greater equality for American women.[74] He was a leading architect of the United States Constitution, and thus, it could be suggested that Wilson's "brain conceived and created the nation."[75] Wilson "wove the intellectual threads of his generation into a theory of popularly based government wedded to the rule of law."[76] The claim made here, however, is that he deserves our attention as the first

---

hard. Thereafter, the overleveraged Supreme Court justice, now hounded by creditors on all fronts, had no choice but to flee his pursuers, leading to arrests and two separate imprisonments. Hiding in a North Carolina tavern with his wife, he died of malaria on August 21, 1798." Wilson was "the only sitting Justice of the Supreme Court to spend time in prison," and "died in abject poverty." Ewald, *supra* note 65, at 914–915. Ewald suggests that had he lived he "likely would have been impeached." *Id.*, at 915.

[71]   Pedersen, *supra* note 68, at 268, 271–272, 288.

[72]   Ewald, *supra* note 65, at 902. But see *id.*, at N. 54, for a very useful summary of recent scholarship on Wilson which strongly suggests that neglect of Wilson is becoming a thing of the past.

[73]   Though Wilson himself did own a slave for a quarter of a century, which slave he freed shortly after marrying his wife, a Quaker. Pedersen, *supra* note 68, at 275.

[74]   Pedersen, *supra* note 68, at 273–279.

[75]   L.H. Alexander, James Wilson, Nation Builder 13 (1907), quoted in Maynard Garrison, Collector's Foreword, xi 1 The Collected Works of James Wilson (Kermit L. Hall & Mark David Hall, eds. 2007). Wilson was one of only six people to have signed both the Declaration and the Constitution. Kermit L. Hall, Introduction, *id.*, at xiii.

[76]   Garrison, *supra* note 75, at xi. Wilson "stood out among the framers of the Constitution as the most thoroughgoing advocate of democracy." Wendell Bird, Press and Speech Under Assault: The Early Supreme Court Justices, the Sedition Act of 1798, and the Campaign against Dissent 162 (Oxford, 2016).

of the great American law professors, or, as one biographer of Wilson has put it, in light of Wilson's setting up "a department of law at [what eventually became] the University of Pennsylvania," he was "the very founder of the American legal academy."[77]

A review of Wilson's law lectures[78] and of his grand jury charges,[79] shows that in a manner similar to that of Blackstone, Wilson laid the basis for an American law which embraced the international law of nations and adopted, for the most part, the common law of England, although a common law shorn of its aspects of monarchy and aristocracy. Indeed, for Wilson, as for Jefferson, the common law adopted by the Americans bore "in its principles and in many of its particulars, a stronger and a fairer resemblance to the common law as it was improved under the [Saxons], than to that [common] law as it was disfigured under the [Normans]."[80] Moreover, as did

---

[77]   Garrison, *supra* note 75, at n.133. Wilson was not, however, the first American law professor. There were at least two earlier ones; George Wythe, who taught at William and Mary and Tapping Reeve who taught at Litchfield (in Connecticut). Bird, *supra* note 76, at 164, n.417.

[78]   It was recently said of these lectures that they "displayed genteel manners and refined learning in philosophy, history, literature, and English jurisprudence." Knapp, *supra* note 66, at 190. Knapp calls the law lectures "Wilson's highest intellectual achievement. . . ." Bird notes that the lectures were "viewed as sufficiently important that the audience for the first lecture included President Washington, Vice President Adams, and a number of members of Congress." Bird, *supra* note 76, at 167.

[79]   For our purposes the most important one of these charges is the one he gave in the famous *Henfield* case, "Charge of Judge Wilson, as President of a special Court of the United States for the Middle Circuit and Pennsylvania district, holden at the Court House, in the city of Philadelphia, on the 22nd day of July, 1793, to the Grand Jury of said Court," reprinted in Francis Wharton, ed., State Trials of the United States During the Administrations of Washington and Adams (Philadelphia: Carey & Hart, 1849), at 59–66.

[80]   Wharton, *supra* note 79, at 61. It should be noted, however, that Wilson believed that Blackstone got some things wrong, for example the law of seditious libel. See, e.g., Bird, *supra* note 76, at 168–169. For Blackstone generally see Chapter 1, *supra*.

Blackstone, Wilson believed the law of nations, an aspect of "the law of nature" which was incorporated into the American common law, as it was into English common law, was the birthright of Americans, was of "obligation indispensable" and of "origin divine."[81] The obligation to follow the law of nations, for Wilson (and Blackstone) like that of the obligation to follow the law of nature was also "[u]niversal and unchangeable."[82]

Moreover, as was true for Jefferson when he drafted the Declaration of Independence, Wilson believed that the basic principles of the law of nations were "the sacred precepts of nature and of nature's God."[83] In this Wilson was, as Roscoe Pound[84] has pointed out, borrowing deeply from the Civil Law tradition (the law that applied in much of Continental Europe), as well as that of the common law of England. Thus, as Pound explains, "in Wilson's Law Lectures (1791) Pufendorf is cited twenty-nine times and there are ten references to Grotius, ten to Vattel, four to Burlamaqui, and five to Rutherforth's Institues of Natural Law, an exposition of Grotius."[85] These four great Civilians (as expositors of the Civil Law are called), Pufendorf, Grotius, Vattel, and Burlamaqui, worked out elaborate explanations of a law that governed all nations, a universally applicable body of rules that was based in a divinely-created natural law. Wilson deserves a great deal of credit for the fact that though we rebelled against Great Britain, we kept, for ourselves, much of British law, because of a belief common among eighteenth-century American elite statesmen, like

---

[81] Wharton, *supra* note 79, at 62.

[82] *Id.*, at 62.

[83] *Id.*, at 63.

[84] On Pound, see Chapter 7, *infra*.

[85] Roscoe Pound, The Formative Era of American Law 24 (1938).

Wilson, that the English common law, which incorporated the law of nations, was, at least in part, the word of God.[86]

Born in 1742, "to a religious household of modest means" in the village of Ceres,[87] in the Scottish lowlands,[88] and educated at the University of St. Andrews, which at the time was a superior university to Oxford and Cambridge, "to say nothing of the education available in the American colonies,"[89] Wilson did not arrive in America until 1765. He successfully began the practice of law in Pennsylvania after studying, beginning in 1766, with the prominent Philadelphia attorney John Dickenson.[90] In 1774, Wilson published a pamphlet denying the authority of Parliament to legislate for the colonies, which "may have influenced" Jefferson's "We hold these truths" paragraph of the Declaration of Independence,[91] and which established Wilson "as one of the leading political thinkers of the [American] Revolution."[92] Wilson's first political position in America was as a member of the first provincial convention in Pennsylvania in 1774, and he was to prove a crucial advocate for American independence from Great Britain,[93] then, once independence was achieved, he became an important figure pressing for a strong Central government

---

[86] There was a religious foundation, for Wilson, to our most basic rights. Thus, for him, "liberty and life," were the "gifts of heaven." Bird, *supra* note 76, at 168.

[87] Pedersen, *supra* note 68, at 261.

[88] Ewald, *supra* note 65, at 902.

[89] *Id.*, at 902.

[90] *Id.*, at 904.

[91] *Id.*, at 904–905.

[92] *Id.*, at 904.

[93] Pedersen, *supra* note 68, at 265–266.

for the newly independent thirteen states, and was a leading debater at the Constitutional Convention of 1787.[94]

It appears that of all the delegates to the Philadelphia Convention, "Gouverneur Morris spoke the most frequently (173 times), followed by Wilson (168) and Madison (161)."[95] While Madison is nearly universally accorded the most prominence with regard to articulating a coherent political theory to the Constitution,[96] one could still build a case, as some have, that Wilson was the theorist with more "imagination," and, indeed, the "intellectual superior" of Madison,[97] if not himself the true father of the Constitution.[98] It appears that the earliest drafts of the document that was to become the Federal Constitution of 1787 are in Wilson's handwriting, thus suggesting his central role in the drafting of the document.[99]

More important, perhaps, than Wilson's early role in drafting the document is what he actually had to say in the Constitutional deliberations, and the philosophy of government that guided his contributions to the debates and to the Constitution itself. The principal point which

---

[94]   See generally Charles Page Smith, James Wilson, Founding Father 1742–1798 (1956), described as the first biography of this important, though usually neglected framer. See, e.g., Merrill Jensen, Book Review, 80 Pa. Mag.Hist. & Biog. 521 (1956). Smith's was the only full-length biography of Wilson as late as 1989. See Conrad, *supra* note 64, at n.1.

[95]   Ewald, *supra* note 65, at n.35, citing Clinton Rossiter, 1787: The Grand Convention 252 (1966, W.W. Norton reprint, 1987).

[96]   One of the most careful students of the Convention, however, the brilliant historian Forrest McDonald, has concluded that Madison's reputation as "the Father of the Constitution" is a "myth," since Madison's specific proposals for the Constitution were generally defeated. See Ewald, *supra* note 65, N. 43, citing Forrest McDonald, *Novus Ordo Seclorum:* The Intellectual Origins of the Constitution 205 (University Press of Kansas, 1985).

[97]   Ewald, *supra* note 65, at 918 (purportedly basing this view on the comments of Max Farrand).

[98]   Pedersen, *supra* note 68, at 269.

[99]   Pedersen, *supra* note 68, at 259.

Wilson argued in those debates was that the new Constitution had to be based "broad and deep" by founding it on the principle of popular sovereignty, by "basing it on the people themselves."[100] "In a time when most members of the ruling class considered commoners inherently inferior . . . , [Wilson] advocated placing as much power as was feasible" with the American people.[101] He "helped attain proportional representation in the House of Representatives,"[102] and, rejecting the view of his colleagues who wanted the federal legislature to elect the nation's Chief Executive, he invented the Electoral College, which gave voters at least indirect influence over the election of the President.[103] And he had wanted more.

Wilson "designed the Electoral College . . . only because it was the most democratic mechanism he could persuade his aristocratic colleagues [at the Constitutional Convention] to accept."[104] Even though it struck his fellow delegates as a "chimerical" suggestion, Wilson unsuccessfully argued for the proposed federal executive to be elected directly by the American people.[105] Similarly, he believed that there should be "direct popular election of the Senate, and, indeed, he advocated a consistent application of the principle of 'one man, one vote.' "[106] "On each of these points," William Ewald, Wilson's much later successor as a Professor of Law and Philosophy at the University of Pennsylvania, properly concludes that Wilson's proposals "were still-born, but on each subsequent experiences have

---

[100]   Ewald, *supra* note 65, at 916.

[101]   Pedersen, *supra* note 68, at 258.

[102]   *Id.*, at 269.

[103]   *Id.*, at 269–270.

[104]   *Id.*, at 319.

[105]   Ewald, *supra* note 65, at 921–922.

[106]   *Id.*, at 922.

tended to vindicate Wilson's practical insight, not that of his colleagues."[107] Still, "Wilson alone, who wielded his formidable intellect on behalf of democracy throughout the Convention, is a major part of the reason why the Constitution ended up as democratic a document as it did."[108] And that, possibly, might be too modest praise of Wilson. According to one recent commentator, "History has vindicated [Wilson] so many times, showing him to have been startlingly ahead of the curve on issue after issue in a way that no other Founder ever was. . . . He was a political Leonardo da Vinci."[109]

Even if Wilson did not persuade his colleagues at the Constitutional Convention to embrace popular sovereignty to the extent he would have wished, Wilson's law lectures, which he delivered as the first law professor at what is now the University of Pennsylvania,[110] became an essential work on the new Federal Constitution, and, as Ewald and others have suggested, he has thus justly been regarded as an important framer of American public law. Equally important for our purposes, however, is that Wilson probably also deserves much of the credit for transplanting the Blackstonian system of the common law onto American soil, so that his influence over private law is every bit as important as it is over public law.[111] Shortly after American independence, every new American state passed a statute adopting the English common law, insofar as it was

---

[107] *Id.*, at 922.

[108] Pedersen, *supra* note 68, at 270.

[109] *Id.*, at 259.

[110] Conrad, *supra* note 64, at 189.

[111] As Knapp explains, "Wilson's jurisprudence, moreover, helped rehabilitate the common law against repeated nativistic attacks from post-Revolutionary law reformers by republicanizing and thereby rendering it culturally durable at a moment when it might have met its permanent demise on American shores." Knapp, *supra* note 66, at 197.

applicable to American institutions, but no one really knew what that meant. Some things were obvious—of course, in this country there was no established national church, nor was there a monarchy or a titled aristocracy, and this meant that those branches of the Blackstonian common law that dealt with those institutions had no force here. But how, then, were we tell what parts of the English common law were free from the taint of aristocracy and monarchy?

Though Wilson may not have succeeded in promoting Constitutional provisions which reflected direct democracy, it nevertheless remained true that American law had to be bottomed on popular sovereignty, but how, then, would we reconcile republican needs with what might well be regarded as an essentially aristocratic body of English common law doctrines?[112] Realizing this problem, some of Wilson's Pennsylvania contemporaries proposed simply cashiering the common law, and replacing it with a statutory code, but Wilson and other conservatives resisted this, believing it was a prescription for anarchy and chaos. Indeed, Wilson had earlier lost some confidence in his Pennsylvania contemporaries, who failed to reelect him to the Continental Congress in 1777 after he had opposed the new 1776 Pennsylvania Constitution "apparently because its unicameral legislature and subordination of executive and judicial functions put too much faith in the people."[113] According to one recent student of Wilson's life and jurisprudence, "Wilson's social position as a wealthy

---

[112] For Knapp, "As the first sustained attempt by a native jurist in American history to reflect systematically on the nature of American law as distinct from its English counterpart, Wilson's law lectures gave birth to American jurisprudence as such." *Id.*, at 194. For the English common law, as expounded by Blackstone, see Chapter 1, *supra.*

[113] Knapp, *supra* note 66, at 200–201. For an edited text of the 1776 Pennsylvania Constitution, and some evaluation of its provisions, see, e.g., Stephen B. Presser and Jamil S. Zainaldin, Law and Jurisprudence in American History 122–134 (West Publishing, 8th ed. 2013).

Philadelphia lawyer, his delay in voting for Independence," his "leadership of the campaign to repeal the radical Constitution of 1776," and his successful defense of several men accused of treason to the new state of Pennsylvania, "pushed the limits of prudence" for Wilson, who "found himself threatened by an armed mob, in the course of which threat six people lost their lives, and Wilson was temporarily forced into hiding."[114] And, yet, especially in his later years, it was clear for Wilson that the only legitimate sovereign in America was the American people themselves.[115]

Moreover, Wilson sympathized at least in part with some American critics of the English common law who condemned its esoteric and essentially class-biased nature. So for Wilson, then, the task became not only to simplify and clarify the law for Americans, but "His larger philosophical vision endeavored to transform the Anglicized common law-based jurisprudence passed down from the colonial period, a jurisprudence that originated in England and that only an elite corps of legal professionals could understand and apply, into an Americanized humanistic jurisprudence created, understood, and applied by a broad cross-section of the citizenry, and oriented toward the American future."[116]

Wilson's law lectures, the vehicle for this transformation, were "intended to make him the American equivalent of Sir [William] Blackstone,"[117] but Wilson, in his lectures, drew some distinctions between his conception

---

[114]   Ewald, *supra* note 65, at 907–908.

[115]   As Knapp puts it, "[O]n December 1, 1787, James Wilson literally invented the American people as a unitary sovereign entity." Knapp, *supra* note 66, at 229.

[116]   Knapp, *supra* note 66, at 237.

[117]   Hall, Introduction, *supra* note 75, at xiv.

of law and that of Blackstone. While Blackstone had based the legitimacy of law on the commands of an omnipotent sovereign, or, perhaps, the dictates of the Deity, Wilson chose to ground the law in the consent of the governed, the American people.[118] It was the principle of popular sovereignty that allowed Wilson to endorse the strong central government that emerged out of the Convention in 1787, since, for Wilson, the entire body of the American people themselves, where, according to Wilson sovereignty actually vested in the newly independent United States, could restrict the operations of the state governments.[119] This according to venerable American historian Merrill Jensen, was an act of "sheer political genius."[120]

It was a little bit theoretically trickier to come up with a means of reconciling popular sovereignty with the English common law. Could it be said that the now sovereign American people really consented to the adoption of that common law? At one level it certainly could be said that they did, since every single newly independent state legislature passed a statute adopting the English common law insofar as it was consistent with American institutions.[121] But even if this had not been the case, it appears that Wilson believed that the consent of the American people to the English common law could be expressed by a history of behavior, and by consistent adherence to "Long and general

---

[118] Knapp, *supra* note 66, at 257–258. It should be recognized, however, that Blackstone himself, as Conrad puts it, "did pay eloquent lip service to the principle of consensual obligation, foremostly in rehearsing the common-law tenet that 'custom' evinces 'consent.' " Conrad, *supra* note 64, at 199, citing 1 W. Blackstone, Commentaries on the Laws of England—A Facsmile of the First Edition of 1765–1769, at 74 (1979).

[119] See, e.g., Jensen, *supra* note 94, at 523.

[120] *Ibid.*

[121] For some sample reception statutes, see, e.g., http://www.iuslaw.org/ reception_statutes.php (Virginia, Delaware, Pennsylvania, New York, North Carolina, Massachusetts) (accessed 2 March 2016).

custom,"[122] which custom, of course, was an established basis, even in Blackstone, for the English common law. It thus became possible, through the device of adherence to custom, for Wilson to claim popular acceptance of, and thus the legitimacy of, the English common law in America.[123] Indeed, it appears that for Wilson the maxim that "a free people are governed by laws, of which they approve," was of "prime importance" to the extent that "*[C]onsent* is the sole obligatory principle of human government and human laws."[124]

For Wilson, however, there was more to the common law than simply a reflection of the consent of the governed. Indeed, Wilson's highest regard, according to a provocative piece by Stephen Conrad, was for the common law, and, according to Conrad, "Wilson held the common law not only over and above statutory law, but also perhaps—and Wilson's apparent ambiguity is at the heart of the matter— over and above what we now call *constitutional* law."[125] This affection of Wilson's was expressed in words verging on the poetic. As Conrad suggests, "With language that anticipated Keats himself, [Wilson] praised the Common Law as not only 'just' but 'beautiful'; indeed 'to every age,' [Wilson] said, 'it has disclosed new beauties and new truths.' "[126] Conrad agrees with Aaron Knapp that the argument from custom was important to Wilson, and, indeed, Conrad asserts that "the character of the common law as customary law moved Wilson to the language of superlatives."[127] Still, Conrad explains, what Wilson really

---

[122] Knapp, *supra* note 66, at 261.

[123] Knapp, *supra* note 66, at 262.

[124] Quoted by Conrad, *supra* note 64, at 199 (emphasis in original).

[125] *Id.*, at 187 (emphasis in original).

[126] *Id.*, at 189.

[127] *Id.*, at 190–191.

wanted, in the process of reconceiving the English common law as fit for America was "to incorporate into American constitutionalism something of the proverbial political virtues of aristocracy—namely, wisdom and knowledge," but in a manner that would still be "compatible with the fortunes of thoroughly *popular* republicanism."[128]

This was no easy task, apparently, and required departing from the Blackstonian conception of absolute sovereignty and discretion vesting in the legislature, in the case of England, of course, in King, Lords, and Commons.[129] For Wilson, the common law became the supreme legal authority by virtue not only of its resting on consent, but also because it embodied what might be referred to as the "historical science" or "the science of human nature," gained by experience over the ages, "from the Greeks and Romans, to the Druids, and through the Saxon, Norman and later epochs of the British constitution, down to 'the common law, as now received in America.' "[130] Thus the common law teaches us the essential truths of human nature, as revealed by experience over many ages. One of these truths, it would seem, was the primacy of what Wilson called "manners," which we would understand as the "mores"[131] or the social obligations of the members of society, the moral obligations that each owes to the other, obligations, really, that are the foundation of law. Or, as Conrad explained it, Wilson understood that in an America, guided by the wise precepts of the common law and accumulated knowledge

---

[128] *Id.*, at 198.

[129] *Id.*, at 200. For this classical conception as limned by Blackstone, see Chapter 1, *supra*, text accompanying notes 49–52. This classical conception of the English Constitution has recently been dramatically altered in practice. *See generally* Erin F. Delaney, Judiciary Rising: Constitutional Change in the United Kingdom, 108 Nw.U.L.Rev. 543 (2014).

[130] Conrad, *supra* note 64, at 202.

[131] *Id.*, at 208.

"progress in virtue," and "progress in knowledge" could be attained together.[132]

While, then, Wilson's jurisprudence may have ultimately rested on the consent of the governed, there was also a realization in Wilson's thought that the sources of discriminating between right and wrong among the sovereign American people included a moral sense placed in each of us by a benevolent Creator. The law employed this divinely-inspired moral sense just as it employed reason to achieve its objectives of liberty and the rule of law.[133] Wilson clearly believed in natural rights, as well as he believed in popular sovereignty, and his belief in natural rights was a belief grounded, "in the immediate evidence arising from the most basic and natural of the human inclinations," as understood, for example, in the Scottish common-sense philosophy of Thomas Reid.[134] As Kermit Hall has explained, "While Wilson owed a great deal to the Scottish Moral Enlightenment, he also infused his lectures with ideas drawn from John Locke, insisting that government depended on a voluntary compact that included the right and duty of every citizen to act in ways that conformed to the laws of God and nature."[135] Thus, as did Jefferson in the Declaration, Wilson recognized these human inclinations, which led to the creation of natural rights, were creations of nature's God. Wilson's project in his Lectures in particular, as Hall explained, was "to synthesize principles of natural

---

[132] *Id.*, at 213.

[133] See, e.g., Knapp, *supra* note 66, at 266–270.

[134] For the influence of Scottish common-sense philosophy and Thomas Reid in particular on Wilson, see, e.g., Daniel N. Robinson, Do the people of the United States form a nation? James Wilson's theory of rights, 8 Int.J. Constitutional Law 287 (2010). The quote in the text appears *id.*, at 292.

[135] Hall, *supra* note 75, at xxi. For the influence of the Scottish Enlightenment on American Constitutional thought generally, see, e.g., the path-breaking article, James E. Pfander & Daniel D. Birk, Article III and the Scottish Judiciary, 124 Harv. L. Rev. 1613 (2011).

law and popular will," resulting in Wilson's "most definitive statement about the character of American law."[136] In this manner, Wilson was able to arrive at a similar point to that of Blackstone, to wit, that American law (like the English law) included a component of divine natural law. A generation later this notion that morals and religion were inseparable even from Constitutional law was taken up by Joseph Story.

---

[136] Hall, *supra* note 75, at xiv.

CHAPTER 3

TOWARDS AN AMERICAN COMMON AND CONSTITUTIONAL LAW

EARLY NINETEENTH CENTURY

Joseph Story
(Harvard)

■ ■ ■

Joseph Story (1779–1845)
Engraved by G. Parker from a painting by Chester Harding.
Historical & Special Collections, Harvard Law School Library.

Supreme Court Associate Justice Joseph Story was one of the earliest teachers to hold a chair devoted to law at an American University. Story became the Dane professor of law at Harvard in 1829, and the donor of that chair, Nathan Dane, who designated Story as the first occupant of the chair, was the enormously successful author of a law book, Dane's *General Abridgement and Digest of American Law.* This was an echo of Blackstone's Vinerian chair at Oxford, donated by Charles Viner, who had written a very successful *General Abridgement* of *English Law*. At Harvard "Story proved to be an extremely popular teacher, and his efforts and prestige were a major factor in the Harvard Law School's flourishing state during the sixteen years that he served as Dane Professor."[137]

Story began the tradition of American law professors writing learned treatises on the law to be used by judges and practitioners (he wrote nine of them on different topics),[138] Story's latter-day successor at Harvard, Roscoe Pound[139] gives these treatises credit for the successful reception of the common law in America,[140] and Story, though he was appointed to the Supreme Court in 1811 by the Republican James Madison, probably did more than anyone else to enshrine the Federalist views of Alexander Hamilton into the United States Constitution. He was, for many years, a colleague of the great Chief Justice John Marshall on the United States Supreme Court, and while Marshall gets most of the credit for forming a nationalist jurisprudence that enabled commerce to flourish and the federal legislature to flex its muscles, the intellectual underpinnings of Marshall's soaring phrases can be found in the more erudite opinions and dense treatises written by

---

[137] H. Jefferson Powell, Joseph Story's Commentaries on the Constitution: A Belated Review, 94 Yale L. J. 1285, 1291 (1985). For the details regarding Dane's endowing what was known for some time as the "Dane Law School," see Daniel R. Coquillette and Bruce A. Kimball, On the Battlefield of Merit: Harvard Law School, The First Century 131–138 (Harvard 2016). On Story's tenure as Dane Professor, see *id.*, at 139–144.

[138] Including Bailments (1832), Constitutional Law (1833), Conflict of Laws (1834), Equity Jurisprudence (1836), Equity Pleading (1838), Agency (1839), Partnership (1841), Bills of Exchange (1843), and Promissory Notes (1845). Roscoe Pound, Formative Era of American Law 140–141 (Little Brown, 1938), Powell, *supra* note 137, at n.41.

[139] See Chapter 7, *infra.*

[140] Pound, Formative Era, *supra* note 138, at 145.

Story.[141] A case could be made that Story was the more significant jurist, or at least the more courageous or outrageous, as it was said that "Marshall avoided controversy when he could and was not fond of 'butting his head against a wall in sport'" but Story "who wrote about everything, [and] took on anyone," was so inclined to act that "if someone brought a cob in a bucket of water into his courtroom he would instantly assume admiralty jurisdiction over it."[142]

And yet, in the early twentieth century, the view that some American lawyers took of Story was anything but benign. John Chipman Gray, Louis Brandeis, and Oliver Wendell Holmes, Jr. condemned Story's views on the common law, prompted, they suggested, by his "restless vanity," and resulting in what they regarded as his infamous decision in *Swift v. Tyson*,[143] which held that there was a "federal common law" which ought to govern commercial disputes. This was supposedly corrected by *Erie v. Tompkins*,[144] which confirmed state law as the source of common law commercial doctrines, but more recent sensitive scholarship has suggested that Story actually had the better of the argument.[145]

---

[141] See generally, Stephen B. Presser, Resurrecting the Conservative Tradition in American Legal History, 13 Reviews in American History 526 (1985) (Reviewing R. Kent Newmyer, Supreme Court Justice Joseph Story: Statesman of the Old Republic (North Carolina, 1985)).

[142] Presser, *supra* note 141, at 526.

[143] Swift v. Tyson, 41 U.S. 1 (1842).

[144] Erie Railroad Co. v. Tompkins, 304 U.S. 64 (1938). On Erie and the lingering possibilities of a federal common law see the famous article, Henry J. Friendly, In Praise of *Erie* and of the new Federal Common Law, 39 N.Y.U. L. Rev. 383 (1964).

[145] See, e.g., Randall Bridwell & Ralph U. Whitten, The Constitution and the Common Law (Lexington Books, 1977), Tony Freyer, Harmony and Dissonance: The Swift and Erie Cases in American Federalim (New York University Press, 1981), and [Mark Tushnet], Note, Swift v. Tyson Exhumed, 79 Yale L. J. 284 (1969).

Nevertheless, as already indicated, Story has had his stout defenders. Roscoe Pound, in his *The Place of Judge Story in the Making of American Law* (1914),[146] "claimed that it was Story who almost single-handedly saved the American common law from the contagion of the dangerously democratic French-inspired modern Civil Law, debasement from an untrained judiciary, premature or crude codification, and from its total fragmentation into separate local legal systems."[147] Pound underscores that if Story the judge in *Swift v. Tyson* failed to create a federal commercial common law, "What Story the judge could not do, Story the text writer largely accomplished."[148] Pound claims that Story's treatise on Equity (that body of English precedents which gave judges discretion to supplement the rules of the common law) was "the decisive factor in the American reception" of English Equity jurisprudence. This was because "With much art, whether conscious or unconscious, [Story] made it seem that the precepts established by the decisions of the English Court of Chancery [the highest court of equity in England] coincided in substance with those of the Roman law as expounded by the civilians and hence were but statements of universal principles of natural law universally accepted in civilized states."[149]

In what he called "A Belated Review" of Story's *Commentaries on the Constitution* (1833), the astute constitutional historian H. Jefferson Powell, writing in 1985, paid particular attention to the manner in which Story's 1833 book rejected the "Compact" theory of the

---

[146] Roscoe Pound, The Place of Judge Story in the Making of American Law, 48 Am.L.Rev. 676 (1914).

[147] Presser, *supra* note 141, at 526–527.

[148] Pound, Formative Era, *supra* note 138, at 154.

[149] *Id.*, at 156. Compare Ronald Dworkin's approach to jurisprudence, limned in Chapter 12, *infra*.

Constitution put forward by Thomas Jefferson, James Madison, and later John Calhoun. The constitutional hermeneutic of these three men of the South emphasized the pre-eminence of the states in implementing our constitutional system, and their theory suggested that any state could judge for itself whether other states were complying with their original "compact," and could nullify federal legislation (or even secede from the Union) if the original compact was not properly enforced. Story, instead, in a manner somewhat similar to that engaged in by Wilson, suggested that "We the People," who adopted the 1789 Constitution, created a powerful and majoritarian, and, indeed a "curiously modern" national government, which only the American people, acting collectively, could unmake.[150] Story's theory, of course, became the basis of Lincoln's claim that he could nullify by armed force the South's attempt at political nullification when the Southern States seceded.

Powell's interpretation of Story departs from an earlier view of Story as something of a tool of mercantile and Northern interests, and as an enemy of democracy. For Powell, Story's *Commentaries* "was not an immutable barrier against popular rule but rather a flexible instrument guided by the dictates of republican and majoritarian rule."[151] Powell demonstrates nicely how Story's *Commentaries on the Constitution* "provided nationalists with a detailed refutation of the historical and theoretical underpinnings of the states' rights theory of the Constitution [set forth by Jefferson, Madison, and Calhoun], and supplied supporters of an expansive domestic

---

[150] H. Jefferson Powell, Joseph Story's Commentaries on the Constitution: A Belated Review, 94 Yale L. J. 1285 (1985). On Wilson, see Chapter 2, *supra*.

[151] *Id.*, at 1288.

role for the federal government with a vigorous assertion of the federal government's powers and responsibilities."[152]

Kent Newmyer's monumental work on Story[153] is very much in this positive vein, although his Story, his "Statesman of the Old Republic," is a "proud leader of the [American] bench and bar, a man who stands for everything noble in the legal profession," a veritable "Tocquevillian portrait in aristocratic lawyering."[154] For Newmyer, Story's most comprehensive and brilliant biographer, Story was not simply a majoritarian, rather he was "a figure who tried to be above democratic politics and to infuse American public and private law with 'old Republican' selfless virtues."[155] These were the beliefs manifested as well by the great Federalist theorists and judges such as Alexander Hamilton and John Marshall, and by some of the New England Whigs in the 1820s and 1830's, and, in particular, Story's Massachusetts colleague, Daniel Webster. They and Story "stood for binding the nation together through the use of a commercial and national elite, 'the good, the wise, and the elevated,' in Story's phrase, who would provide prosperity, and to whom a virtuous citizenry would naturally defer."[156]

The elitism of the Old Republic is now out of favor and fashion, of course, but for Story it resulted in a creative and sensible Constitutional and private law jurisprudence. As Newmyer demonstrated, unlike what Brandeis, Holmes, and Gray believed, the foundation of Story's view of commercial law was not some sort of oppressive "brooding omnipresence," but was "rather a carefully-crafted attempt

---

[152] Id., at 1293–94.

[153] R. Kent Newmyer, Supreme Court Justice Joseph Story: Statesman of the Old Republic (North Carolina, 1985).

[154] Presser, supra note 141, at 528.

[155] Id., at 528.

[156] Quotations are from id., at 528.

to capture the actual custom of New England merchants and bankers."[157] It could be suggested that Story's commercial jurisprudence, by furthering the growth of the nineteenth-century economy, resulted eventually in benefits for all, but it has been argued that some disproportionately partook of those benefits. More troubling for Story's legacy was that he did not hesitate to make clear what he detested, and this included "Thomas Jefferson, Andrew Jackson, and the misguided mobs" their political allies "fomented and encouraged."[158]

Story's *Commentaries on the Constitution*, available for many years in a one-volume student edition,[159] shaped the beliefs of a generation of law students, politicians and statesmen. It is likely that Tocqueville's famous observation that lawyers serve as the only true aristocrats in America is, at least in part, attributable to the fact that while Tocqueville was conducting his survey of Americans in the early 1830's, he spent some time with Story, who guided the French visitor's reading and contributed to his appreciation of American law and legal institutions.[160]

Still, as Morton J. Horwitz and others have shown, while Story's constitutional jurisprudence may have been

[157] *Id.*, at 529.

[158] *Ibid.*

[159] Reprinted as Joseph Story, A Familiar Exposition of the Constitution of the United States (1986 reprint of the 1840 edition by Regnery Publishing, Inc. for the Conservative Book Club, with a forward by Edwin Meese III).

[160] See, e.g., Adam Cohen, Democracy in America, Then and Now, a Struggle Against Majority Tyranny, New York Times, January 23, 2006 ("Tocqueville, who was born into the French aristocracy, was just 25 years old when he landed in Newport, R.I., in 1831 with the professed aim of studying the American penal system. In his travels, he visited prisons, but he also interviewed important personages, including President Andrew Jackson, former president John Quincy Adams and Supreme Court Justice Joseph Story.") Available on the web at http://www.nytimes.com/2006/01/23/opinion/23mon3.html?_r=0 (accessed 20 February 2016).

deeply conservative, and deeply influenced by English thinkers such as Blackstone and Edmund Burke, his work on the common law was subtly, and in some cases even brazenly, transformative.[161] Story's transformative work, taking the English common law materials, as he and some of his contemporaries such as the great New York Chancellor James Kent did, and, as indicated earlier, borrowing from other jurisprudential traditions to arrive at a new American synthesis, was appreciated as early as 1938 in the work of Roscoe Pound, who wrote that

> Not the least of the means by which Kent and Story did so much to insure the general reception of English common law was a skillful use of comparative law, seeming to show the identity of an ideal form of the common-law rule with an ideal form of the civil-law rule, and thus demonstrating the identity of each with a universally acknowledged law of nature.[162]

The realization of that phenomenon, of American judges creatively transforming the law, and idealist borrowing from other traditions, was later to provide a basis for

---

[161] For Horwitz's take on Story's transformative jurisprudence see his Bancroft Prize-winning work, Morton J. Horwitz, The Transformation of American Law 1780–1860 (Harvard, 1977), and for Horwitz's notable disparagement of two Story biographers see his seminal essay, Morton J. Horwitz, The Conservative Tradition in the Writing of American Legal History, 17 Am. J. Leg. History 275 (1973). The two biographies Horwitz criticized give a clear picture of the conventional view of Story as an orthodox lawyers' icon—Gerald T. Dunne, Justice Joseph Story and the Rise of the Supreme Court (Simon & Schuster, 1970) and James T. McClelland, Joseph Story and the American Constitution (Oklahoma, 1971). See also Newmyer, *supra* note 153. For James Kent's failures as a law professor at Columbia, and for his success through his *Commentaries on the American Law* in influencing Joseph Story's work at Harvard see Coquillette and Kimball, *supra* note 137, at 144–146. Coquillete and Kimball limn Kent's three principles regarding the teaching of law of universality, political liberalism, and utility. *Id.*, at 145–146.

[162] Pound, *supra* note 138, at 107.

twentieth-century academics successfully to argue for a radical transformation in American law, one that doubtless would have horrified Blackstone and Story.[163]

Story, then, should be seen as one of the seminal figures in the forming of an American jurisprudence, one purportedly anchored in universal principles, and like Blackstone and like Wilson, Story understood that divine authority undergirded the doctrines of the law. In his *Constitutional Commentaries*, Story even took the position that it was the job of government to promote religion, and, indeed, an explicitly Christian version of religion. This may have been put most pithily by Story in his *Familiar Exposition of the Constitution*,[164] where he wrote, discussing the First Amendment:

> How far any government has a right to interfere in matters touching religion, has been a subject much discussed by writers upon public and political law. The right and the duty of the interference of government, in matters of religion, have been maintained by many distinguished authors, as well those, who were the warmest advocates of free government, as those, who were attached to governments of a more arbitrary character. Indeed, the right of a society or government to interfere in matters of religion will hardly be contested by any persons, who believe that piety,

---

[163] For that development, see, e.g., Note, 'Round and 'Round the Bramble Bush: From Legal Realism to Critical Legal Scholarship, 95 Harv. L. Rev. 1669, 1678 (1982) ("By demonstrating that first principles, not only doctrinal details, are products of historical circumstance and historically specific modes of legal reasoning, the critical legal scholar uses history to disclose that the underlying assumptions of doctrinal fields lack the necessity sometimes claimed for them—to demonstrate that such assumptions represent mere choices of one set of values over another.") For more on Critical Legal Studies, see Chapter 14, *infra*.

[164] *Supra* note 159.

religion, and morality are intimately connected
with the well being of the state, and indispensable
to the administration of civil justice. The
promulgation of the great doctrines of religion, the
being, and attributes, and providence of one
Almighty God; the responsibility to him for all our
actions, founded upon moral freedom and
accountability; a future state of rewards and
punishments; the cultivation of all the personal,
social, and benevolent virtues;—these never can be
a matter of indifference in any well ordered
community. It is, indeed, difficult to conceive, how
any civilized society can well exist without them.
And at all events, it is impossible for those, who
believe in the truth of Christianity, as a divine
revelation, to doubt, that it is the especial duty of
government to foster, and encourage it among all
the citizens and subjects. This is a point wholly
distinct from that of the right of private judgment
in matters of religion, and of the freedom of public
worship according to the dictates of one's
conscience.[165]

Story added that "Probably, at the time of the adoption of
the Constitution, and of the [First Amendment] . . . the
general, if not the universal, sentiment in America was that
Christianity ought to receive encouragement from the
State, so far as such encouragement was not incompatible
with the private rights of conscience, and the freedom of
religious worship. An attempt to level all religions, and to
make it a matter of state policy to hold all in utter
indifference, would have created universal disapprobation,

---

[165] *Id.*, at 314–315. This passage also appears (in identical language) in
Story's more famous *Commentaries on the Constitution* (1833).

if not universal indignation."[166] Story would have been
surprised, if not shocked and dismayed, that the modern
United States Supreme Court majority now believes that
the Constitution's First Amendment was designed, for all
practical purposes, to banish religion from the public
square, or at least to prevent the government from
promoting belief in the Deity.[167]

Story's contemporary, Robert Rantoul,[168] a defender of
the laboring classes, and perhaps even a prototype of the
modern public interest lawyer such as Ralph Nader,[169]
picked up where Bentham left off, so to speak, and
condemned the English common law as the product of
barbarism and feudalism, and as wholly inappropriate for a
modern American republic.[170] Influenced by events in early
nineteenth-century France, where Napoleon had

---

[166] Story, *supra* note 159, at 316.

[167] For one of the clearest recent Supreme Court statements that the
government is forbidden from taking the side of religion against non-believers,
see, e.g., Lee v. Weisman, 505 U.S. 577 (1992) (Forbidding a prayer at a middle
school graduation ceremony). For an argument that the government must be
neutral in matters of religion, and yet extend protection to religion to prevent
it from being manipulated by politicians, see Andrew Koppelman, Defending
American Religious Neutrality (Harvard, 2013). For an empirical study
suggesting that judicial ideology is determining outcomes in establishment-
clause cases in the lower courts, see Gregory C. Sisk, and Michael Heise,
Ideology 'All the Way Down'? An Empirical Study of Establishment Clause
Decisions in the Federal Courts, 110 Mich.L.Rev. 1201 (2012).

[168] There is, as yet, no modern scholarly biography of Rantoul. For the
facts of his life and some of his writings, see Luther Hamilton, ed., Memoirs,
Speeches, and Writings of Robert Rantoul, Jr. (Boston, John P. Jewett & Co.,
1854). Available in a digitized version on the web at https://archive.org/
details/memspeeches00rantrich (accessed 3 August 2016).

[169] For Nader's career as a champion of the public interest, see, e.g.,
Charles McCarry, Citizen Nader (Saturday Review Press, 1972).

[170] This attitude is to be found in Rantoul's famous Fourth of July 1836,
"Oration at Scituate," reproduced in part in Stephen B. Presser and Jamil S.
Zainaldin, Law and Jurisprudence in American History 305–307 (West
Publishing, 8th ed. 2013). For the entire text see, e.g., Hamilton, *supra* note
168, at 251–296. For Bentham, see Chapter 1, *supra*, on Blackstone.

supervised the promulgation of a code, an assemblage of statutes, to replace the aristocratic and monarchical legal system of the *Ancien Regime*, Rantoul argued that democracy in America also required such a code—"the whole body of the law must be codifed,"[171] into statute form, Rantoul explained, and our law should not be "ambiguous base-born, purblind, perishable common law,"[172] but Story disagreed.

Still, Story appeared ready to concede that certainty for law in the new republic might require that some legal rules be written down, and while he did even cooperate with the Massachusetts legislature in seeking to codify some of the important common law rules,[173] it might better be said that his many treatises went far toward giving the law a coherent written formulation. It does, in fact, seem possible, as Pound hinted, that the reason why the common law lingered so long as the basic legal authority in America was its promulgation and enshrinement in the series of legal treatises produced by Story and others in the nineteenth and twentieth centuries in America, and widely available to American lawyers, judges, and academics.[174]

More importantly, riding Circuit, Story demonstrated that English common law doctrines did not necessarily bind

---

[171] Hamilton, *supra* note 168, at 281.

[172] Hamilton, *supra* note 168, at 279.

[173] Codification of the Common Law: Report of Joseph Story, Theron Metcalf, Simon Greenleaf, Charles E. Forbes, and Luther S. Cushing, Made to the Legislature of Massachusetts in 1836 (Martin B. Brown, 1887).

[174] The greatest of these treatises was the multi-volume treatise on evidence, produced by John Henry Wigmore. See *infra*, Chapter 6. For the rise and fall of what might be regarded as the legal treatise tradition, see, e.g., A.W.B. Simpson, The Rise and Fall of the Legal Treatise: Legal Principles and the Forms of Legal Literature, 48 U. Chi. L. Rev. 632 (1981); Morton J. Horwitz, Treatise Literature, 69 Law Libr. J. 460 (1976), and, especially, Richard A. Danner, Forward: Oh, the Treatise!, 111 Michigan Law Review 821 (2013).

Americans if they were contrary to American needs. Thus, for example, in the great case of *Van Ness v. Packard*,[175] Story rejected the English doctrine that would not permit a tenant to remove trade fixtures used for agricultural purposes (the English doctrine held, essentially, that all such fixtures, once erected, belonged to the landlord), both because the established custom in America was different, and because the purposes the law served in England might not necessarily be right for America. The American Common Law, in short, could be used to fashion rules for a republic, even if its origin, the English Common Law doctrines, was in an aristocratic feudal society. Story seemed to understand that this task was a creative one, insofar as it would result in an American Common Law different from that of England, but Story never suggested that this required the judge self-consciously to engage in legislation. Rather, it would seem, Story assumed that a sensible judge would understand, as a matter of logic and common sense, that some English rules were simply inapplicable in America.

Story also believed that certainty in the commercial law (an important topic for a man who had authored a treatise on Bills and Notes and who, while a Supreme Court Justice, also served not only as Dane Professor of Law at Harvard, but also as the President of the Merchant's Bank of Salem and the Vice-President of the Salem Savings Bank) required that the Common Law that governed, for example, the law of negotiable instruments, ought to be national rather than local. Believing that the commercial law was, like the law of nations, something that had to be expected to apply to cross-border transactions, in one of his most famous opinions, *Swift v. Tyson*,[176] Story held that the general commercial

---

[175] Van Ness v. Pacard, 27 U.S. (2 Pet.) 137 (1829).

[176] Swift v. Tyson, 41 U.S. 1 (1842).

Common Law ought to trump the law of New York, thus creating something that has come to be a called a "federal common law." Story also believed in a federal criminal Common Law, one that reflected universal principles of criminal jurisprudence, but the Supreme Court had explicitly rejected that view in 1812.[177] As indicated earlier, Story's federal commercial common law endured until *Erie Railroad v. Tompkins*,[178] in 1938, when the United States Supreme Court, perhaps exemplifying the view earlier attributed to Gray, Brandeis, and Holmes, and not understanding that Story actually had a fairly limited view of federal Common Law, rejected it.

In the first part of the nineteenth century, during the period of the great decisions of the Marshall court, including *Dartmouth College*,[179] *Gibbons v. Ogden*,[180] and *Swift v. Tyson*, Story (and Marshall) were in the ascendance, conducting something of a rear-guard action against the Jacksonians for the protection of private property, and for the maintenance of the certainty and stability of the economic order. As the century wore on, however, and as Democratic Presidents began to nominate a majority of the Supreme Court, this changed. By 1837, with the new Chief Justice Roger Taney, former attorney general to Andrew Jackson, the Court's position on these issues was undergoing an important alteration. In an extraordinary decision, the *Charles River Bridge* case,[181] pursuant to a majority opinion written by the new Chief Justice Taney, the Court, in effect, eviscerated Massachusetts's grant of a

---

[177]   United States v. Hudson and Goodwin, 11 U.S. 32 (1812). For Story's belief in the federal Common Law of crimes, see United States v. Coolidge, 25 F. Cas. 619, 621 (C.C.D. Mass. 1813) (No. 14,857) (opinion of Story, J.).

[178]   Erie R. Co. v. Tompkins, 304 U.S. 64 (1938).

[179]   Trustees of Dartmouth College v. Woodward, 17 U.S. 518 (1819).

[180]   Gibbons v. Ogden, 22 U.S. 1 (1824).

[181]   Charles River Bridge v. Warren Bridge, 36 U.S. 420 (1837).

monopoly to one bridge company, by allowing a competing bridge to operate, in a decision with clear populist and anti-monopoly Jacksonian undertones. The decision has been aptly called "Creative Destruction,"[182] as it promoted competition, and, theoretically, at least, economic progress. But the Supreme Court's opinion also upset commercial predictability, and seemed to presage what Samuel Chase once called, "mobocracy, the worst of all possible governments."[183] Chagrined, Story gloomily dissented, and wrote that he would have simply enforced the clear property rights originally granted by Massachusetts.

Story's career may thus have ended in something close to despair. Story set out, and to a great extent probably succeeded, in creating a national law of commerce, and, indeed, quite possibly "making the country safe for New England capital."[184] But what Story may not have understood (and what Tocqueville did) was that "by encouraging the rise of acquisitive, individualistic industrial capitalists," Story may also have "run the risk of creating a society in which the values [that he cherished] of republican deference, reciprocity, civility, artistic aspiration, and even Christian charity . . . might be undermined."[185] Perhaps Story was cheered by the words of one of his admirers, Charles Sumner, who told him that reading Taney's majority opinion after reading Story's dissent in *Charles River Bridge* was like drinking "hog wash

---

[182]   Stanley I. Kutler, Privilege and Creative Destruction: The Charles River Bridge Case (Johns Hopkins University Press, 1989).

[183]   This suggestion was made in Chase's ill-fated charge to the Baltimore Grand Jury in 1803, which inexorably led to his impeachment, the only such proceeding ever brought against a Supreme Court Justice. The Senate failed to convict by the requisite two-thirds vote, however, and Chase remained on the bench. The Grand Jury Charge is excerpted in Presser & Zainaldin, *supra* note 170, at 269–271.

[184]   Presser, *supra* note 141, at 532.

[185]   *Id.*, at 532.

after champagne,"[186] but the times finally may have been moving beyond Story.

There were some other notable nineteenth century teachers of law[187] but for our purposes it is not until the late nineteenth century when two major thinkers, Christopher Columbus Langdell, and Oliver Wendell Holmes, Jr. exerted an influence which still lingers today, and it is to them we next turn. We might pause a moment before leaving Story, a great Burkean, and a great conservative, to contemplate the caution of Story's great biographer, Kent Newmyer. Newmyer "made clear his belief that Story's conservatism" would be "no comfort for those modern conservatives who seek to shackle the Supreme Court and who believe that 'plumbers are corrupt and grape pickers overpaid.' "[188] But this characterization of conservatives might well miss the mark. What Story really stood for was a nobler vision of conservatism, one that is not wholly absent in the work of other "Republican" [in both the old and new senses of the term] Justices, such as Samuel Chase, Richard Peters, Rufus Peckham, and more recently, William Rehnquist, Antonin Scalia, and Clarence Thomas, who may well have wished to recapture Story's vision of a "moral, altruistic Burkean legal aristocracy."[189]

---

[186] Gerald T. Dunne, Justice Joseph Story and the Rise of the Supreme Court 365–366 (Simon & Schuster, 1970).

[187] See, e.g., David M. Rabban, Law's History: American Legal Thought and the Transatlantic Turn to History (Cambridge, 2013) (Discussing several important nineteenth-century thinkers) and see also, Stephen A. Siegel, Historicism in Late Nineteenth-Century Constitutional Thought, 1990 Wis. L. Rev. 1431, Duncan Kennedy, The Rise and Fall of Classical Legal Thought (Beard Books, 2006), and William M. Wiecek, The Lost World of Classical Legal Thought (Oxford, 1998).

[188] Presser, *supra* note 141, at 533, citing Newmyer, *supra* note 141, at 390.

[189] Presser, *supra* note 141, at 533.

CHAPTER 4

LAW AS SCIENCE?

LATE NINETEENTH CENTURY

Christopher Columbus Langdell
(Harvard)

■ ■ ■

Christopher Columbus Langdell (1826–1906)
Oil painting by Frederick Porter Vinton (1892).
Historical & Special Collections, Harvard Law School Library.

If James Wilson and Joseph Story were the most prominent examples of early American law professors, with Christopher Columbus Langdell, we reach a recognizably more modern model, and while Blackstone, Wilson, and Story, or at least the ideals they espoused, retain some lasting influence on American legal learning, it is clear that Langdell's original and continuing impact on American legal education is unparalleled. "The appointment of Langdell as Dane Professor at Harvard Law School on January 6, 1870, is widely acknowledged to mark the beginning of the modern American law school."[190] As Robert Gordon has observed, Langdell's Harvard model, by 1900, was becoming universal in American legal education. Harvard's "example—sometimes transmitted by Harvard's own former faculty as pro-consular deans, such as William Keener at Columbia and Joseph Beale at Chicago—spread to other leading law schools between 1895 and 1925; and between 1925 and 1950 virtually every full-time university-based law school in the country had adopted the Harvard model's basic elements."[191]

Langdell, the father of the Harvard "method," was the first American law professor to write a modern law school casebook[192] (which form is still the most-employed teaching tool for American law), and the founder as well, it is said, of the law school Socratic method, long the dominant classroom style in American law schools. Langdell's Harvard was "the prototype for modern legal education in the United States: the three-year postgraduate sequenced curriculum of private-law courses staffed by a faculty of full-time academics. . . ."[193] It was a serious program of academic study with rigorous examinations in discrete courses, and "a high flunk-out rate for those who failed them. (This replaced the casual system in which students

---

[190] William P. LaPiana, Logic and Experience: The Origin of Modern American Legal Education 3 (Oxford, 1994).

[191] Robert W. Gordon, The Geologic Strata of the Law School Curriculum, 60 Vand.L.Rev. 339, 340 (2007). See also Paul Carrington, Diversity, 1992 Utah L. Rev. 1105, 1187 ("The three-year curriculum was first made a firm requirement at Harvard in 1899. By the beginning of World War I, most of its students were also college graduates. The gradual movement of other schools in the direction of a seven-year total requirement proceeded for decades, but it was not until the Great Depression inspired fears of overcrowding in the bar that the American Bar Association imposed the three-year law requirement on all approved schools.") (footnotes omitted).

[192] Christopher Columbus Langdell, Selection of Cases on the Law of Contracts (Boston: Little Brown, 1871).

[193] Robert W. Gordon, Book Review, 93 Mich. L. Rev. 1231 (1995).

could casually drop in, attend a course of lectures, and then drop out.)"[194] In the late nineteenth century, Langdell was the most famous American law professor to claim that the law ought to be studied empirically, much as the natural sciences were beginning to be studied (in Germany and America) as physical phenomena revealing constant rules and principles.

As scientists in physics and biology, then, could study natural phenomena inductively to reveal essentials, Langdell believed that there were discoverable basic principles inherent in the reports of cases which comprise the English and American common law, and that these principles could be discovered by the close analysis of the opinions of courts in appellate cases. Study of these cases by law students, he maintained, would reveal to them the unique principles and the unique shared logic of American and English common law. Langdell believed, in other words, that law students could understand the ways of the law by studying reports of cases as if they were reports from the field, as if they were the results of scientific experiments. From the cases, he thought, the students could derive the "few" "ever-evolving" and "fructifying" principles of the common law.[195]

Much of American legal scholarship in the twentieth century was devoted to debunking Langdell's views. For example, in a recent sharp evaluation of Langdell, Wake

---

[194] Gordon, Geologic Strata, *supra* note 191, at 341.

[195] See, e.g., perhaps the most famous summary of Langdell's views on this point, that to be found in Lawrence Friedman's A History of American Law (Simon & Schuster, 1973): "Langdell had a theory for his emphasis on the case method. He believed that law was a 'science;' it had to be studied scientifically, that is, inductively through primary sources. These sources were the printed cases; they expressed, in manifold dress, the few, ever-present, and ever-evolving and fructifying principles, which constituted the genius of the common law." *Id.*, at 531.

Forest Law Professor Harold Anthony Lloyd argues that the three basic Langdellian notions of legal education—to wit, that "(1) law is a science of principles and doctrines known with certainty and primarily traced through case law, (2) studying redacted appellate cases is 'much the shortest and best, if not the only way' learning such law, and (3) despite Langdell's own roughly fifteen years of practice experience, practice experience taints one's ability to teach law" are all "wrong and counterintuitive" and have done "longstanding, substantial damage . . . to law schools and to legal education."[196] The notion that Langdellian analysis is misleading might be seen as culminating, perhaps, in Secretary Panetta's jibe,[197] repeated in the Introduction, about "the logic of a law professor," but for his time, Langdell's legal educational reforms can be understood to be quite revolutionary (as some more recent scholarship on Langdell has shown). Indeed, Langdell can be seen as the precursor of important empirical movements in twentieth-century law.

Charles Eliot, Harvard's President, having been impressed by the sophisticated approach to scientific knowledge he had found observing the late nineteenth-century teaching in German Universities, determined to create, in Cambridge, a great laboratory for the study of social science. Harvard Law School, at that point, was a moribund institution, requiring no college degree, and offering no significant academic distinction. With the appointment of Langdell, however, everything changed. Langdell was ripe for the picking, having apparently become somewhat frustrated with New York law practice, and having developed a "hearty disgust for the means &

---

[196] Harold Anthony Lloyd, Raising the Bar, Razing Langdell, 51 Wake Forest L. Rev. 231 (2016).

[197] Text accompanying note 1, *supra*.

methods by which business, place & reputation are ...
gained" at the New York bar.[198]

Somewhat in the manner that Blackstone had done,
but on a narrower scale, and focused on a particular area of
the common law, Langdell marked out a doctrinal area of
the law—"contracts" (the law of enforceable agreements)—
and sought to demonstrate that this body of doctrine had an
internal logic, and could be understood as a means of solving
practical legal problems in a more coherent manner than
had previously been suggested. For the most part, until
Langdell began teaching, law professors lectured (as had
Blackstone, Wilson, and Story), but Langdell's Socratic
method led students to explore for themselves the nature of
law.

The principles that Langdell sought to reveal, however,
were not "grand principles related to the ultimate ordering
of society," as one might find, for example, in Blackstone,
but rather "the narrow, technical principles that make up
the real work of the lawyer, which courts use to decide real
cases."[199] Before Langdell, law professors' lectures had
reflected the archaic English Common Law practices
involved in pleading cases, and had, for example, listed the
nearly innumerable back and forth forms of the Common
Law writ system and their subtle nuances. With Langdell's
method of analysis, students began to see that whatever the
historical forms of pleading, the cases themselves revealed
the dynamic qualities of bargaining behavior. Accordingly,
the law of contracts could be understood not simply as a set
of pleading requirements necessary to settle the outcome of
litigation, but, rather, as the articulation of a set of steps to

---

[198] La Piana, *supra* note 190, at 12, quoted by Gordon, *supra* note 193, at
1232.

[199] La Piana, *supra* note 190, at 57–58, quoted by Gordon, *supra* note 193,
at 1234.

present, precisely determine, and then execute mutual assent, mutual exchange, and conditions of performance. Langdell's critics then, and more recently, claimed that Langdell was reading things into the cases that actually weren't there, and that, as the famously caustic Yale Law Professor Grant Gilmore remarked, Langdell made the cases fit his doctrinal notions rather in the manner that Procrustes made his guests fit his bed,[200] but this is almost certainly and stunningly wrong.[201]

What Langdell, who, before he came to Harvard, was a talented appellate commercial lawyer in New York and a man quite familiar with the nuances of business legal practice, was actually seeking to do at Harvard was not some nefarious Procrustean pursuit, but rather Langdell simply sought to explain how contracts jurisprudence could lend certainty and predictability to the creation, performance, and the substance of actual business agreements. In seeking to break the law of contracts down into its component parts, Langdell was actually formulating a dynamic and flexible system of legal doctrine that could

---

[200] Gilmore's famous fulminations against Langdell are to be found in his Death of Contract (originally published 1975, 2nd ed., Ronald K.L. Collins, ed., 1995). For the comments about Procrustes, see *id.*, at 107–108.

[201] While Gilmore's book may be inaccurate, it was, quite possibly because of its great readability (especially for a book by a law professor) highly influential. For a fine evaluation of the book, and what it represented, see generally the symposium marking the book's 20 year anniversary in the Northwestern University Law Review in volume 90, and in particular, the article by Daniel Farber, The Ages of American Formalism, 90 Nw.U.L.Rev. 89 (1995). Farber's footnote 2, *id.*, at 89, nicely captures the criticism of Gilmore ("One reviewer referred to Gilmore's analysis as 'strikingly unhistorical.' Morton S. Horwitz, Book Review, 42 U. Cm L. Rev. 787, 794 (1975); see also Richard Danzig, The Death of Contract and the Life of the Profession: Observations on the Intellectual State of Legal Academia, 29 STAN. L. Rev. 1125, 1130 (1977) (describing the book as 'classroom history'); Richard A. Epstein, Book Review, 20 AM. J. LEGAL Hist. 68, 69 (1976) (observing that a 'wealth of precedent' cuts against Gilmore's historical analysis); James R. Gordley, Book Review, 89 Harv. L.Rev. 452, 453 (1975) (Gilmore's historical 'view of legal theorizing is parochial.').").

help order business transactions, and one that could more easily be understood by those engaged in and evaluating such arrangements.

Remarkably, modern legal historians such as the extraordinarily talented, if occasionally slightly opinionated Lawrence Freidman, have charged that Langdell's legal science, based, as they believed, on abstract theory, was like an astronomy without stars, or a geology without rocks. But more sensitive interpreters of Langdell, such as William LaPiana,[202] Marcia Speziale, Bruce Kimball,[203] and Anthony Chase, have actually understood the practical applicability of what Langdell was doing, and its basis in the actual needs of commercial actors, so that his legal science was better described as "a geology with nothing but rocks and an astronomy with nothing but stars."[204] Or, as one of the most astute and fair Critical Legal Studies scholars, Robert Gordon, explained, "Langdell was no fool; indeed, he was an accomplished practitioner whose ideas about law and how to study it not only were well grounded in contemporary jurisprudence but also strongly reflected

[202] See generally, LaPiana, *supra* note 190.

[203] Marcia Speziale, "Langdell's Concept of Law as Science: The Beginnings of Anti-formalism in American Legal Theory," 5 Vermont Law Review 1 (1980). For a further discussion of recent revisionist scholarship on Langdell see, e.g., Bruce A. Kimball, The Langdell Problem: Historicizing the Century of Historiography, 22 L. & Hist. Rev. 277 (2004). For Kimball's impressive book-length study of Langdell and his Harvard reforms, see Bruce A. Kimball, The Inception of Modern Professional Education: C.C. Langdell, 1826–1906 (UNC Press, 2009). And for Kimball and his co-author's take on the Harvard Law School itself, see Daniel R. Coquillette and Bruce A. Kimball, On the Battlefield of Merit: Harvard Law School, The First Century (Harvard, 2016).

[204] See generally Anthony Chase, "The Birth of the Modern Law School," 23 Am.J.Legal History 329 (1979), "Origins of Modern Professional Education: The Harvard Case Method Conceived as Clinical Instruction in Law," 5 Nova Law Journal 323 (1981), and "American Legal Education Since 1885: The Case of the Missing Modern," 30 N.Y.L.S.L.Rev. 519 (1985).

the experience of practice under the great changes wrought by code pleading."[205]

As Bruce Kimball recently observed, "[A] more faithful and complex picture of Langdell—the student, lawyer, professor, and dean—will emerge, as scholars overcome the ironic reluctance for the past ninety years to examine the available evidence. The irony resides in the fact that the law professor who taught his profession to scrutinize every general proposition in light of the original sources about specific cases has had his story told and his legacy shaped by many who flouted his most fundamental principle. Surely there is no greater justification for the study of Langdell to continue."[206] As Robert Gordon put it, "Langdell's Harvard experiment succeeded and spread . . . because it was able to develop a better professional product—a more rigorous and practical legal science and teaching method than its predecessors and rivals. Harvard also succeeded in creating the right niche market for its product: an elite postbellum bar anxious to upgrade its prestige and supply certifiably smart talent to the new corporate law firms."[207] The echoes of Blackstone's understanding that it was his job to inculcate an English aristocracy into the nuances and genius of the English Common Law are clearly audible.

Latter-day critics of Langdell have been particularly disparaging of his selection of appellate cases as the main matter of scrutiny for students. Langdell's belief, as indicated, was that from these cases, one could tease out the

---

[205] Robert M. Gordon, Book Review [Of LaPiana, *supra* note 190, summing up the author's thesis], 93 Mich. L. Rev. 1231, 1232 (1995). Code pleading was the result of reformist efforts that eliminated the archaic forms of common law pleading, and replaced them with more simplified, clearer, and more flexible means of initiating and conducting litigation.

[206] Kimball, Langdell Problem, *supra* note 203, at 331.

[207] Gordon, *supra* note 193, at 1232–33 (footnotes omitted).

"ever-fructifying" principles of the law, but as time wore on, it became clear that appellate cases were not necessarily reflective of the actual application of legal rules to everyday life. These days, empiricists have demonstrated, while millions of legal disputes are initiated in state and federal courts each year, a dazzling 90-something percent of them are withdrawn by the parties before there is even a trial court decision on the matter, pursuant to agreed-upon settlements.[208] In those cases that do go to trial, litigants can appeal an adverse decision reached by the trial court judge (generally limited to matters of granting or denying motions, including or excluding evidence, or the content of instructions on law given to juries), although they may not, generally speaking, challenge the factual findings of a jury. Hundreds of thousands of appeals from the state and federal trial courts are actually filed each year, but the overwhelming majority of those appellate proceedings (much like the trial court proceedings), are also withdrawn by the parties before an appellate court issues a final ruling on the dispute.[209] There is, in both the state and federal system, a second appellate review that is possible for

---

[208] See, e.g., What Percentage of Lawsuits Settle Before Trial? What Are Some Statistics on Personal Injury Settlements? http://thelawdictionary.org/article/what-percentage-of-lawsuits-settle-before-trial-what-are-some-statistics-on-personal-injury-settlements/ (accessed 31 January 2016) (about 95% of lawsuits are settled before trial). See also, for estimates of settlements in the federal trial courts, Gillian K. Hadfield, Where Have All the Trials Gone? Settlements, Nontrial Adjudications and Statistical Artifacts in the Changing Disposition of Federal Civil Cases, 1 J. Empirical Legal Stud. 705 (2004).

[209] The settlement figure is not quite as dramatic as it is for cases brought in the trial courts, but it appears to be something close to 80%. See generally Theodore Eisenberg, Appeal Rates and Outcomes in Tried and Nontried Cases: Further Exploration of Anti-Plaintiff Appellate Outcomes, 1 Journal of Empirical Legal Studies 659 (2004) (Reporting that only 22.7% of Appellate cases, where there has been a final trial court determination reach a final decision by those appellate courts; for cases appealed before there has been a final trial court determination the completion rate in the appellate court is only 10.2%).

disappointed litigants, although that second appellate review is generally discretionary both with the state Supreme Courts and the United States Supreme Court. For example, in the past few years approximately 10,000 requests for this second appellate review (usually called "a petition for a writ of certiorari") are filed each year with the United States Supreme Court, but it grants fewer than 100 of them each year.[210]

There is, then, not a little irony in the fact that most of what modern law students read to learn the law is the decisions of appellate courts, and, to a surprising extent, the opinions of state and federal Supreme Courts. Since most rational people settle their legal disputes before they reach these august bodies, students are taught by examining the products of irrationality or caprice. The cases that are not settled generally involve either extremely thorny issues of law or, perhaps, litigants who are proceeding out of perversity, spite, or similarly idiosyncratic emotional or mental conditions. To use these twisted products of litigational misadventure as the basis for learning the law would seem to render something of a warped perspective, so that perhaps Langdell's critics had a point after all, and perhaps those, like Secretary Panetta who disparage the "logic of a law professor" are reflecting the irony of a legal educational system that explores non-representative, strange, and weird materials.

Robert Gordon notes the related irony that Langdell's appellate practice-centered system of legal education emerged at the same time that the job of the professionally-ascendant lawyers Harvard increasingly was training saw a "shift of elite practice from the courtroom to the

---

[210] See, e.g., http://www.conservapedia.com/Certiorari (accessed 31 January 2016) (The rate of granting of petitions of certiorari is about 1%, fewer than 100 petitions are granted each year).

boardroom, from appellate argument to corporate reorganization practice, and from litigation to counselling and deal-making. About this emerging world of corporate practice," Gordon acidly remarks, "Langdell's school taught absolutely nothing,"[211] It remains even more true today that once most law students get into practice they discover that their job is to keep their clients out of court, and not to be litigators, and if they are litigators, much more often than not, they find themselves settling their cases. And yet, Langdell's Harvard became the successful model for American legal education, and, to a powerful extent it still is.

How can this be? Was there something about appellate case analysis that, whether or not it really was relevant for practice, sharpened the minds of law students and somehow made them better lawyers? Was this like the teaching of Latin and Greek in English Universities to men who became senior civil servants where those skills were not of immediately apparent use, but may have created a culture that worked imperial marvels?[212] Perhaps it was, as N.E.H. Hull argues, that Langdell's innovations at Harvard met the needs of the times. As she explains, "The law school replaced law office apprenticeship for two reasons: the law schools could meet the increased market demand for lawyers by a kind of mass production of lawyers that the former and time-honored method of training could not begin to approach, and the abstract analytical approach of

---

[211] Gordon, *supra* note 193, at 1244.

[212] See Gordon, *supra* note 193, at 1240–1241. ("[T]he English universities since the nineteenth century have prepared candidates for the upper civil service by teaching them Latin and Greek. That curriculum was eminently 'practical' in the indirect sense that it was rigorous and exclusive; it sorted the candidates by general intelligence and class background. But only its most generous admirers ever claimed that it taught them much of immediate utility about the governance of a nation and empire.")

Langdell's case and Socratic methods of teaching
encouraged the kind of rational reasoning that could create
legal innovation for the new [late nineteenth century]
business environment."[213] It may also be that Langdell's
analysis was much richer than his latter-day critics
understood. Bruce Kimball, probably the deepest analyst of
Langdell's work and thought, concludes that Langdell's
"jurisprudence is actually three-dimensional, exhibiting a
comprehensive yet contradictory integration of induction
from authority, deduction from principle, and analysis of
justice and policy."[214] It would be difficult to ask for more
from a system of legal education.[215]

Even the deeply skeptical Gordon concedes that
Langdell's case method was "a genuinely fruitful innovation
in pedagogy that encouraged active rather than passive
learning and that motivated the students to engage
firsthand with at least some—if deplorably few—of the
primary materials of their trade."[216] Roscoe Pound, who
brought Langdell's methods to Nebraska when he was Dean
there, in the early twentieth century, called Langdell's
pedagogy "the best system of teaching law [which] has
revolutionized its study [and] has placed the Harvard Law

---

[213] N.E.H. Hull, Roscoe Pound & Karl Llewellyn: Searching for an
American Jurisprudence 27 (Chicago, 1997).

[214] Kimball, Inception, *supra* note 203, at 6.

[215] In Kimball's book, Inception, *supra* note 203, he argues persuasively
that Langdell's Law School served as a general model for university
professional schools, and that Langdell's innovations for such schools
amounted to a "new system" of "academic meritocracy," which included "the
admissions requirement of a bachelor's degree or its equivalent, the sequenced
curriculum and its extension to three years, the inductive pedagogy of teaching
from cases, the hurdle of written examination posing hypothetical problems,
the program of study leading to academic honor, the independent career track
for faculty, the transformation of the library from a textbook dispensary to a
scholarly resource, and the national alumni association actively supporting the
school." *Id.*, at 7.

[216] Gordon, *supra* note 193, at 1259.

School in its well recognized position as the leading institution in the world for the teaching of the Common Law." For Pound, "[T]he system [of Langdell] substitutes thinking, criticism, [and] analysis, for memorizing[.]"[217] William LaPiana concludes that Harvard's success under Langdell "rested on the service it performed, both in meeting the needs of the bar for social position and prestige and in training young men for the realities of practice in a legal world transformed by an early version of the information explosion."[218] Bruce Kimball observes that "Langdell's life and work reveal that there has never existed a moment, even at its inception, when the formal system of academic meritocracy in professional education operated free of the interests, values, and prejudices of those who conceived, built, and operated the system." But he still concludes that critics of the "Langdellian orthodoxy" have failed to realize that the alternatives to what Langdell created might have included a legal profession characterized by a lack of sophistication or even political corruption. Kimball ends his consideration of Langdell by suggesting that "We must therefore consider whether, like democracy in political life, academic meritocracy may still be the best of the worst ways of organizing professional life."[219]

Gordon shrewdly notes that while Langdell's conception of the case method may have been a means, for him, of teaching about the evolution of important principles which were the bedrock of law, in his own time, even some of his colleagues had begun instead to treat cases, "simply as a means of exercising mental muscles and teaching legal

---

[217] Hull, *supra* note 213, at 52, quoting Pound.

[218] LaPiana, *supra* note 190, at 5.

[219] Kimball, Inception, *supra* note 203, at 346.

reasoning—how to 'think like a lawyer.' "[220] Moreover, "[b]y the 1920s and 1930s Legal Realist law teachers [of whom more soon] used cases largely as storehouses of facts about disputes and treated the actual opinions (except for those of a handful of judge-heroes) as examples of unsatisfactory formalist analysis. . . ." Still, Gordon goes on to suggest that Realist law teachers could, after exposing the shortcomings of opinions, get their students to "craft context-and policy-based rationales that would provide better bases for decisions," and that "this use of cases continues today."[221]

Langdell's method, then, still endures, albeit in somewhat altered form. More importantly, we are coming now to understand that Langdell was one of the key nineteenth-century American educators who learned from Continental efforts, and shifted the nature of legal analysis from deductive to inductive principles. As one of the leading intellectual historians of legal theory, David Rabban, tells us:

> Recent revisionist scholarship on Langdell has emphasized the inductive aspects of his thought, minimizing or sometimes denying entirely the dominant concept of him as the exemplar of deductive formalism. Langdell's conception of legal science, revisionists have observed, typified late nineteenth-century views of science generally, replicating the focus on induction from empirical evidence and on the evolution of organic principles. Whereas traditional scholarship on Langdell often stressed the mathematical or geometric structure

---

[220]   Gordon, Geologic Strata, *supra* note 191, at 342.

[221]   *Ibid*. On the Legal Realists see, in particular, Chapter 8, *infra*.

of his legal thought, the revisionists detected a much closer analogy to experimental biology.[222]

Langdell anticipated, then, the work that Roscoe Pound (see Chapter 7) would perform a generation later. Why then, the nearly universal disparagement of Langdell in so many elite quarters of contemporary legal education? Why the sentiment, as it was recently expressed, that Langdell's approach fails to take account of crucial questions of context, and thus "masks questions of great importance" such as "whether following the rule of law really weakens us."[223] Why the consensus, as William LaPiana puts it "that the case method lacks *something* and that Langdell took too narrow a view of legal education."[224] Why the persistent notion that Langdell was "perverse," and that "His thought—and by extension the form of legal education he helped create—has been identified as one of the principal sources of the sterile formalism that supposedly marked late nineteenth-century American legal thought[?]"[225] To begin to understand this we might turn to the first and probably still the greatest of Langdell's critics, Oliver Wendell Holmes, Jr. What Bentham was to Blackstone, Holmes was to Langdell.

---

[222] David M. Rabban, Law's History: American Legal Thought and the Transatlantic Turn to History 484 (Cambridge, 2013) (footnotes omitted).

[223] To put this precisely in context, the quoted author, Harold Anthony Lloyd, was asking whether Langdell's method could really help us understand a troubling Supreme Court case such as Hamdi v. Rumsfeld, 542 U.S. 507 (2004), where the court had to make a difficult choice between following the rule of law or authorizing "violence" as "the only effective answer to human evil." Lloyd, *supra* note 196, at 234–35, relying on a piece by Linda H. Edwards, Where Do the Prophets Stand? Hamdi, Myth, and the Masters' Tools, 13 ConnPub.Int.L.J. 43 (2013).

[224] LaPiana, *supra* note 190, at vii (emphasis in the original).

[225] *Id.*, at 3.

CHAPTER 5

THE LIFE OF THE LAW AS EXPERIENCE

LATE NINETEENTH CENTURY

Oliver Wendell Holmes, Jr.
(Harvard, 1882; Boston University,
for one notable 1897 lecture)

■ ■ ■

Oliver Wendell Holmes, Jr. (1841–1935)
Harris & Ewing, Collection of the Supreme Court of the United States.

Oliver Wendell Holmes, Jr. is generally regarded as the
only authentic sage of American law. His colossal
reputation stems principally from his service for 50 years on
the bench, first for 20 years on the Massachusetts Supreme
Judicial Court, and, then, for another 30 on the United
States Supreme Court. Still, one can build an impressive
argument that his work as a student of the law, and briefly
(for three months) as Weld Professor of law at Harvard,
ought similarly to be regarded as important. One of his most

77

sensitive admirers, Richard Posner,[226] suggests that "Although Holmes was a competent and respected legal practitioner, his bent was academic. Considering that most of his working time [during the years after he graduated from Harvard Law School in 1866] was devoted to practice, his scholarly output during this period was prodigious: a distinguished edition of Kent's *Commentaries*, the leading legal treatise in America; many articles, brief notes, and book reviews,"[227] as well as his most important work, widely regarded as the best "book on law ever written by an American,"[228] which appeared just fifteen years after he finished law school. Holmes was a college professor at Harvard who lectured on Constitutional law for one year,[229] and then actually only a law professor at Harvard Law School for a brief period,[230] but given his academic bent, it seems fair to include him in this gallery of law professors.

The book to which Posner referred, Holmes's 1881 work, *The Common Law*,[231] and Holmes's tenure as the

[226] For Posner, see Chapter 15, *infra*.

[227] Richard A. Posner, ed., The Essential Holmes: Selections from the Letters, Speeches, Judicial Opinions and Other Writings of Oliver Wendell Holmes, Jr. x (Chicago, 1992).

[228] *Ibid*. See also David M. Rabban, Law's History: American Legal Thought and the Transatlantic Turn to History 48 (Cambridge, 2013). ("Though more known than read, it remains a classic of American legal scholarship, probably the most famous book about law ever written by an American.")

[229] Rabban, *supra* note 228, at 50. In 1872 "President Eliot appointed him to the faculty of Harvard College as university lecturer on Constitutional law," which position he gave up in 1873 for the full-time practice of law, but "While working in private practice throughout the 1780's, however, Holmes invested his great ambition in legal scholarship, perhaps spending more time on that than on his practice."

[230] *Id.*, at 51. ("Appointed in February 1882, Holmes began attending faculty meetings in March and started teaching in the fall. In December 1882, however, Holmes shocked his colleagues by resigning to accept a position as associate justice on the Supreme Judicial Court of Massachusetts, the highest court of the state.")

[231] Posner, *supra* note 227, at x, referring to Oliver Wendell Holmes, Jr., The Common Law (Little Brown, 1881).

editor of the American Law Review, as well as a speech he
gave at the 1897 dedication of the Boston University School
of Law ("The Path of the Law"[232]) could all be regarded as a
coordinated attack on the jurisprudence and teaching of
Christopher Columbus Langdell.[233] Holmes rejected what
he apparently believed was Langdell's "legal theology," or,
to be more precise, what Holmes perceived to be Langdell's
belief that logic and principle were the most important
factors in the creation and application of legal doctrine.

"The Life of the Law," wrote Holmes, in his most
famous utterance, "is not logic, but experience."[234] Holmes
believed that Langdell had missed the fact that the "felt
necessities of the time" had more to do with the application
of law by the courts than the syllogism. For Holmes, as he
worked out in a striking analysis of the evolution of damage
remedies over hundreds of years, from Greece and Rome
through modern times, legal rules were repeatedly invoked,
but as they served different purposes over time they became
subtly altered.

Thus, as he explained in the first chapter of *The
Common Law*, on torts (the body of law that provides
compensation for injuries inflicted by one private person on
another), the original Roman rule which required the

---

[232] Oliver Wendell Holmes, Jr., The Path of the Law, 10 Harvard Law
Review 457 (1897). Posner says of this piece that it "may be the best article-
length work on law ever written." Posner, *supra* note 227, at x.

[233] See Chapter 4, *supra*.

[234] The first appearance of this aphorism was apparently in a review of
Christopher Columbus Langdell's casebook on contracts. See, for a discussion
of the "Life of the Law" sentence Brian Hawkins, The Life of the Law: What
Holmes Meant (a paper available on SSRN, SSRN-id175389.pdf). The
anonymous book review appeared in *Book Notices*, 14 Am. L. Rev. 233 (1880),
and the sentence was repeated in Oliver Wendell Holmes, Jr., The Common
Law 1 (Little Brown, 1881). The repetition may have been owing to the fact
that "Holmes loved his own ideas and language so much." Hawkins, *supra*, at
n.7, citing G. Edward White, Justice Oliver Wendell Holmes: Law and the
Inner Self 444–45 (1993), and Thomas C. Grey, Plotting the Path of the Law,
63 Brook. L. Rev. 19, 29 (1997).

surrender of a slave who did harm to a person not that slave's owner, in order to provide for vengeance on that slave, evolved into the modern doctrinal rule of *Respondiat Superior*, which made employers liable for the torts of their servants simply because they were the beneficiaries of their employees' labor and they were handy possessors of the resources necessary to meet liabilities. From a rule that implemented the somewhat barbaric value of vengeance, then, came a transformed new rule that implemented the newly-important and rather more civilized rule of monetary compensation.

Just as Sir Edward Coke had recognized that out of the old fields would come new corn, so Holmes saw that old rules could be turned to new purposes, or, as another hoary old common law maxim had it, the common law was always producing and pouring new wine into old bottles. Holmes even threw off a charming animal observation to explain, "just as the clavicle in the cat only tells of the existence of some earlier creature to which a collarbone was useful, precedents survive in the law long after the use they once served is at an end and the reason for them has been forgotten."[235] Still, Holmes went on to add, "when ancient rules maintain themselves in the way that has been and will be shown in this book [*The Common Law*], new reasons more fitted to the time have been found for them, and that they gradually receive a new content, and at last a new form, from the grounds to which they have been transplanted."[236] With an impressive absence of modesty, Holmes announced, in effect, that before he came along to make his observations, this process had been "unconscious," but now he was prepared to strip away the underbrush and

---

[235] Holmes, *supra* note 231, at 35. Holmes may have had a thing about household pets. In another famous remark he observed that "even a dog distinguishes between being stumbled over and being kicked." *Id.*, at 3.

[236] Holmes, *supra* note 231, at 34–35.

reveal the growth of the law for what it actually was—a pragmatic and policy-oriented process. The license this was to give judges (and law professors) for the next century was formidable.

Holmes may not really have given Langdell enough credit for the originality and perception of Langdell's work on Contracts, and, indeed, Holmes's own scholarship on the law of contract is hardly distinguishable from Langdell's.[237] Still, Holmes eventually became an even more important influence on jurisprudence than was Langdell, and Holmes's skepticism and policy-orientation was embraced by a later school of jurisprudence known as "American Legal Realism," and then also, as we will soon see, by a more radical movement known as "critical legal studies."[238] This was true even though Holmes's skepticism may have crossed the boundary into cynicism. For example, in an introduction to a book of essays entitled *Rational Basis of Legal Institutions* (1923), "concerned with the use of legislation as a social control device," as currently favored by Progressives, Holmes remarked that "[E]ven the enlightened reformers that I hear or read seem to me not to have considered with accuracy the means at our disposal and to become rhetorical just where I want figures. The notion that we can secure an economic paradise by changes in property alone seems to me twaddle."[239]

The key to Holmes's incredible lionization in American law schools in the second half of the twentieth century, in spite of his rather dyspeptic attitude, may be that his theory that judges were, essentially, engaged in a legislative task,

---

[237] This point about Holmes and Langdell's sharing ideas about the law of contract is brilliantly explored in Grant Gilmore, *The Death of Contract* (Ohio State University Press, 1974, 2nd ed. 1995).

[238] On Legal Realism see Chapter 8, *infra*, and on Critical Legal Studies see Chapter 14, *infra*.

[239] Quoted in Herbert Hovenkamp, The Opening of American Law: Neoclassical Legal Thought 1870–1970 42 (Oxford, 2015).

was a means of justifying mid and late twentieth-century Constitutional judging by the Warren Court and its successors. That exercise in Constitutional creativity turned the understanding of the Constitution away from its original meaning, in order to promote a vision of social justice more appealing to the Warren Court Justices, and perhaps to enhance the standing of American justice abroad.[240] Holmes was a critic of the pre-New Deal Court's *Lochner*-era jurisprudence, in which the court stymied efforts to regulate the economy in a manner to help labor and restrict the ability of employers to impose onerous contract terms on employees. The principal characteristic of that era in the law was the Court's elevating the principle of "freedom of contract" to paramount status, and thus proclaiming, as the Court did in the now infamous *Lochner* case itself, that it was a violation of "due process" for a state to decide, for example, that bakers could only work a certain number of hours per week, or for a particular minimum wage. This was because maximum hours and minimum wage laws interfered with the bakers' purportedly constitutionally-guaranteed freedom to arrive at contract terms on their own.[241]

For those, like the academic progressive liberals who believed that this notion of "freedom of contract" was a myth or a shibboleth, this was unacceptable because it barred governmental actions to even the playing field by increasing the bargaining power of workers, or by elevating their wages or limiting their hours, to create more humane working conditions. When Holmes declared, in his famous

---

[240] See, e.g., Mary L. Dudziak, "*Brown* as a Cold War Case," 91 Journal of American History 32–42 (2004) and see also Mary L. Dudziak, Cold War Civil Rights: Race and the Image of American Democracy (Princeton, 2011).

[241] See generally, Lochner v. New York, 198 U.S. 45 (1905).

and now exceptionally venerated,[242] *Lochner* dissent that the Constitution did not impose any particular economic theory—neither the *laissez-faire* social Darwinist approach of Herbert Spencer's *Social Statics*, or the top-down central planning of the socialist "organic state"[243]—Holmes seemed to suggest that the Constitution permitted this kind of economic regulation of wages and hours, and, in retrospect, it looked as if Holmes was favoring the similar liberal measures that later came to constitute the New Deal. This was particularly impressive to academics such as Felix Frankfurter, who must have had this sort of view of Holmes's in mind, when Frankfurter declared that Holmes possessed the qualities of "personal genius . . . perhaps in richer measure than any member in the Court's history."[244]

At bottom, however, there was perhaps even more than cynicism, there may have been something that could be described as closer to a monstrous strain in Holmes's approach to the law, which Albert Alschuler recently and brilliantly explored in his important book, *Law Without Values*.[245] Holmes remains the hero of such prominent American jurisprudes as Richard Posner, but Alschuler's devastatingly critical view, at this point in the history of jurisprudence, seems closer to the mark. Moreover, it does appear that for whatever reason, Holmes either misunderstood what Langdell was doing, or overstated his

---

[242] See, e.g., Richard A. Posner, Law and Literature 271 (Harvard, 1998) where Holmes's dissent in *Lochner* is called "the greatest judicial opinion of the last hundred years."

[243] *Lochner*, 198 U.S., at 75 (Holmes, J., dissenting).

[244] Felix Frankfurter, Mr. Justice Holmes and the Supreme Court 46 (Atheneum, 2nd ed. 1965). Frankfurter explained that for him the qualities of "personal genius," were manifest when "a man's genius breaks through a collective judgment, or his . . . life before he went on the bench serves as commentary, or as he expresses individual views in dissent or through personal writings." *Id*. On Frankfurter see Chapter 9, *infra*.

[245] Albert W. Alschuler, Law Without Values: The Life, Work, and Legacy of Justice Holmes (Chicago, 2000).

attack on the Harvard Dean to call attention to himself. Alschuler also manages to raise some doubt about the quality of Holmes's writing, perhaps his chief claim to fame, by suggesting (with much truth—see for yourself) that much of *The Common Law* is nearly unreadable,[246] although, Alschuler concedes, it does contain five brilliant and timeless paragraphs.

As did some of Holmes's earlier critics, most notably H.L. Mencken, Alschuler realized that Holmes was not the great liberal some of his twentieth-century admirers (most notably Felix Frankfurter and Harold Laski) had made Holmes out to be, but, rather he was a Justice who was prepared to approve of virtually anything any legislature did. In Mencken's wonderfully biting words[247]:

---

[246] Alschuler's critique of Holmes's writing is worth reproducing in full, as it points out alternatives for the student seeking laudable legal prose:

> People who know Holmes's frequently masterful style may find it difficult to realize how ponderous and dense his book is until they try to read it. Although this book contains five paragraphs of Holmes at his best, it contains hundreds of paragraphs of Holmes at his worst. Moreover, perhaps because Holmes had a deadline, the quality of his writing deteriorated throughout the volume. Holmes's prose was, to be sure, no more dreary than that of Langdell, Beale, and other writers of his era, but anyone who suspects that only our distance in time accounts for the flatness and obscurity of Holmes's language ought to consider the clear engaging prose of a classic fully twice as old as The Common Law, Blackstone's *Commentaries.* Or that reader might examine the still-crisp prose of Holmes's English contemporaries Pollock, Stephen, and Maitland—or the writings of outstanding American legal and political authors prior to Holmes such as Madison, Marshall, Tucker, Pomeroy, and Lincoln. Classics are timeless, and Holmes's five great paragraphs *are.* The bulk of his book isn't.

Alschuler, *supra* note 245, at 228 (emphasis in original).

[247] H.L. Mencken is relatively unknown today, but his life's work was, as his anthologist, the esteemed British transplant Alistair Cooke, put it, to be "the native American Voltaire, the enemy of all puritans, the heretic in the Sunday school, the one-man demolition crew of the genteel tradition, the unregenerate neighborhood brat who stretches a string in the alley to trip the bourgeoisie on its pious homeward journey." Henry Lewis Mencken, The Vintage Mencken: Gathered by Alistair Cooke ix (Vintage Books 1955)

[Holmes] believed that the law-making bodies should be free to experiment almost *ad libitum*, that the courts should not call a halt upon them until they clearly passed the uttermost bounds of reason, that everything should be sacrificed to their autonomy, including apparently, even the Bill of Rights. If this is Liberalism, then all I can say is that Liberalism is not what it was when I was young.[248]

For Mencken, Holmes's jurisprudence included the doctrine that "it is the chief business of the Supreme Court to keep the Constitution loose and elastic so that blasting holes through it may not be too onerous."[249] And Mencken was on to something, for as Holmes famously remarked in a letter to his friend Laski, "I always say, as you know, that if my fellow citizens want to go to Hell I will help them. It's my job."[250]

This attitude was also the essence of what led Alschuler to describe Holmes's jurisprudence as being "without values," and Holmes himself boldly proclaimed that absence of values as his perspective, explaining in his most famous lecture, *The Path of the Law*, that law was best understood the way a "bad man" would understand it. Such a man, said

---

(Introduction by Alistair Cooke). Mencken's eye was discerning, and he splendidly and accurately took the measure of Holmes.

[248] Henry Lewis Mencken, "Mr. Justice Holmes," reprinted in The Vintage Mencken, *supra* note 247, at 190 (1955).

[249] *Id.*, at 191. Mencken thought that Holmes's mistake was to think that legislatures spoke with the voice of the people, but for Mencken legislatures had clearly been captured by what we now refer to as "special interests," and thus that American legislators were, essentially, bought and paid for. "The typical lawmaker of today," Mencken wrote, "is a man wholly devoid of principle—a mere counter in a grotesque and knavish game. If the right pressure could be applied to him, he would be cheerfully in favor of polygamy, astrology, or cannibalism." *Id.*, at 192.

[250] Oliver Wendell Holmes, Jr. to Harold J. Laski (March 4, 1920); reprinted in Mark DeWolfe Howe, ed., Holmes–Laski Letters (Harvard, 1953), vol. 1, p. 249.

Holmes, cared nothing for jurisprudential niceties or principles but was interested only in what the courts will do in fact.[251]

Precisely where this rather unsavory quality of Holmes—Alschuler regards him as ineffably ghoulish—came from is open to some doubt. Some have attributed it to his stoic behavior as a wounded soldier fighting for the North in the Civil War[252]—if the government could demand the sacrifice of Holmes and his fellow soldiers' lives then, it was only just to allow government the maximum of freedom to legislate during peacetime, and for citizens to defer to their government. Others have observed that it may have been aspects of this dyspeptic personality which prevented Holmes from ever having children, as he explained, because he couldn't bear to bring them into this world.[253] Still others have pointed to Holmes's obsession with science, and perhaps even an impersonal economic approach to the law (this might be what attracts Richard Posner to the man), which have led Holmes to be perceived as cool and indifferent to much human travail. This view of Holmes does seem to be exemplified, for example, not only in his bad man theory of the law, but also in his judicial enforcement of eugenics, and his apparent approval of forced sterilization of substandard parents, as he remarked,

---

[251] Oliver W. Holmes, Jr., The Path of the Law, Address at the Dedication of the New Hall of the Boston University School of Law (Jan. 8, 1897), in 10 Harv. L. Rev. 457, 460–61 (1897).

[252] This appears to have been Mencken's view. Holmes, he thought, was not a liberal, a *litterateur*, a reformer, a sociologist, a prophet, an evangelist, or even a metaphysician, he was, simply, a soldier. Mencken, *supra* note 247, at 193. Said Mencken, he was "a soldier extraordinarily ruminative and articulate—in fact, so ruminative and articulate as to be, in the military caste, almost miraculous," but still he was a soldier "whose natural distaste and contempt for civilians, [included a] corollary yearning to heave them all into Hell." *Ibid.* See, on this point, text accompanying note 250, *supra.*

[253] See generally for another penetrating study of Holmes's personality, and for Holmes's possible reluctance to have children, G. Edward White, Justice Oliver Wendell Holmes: Law and the Inner Self 106 (Oxford, 1993).

upholding Virginia's eugenics statute in the notorious *Buck v. Bell* case, that "three generations of imbeciles are enough."[254]

Perhaps at bottom Holmes's theory of the law was, essentially, Thrasymachian, and perhaps the main characteristic of Holmes's jurisprudence was, then, as Mencken and Alschuler described it, or, as Robert Burt called it, a "cosmically detached" pessimism.[255] Whatever Holmes's essential thinking on the law was, though, it was sometimes stated with much eloquence, albeit not without a little prestidigitation or subtle duplicity. Let's consider the eloquence first, by quoting the "five paragraphs," from *The Common Law*, which even Alschuler does consider to be timeless and great, and which contain, in essence, Holmes's theory of jurisprudence, which theory was to be embraced by the Legal Realists and, later, by the Critical Legal Studies scholars. The First of these five luminous Paragraphs is the opening paragraph of the book:

> The object of this book is to present a general view of the Common Law. To accomplish the task, other tools are needed besides logic. It is something to show that the consistency of a system requires a particular result, but it is not all. The life of the law has not been logic: it has been experience. The felt necessities of the time, the prevalent moral and political theories, intuitions of public policy,

---

[254] Buck v. Bell, 274 U.S. 200, 207 (1927).

[255] Robert A. Burt, Two Jewish Justices: Outcasts in the Promised Land 123 (California, 1988). Some critics of Holmes appear to believe that his attitude was ultimately one of indifference. Thus, see Louis Menand, American Studies 33 (Farrar, Straus, and Giroux, 2002) (Holmes "almost never cared, in the cases he decided, about outcomes. . . . [H]e was utterly, sometimes fantastically, indifferent to the real-world effects of his decisions.") quoted in the very perceptive and provocative Allen Mendenhall, Justice Holmes and Conservatism, 17 Texas Review of Law and Politics 305, 308 (2013) (Arguing that Holmes should not be viewed as either a doctrinaire liberal or conservative, but as a nuanced pragmatist).

avowed or unconscious, even the prejudices which judges share with their fellow-men, have had a good deal more to do than the syllogism in determining the rules by which men should be governed. The law embodies the story of a nation's development through many centuries, and it cannot be dealt with as if it contained only the axioms and corollaries of a book of mathematics. In order to know what it is, we must know what it has been and what it tends to become. We must alternately consult history and existing theories of legislation. But the most difficult labor will be to understand the combination of the two into new products at every stage. The substance of the law at any given time pretty nearly corresponds, so far as it goes, with what is then understood to be convenient; but its form and machinery, and the degree to which it is able to work out desired results, depend very much upon its past.[256]

Following his exposition in the first chapter of *The Common Law*, in which Holmes demonstrated, as indicated earlier, that what we now know as the torts rule of *respondiat superior*, which imposes liability on the employer for the acts of the employee (and which meets the economic needs of our time), grew out of an earlier Roman rule which had to do with completely different policies and effects grounded in religion and vengeance, Holmes elaborates the themes set forth in his opening paragraph, in four close to the end of the chapter:

The foregoing history, apart from the purposes for which it has been given, well illustrates the paradox of form and substance in the development of law. In form its growth is logical. The official

---

[256] Oliver Wendell Holmes, Jr. The Common Law, *supra* note 231, at 1–2.

theory is that each new decision follows syllogistically from existing precedents. But just as the clavicle in the cat only tells of the existence of some earlier creature to which a collar-bone was useful, precedents survive in the law long after the use they once served is at an end and the reason for them has been forgotten. The result of following them must often be failure and confusion from the merely logical point of view.

On the other hand, in substance the growth of the [Common Law] is legislative. And this in a deeper sense than that what the courts declare to have always been the law is in fact new. It is legislative in its grounds. The very considerations which judges most rarely mention, and always with an apology, are the secret root from which the law draws all the juices of life. I mean, of course, considerations of what is expedient for the community concerned. Every important principle which is developed by litigation is in fact and at bottom the result of more or less definitely understood views of public policy; most generally, to be sure, under our practice and traditions, the unconscious result of instinctive preferences and inarticulate convictions, but none the less traceable to views of public policy in the last analysis. And as the law is administered by able and experienced men, who know too much to sacrifice good sense to a syllogism, it will be found that, when ancient rules maintain themselves in the way that has been and will be shown in this book, new reasons more fitted to the time have been found for them, and that they gradually receive a new content, and at last a new form, from the grounds to which they have been transplanted.

But hitherto this process has been largely unconscious. It is important, on that account, to bring to mind what the actual course of events has been. If it were only to insist on a more conscious recognition of the legislative function of the courts, as just explained, it would be useful, as we shall see more clearly further on. [footnote omitted]

What has been said will explain the failure of all theories which consider the law only from its formal side, whether they attempt to deduce the *corpus* from *a priori* postulates, or fall into the humbler error of supposing the science of the law to reside in the *elegantia juris*, or logical cohesion of part with part. The truth is, that the law is always approaching, and never reaching, consistency. It is forever adopting new principles from life at one end, and it always retains old ones from history at the other, which have not yet been absorbed or sloughed off. It will become entirely consistent only when it ceases to grow.

These five paragraphs lay out a theory of the law in which the judge functions as a legislator, wisely adjusting the legal rules to meet the needs of the times, albeit somewhat constrained by the forms of the past. This view of the law gives the judge power to change it, and seems to suggest that the law is, really, anything the judge wants it to be. It is a profoundly positivistic conception of the law, and that positivism—looking at the law simply as it actually was[257]—appears as one powerful strain in Holmes's thought. Thus, in his famous *Path of the Law* Essay, for example, most of the exposition, centered around the "bad man" theory of the law, invoked a jurisprudence in which

---

[257] For an explanation and examination of American judicial theories of positivism, see, e.g., Anthony J. Sebok, Legal Positivism in American Jurisprudence (Cambridge, 2008).

the only interest was "in what the courts would do in fact," not in any elegant theories of the law. Still, at the end of the *Path of the Law* essay, in a rather unsettling *volte face*, Holmes indicated that one studied law in order to realize that it contained universals, that there was a constant manner in which the law changed, and that by careful observation one could, when one marveled at the work of courts, even hear "echoes of the infinite." Holmes could thus be pointed to as a champion for the natural lawyers as well as the positivists. Like another great American, Thomas Jefferson, who at various points in his political career covered all the bases, Holmes was untroubled by inconsistency.[258] His Olympian detachment has, it must be said, garnered myriad admirers in the professoriat.[259] Perhaps the best way to describe Holmes's jurisprudence is to say that there was not really a guiding principle to it at all. Thus, it can be said that Holmes offered a "grab-bag" of "forces that shaped the law," including "necessity, history, public policy, moral consensus, and even the prejudices of particular judges, yes—logic, no."[260]

Yet, somehow, Richard Posner, the most influential law professor of the twentieth and early twenty-first centuries,[261] could write, flat out, that Holmes was "the

---

[258] Posner suggests that "The sheer bulk of Holmes's *oeuvre* evidently precludes complete consistency, which may make the skeptical reader wonder whether there is, as my title posits, an 'essential' Holmes." Posner, *supra* note 227, at xii. *Indeed.*

[259] "Olympian" seems an uncommonly popular adjective to apply to Holmes. See, e.g., Catherine Drinker Bowen, Yankee from Olympus: Justice Holmes and His Family (First Edition, 1944), or Robert A. Burt, Two Jewish Justices: Outcasts in the Promised Land 19 (California, 1988) "Holmes . . . had found a home for himself outside—as others have put it, outside and above, gazing skeptically down 'as from Olympus.'" (quoting from W. Mendelson, "The Influence of James B. Thayer upon the Work of Holmes, Brandeis and Frankfurter," 31 Vand. L. Rev. 71, 75 (1978)).

[260] N.E.H. Hull, Roscoe Pound and Karl Llewellyn: Searching for an American Jurisprudence 32 (Chicago, 1997), quoting G. Edward White, Justice Oliver Wendell Holmes: Law and the Inner Self 151, 153 (Oxford, 1993).

[261] See Chapter 15, *infra*.

most illustrious figure in the history of American law."[262]
Summing up Holmes's contribution, and referring to both
The Common Law and *The Path of the Law,* Posner states
that "Book and article are similar in theme as well as in
distinction. Together they supplied the leading ideas for the
legal-realist movement (more accurately, the legal-
pragmatist movement)—the most influential school of
twentieth-century American legal thought and
practice. . . ."[263] Indeed, in what may be a bit more
controversial set of assertions Posner also claims that
Holmes "created the modern theory of federalism, the
theory of judicial self-restraint (though here he was
borrowing heavily from James Bradley Thayer), and the
idea of the 'living Constitution'—the idea that the
Constitution should be construed flexibly, liberally, rather
than strictly, narrowly."[264]

Still, perhaps more of an explanation is needed for how
a man whose jurisprudence was essentially empty, if not, as
Alschuler suggests, ghoulish, could still be so idolized. One
is tempted to wonder if the explanation is that with his
flowing mustaches and long white hair, Holmes could have
posed as the model for Michelangelo's Sistine Chapel's God
the Father. Maybe the way ultimately to succeed as a
jurisprude is to be a dead ringer for the Deity. More likely,
the elements in Holmes's five great paragraphs, setting
forth a theory of the judge as legislator, served as a
justification for those, like the progressive critics of the
Lochner court, who wanted to change the law to better meet
the needs of labor, or those, like the proponents of the
jurisprudence of the Warren Court, who wanted to see
Constitutional law moved more in the direction of
protecting insular minorities, to get judges actually to

---

[262] Richard A. Posner, ed., The Essential Holmes, *supra* note 227, at ix.
[263] *Id.*, at xi.
[264] *Id.*, at xii.

become legislators to start on what they perceived to be the necessary work of redistribution. Holmes anticipated what the Courts would do in the second half of the twentieth century, and praising him perhaps helped to justify that conduct. Unhappily for those who yearned (as Holmes thought we should not) for certainty in the law, or for those who thought the law could be objectively applied, these strands of jurisprudence, that Posner suggested Holmes prompted, destroyed the notion that the law could be clear, certain, and fixed, and may have fatally undermined the cherished maxim that ours was a government of laws, not men.

As Posner reminds us, Holmes pointed the way to the flexibility of twentieth- and twenty-first-century Constitutional law. His influence was incalculable. Even a jurisprude as committed to natural law as Lon Fuller, in words that could be applied to Holmes, could be said, really, to have "conceived of the legal scholar's role as at least in part that of clarifying and improving legal doctrine by identifying and tracing out the practical purposes that actually motivated courts to decide cases the way they did, rather than by deducing results from the 'nature' of particular concepts."[265] No less could this be said of Richard Posner, who, following Holmes, conceived of the judge's task as one of, essentially, pragmatic problem solving, using the flexible method of the common law.

Still, one has to ask whether flexibility in the service of pragmatism is all there is to law. In his superbly titled dissection of Holmes, *Law Without Values*, Albert Alschuler observed that Holmes, since he was over 6 feet tall, was not short, and was clearly too cultivated to be nasty, but, nevertheless, he was certainly brutish. The Holmes

---

[265] Charles L. Barzun, Jerome Frank, Lon Fuller, and a Romantic Pragmatism, University of Virginia School of Law, Public Law and Legal Theory Research Paper Series 2016–6, January 2016, at 14.

Alschuler wrote about took credit for others' work, had boundless ambition, failed to come up with a single original idea, wrote generally utterly incomprehensibly, was possibly perverted, delighted in eugenics, was probably a racist and maybe an anti-Semite, and, as we have seen, allowed legislatures *carte blanche*, and believed that law students could only come to appreciate law if they thought about it the way a "bad man" would. Alschuler asked as the title for his Chapter Three, "Would You Have Wanted Holmes as a Friend?" and his answer was a resounding, "No!"[266] One who apparently did want Holmes as a friend, however, was John Henry Wigmore, to whom we now turn.

---

[266] Parts of this paragraph were taken from my review of Alschuler's book, which is available, *inter alia*, at http://h-net.msu.edu/cgi-bin/logbrowse. pl?trx=vx&list=h-law&month=0208&week=b&msg=2c10h52si%2BpgO2dqK wYBmQ&user=&pw= (accessed 2/14/15).

CHAPTER 6

AN ELITE LEGAL INTELLECTUAL AS MORALIST AND REFORMER

EARLY TWENTIETH CENTURY

John Henry Wigmore
(Northwestern, 1893–1929)

■ ■ ■

John Henry Wigmore (1863–1943)
From a painting by Arvid Nyholm (1911).
Historical & Special Collections, Harvard Law School Library.

Partly because it has produced so many graduates, we tend to think of Harvard as the most important American law school,[267] and perhaps it is (especially since so many law professors at other schools here and abroad studied there), but one of the things that these chapters have sought to demonstrate is that the work of law professors active at

---

[267] See generally, Daniel R. Coquillette and Bruce A. Kimball, On the Battlefield of Merit: Harvard Law School, The First Century (Harvard, 2016), the book jacket of which notes that "Harvard Law School is the oldest and, arguably, the most influential law school in the nation."

institutions other than just Harvard and Yale had a profound effect on American Legal Education. One such individual, albeit one trained at Harvard, was John Henry Wigmore, a graduate of Harvard College and Harvard Law School, and one of the founders of the Harvard Law Review, now one of the most prestigious legal publications. Wigmore achieved renown not because of his Harvard connections, however, but because he was the "country's best known scholar of scientific criminal evidence,"[268] and the Dean of Northwestern University School of Law (1900–1929). It is a mark perhaps of the importance of Harvard and its tendency to overshadow other institutions that has led to such things as the recent author of a biography of Antonin Scalia claiming that Wigmore was "Harvard's legendary law school dean."[269] For Wigmore, though, Northwestern was the place to be (or, perhaps, the place to build), and, over the course of his career as Dean, he turned down offers to move to the University of Chicago, Columbia University, and Yale.[270]

Wigmore was an astonishingly prolific legal scholar,[271] and, in his time, a towering figure of jurisprudence. Herbert

[268] Herbert Hovenkamp, The Opening of American Law: Neoclassical Legal Thought 1870–1970 49 (Oxford, 2015).

[269] Bruce Allen Murphy, Scalia: A Court of One 158 (Simon and Schuster, 2014). When this was pointed out to Professor Murphy, he graciously acknowledged the error and promised to correct it in future editions. Email correspondence between Bruce Murphy and Stephen Presser, June 17, 2014, in the possession of the author.

[270] William R. Roalfe, John Henry Wigmore: Scholar and Reformer 69–70 (Northwestern University Press, 1977).

[271] According to one source on the web, "He produced 46 original volumes of legal scholarship, 38 edited volumes, and more than 800 articles, pamphlets, and reviews." Wigmore, John Henry, an entry in The Free Dictionary, http://legal-dictionary.thefreedictionary.com/John+Henry+Wigmore, accessed November 1, 2014. One of his successors as Dean at Northwestern, James A. Rahl, claimed that Wigmore's writings "probably were more voluminous than those of any other known writer in any field in history." James A. Rahl, "Forward" to Roalfe, *supra* note 270, at ix. Roalfe notes that "during the two decades ending in 1920, Wigmore produced, in the field of evidence alone, eleven books, one pamphlet, eleven articles, thirty-four case comments, six notes, two

Hovenkamp, in his work on "neoclassical legal thought," recognizes Wigmore as one of the "elite legal intellectuals" in the pre-New Deal period "who had good educations . . . and read widely," and lumps Wigmore in with a group of six that also included "Oliver W. Holmes, Jr.,[272] Francis Wharton, James G. Carter, Roscoe Pound,[273] and Jerome Frank," an exceptionally influential set.[274] Still, Wigmore's biographer complained in 1977 that "Wigmore the man is . . . perhaps the most neglected and the least appreciated major figure in the broad arena to which he made such a lasting contribution."[275] Wigmore is today remembered for his work on the law of evidence, but not for much else, but much else there was.

Like Langdell (if not Holmes), Wigmore believed that there was or could be a logic to the law, and his multi-volume treatise on the law of evidence is a staggering achievement in making that argument. Like Joseph Story,[276] Wigmore was a prominent conservative,[277] and, like James Wilson[278] and unlike Holmes, Wigmore saw law as a repository of noble and perhaps unchanging values. Wigmore also taught at a Japanese Law School, and was one of the first in the early twentieth century to conceive of American law as part of a broader global jurisprudential

---

introductions, two book reviews, one address, and one translation." *Id.*, at 82. For other exceptionally prolific legal scholars, see, e.g., Chapter 15 (Richard Posner) and Chapter 22 (Cass Sunstein).

[272]   See Chapter 5, *supra*.

[273]   See Chapter 7, *infra*.

[274]   Hovenkamp, *supra* note 268, at 10.

[275]   Roalfe, *supra* note 270, at iii.

[276]   See Chapter 3, *supra*.

[277]   Though he did, apparently, vote for Franklin D. Roosevelt. Rahl, *supra* note 271, at ix. Wigmore's credentials as a thoroughbred of Anglo-American stock are strong. His biographer reports that "The Wigmore family can trace its ancestry back to the time of William the Conqueror." Rolfe, *supra* note 270, at 4.

[278]   See Chapter 2, *supra*.

tradition.[279] "He was accomplished in a dozen languages and traveled with his wife to most parts of the world."[280] Moreover, he was, in a century when law professors were, as a rule, rather narrowly focused, clearly a polymath. One of his successors as Dean, who knew him well, reports that "he wrote numerous songs for lawyers and students and played them on the piano at all kinds of professional gatherings."[281] Legend at Northwestern has it that he composed the Northwestern Law School school song, sung it with great gusto at appropriate times, and even built chimes that would play the law school song in the law school's main building every day at noon.[282]

Wigmore was a friend of the great and the near great, including the jurists Oliver Wendell Holmes, Jr., Louis D. Brandeis[283] and Felix Frankfurter.[284] His professional activities were myriad—he was one of the organizers, along with Roscoe Pound and the famous trial lawyer Clarence Darrow, of the American Institute of Criminal Law and Criminology.[285] While he was Dean, Northwestern began to

---

[279] See, e.g., John H. Wigmore, A Panorama of the World's Legal Systems (West Publishing Co., 3 vols. 1928). This was, of course, Story's view as well. See generally Chapter 3, *supra*.

[280] Rahl, *supra* note 271, at ix.

[281] *Id.*

[282] One could still hear them as late as the late seventies, I can report from personal experience. Unhappily, the machinery seems to have failed shortly thereafter. In any event, the legend appears true. Wigmore's biographer reports that, in all, Wigmore's musical compositions, published in 1914, included "a madrigal, eleven ballads, two processional hymns, and three law-student choruses. . . ." Roalfe, *supra* note 270, at 67.

[283] Brandeis was the first Jew to be appointed to the United States Supreme Court, and might have been the subject of a chapter here but for the fact that he turned down an invitation to teach at the Harvard Law School. See generally Robert A. Burt, Two Jewish Justices: Outcasts in the Promised Land 6 (California, 1988).

[284] Rahl, *supra* note 271, at ix. On Frankfurter, see Chapter 9, *infra*.

[285] Hovenkamp, *supra* note 268, at 47.

be intimately connected to the well-off, well-connected and powerful in Chicago.

Wigmore grew up in San Francisco, where his family had accumulated some wealth from farming and the retail trade in furniture and hardware. He attended a private school, The Urban School, where he acquired a reputation, according to his brother, "for erudition and phenomenal attainments,"[286] and then matriculated at Harvard College, where, curiously, his mother proceeded to bring his entire family to Cambridge, because, according to Wigmore's biographer, she was "unable to bear the thought of separation from her firstborn."[287] After Wigmore's four years at Harvard College, the family returned to San Francisco, and, after one more year there, Wigmore began Harvard Law School in the fall of 1884.[288] His grades put him at the top of his class the first year, and near the top the second, and, in 1886, he and his classmates Joseph E. Beale and Julian W. Mack, who also went on to distinguished academic careers, were among the small group who founded the Harvard Law Review, and, in Wigmore's case, began a section of the magazine called "Recent Cases," which was soon replicated in similar publications.[289] In his last year at the Law School, Wigmore published two pieces in the then leading law review, The American Law Review, which were favorably reviewed by Oliver Wendell Holmes, Jr. himself (who had earlier served as editor of that review).[290]

---

[286] Roalfe, *supra* note 270, at 5.

[287] *Id.*, at 7.

[288] *Id.*, at 9.

[289] *Id.*, at 11.

[290] *Id.*, at 12. For Holmes's editorship of the American Law Review during the years 1870–1873, see, e.g., Edmund Fuller, Oliver Wendell Holmes, Jr. Encyclopedia Britannica, http://www.britannica.com/EBchecked/topic/269514/ Oliver–Wendell–Holmes–Jr (accessed January 21, 2015).

Following graduation from Harvard Law School, Wigmore remained in Boston and began the practice of law, or at least the practice of legal research, having been employed for that purpose by both the distinguished New Hampshire Judge, Charles Doe, and the even more distinguished lawyer, and eventual Supreme Court Justice, Louis Brandeis.[291] Wigmore also began increasingly to publish on legal and political topics, and, in 1889, he was offered a three year assignment in "the post of chief professor of Anglo-American law at Keio University in Tokyo."[292] As a means of staying in touch with American developments, and making the most of his time abroad, Wigmore managed to get himself appointed as the regular Japanese correspondent for *The Nation*, and a stringer for other publications, including *The New York Evening Post*, the *New York Times*, *Scribner's Magazine*, and for the *Green Bag* (a legal periodical),[293] and he wrote as well for the *Boston Herald* and the *Japan Daily Mail*.[294] Wigmore was thus developing a talent for popular as well as scholarly commentary. In Japan, Wigmore "was virtually the founder of the law department" at Keio University, where, in effect, following Langdell's innovation, he replicated the three-year course taught at American law schools.[295] During his three years in Japan Wigmore continued to produce works targeted at legal professionals in America, as well as to write and research on Japanese legal institutions and legal doctrines, learning Japanese in the process.[296] His work, which again won the praise of Justice Holmes, was the

---

[291] Roalfe, *supra note* 270, at 12–14.

[292] *Id.*, at 17.

[293] *Id.*, at 18.

[294] *Id.*, at 25.

[295] *Id.*, at 25. For Langdell, see Chapter 4, *supra*.

[296] Roalfe, *supra* note 270, at 24–28.

beginning of Wigmore's expertise in the newly emerging field of comparative law.[297]

Wigmore declined a three-year renewal of his assignment in Japan, and, back in the United States, and failing to find a "suitable opening" at Harvard or in New York, Wigmore decided to accept an offer from the President of Northwestern University to join its law school, first as a teacher and "secretary to the faculty,"[298] and then, soon after, as Dean. Aided by his close relationship with some faculty members at Harvard, and, in particular, its Dean, James Barr Ames, Wigmore adopted the case method of instruction he learned at Harvard, and immediately set to work building up the law school by increasing its faculty.[299] As indicated earlier, Wigmore was eventually to become famous for his specialization in the law of evidence, and it was a topic that he taught during his early years at Northwestern, along with Torts. Remarkably, however, in this present age of extreme doctrinal specialization among law professors, Wigmore also taught courses in common law pleading, conflict of laws, quasi-contracts, the Law of Persons, International Law (Public and Private), domestic relations, bailments and carriers, and master and servant (employment law).[300] Such a range would be unheard of at an elite law school today.

Wigmore continued to write academic articles in his first years teaching at Northwestern, including some in the Harvard Law Review on Torts, which were favorably noted by the famous English scholar Sir Frederick Pollock, by Harvard's Dean Ames, and, again, by Wigmore's sometime idol, Oliver Wendell Holmes, Jr.[301] Then, in 1899, Wigmore

---

[297]   *Id.*, at 28–29.
[298]   *Id.*, at 32–22.
[299]   *Id.*, at 35–37.
[300]   *Id.*, at 37.
[301]   *Id.*, at 40–41.

completed a revision for the house that became his
publisher, Little Brown, of volume one of the nineteenth-
century treatise (first published in 1842), *Greenleaf on
Evidence*.[302] Wigmore's revision of Greenleaf was described
by one reviewer as "monumental,"[303] but that work paled
when compared to what Wigmore soon began, his own
multi-volume work on the law of evidence. In the meantime,
however, Wigmore's work on Greenleaf won Harvard's
Ames Prize in 1902, "awarded by the Harvard Law School
faculty every four years for the most meritorious law book
or legal essay in English that had been published not less
than one year or more than five years before the award,"
and Wigmore continued to produce published pieces on
comparative law, Japanese law, and legal education.[304]

In 1901, Northwestern's Trustees offered Wigmore the
Deanship of the law school.[305] He accepted, although he was
apparently under no illusions regarding the difficulty of the
task he was assuming, as the school was in a "chaotic"
situation, having been without "an effective head for almost
a decade,"[306] and being faced with new competition from the
recently formed law school of the University of Chicago,
whose aim, Wigmore's biographer reports, was to destroy
Northwestern's Law School by raiding its faculty.[307]
Amazingly, Wigmore himself turned down an offer to move
to Chicago's new law school, to bring with him a couple of
his colleagues, and to name his salary.[308] Wigmore stayed
at Northwestern, which soon provided an increase in
funding and a new building, with space "more than seven

---

[302] Simon Greenleaf, A Treatise on the Law of Evidence, edited by J.H.
Wigmore (Little Brown, 1899).

[303] Roalfe, *supra* note 270, at 42.

[304] *Id.*, at 43.

[305] *Id.*, at 45.

[306] *Id.*, at 45.

[307] *Id.*, at 46.

[308] *Id.*, at 46.

times as large as the previous quarters."[309] Oliver Wendell Holmes, Jr., who had just become a Justice on the United States Supreme Court, and who was, at the time, already the most famous figure in American law, spoke in 1902 at the dedication of the new building, at the invitation of Wigmore, and, in particular, to give a boost to Wigmore's career and his Deanship.[310] Wigmore had secured additional funding from the University, he now had a full-time faculty of six (including, for two years, Roscoe Pound,[311] until Pound was poached by the University of Chicago's law school, and then, one year later, moved on to Harvard).[312] Wigmore proceeded to embark on the building of a network of alumni and community support, including, for example, generous contributions from Elbert H. Gary, then the chairman of the board of U.S. Steel.[313] Gary's contributions were particularly useful to Wigmore in building Northwestern's law library (now in part named the Gary Library), as Wigmore built what was, at the time, probably the country's greatest collection of works on Continental law.[314] Wigmore himself believed that he had acquired "the most unique Law Library in this country, outside of Harvard University and [The Library of] Congress."[315]

Not only was Wigmore a scholar and a distinguished administrator, but he was, as well, a notable classroom performance artist, who might have served as a

---

[309] *Id.*, at 47.

[310] *Id.*, at 47–48.

[311] See Chapter 7, *infra*.

[312] Roalfe, *supra* note 270, at 50–51. See also, on Pound and Wigmore, David M. Rabban, Law's History: American Legal Thought and the Transatlantic Turn to History 426 (Cambridge, 2013). ("Lured to Northwestern Law School by Wigmore in 1907, Pound moved to the University of Chicago in 1909 and Harvard in 1910.")

[313] Roalfe, *supra* note 270, at 49.

[314] *Id.*, at 57.

[315] Quoted *id.*, at 58.

Kingsfieldian[316] model for the practitioner of the Socratic method. One of his classrooms at Northwestern contained a bust of Sir William Blackstone,[317] and there is a report that "When a student made a particularly inept recitation, the Dean would shake his head, walk over to the bust of Blackstone and turn Blackstone's face to the wall."[318]

Felix Frankfurter,[319] in a letter he wrote to Wigmore in response to the latter's congratulation on Frankfurter's appointment to the Harvard Law School faculty, expressed his gratitude based on Wigmore's standing as "among the deepest sources of professional inspiration, and one of the profoundest leaders in the task of shaping the law to meet the needs of the modern state."[320] Frankfurter may have been given to shameless flattery,[321] but he had a point.

As indicated earlier, Wigmore's fame, such as it is today, is due to the treatise on Evidence, on which he worked for fifteen years, and which appeared in a four-volume edition in 1904–1905.[322] Another volume, a supplement covering the years 1904–1907 was published in 1908, and still another, a cumulative supplement, covering evidence cases decided from 1904–1914 appeared in 1915.[323] Several revisions of the treatise were done in the following decades, and it remains in print today.[324] Praise

---

[316] See Chapter 13, *infra*, on the fictional law professor, Charles Kingsfield.

[317] For the image see the illustration in Chapter 1, *supra*.

[318] Roalfe, *supra* note 270, at 54.

[319] See Chapter 9, *infra*.

[320] Quoted by Roalfe, *supra* note 270, at 53.

[321] See *infra*, Chapter 9.

[322] Roalfe, *supra* note 270, at 77.

[323] *Ibid.*

[324] The Fourth edition, in 13 hardcover volumes, now updated twice annually, is available from a distinguished law book publisher for the modest sum of $3185. See generally http://www.wklawbusiness.com/store/products/wigmore-evidence-set-fourth-prod–0316939706/hardcover-item–1–0316939706 (accessed February 13, 2015).

for the treatise knows few bounds. Quoting two prominent evidence scholars who wrote reviews of the Treatise, two recent commentators on evidence scholarship observed "Joseph Beale wrote, 'It is hardly too much to say that this is the most complete and exhaustive treatise on a single branch of our law that has ever been written[,]"[325] and "[o]f the third edition, Edmund Morgan wrote: 'Not only is this the best, by far the best, treatise on the Law of Evidence, it is also the best work ever produced on any comparable division of Anglo-American Law.' "[326]

The treatise did not win immediate acceptance,, perhaps due to the fact that it introduced a new classification system, new terminology, and advocated the implementation of principles of law that were as yet, unsupported by either logic or court authority.[327] Wigmore introduced concepts such as "retrospectant evidence, prophylactic rules, viatorial privilege, integration of legal acts, and autoptic preference," which to most professors and practitioners were not only novel, but possibly "repellant."[328] Nevertheless, within a few years it did

---

[325] Roger C. Park and Michael J. Saks, Evidence Scholarship Reconsidered: Results of the Interdisciplinary Turn, 46 B.C. L. Rev 949, 951 n6, Quoting J.H. Beale, Book Review, 18 HARV. L. REV. 478, 478 (1905) (reviewing John Henry Wigmore, A Treatise On The System Of Evidence In Trials At Common Law (Little Brown, 1905)).

[326] Ibid., quoting Edmund M. Morgan, Book Review, 20 B.U. L. REV. 776, 793 (1940) (footnote omitted).

[327] Roalfe, supra note 270, at 79.

[328] Id., at 79, quoting Joseph H. Beale. For a penetrating relatively recent look at the project of evidence law reformers, of whom Wigmore may have been the most prominent, which analysis uses the insights of Critical Legal Studies (see Chapter 14, infra), and implies that the law and scholarship of evidence suffers from a failure really to understand what is going on in trials, see Michael S. Ariens, The Law of Evidence and the Idea of Progress, 25 Loy. L.A. L. Rev. 853 (1992). For the most important recent work on the modern American trial experience, see Robert P. Burns, A Theory of the Trial (Princeton, 1999). And, for the provocative argument that trial lawyers can learn a lot from poker players, see Steven Lubet, Lawyers' Poker: 52 Lessons that Lawyers Can Learn from Card Players (Oxford, 2006).

become the standard reference in the law of evidence for practitioners and judges, and it remains one of the most acclaimed and successful legal treatises ever published.[329] Henry Friendly, arguably the greatest judge never to sit on the United States Supreme Court, believed that Wigmore's treatise was among the most "stimulating and exciting" law books he had ever encountered, although this view may be debatable.[330] It is possible, however, that Wigmore's greatest contribution to the law was not his work in evidence, but rather, as Michigan's law school's Dean (a graduate of Northwestern, but before Wigmore's time), put it, Wigmore's "leadership in the movement to strike the fetters of intellectual and legal [provincialism] from the bar and in pointing out the way to a conservative and scientific reform and progress in our jurisprudence."[331]

There is one biography of Wigmore,[332] but today, except for evidence scholars,[333] there is very little attention paid to this early twentieth-century legal titan. He was, nevertheless, an important pioneer in comparative law and legal empiricism, and while he paid attention to historical development of the law, he did so as a reformer attracted to the "practical or sociological side" rather than "to the outmoded views of historical jurisprudence."[334] Wigmore had eclectic tastes, and he was sensitive to the need to link what was being done in the law schools to the broader world.

---

[329] See, e.g., Roalfe, *supra* note 270, at 80.

[330] For that view of Friendly's, see David M. Dorsen, Henry Friendly: Greatest Judge of His Era 78 (Harvard, 2012). Dorsen dissents, and calls *Wigmore on Evidence* "dry and demanding reading, to say the least." *Id.*, at 389 n.1.

[331] Roalfe, *supra* note 270, at 104, quoting a 1914 letter to Wigmore from Henry M. Bates.

[332] Roalfe, *supra* note 270.

[333] See, e.g., William Twining, Theories of Evidence: Bentham & Wigmore (Stanford, 1986).

[334] Rabban, *supra* note 312, at 466, discussing Roscoe Pound's views of Wigmore's scholarship. On Pound, see Chapter 7, *infra*.

He initiated an interest in other social science fields that is still characteristic of Northwestern. For example, to celebrate the 50th anniversary of the founding of the law school, in 1909, he helped institute a conference on Criminal Law and Criminology at the school that would incorporate insights from "the contributory sciences of law, sociology, medicine, psychology, penology, police and philanthropy."[335] This conference led to the publication of the Journal of Criminal Law and Criminology, in May, 1910,[336] and it continues to be the premier specialized journal in its discipline.

Wigmore's work laid out an intriguing path for the law and legal education which has come to be more influential than is now generally appreciated. Some of my colleagues at Northwestern, consciously or unconsciously carrying on Wigmore's tradition of empirical studies, now believe that the future of legal education lies with those who engage in quantitative analysis of the law, and, it almost seems, at times, they virtually refuse to consider as serious scholarship anything that is not peppered with Greek letters and complex mathematical formulae.[337]

---

[335]　Roalfe, *supra* note 270, at 60.

[336]　*Id.*, at 61.

[337]　The most prominent of Northwestern's Empirical scholars of the law is currently Bernard S. Black, the Nicholas D. Chabraja Professor at Northwestern's Pritzker School of Law and Kellogg School of Management. He is the managing director of the Social Science Research Network and the founding chairman of the annual Conference on Empirical Legal Studies. For a sample of Professor Black's work (complete with Greek letter formulae), see, e.g., Zenon Zabinski and Bernard S. Black, The Deterrent Effect of Tort Law: Evidence from Medical Malpractice Reform, Northwestern University Law School Law and Economics Research Paper No. 13–09 (Draft, February 2015), available on the web at http://papers.ssrn.com/sol3/papers.cfm?abstract_id= 2161362 (accessed 5 March 2016) (Concluding that there is evidence that "reduced risk of med[ical] mal[practice] litigation, due to state adoption of damage caps, leads to higher rates of preventable adverse patient safety events in hospitals." *Id.*, at 26). To similar effect, see the research by one former and one current Northwestern University School of Law members, Ronen Avraham and Max Schanzenbach, The Impact of Tort Reform on Intensity of Treatment:

Like his friend Oliver Wendell Holmes, Jr., Wigmore undoubtedly thought of himself as a reformer (and he was). For example, when Roscoe Pound was appointed to the Harvard Law faculty in 1910, Wigmore expressed "the hope that you will not allow the traditions and inertia and complacency of an age-honored institution to congeal or ossify your living zeal or any of your well-defined views. You know what the usual fate of the opposition is when it accepts office as the party in Power."[338] Wigmore appears to have believed that the law "should be coherently ordered into abstract concepts," but he was not necessarily committed to the belief that these concepts could yield "axiomatic general truths," or that "a deductive system of

---

Evidence from Heart Patients in 39 Journal Of Health Economics 273 (2015) (Suggesting that treatment intensity declines after a cap on non-economic damages.) For a provocative empirical study by another Northwestern faculty member, powerfully suggesting that Sarbanes-Oxley, a much touted federal regulatory measure, actually inhibits risk-taking (and therefore eventual financial rewards for shareholders) among managers, see Kate Litvak, Defensive Management: Does the Sarbanes-Oxley Act Discourage Corporate Risk-Taking?, 2014 U.Ill. L.Rev. 1663. See also, for a different approach to empirical studies, the Chicago Homicide Project, under the direction of Northwestern's Leigh Bienen, which has been accumulating and making available to scholars a rich trove of data on murders in the windy city. See, e.g., Leigh B. Bienen and Brandon Rottinghaus, Learning from the Past, Living in the Present: Understanding Homicide in Chicago, 1870–1930, 92 J. Crim. L. & Criminology 437 (2002). For a sampling of still other empirical social-science approaches to the law by Northwestern's faculty, see, e.g., Tonja Jacobi & Emerson H. Tiller, Legal Doctrine and Political Control, 23 J.L. Econ. & Org. 326 (2007), Shari Seidman Diamond, Truth, Justice, and the Jury, 26 Harv.J.Law & Public Policy 143 (2003), Janice Nadler, Flouting the Law, 83 Tex.L.Rev. 1399 (2005), David L. Schwartz, Practice Makes Perfect? An Empirical Study of Claim Construction Reversal Rates in Patent Cases 107 Mich.L.Rev. 223 (2008), and John P. Heinz and Edward O. Laumann, Chicago Lawyers: The Social Structure of the Bar (Rev.ed. Northwestern University Press, 1994).

[338] Rabban, *supra* note 312, at 470, quoting Wigmore to Pound (March 29, 1910). Rabban notes Morton Horwitz's observation in his The Transformation of American Law 1870–1960 217–219 (Oxford, 1992), that once Pound became Dean "he did not follow through on his own hopes for sociological jurisprudence and by the late 1930's eventually manifested . . . an intellectual 'about face.' " Rabban, *ibid.*

formal reasoning can apply them to decide new cases."[339]
Wigmore was a bit like his friend Holmes in rejecting the
notion that the law inevitably was "logic," but unlike
Holmes (if Alschuler is right, and he is), Wigmore never lost
sight of the fact that the attempt to separate law from
morals was dangerous. Wigmore lamented what he thought
was "a voluntary divorce of the judicial pronouncements
from morality and reality. The judge conceives it his part,"
Wigmore wrote, "neither to allude to the one nor to seek for
the other. He prefers to keep himself retired within the dry
logical network of his legal system. He is disinclined to keep
obviously and frankly in touch with morality and with
reality. Has not the time come for a different attitude?"[340]
Perhaps in his insistence that the law be not separated from
morality Wigmore was something of a conservative, but in
his time he was perceived as more of a reformer, and
perhaps this is true as well of the man for whom Wigmore
was a mentor,[341] Roscoe Pound.

---

[339] Rabban, *supra* note 312, at 483, using the categories of "formalism"
and "conceptualism" to be found in Thomas C. Grey, Langdell's Orthodoxy, 45
U.Pitt.L.Rev. 1 (1983).

[340] Roalfe, *supra* note 270, at 95, quoting from a 1915 piece in the Illinois
Law Review (now the Northwestern University Law Review), "Justice,
Commercial Morality and the Federal Supreme Court: The Waterman Pen
Case," 10 Ill.L.Rev. 178, 189 (1915).

[341] Rabban, *supra* note 312, at 466.

CHAPTER 7

TOWARDS SOCIOLOGICAL JURISPRUDENCE

EARLY TWENTIETH CENTURY

Roscoe Pound
(Nebraska, 1895–1907; Northwestern, 1907–1909;
Chicago, 1909–1910; Harvard, 1911–1964)

■ ■ ■

Roscoe Pound (1870–1964)
Photograph taken while Pound was
Dean of the University of Nebraska Law School, c. 1906.
Historical & Special Collections, Harvard Law School Library.

These days, Roscoe Pound[342] probably gets most of the
credit for advancing jurisprudence and law reform in the
early twentieth century that might, at least in part, be
properly owing to Wigmore, if for no other reason than
Wigmore gave Pound the momentum to move himself into

---

[342] A useful biography of Pound is David Wigdor, Roscoe Pound,
Philosopher of Law (Westport, Conn.: Greenwood Press, 1974). An earlier, less
critical work, is Paul Sayre, The Life of Roscoe Pound (Iowa, 1948).

the highest regions of the legal academy.[343] Pound was, admittedly, a figure of extraordinary talent. He was "voraciously curious," he had the "ability to speed read, [the] command of every European language and [a] photographic memory."[344] Wigmore brought Pound to teach at Northwestern, and, to Pound's credit, he is reported to have stated that "I always remember my short time at Northwestern . . . as one of the high water marks of my career,"[345] but, after only two years, Chicago soon hired him away, and finally Pound came to rest at Harvard, where he became its most famous Dean (1916–36) since Langdell. "Through his work in building faculty and programs and in seeking international students, he made Harvard the first of the world-class American law schools. His name now graces one of Harvard's buildings, an honor accorded to only a handful of legal greats."[346] Pound's father was a prominent Nebraska judge, and wanted his son to follow in his chosen profession. Pound at first resisted this directive, although he did attend Harvard Law School for one year,

---

[343] Pound acknowledged Wigmore's contribution to a critical and needed approach to the law of evidence. See, e.g., Pound, Mechanical Jurisprudence, 8 Col. L. Rev. 605, 620 n.59 (1905) (noting Wigmore's "excellent critical discussion" in his evidence treatise of the information that should be offered jurors when confronted with scientific and technical matters of dispute). Could Pound's praise of Wigmore in 1905 have something to do with Wigmore's bringing Pound to Northwestern in 1907? In any event, Pound's respect for Wigmore endured. In 1938 Pound credited Wigmore with participating in a "revival of doctrinal writing" (along with Williston on Contracts and Beale on the Conflict of Laws) which resulted in "permanent contributions to our law." These three "put the matured nineteenth-century law in form to be used in a new era of growth." Roscoe Pound, Formative Era of American Law 165 (Little Brown, 1938).

[344] N.E.H. Hull, Roscoe Pound and Karl Llewellyn: Searching for an American Jurisprudence 12 (Chicago, 1997) (See also id., at 46, indicating Pound's fluency in Greek, Latin, German and French).

[345] William R. Roalfe, John Henry Wigmore: Scholar and Reformer 51 (Northwestern University Press, 1977).

[346] Stephen Presser, Forward to Roscoe Pound, The Ideal Element in American Law (Liberty Fund, 2002), available on the web, at http://oll.liberty fund.org/pages/pound-and-the-law (accessed January 2, 2016).

and he did practice law for a time in his father's firm.[347] It appeared for a while, however, as though Pound had embarked on a career as a botanist. Much of his early interest was in plant life, he received both a BA and a Ph.D. in botany from the University of Nebraska,[348] and, indeed, his co-authored book on the plants of his native Nebraska, Phytogeography of Nebraska (1898),[349] might still be regarded as a classic of the genre.

Pound's early training as a natural scientist, and as a Darwinist, under the influence of his mentor in Botany at the University of Nebraska, Charles Bessey, predisposed him to see the law in terms of organic growth and to understand that only those parts of the law should survive that were useful. Pound's "work with Bessey," writes N.E.H. Hull, "had been on the frontier of a new discipline—ecological mapping—and what Pound seemed to see in law was an ecological process, a contextualized growth fostered and hindered by the cultures that surrounded law."[350] When Pound thought of the law as "organic," he "meant not an organism already evolved and now fixed in its morphology, but rather a living organism, changing and adopting."[351] As Hull further explains, "The organic model was the 'in' thing,

---

[347] This was apparently not a happy time for Pound. Hull, *supra* note 344, at 41, quotes a 1915 letter in which Pound writes that "I shall always remember the years in which I was a combined collector of bad debts, messenger boy and stenographer in a big law office as the most irksome of my existence." Pound was not the last law professor whose years of practice were not the subject of fond remembrance.

[348] Presser, *supra* note 346. Pound's Ph.D. in botany was "the first in the subject granted in Nebraska (and the second Ph.D. given there)." Hull, *supra* note 344, at 48.

[349] Roscoe Pound and Frederic E. Clements, The Phytogeography of Nebraska (The Seminar, 1898). This work treated botany "not as a sterile field concerned only with taxonomy and classification, but rather encompassing an understanding of the organic and evolutionary relationship among all plant life." Presser, *supra* note 346. Compare the wonderful old lawyers' maxim that the law is a "seamless web."

[350] Hull, *supra* note 344, at 49.

[351] *Id.*, at 44.

and Pound's recourse to biology in an age when Darwinian models of human progress were all the rage could hardly be called original, but his gift was to catch the academic tide as it surged, not to anticipate it."[352] This was a perspective he never abandoned.

While Pound understood the fact of organic change in botany and law, he never wavered from a conviction that in both fields of study there were constant principles which determined change, a constant striving toward stability and equilibrium, and a constant existence of underlying truths which could be revealed by careful observation, classification, and analysis.[353] From his botanical work came, perhaps, a faith that forces of nature caused evolution and change, and it was that insight that appears to have driven Pound's analysis of both common law and jurisprudence. And yet there are puzzles in Pound's view of the law. Hull, one of Pound's most insightful expositors, discerns a "dual strain in his jurisprudential nature," seeing him both in his early and later years as a conservative who "despised violent change and lauded systematization and classification," but also as someone who for "three or more decades" would espouse "a progressive-pragmatic doctrine of jurisprudence that seems at odds with these fussy taxonomies."[354]

There are at least three interesting and distinct strains in Pound's influential, and, as Hull hints, somewhat contradictory work. The first, drawing from his early study of biology, is what might be regarded as his evolutionary writing on Jurisprudence. In his monumental five volume treatise on jurisprudence,[355] for example, which Pound

---

[352] *Id.*, at 45.

[353] The first part of this paragraph is adopted from Presser, *supra* note 346.

[354] Hull, *supra* note 344, at 41.

[355] Roscoe Pound, Jurisprudence (5 vols) (West Publishing Co. 1959).

published at the age of 89, Pound followed ideas he had articulated as early as 1893,[356] and argued that an internal dynamic caused the substance of legal regimes to change, but never explained why that change happened. Reworking his notions about legal change in a piece he published in 1904, in the course of "a sound analysis of positive law, legislation, and judicial discretion from the Romans through Jeremy Bentham, Austin, and everyone else, he asserted that the progress of the law was cyclical."[357] He wrote, "In the history of jurisprudence periods of legislation and codification in which the imperative theory of law has been predominant, have always been periods of stagnation. The law has lived and grown through juristic activity under the influence of ideas of natural right and justice or reasonableness, not force, as the ultimate source of authority."[358]

In a second subject matter area, Pound wrote on American Legal History, most prominently in his 1938 volume, *The Formative Era of American Law*,[359] which period, he said, ran from "independence to the time of the Civil War,"[360] chronicling, apparently, one of his eras of "juristic activity under the influence of ideas of natural right and justice or reasonableness," and crediting profound American legal doctrinal change to brilliant and creative nineteenth-century American common law judges. *Formative Era* was also notable for Pound's firm rejection of Marxist explanations for change in nineteenth-century American law. Pound's four lectures which became *Formative Era* were delivered at Tulane Law School in

---

[356] Hull, *supra* note 344, at 46.

[357] *Id.*, at 57.

[358] Roscoe Pound, "A New School of Jurists," 4 University Studies 249, 250, 265 (July 1904), quoted by Hull, *supra* note 344, at 57.

[359] Roscoe Pound, The Formative Era of American Law (Little, Brown & Co. 1938).

[360] *Id.*, at 3.

1936, and were described as "the first serious and the first comprehensive account of the formative period of American legal history."[361] At the time of this lecture series Pound was introduced as "the great American jurist of our time."[362]

According to Pound, the great nineteenth-century American common law judges, men such as James Kent, Joseph Story,[363] John Bannister Gibson, and Lemuel Shaw,[364] were articulating a "taught legal tradition."[365] Pound suggested that this "taught legal tradition" could, and ought to be, distinguished from what he described as "recent theories of law as formulated class self-interest, or as a product of individual judicial psychology governing the behavior of the judge, or as a disappearing phenomenon in the society of the future."[366] Those who articulated this "taught legal tradition," in the nineteenth century were drawing inspiration from an ideal of individual freedom, or, as Pound also described it, an "ideal society in which there was a maximum of abstract free individual self-assertion," which the judges thought was " 'liberty' as secured in bills

[361] *Id.*, at x (Introduction by Rufus C. Harris, President of Tulane University).

[362] *Ibid.*

[363] See Chapter 3, *supra.*

[364] Pound actually listed 10 men whom he stated were "the ten judges who must be ranked first in American judicial history," Pound, *Formative Era, supra* note 359, at 4. These were Chief Justice of the United States, John Marshall, James Kent (Chief Justice of the New York Supreme Court and afterwards its greatest Chancellor), Joseph Story (Supreme Court of the United States), John Bannister Gibson (Supreme Court of Pennsylvania), Lemuel Shaw (Chief Justice of the Supreme Judicial Court of Massachusetts), Thomas Ruffin (Chief Justice of the Supreme Court of North Carolina), Thomas McIntyre Cooley (Supreme Court of Michigan and member of the Interstate Commerce Commission), Charles Doe (Chief Justice of the Supreme Court of New Hampshire), Oliver Wendell Holmes, Jr. (Supreme Judicial Court of Massachusetts and United States Supreme Court), and Benjamin Nathan Cardozo (Court of Appeals of New York and United States Supreme Court). Of this list, all but Holmes and Cardozo served principally in the nineteenth century. *Id.*, at 30–31, fn. 2.

[365] *Id.*, at vii.

[366] *Id.*, at vii–viii.

of rights."[367] Still, Pound understood that in his own time, natural law notions favoring collective values which placed the state over the individual and those emphasizing the values of civilization itself might have been in the ascendance.[368]

Pound recognized that nineteenth-century American judges—like Lemuel Shaw, John Bannister Gibson, and Thomas Ruffin, in particular[369]—had profoundly altered the common law, but Pound argued that these judges had done no more than to permit American legal doctrines to respond to American conditions which differed from those of England. As he put it, American judges and doctrinal writers had to develop an American common law, a body of judicially declared or doctrinally approved precepts suitable to America, out of the old English cases and the old English statutes. "Tenacity of a taught legal tradition," he argued, "is much more significant in our legal history than the economic conditions of time and place."[370] Still, Pound suggested, nineteenth-century judges and treatise writers "reworked the common law, and did it thoroughly, in about three quarters of a century."[371] Their activity, for Pound, was that of neutrally acting professionals, who were simply responding to:

> Pressure of new demands, problems created by the development of transportation, the effect of inventions, and the rise of industry in some sections and growth of trade in others, [which] called for new reasoned applications of the technique in which these judges had been trained to the body of legal precepts and established legal

---

[367] *Id.*, at 98.

[368] *Id.*, at 19.

[369] See, e.g., *id.*, at 82–86.

[370] *Id.*, at 82.

[371] *Id.*, at 20–21.

analogies which had been taught them. This, rather than the Marxian class struggle is the economic interpretation of American law in its formative era.[372]

Pound was prepared to concede that "American legislation of the formative era may be understood to a large extent through a conventional economic interpretation,"[373] because legislators responded to some "group or class" like, for example, "a politically dominant class of farmers."[374] For Pound, however, the real legal professionals, the judges and treatise writers, simply fitted legal changes "into the traditional system in their interpretation and application, and [affected] slowly or very little the principles, conceptions and doctrines which are the enduring law."[375] Responding to Marxist critics of these nineteenth-century judges,[376] which critics argued that American law had been transformed in a manner that favored capitalists and entrepreneurs, Pound replied that the Marxists simply found it impossible to understand "an honest man," such as Massachusetts Supreme Judicial Court Chief Justice Lemuel Shaw,[377] who, according to Pound, even-handedly applied and articulated the law, following the "taught legal tradition," in a manner that promoted the interests of both workers and capitalists.

---

[372] *Id.*, at 86–87.

[373] *Id.*, at 91.

[374] *Ibid.*

[375] *Id.*, at 83.

[376] Pound singles out for excoriation Walter Nelles, a law professor at Yale, and one of the founders of the organization that became the American Civil Liberties Union, and, in particular, Pound is critical of Nelles, Commonwealth v. Hunt, 32 Col.L.Rev. 1128 (1932). See Pound, Formative Era, *supra* note 359, at 129, n.11–12, and accompanying text (*id.*, at 86–87).

[377] Shaw is the subject of one of the best judicial biographies ever written, Leonard W. Levy, The Law of the Commonwealth and Chief Justice Shaw (Harvard, 1957, reprinted Oxford, 1987).

It does appear difficult to deny that Shaw was struggling to meet the needs of his time, and equally difficult to deny that he understood he was faced with the task of reconciling competing economic interests. While it is true, for example, that he was the author of the notorious decision in *Farwell v. Boston & Worcester R.R.*,[378] which implemented the English "fellow-servant" rule for America, denying the right of a worker to sue an employer for injury caused by a negligent "fellow servant," Shaw was also the author of an equally famous decision, *Commonwealth v. Hunt*,[379] in which Shaw decided that members of workers' associations (the predecessors of what were eventually to become unions) were free to refuse to work for employers who hired workers who were not members of their association. This was a departure from the existing rule of the English common law, which had a tendency to regard any combination of workers as an unlawful conspiracy to raise wages. Shaw seemed to go out of his way to suggest there were benevolent reasons for workers to wish to associate in "closed shops," for example to avoid working with colleagues who might be tempted to imbibe alcohol. Shaw may have been taking this almost whimsical move in order slightly to tweak the counsel for the workers, an early nineteenth-century public interest lawyer of sorts, Robert Rantoul, who was a well-known temperance advocate.[380]

Some of the most recent critics of Roscoe Pound, such as Morton Horwitz of Harvard, a leading figure in the Critical Legal Studies movement, to be discussed, *infra*,[381] have given Pound credit for recognizing the dynamic aspect of jurisprudence—indeed, Pound's five volume history of jurisprudence does a magnificent job in suggesting that

---

[378] Farwell v. Boston & Worcester R.R. Corp, 45 Mass. 49 (Mass. 1842).

[379] Commonwealth v. Hunt, 45 Mass. 111 (1842).

[380] On Rantoul, see Chapter 3, *supra*, text accompanying notes 168–172.

[381] See Chapter 14, *infra*.

laws change over time—but have faulted him for failing to explain why this legal change comes about.[382] As already suggested, perhaps Pound's early training as a botanist prepared him to see that the law could evolve organically, that it could be, so to speak, a machine that would go of itself, but, so the criticism goes, other than suggesting that the law springs from the desires of the Creator (as does the natural world), Pound had no theory of legal development. For Horwitz, of course, Pound was an apologist for the existing legal order, and like earlier Marxist critics of Pound, Horwitz appeared to be arguing that Pound, and writers of legal history like him, were inappropriately insensitive to the injustice wrought by the modern system of law. Thus Horwitz, in his *The Transformation of American Law 1780–1860* (1977), took the same period Pound analyzed in *Formative Era*, analyzed the work of many of the judges Pound did, and concluded that it was economic interests of lawyers and the entrepreneurs and the manufacturers they came to serve rather than a "taught legal tradition" that explained these decisions. It might be said by one sympathetic to Horwitz's efforts that Horwitz set Pound on his feet much the same way Marx did to Hegel. Put slightly differently, Horwitz brilliantly took Pound's materials and used them to argue that Walter Nelles & Co. were correct after all.[383]

In what might be regarded as a third set of writings, Pound argued for "sociological jurisprudence," a realistic approach to what the courts were actually doing, moving away from what Pound believed to be Langdell's misguided

---

[382] For some of Horwitz's criticism of Pound, see, e.g., Morton J. Horwitz, The Conservative Tradition in the Writing of American Legal History, 17 American Journal of Legal History 275 (1973) and Morton J. Horwitz, The Transformation of American Law, 1870–1960: The Crisis of Legal Orthodoxy (Oxford, 1992).

[383] See Horwitz, Conservative Tradition, *supra* note 382, and see also, Morton J. Horwitz, The Transformation of American Law 1780–1860 (Harvard, 1977).

notion that the life of the law was logic, not experience. In this, of course, Pound was rather like Holmes, but, curiously, over the years, Pound has come to be perceived (especially by the legal realists[384] and the Critical Legal Studies scholars (of whom more soon))[385] as something of a conservative "naive prattler." As Hull hints, though, Pound resists easy labelling. One can discern, even in Pound's writing on American legal history, a core belief that the law should not be separated from morals, and that mechanical application of legal rules, such as prevailed in the late nineteenth and early twentieth century on the United States Supreme Court (presumably even those that dictated enforcement of "liberty of contract") was really not in the interests of the polity.[386]

Nevertheless, especially when he was writing what became his "sociological jurisprudence," Pound was something of a courageous legal reformer, and one well ahead of his time. One brilliant legal scholar, in his sweeping analysis of one hundred years of American legal thought, goes so far as to place Pound among a group of "Progressive" legal thinkers, with a "radical agenda."[387] Another iconoclastic legal scholar, understanding Pound's international outlook, and his reformist beliefs, writes that "Like many intellectuals in Europe and the United States, including the leading German and English legal scholars,

---

[384] Pound's thought, and that of the legal realists, is superbly analyzed in Hull, *supra* note 344.

[385] Chapter 14, *infra*.

[386] See, e.g., *Formative Era*, *supra* note 359, at 98–100, implicitly criticizing cases such as Lochner v. New York, 198 U.S. 45 (1905), and citing in support of such criticism, *id.*, at 131 n.39, Roscoe Pound, Mechanical Jurisprudence, 8 Col. L.Rev. 605 (1908).

[387] Herbert Hovenkamp, The Opening of American Law: Neoclassical Legal Thought 1870–1970 4 (Oxford, 2015) (Commenting on a group of Progressive Legal Scholars, who embraced Darwinism to achieve a "radical agenda for social experimentation," which scholars, Hovemkamp writes, included Lester Frank Ward, Edward A. Ross, Richard T. Ely, and Roscoe Pound).

Rudolf von Jhering and Frederic Matiland, Pound believed that traditional conceptions of individualism and individual rights impeded the attention to collective interests required in the modern world."[388]

While serving as Dean of the University of Nebraska, In August 1906, Pound addressed the annual convention of the American Bar Association in St. Paul, Minnesota. His talk was titled "The Causes of Popular Dissatisfaction with the Administration of Justice," and was his first major exposition of what would become known as "sociological jurisprudence." In that talk Pound declared that "The most important and most constant cause of dissatisfaction with all law at all times is to be found in the necessarily mechanical operation of legal rules."[389] Because his talk, and his railing against "mechanical" jurisprudence, advocated what appeared to be major changes in American law and legal practice, in order to take advantage of modern science, it struck many of Pound's listeners as radical, and some objected to the talk's publication, presumably fearing the negative light it might cast on the then rather conservative American Bar Association. Nevertheless, others who heard the talk, or were later to read the text, understood that Pound was one of the most significant contemporary legal thinkers, and it immediately catapulted Pound to national notice. One important result of the talk was the offer, as noted earlier, from the dean of the

---

[388] David M. Rabban, Law's History: American Legal Thought and the Transatlantic Turn to History 8 (Cambridge 2013). Rabban's book, crucial for an understanding of nineteenth-century transatlantic intellectual history, legal history, doctrinal thought, jurisprudence and legal education, is a needed corrective to the more common disparagement of Pound in the twentieth and twenty-first century, and a refreshing look at a whole host of previously neglected American legal and historical thinkers. For Rabban's evaluation of Pound see especially *id.*, at 423–469.

[389] Quoted, e.g., in N.E. Hull, *supra* note 344, at 64.

Northwestern University School of Law, John Henry Wigmore,[390] to join Northwestern's faculty.[391]

Pound died before his fellow Harvard Professor Horwitz lodged his charges against him, but, in his own time, Pound was lambasted by the great "legal realist" Jerome Frank[392] for naively believing that there was clear and certain content in at least some legal doctrines. Legal Realists like Frank sought other explanations besides the "taught legal tradition," or neutral applications of legal rules, for legal decisions, and Frank himself argued that Pound's notions were like the prattling of a small boy, mistaking the law for the purportedly omnipotent father Frank thought we all sought in childhood. For Frank, belief in the certainty of law, such as that displayed from time to time by Pound, was simply a substitute for a childhood belief in an infallible parent, much as, in Frank's view, religious belief could also be. The suggestion that childhood problems could result in adult difficulties, the Freudian notion that the "child is father to the man," on which Frank apparently relied, was clearest to Frank, perhaps, in the thought of the Freudian-influenced Psychologist, Jean Piaget.[393]

Pound had little tolerance for acerbic legal realists such as Frank, as he worried that their more extreme claim that

---

[390] Chapter 6, *supra*.

[391] This paragraph is principally drawn from Presser, *supra* note 346.

[392] Jerome Frank is generally regarded "as an 'extreme' [legal] realist," who, pursuant to one strain of belief in that early twentieth-century movement in legal thought, believed that judges decided cases "on the basis of irrational biases." Charles L. Barzun, Jerome Frank, Lon Fuller, and a Romantic Pragmatism, University of Virginia School of Law Public Law and Legal Theory Research Paper Series 2016–6, January 2016, at 2. On "Legal Realism" generally, see, e.g., Hull, *supra* note 344.

[393] Frank's extraordinary criticism of Pound's "prattling" can be found in his controversial Jerome Frank, Law and the Modern Mind (Brentano's Inc., 1930), which is, essentially, a psychological explanation for the obscurity of law. See, e.g., *id.*, at 307. For an insightful rumination on the nature of Frank's legal realist thought see Barzun, *supra* note 392.

judicial decisions were nothing but after-the-fact rationalizations threatened to undermine what Pound regarded as the benign organic character of the law, and might well give license to arbitrary and dangerous judicial behavior.[394] Still, Pound did go out of his way to engage with the more sophisticated members of the legal realist group, such as Karl Llewellyn, and a fair appraisal of Pound might also acknowledge that some of Pound's work laid the foundation for what was to become legal realism and "progressive legal thought."[395]

In an extraordinary piece which he apparently later admitted was "written in haste" amidst a plethora of administrative and consulting obligations,[396] an obviously stung Pound chided the new "legal realists" for failing to realize that he and his earlier cohort had been concerned with the same failures of the law to meet the needs of the times. He railed against this new rising group of law professors for what he appeared to believe was their naïve

---

[394] For one of Pound's most carefully constructed arguments against Frank and the more extreme legal realists see generally, The Ideal Element in Law, *supra* note 346, a series of lectures Pound delivered in India in 1948, when Pound was 76, a mature thinker, but still in full command of his powers. Ten years earlier he sounded a similar theme. See *Formative Era, supra* note 359, at 27–28. ("Today rationalism is under attack from another quarter. A psychological realism is abroad which regards reason as affording no more than a cover of illusion for processes judicial and administrative which are fundamentally and necessarily unrational. But merely destructive so-called realism makes neither for stability nor for change since it gives us nothing in place of what it would take away.")

[395] See, e.g., Eben Moglen, The Transformation of Morton Horwitz, 93 Colum. L. Rev. 1042, 1045 n.7 (1993). (Reviewing Horwitz, *supra* note 382, and explaining that, according to Horwitz, *id.*, at 33–34, Pound's criticism of Lochner expressed in his "famous article Liberty of Contract, 18 Yale L.J. 454 (1909)" was "the effective beginning of Progressive Legal Thought.")

[396] Roscoe Pound, The Call for a Realist Jurisprudence, 44 Harv.L.Rev. 697 (1931). For the genesis of this piece, see, e.g., William Twining, Karl Llewellyn and The Realist Movement 72 (Weidenfeld and Nicolson, 1973). The second edition of Twining's classic work, published by the Cambridge University Press in 2012, contains a fine introduction by Frederick Schauer, one of the leading contemporary scholars of jurisprudence, analyzing the importance, the history, and the development of legal realism.

acceptance of psychological (presumably Freudian) theories as adequate explanations for what judges do, but he acknowledged the need for more serious study of what legal institutions actually were doing, and whether (as the legal realists believed) the rationales judges offered were really the explanations for the decisions they rendered.[397]

Pound seems to have been most irked by the charges lodged against him by Jerome Frank,[398] but, curiously, as indicated earlier, he maintained quite a cordial relationship with Karl Llewellyn. Llewellyn, like the young Pound when he was a champion of sociological jurisprudence, recognized the important role of stable, traditional elements in American law, and also the obvious fact that many areas of the law did allow courts to engage in certain and sensible decision making.[399] Unlike Frank, who alienated Pound, Llewellyn enjoyed his friendship with the older man, and, to a certain extent, Llewellyn benefited from the patronage of Pound, and was prepared to concede that the legal rules were, in the main, actually the cause of particular legal decisions. Still, Llewellyn was aware that American legal institutions could be encouraged to develop law that was more in keeping with twentieth-century needs. Llewellyn, then, like the mature Pound, appreciated both the traditional and organic as well as the evolutionary nature of the law, and Pound was determined to further efforts like Llewellyn's and disparage those like Frank's.[400] It is to Karl Llwellyn to whom we next turn, but before making that turn, we might pause to consider the prescience of a

---

[397] See generally Pound, *supra* note 396.

[398] Presumably in Law and the Modern Mind, *supra* note 393.

[399] See, e.g., Karl N. Llewellyn, The Common Law Tradition: Deciding Appeals (Little, Brown, 1960). For Llewellyn, see Chapter 8, *infra*.

[400] For the interesting triangular relationship among Pound, Frank, and Llewellyn, see Hull, *supra* note 344, at 173–222. Much of this paragraph is taken from Presser, *supra* note 346.

warning that Pound made in his lectures, delivered in India in 1948.[401]

By the time Pound gave these lectures, of course, the stunning expansion of the federal government that was the New Deal was well underway, but Pound argued that the welfare state (or the "service state" as he called it) cannot do everything. As Professor Jeremy Kessler has recently reminded us, Pound was "one of the most vociferous anti-New Deal voices,"[402] and Pound's 1948 lectures, *The Ideal Element in Law*, were a powerful argument against redistribution, or what Pound calls the "Robin Hood" principle.[403] From the beginning of his work in the law, Pound was skeptical of populism, its expressed desire for redistribution, and its attacks on established centers of wealth and power in society. In *The Ideal Element*, Pound devotes substantial space to expounding his lifelong view that the desire for equality should not be pushed so far that it ends up destroying liberty, and Pound hints darkly that in 1948 we had already gone too far down that road, with the New Deal probably in his mind as a prime exhibit.[404] In those 1948 lectures he provides very good examples not only from political mistakes of European nations, but also from the common law doctrines themselves, as they have been recently skewed in American jurisprudence, most clearly in torts and contracts. What Pound said in 1948 still rings remarkably true in the early twenty-first century. Indeed, what Pound railed against in his 1948 lectures as the

---

[401] Pound, *supra* note 346.

[402] Jeremy K. Kessler, Book Review: The Struggle for Administrative Legitimacy (Reviewing Daniel R. Ernst, Tocqueville's Nightmare: The Administrative State Emerges in America 1900–1940 (Harvard, 2014)), 129 Harv. L. Rev. 718, 757 (2016).

[403] See, e.g., The Ideal Element in Law, *supra* note 346, at 340, 357–67.

[404] For the struggle of elite lawyers against the encroaching administrative state, in which Pound played a prominent part, see generally Daniel R. Ernst, Tocqueville's Nightmare: The Administrative State Emerges in America 1900–1940 (Harvard, 2014).

"sporting theory of litigation," the notion that litigation ought to be a ruthless tool to achieve partisan ends, now is everywhere in evidence in twenty-first-century America, extending even, in 2000, to the election of the United States president.[405]

As suggested earlier, Pound appears to have shared at least some of the late nineteenth and early twentieth century progressives' faith in the ability of experts to reformulate American law. Thus, he repeatedly called for "ministries of justice" at both the federal and state levels to help in the formulation and interpretation of the legislation that he thought was required in twentieth-century America. He was chagrined in a manner that remarkably foreshadows that of Richard Posner[406] at the failures of American legislatures. In 1938 Pound stated that:

> We cannot overlook that such [American legislative] assemblies have not been too likely to choose the most expert advisers or reporters to draft laws, that the formulating process which goes before their action has involved grave defects, that politics may play an unhappy role where it should be excluded, that there has been legislative carelessness far beyond anything exhibited in judicial decision, and that the system of informing the legislative lawmaker upon the matters to which he is to legislate is usually crude and inadequate.[407]

To fix this problem of legislative incompetence and legislative failure Pound proposed the development of "competent, scientific, impartial agencies of [statutory] preparation," which agencies could search out better

---

[405] Bush v. Gore, 531 U.S. 98 (2000).

[406] See Chapter 15, *infra*.

[407] Pound, Formative Era, *supra* note 359, at 64–65.

materials, and could aid legislators in creating more effective means of drafting and implementing legislation.[408] Pound apparently believed that judicial creativity was adequate to transform American law in the nineteenth century, but that substantial reform for the twentieth would have to come from a legal system with far more sophisticated legal institutions.

While in his later years Pound appeared to grow more conservative, still, he was a reformer of legal education from an early point in his career. As early as 1903, when he became Dean at the law school of the University of Nebraska, Pound sought to expand the curriculum to move beyond traditional legal doctrinal topics in order to include "allied fields of study already taught in great universities," and, specifically, Pound "wanted legal history and jurisprudence, two subjects practitioner-teachers shunned, added to the required course list."[409] At Harvard, Pound pioneered an interdisciplinary approach to law. "For his seminar in legal and political philosophy, Pound brought together and regularly networked with Harvard professors Gordon Allport (psychology), Talcott Parsons (sociology), B.F. Wright (government), and O. H. Taylor (economics). By so doing, Pound linked the law school to the rest of what was becoming the foremost research university in the country."[410] But while Pound was thus capable of looking outside the law in an effort to reform it, his 1948 lectures reflect the conservatism that characterized his later years. Perhaps it is fair to say that a healthy dose of Pound's mature wisdom, available in these 1948 lectures and elsewhere, might be useful in reminding a new generation of American law students and lawyers how law ought

---

[408] *Id.*, at 71–72.

[409] Hull, *supra* note 344, at 52.

[410] *Id.*, at 6–7 (1997) (footnote omitted).

properly to be used to preserve and protect American traditions, the rule of law, and liberty.[411]

Summing up, then, Pound, while he might have been a progressive in his youth, quite clearly eventually turned against the modern administrative state. He and men like him, suggests Professor Hovenkamp, "believed the [administrative] agencies threatened absolutism and arbitrary decision-making."[412] It is a very nice question, however, whether these latter-day conservative views are most characteristic of Pound, and whether Pound ought really to be viewed as a champion of tradition, the rule of law, and liberty, because it remains true that Pound might also be seen to be the progenitor of what came to be known, in general, as "progressive" legal thought[413] (both in the early twentieth century and in our day) and "legal realism" in the 1930's. Indeed, in his 1905 Columbia Law Review article, "Do We Need a Philosophy of Law,"[414] Pound even suggested that the times called for a "balance between individualism and socialism," which might be achieved through "training the rising generation of lawyers in a social, political, and legal philosophy abreast of our time."[415] Perhaps the most accurate and nuanced assessment of Pound's thought is that offered by N.E.H. Hull, who states that "Pound changed his thinking over time in quite distinct ways. . . . [T]here was no consistent underlying legal philosophy in Pound, although there always was a disposition to piece together, to listen, to reflect, and, at his

---

[411] The latter part of this paragraph is taken from Presser, *supra* note 346.

[412] Hovenkamp, *supra* note 387, at 308.

[413] See, e.g., note 395, *supra* (Eben Moglen's observation that Morton Horwtiz gives Pound credit for beginning the tradition of progressive legal thought).

[414] 5 Columbia Law Review 342 (1905).

[415] Hull, *supra* note 344, quoting Pound, *supra* note 414.

best, to see deeper meanings. Pound changed from conservative to liberal to conservative. Period."[416]

In any event, a hallmark of this "progressive" thinking was that earlier generations had misunderstood the nature of law, and that law needed radically to be altered to meet the needs of the times. Pound understood this, and may have even taken his cue from Holmes. In Pound's lectures on nineteenth-century legal history, for example, while he argued that nineteenth-century judges, lawyers, and teachers were reformulating American law pursuant to an "organizing idea in the theory of natural law,"[417] they were still engaged in "the creative process of applying reason to experience which has been the life of the law."[418] In Pound's 1908 article criticizing "Mechanical Jurisprudence," Pound made clear his belief that the purpose of law was "justice," and that simply applying legal rules, in a mechanical manner, was not enough:

> Law is not scientific for the sake of science. Being scientific as a means toward an end, it must be judged by the results it achieves, not by the niceties of its internal structure; it must be valued by the extent to which it meets its end, not by the beauty of its logical processes or the strictness with which its rules proceed from the dogmas it takes for its foundation.[419]

For Pound the practical function of law was to adjust "everyday relations so as to meet current ideas of fair play."[420] It was inappropriate for the legal system simply "to impose

---

[416] Hull, *supra* note 344, at 56 n.76.

[417] Pound, *Formative Era, supra* note 359, at 12.

[418] *Id.*, at 13 (Compare Holmes's famous dictum from The Common Law 1 (1881)) ("The life of the law has not been logic: it has been experience"). See generally Chapter 5, *supra.*

[419] Pound, *Mechanical Jurisprudence, supra* note 386, at 605.

[420] *Id.*, at 606.

the ideas of one generation upon another."[421] Instead of following the rigid legal rules of the past, in much the same manner Holmes had advocated in 1881, Pound called, in 1908, for a "pragmatic, a sociological legal science,"[422] one that would result in "the adjustment of principles and doctrines to the human conditions they are to govern rather than to assumed first principles; for putting the human factor in the central place and relegating logic to its true position as an instrument."[423] For Pound, in 1908, the legal system had so far failed to bring justice in the areas of "employers' liability," "a uniform commercial law," "a reasonable or certain law of future interests in land," "discrimination by public service companies," "the adjustment of water rights in our newer states," holding "promoters to their duty and to protect the interests of those who invest in corporate enterprises against mismanagement and breach of trust," and, in general, American law had failed to "work out a scheme of responsibility that will hold legal entities, or whose who hide behind their skirts, to their duty to the public."[424] One can discern here, in this lament, not only the perspective of the legal realists like Frank and Llwellyn, but also the advocates of a "living constitution,"[425] and even the yearnings for a legal system that better served the needs of the human heart, as displayed by the Critical Legal Studies school in our own time.[426]

---

[421] *Ibid.*

[422] *Id.*, at 609.

[423] *Id.*, at 609–610.

[424] *Id.*, at 614–615.

[425] Thus, remarkably, Pound refers and praises the efforts of Chief Justice John Marshall "in giving us a living constitution by judicial interpretation." *Id.*, at 615. Again, Pound is railing against Supreme Court doctrines, such as those enunciated in *Lochner*, and allying himself with Holmes's dissent. See *id.*, at 616 n.43 (citing Holmes's *Lochner* dissent).

[426] See Chapter 14, *infra*.

This approach to Pound, as a progenitor of the current academic approach to law, was nicely summarized in an article by one of the leading historians of nineteenth- and twentieth-century legal thought, David Rabban:

> Perhaps most broadly and importantly, legal realism continued Pound's attack on the orthodox legal thought of the nineteenth century, condemning its presumed use of formal deductive logic, its disregard for the social context of law, and its resulting inability to address the pressing social problems of the United States in the twentieth century. Legal realism also extended Pound's emphasis on incorporating social science into legal education and scholarship. It followed Pound in treating the lawyer as a "social engineer." In many respects, the scholars grouped as legal realists viewed themselves as actually pursuing the research agenda that Pound had called for but had not accomplished himself. Many realists attempted to make sociological jurisprudence more concrete.[427]

Pound may well have been the godfather of the legal realists, though it does appear that in their prime, their philosophy may well have driven Pound from the Harvard Law School Deanship.[428] It is time, then, to turn to those "legal realists."

---

[427] David M. Rabban, Pound's Sociological Jurisprudence: European Roots and American Applications, in Le "moment 1900": Critique sociale et critique sociologique du droit en Europe et aux Etats-Unis 113, 140 (2015) (footnotes omitted).

[428] Laura Kalman quotes a letter Pound wrote at the time he gave up the Deanship, in 1936, in which he stated that "Indeed my chief reason for giving up the Deanship is that I do not care to be responsible for teaching that law is simply a pious fraud to cover up decisions of cases according to personal inclinations or that there is nothing in the way of reason back of the legal order but it is simply a pulling and hauling of interests with a camouflage of authoritative precepts." Laura Kalman, Legal Realism at Yale 57 (UNC Press, 1986) (quoting Letter from Roscoe Pound to Spier Whitaker (Aug. 27, 1936) (available at Dean's Files, Harvard University Archives)), also quoted by Joseph William Singer, Legal Realism Now, 76 Cal. L. Rev. 465, 540 n.254 (1988).

CHAPTER 8

ADVANCING AMERICAN LEGAL REALISM

EARLY TO MID-TWENTIETH CENTURY

Karl N. Llewellyn
(Columbia and Chicago, 1925–1962)

■ ■ ■

Karl N. Llewellyn (1893–1962)
Photograph signed and autographed from Llewellyn to Roscoe Pound.
Historical & Special Collections, Harvard Law School Library.

One of the most prolific and frequently-cited of all American legal scholars, Karl Llewellyn is usually associated with the invention of American Legal Realism, a pragmatic strain of jurisprudence, something like Benthamite criticism of the English Common Law. Precisely what the Legal Realists were up to remains shrouded in a bit of doubt,[429] but it seems fair to say that

---

[429] See, e.g., William Twining, Karl Llewellyn and the Realist Movement 80 (Weidenfeld and Nicolson, 1973) ("[J]uristic controversies are prone to be inconclusive and unsatisfactory; of juristic controversies that surrounding

there were at least three aims of the American legal realist scholars. As a perceptive student note linking the legal realists with the critical legal scholars of a later generation[430] suggested, "The Realist methodology was characterized by three tenets: [1] an emphasis on study of the evolution of legal doctrine, [2] a critical approach to the use of formalistic reasoning, and [3] a firm commitment to progressive law reform grounded in social scientific research."[431] Legal Realism, as practiced in the American legal academy, eventually became the most influential body of American legal thought, having, for example, a profound influence on the Warren Court. Legal Realism has even been called the "Only American Jurisprudence."[432] By 1988, talented and creative scholars, such as the then Boston College, now Harvard, Law Professor Joseph William Singer, could declare, "We are all legal realists now."[433] The work of Karl Llewellyn, the avatar of the movement, is part of the reaction against Christopher Columbus Langdell[434]

[American Legal] realism has had more than its share of slovenly scholarship, silly misunderstandings and jejeune polemics. In 1931 public discussion of 'realism got off to a bad start from which it never fully recovered.") See also [Rand Bosenblatt], Note, Legal Theory and Legal Education, 79 Yale L.J. 1153, 1158 (1970). (["T]he realist effort to formulate a general 'scientific' approach to law is now regarded as too abstract and polemical, and the issues involved either inherently unscientific or obvious to the point of sterility.") See also, for a fine introduction to "Legal Realist" thought, Frederick Schauer, "Introduction" to the 2nd edition of Twining, *supra*, published by the Cambridge University Press in 2012.

[430] See Chapter 14, *infra*.

[431] Note, 'Round and 'Round the Bramble Bush: From Legal Realism to Critical Legal Scholarship, 95 Harv. L. Rev. 1669 (1982).

[432] David Van Zandt, The Only American Jurisprudence, 28 Hous. L. Rev. 965, 991 (1991). For the Warren Court and its refashioning of Constitutional Law, see, e.g., Chapter 11, *infra*.

[433] Joseph William Singer, Legal Realism Now, 76 Cal.L.Rev. 465, 467 (1988). Singer's 1988 piece, a book review of Laura Kalman's Legal Realism at Yale: 1927–1960 (1968) is also a very accessible introduction to the thought of Critical Legal Studies. See Chapter 14, *infra*.

[434] See Chapter 4, *supra*.

and classical legal thought, just as Roscoe Pound's[435] work was, and, as already indicated in the preceding chapter, while Llewellyn had a cordial relationship with Pound, other legal realists, most notably Jerome Frank, were anathema to Pound, and this jurisprudential brouhaha had a profound effect on the teaching of law for several decades.

While Llewellyn is not generally known among today's law students, he was probably the most important American legal thinker of the nineteen-thirties, and, as indicated, he had a fascinating and complex relationship with Roscoe Pound, the legal titan of his own earlier age, though Llewellyn was, fundamentally, unlike Pound. As N.E.H Hull astutely observes, while Pound and Llewellyn were both "engaging and powerful men," Pound "was a gentle pedant with a will of iron whose happiest hours were spent at his desk at Harvard Law School," while Llewellyn was "a mercurial romantic whose joy and despair in the law spilled into pages of anguished poetry and exuberant lectures." "Roscoe Pound and Karl Llewellyn," Professor Hull explains, "were the most quoted and admired, the most disputed and abused jurisprudents of their day, and that day spanned the first sixty years of the twentieth century."[436]

Llewellyn wrote a great introduction to the law for first-year law students, called *The Bramble Bush*, and his jurisprudence and influence has been the subject of three of the most incisive and provocative legal scholars, William Twining,[437] Laura Kalman,[438] and N.E.H. Hull.[439] As near

---

[435] See Chapter 7, *supra*.

[436] N.E.H. Hull, Roscoe Pound and Karl Llwellyn: Searching for an American Jurisprudence 1 (Chicago, 1997).

[437] Twining, *supra* note 429.

[438] See, e.g., Laura Kalman, Legal Realism at Yale 1927–1960 (UNC Press, 1986), and The Strange Career of Legal Liberalism (Yale, 1996).

[439] Hull, *supra* note 436.

as I can tell, Llewellyn is also the only American law professor to have fought in World War I on the German side, and surely the only American law professor to write satiric work under the *nom de plume* borrowed from Thomas Carlyle, "Diogenes Teufelsdrockh" (whose last name means, literally, "devil's droppings"). Llewellyn had two things rarely found in modern American law professors, actual cosmopolitanism, and literary talent and flair. He was also a pioneer in legal anthropology, having been the co-author of one of the great works on Native American Jurisprudence, *The Cheyenne Way*.[440]

The Bramble Bush: On Our Law and Its Study[441] was the published version of the lectures that Llewllyn gave to Columbia's entering law students. Almost 90 years later, it can still be read with profit as a means of understanding the late twentieth- and early twenty-first-century process of legal education.[442] This appears to have been a process that Llewellyn was not completely sanguine about, hence the title of the book, drawn from an old Mother Goose Rhyme:

> There was a man in our town[443]
>
> and he was wondrous wise;

---

[440] Karl N. Llewellyn and E. Adamson Hoebel, The Cheyenne Way: Conflict and Case Law in Primitive Jurisprudence (University of Oklahoma Press, 1941).

[441] Karl N. Llewellyn, The Bramble Bush: On Our Law and its Study with a new introduction and notes by Stewart Macaulay (Quid Pro Books, 2012) (Originally published in 1930).

[442] See generally, *id.*, at i–xxi. (Macaulay's introduction, written in 2010, beginning with the suggestion that this "is a book that anyone interested in law schools or law should read. Karl Nickerson Llewellyn was a brilliant man.")

[443] As originally a part of the mother goose rhymes, the first line was most likely "There was a man of Thessaly," rather than "our town," and the penultimate line features "another bush" rather than "another one." There are, however, several variant forms of this ditty. See generally, Iona and Peter Opie, eds., The Oxford Dictionary of Nursery Rhymes 480–481 (Oxford, 1997 ed.). The original meaning of the rhyme did not seem to have anything ostensibly to do with law.

> he jumped into a BRAMBLE BUSH
>
>   and scratched out both his eyes—
>
> and when he saw that he was blind,
>
>   with all his might and main
>
> he jumped into another one
>
>   and scratched them in again.[444]

The little octave is wonderful for a variety of reasons,[445] including the intriguing assertions that one can see that one is blind, and that having become blind one has the power to gain sight right back by the simple act of scratching one's eyes back in, and, further, that someone "wondrous wise" might leap into a bramble bush, knock out his or her eyes, and knock them right back in. Apparently the process of learning the law is, for Llewellyn, and his students, a process of unlearning what you actually know (suspending, perhaps, moral judgment) and then learning really to reason, think, or see like a lawyer (with your eyes scratched back in), by becoming familiar with the language of the law, or at least by becoming familiar with the manner in which courts actually do what they do. The Bramble Bush rhyme, then, is a metaphor for American Legal Realism.

---

[444] This version of the rhyme appears just before Llwellyn's Forward. *Bramble Bush, supra* note 441, at 6.

[445] It may however, have rubbed some the wrong way. There is a curious statement in Richard Posner's blistering critique of the academy as useless to the judiciary, Richard A. Posner, Divergent Paths: The Academy and the Judiciary 274 (Harvard 2016), about Llewellyn. After praising Llewellyn's book The Common Law Tradition: Deciding Appeals (originally published 1960, reissued by Quid Pro, 2012), a foundational text for legal realism, Posner lambastes its "length, style, age, and errant organization," and remarks about Llewellyn, "Though Llewellyn was brilliant, his writing style resembled that of the Dr. Seuss books." There are worse sins. For sheer delight, it's tough to top Dr. Seuss's, Green Eggs and Ham (Random House, 1960) or his One Fish, Two Fish, Red Fish, Blue Fish (Random House, 1960).

For Llewellyn, as for Holmes (who said he meant by law, "what the courts will do in fact,")[446] law was, to paraphrase the most notorious observation in *The Bramble Bush*, "what [legal] officials do about disputes."[447] so that it wasn't the *rules of law* that were of paramount importance, but the *manner in which they were or were not applied or administered*. Llewellyn understood (as he noted in a subsequent edition of his book) that this statement of the core belief of what came to be legal realism was subject to ridicule. Indeed, he suggested that this attitude of his and his colleagues led to "the teapot tempest in which 'realism' (which was and is still an effort at more effective legal technology) was mistaken for a philosophy and made the scape-goat for all the sins (real and supposed) of administrators and autocrats and the ungodly in general)."[448]

But if Llewellyn was, like Holmes, a rule sceptic and a positivist, still, like Holmes, Llewellyn was a clear-eyed thinker, and not insensitive to tradition.[449] In the *Bramble Bush* Llewellyn even begins like Blackstone,[450] clearly demarcating between public and private law, and giving what amounts to a whistle-stop tour of all the basic doctrines of private law, which, for Llewellyn, can be neatly divided into contracts, property, associations, and torts. He then goes on, in *The Bramble Bush*, to explain precisely how trials work, what burdens plaintiffs (those initiating

---

[446] See generally Chapter 5, *supra.*

[447] *Bramble Bush, supra* note 441, at 8. "What these officials do about disputes is to my mind, the law itself."

[448] *Bramble Bush, supra* note 441, at 10.

[449] In an early book review of The Bramble Bush, Llewellyn's fellow legal realist, Jerome Frank, observed that Llewellyn was "one of the ablest subtlest, most hard-working of Holmes' [sic] disciples." Jerome Frank, Book Review [of the Bramble Bush], 40 Yale L.J. 1120, 1125 (1931). Frank said of the Bramble Bush, "It is a worthy successor, for our times, to Holmes' [sic] Path of the Law." *Id.*, at 1120.

[450] See Chapter 1, *supra.*

lawsuits) have to meet in order to prevail, and how distinctions are made in the manner that judges and juries function, and even how the legal system is structured to make sure that the laymen of the jury are not misled about the requirements of the law.

Where *The Bramble Bush* is really dazzling, however, and where the process of scratching out eyes and scratching them back in is most clearly revealed, is Llewellyn's extraordinarily careful examination of the still dominant method of teaching American law, the case method. It is a curiosity of our legal educational system (already remarked upon) that we teach law by the study predominately of appellate opinions, that is to say, the written reviews by judges of what other judges did in the trial courts, even though most cases are settled before trial, much less after one or two appellate reviews.[451] Appellate opinions are the result of challenges to the work of the trial judge in applying the relevant law to the case, and it is one of the marvels of our system that we actually encourage review of trials. Appellate opinions are famously abstruse, not only because they are written in the language of the law, which Llewellyn reminds us, cannot be understood by a layman without a law dictionary, but also because they go to great lengths to winnow out insignificant facts and to discard irrelevant legal doctrines. All of this is undertaken to arrive at a defensible result, based on the law which applies to the particularly important facts of the case before the appellate court, while still laying out general principles that will be relevant for future courts deciding the same or related issues. The complexity of appellate opinions baffles

---

[451] On this point see not only Chapter 4, *supra* on Langdell, but see also *Bramble Bush*, *supra* note 441, at 93, where Llewellyn similarly observes that while it is true that appellate court decisions actually affect few individuals, still appellate courts' records are useful repositories of the law because "the appellate courts make access to their work convenient. They issue reports, printed and bound, to be had all gathered for me in the libraries." *Id.*, at 93–94.

beginning law students, so Llewellyn took pains to supply a clear path to unravelling them.

Llewellyn's twelve-point checklist for "briefing" cases, for him the only indispensable approach to law study, set forth in the pivotal chapter III of *The Bramble Bush*, "This Case System: What to *Do* with the Cases," included, for each case, writing down (1) the title of the case and its page in the student's casebook, (2) the state and date of the case, (3) the precise relief sought by the plaintiff (the complaining or initiating party) in the case, (4) the conduct of the defendant (the party originally sued) that caused the dispute, and the defendant's legal claim to support that conduct, (5) the decision between the plaintiff and the defendant reached by the trial court, (6) the asserted legal error which the appealing party or parties claims, (7) the decision reached by the appellate court on this asserted error, (8) the facts found relevant by the appellate court, (9) the legal determination, the *ratio decidendi* (the ground or reason for the decision), the rule of law applied by the appellate court, (10) the student's assessment of the court's application of the law, in light of other cases studied thus far, (11) what Llewellyn somewhat mysteriously called "the line of argument the court indulged in,"[452] and finally, (12) "highly interesting and informative" general remarks on the nature of law made by the court in the particular case.[453] To do this for every case studied, of course, would consume an extraordinary amount of time for beginning law students, since they consider hundreds of appellate cases each year, but would also lead to an extraordinary understanding of the common law process.

Still, what *The Bramble Bush* was ultimately about was the elusive nature of the law student's task because of

---

[452] *Bramble Bush, supra* note 441, at 55.

[453] These twelve matters for inclusion in briefs, paraphrased here, are to be found on pages 54–55 of *Bramble Bush, supra* note 441.

the inescapable malleability of the common law. So that no matter how clearly and comprehensively a law student mastered what a particular court had said in a particular case, he or she could not be sure that he or she could predict with confidence what would happen when the next case came up, even before that court. This was because, as Llewellyn put it, in his chapter on Precedents (which followed the chapter on briefing cases), it was not really the *rules of law* that determined whether precedents would be followed, but, rather, "the *reactions of judges* to the *facts* and to the *life* around them."[454] If one really wanted to grasp all there was to understand about the law, Llewellyn seemed to be saying, then one would have to conceptualize the law as nothing more than what the courts would do in fact[455] (just as Holmes observed). This meant, as Llewellyn explained in his marvelously comprehensive way, in a suggestively titled chapter called "Ships and Shoes and Sealing Wax," that law students had to "sit back more at our ease, give fancy freer rein, and loaf a little in such pastures of the law as the old nag will take us to."[456]

The meaning of this picturesque and bucolic equine metaphor seemed to be that the law student had to "roam" in many "pastures," including, as Llewellyn listed them, "logic and legal history, and the Register of Writs; law on the Continent, law among the Cheyenne, juvenile courts; Hohfeldian analysis, the federal Constitution; Bracton and Blackstone, Mansfield, Coke and Bentham; how English law came to America; statutes, the judge in politics, legal research; admission to the bar, the bar itself; use of the library, codes, and the law's delay."[457] Making things even

---

[454] *Id.*, at 70 (emphasis supplied).

[455] *Cf. Bramble Bush, supra* note 441, at 87: "A right is as big, precisely, as what the courts will do." See also, *id.*, at 94: "Law *is*, to the community, what law *does*." (emphasis in original).

[456] *Bramble Bush, supra* note 441, at 73.

[457] *Ibid.*

more maddening, as we will see played out in the work of Osborn and Turow, below,[458] Llewellyn, much like the fictional Kingsfield, denied that law professors were even doing teaching. Said Llewellyn, "we do not teach—you learn. *If* you learn, then we may be said to teach; but our part is like the sowing of the wheat: it must be sown, it must be fertile, but the sowing is soon done; time, soil and weather make the crop."[459] There was also some mystery, then, but even some joy, involved in Llewellyn's advice to law students.

Making a move that might upset many politically correct students of the law today, Llewellyn claimed that in the first year of learning law one should set aside one's common sense and one's sense of ethics,[460] and just try to absorb as much of the rules of law that already existed as possible. As he put it, "you must immerse yourself for all your hours in the law. Eat law, talk law, think law, drink law, babble of law and judgments in your sleep. Pickle yourselves in law—it is your only hope."[461] And this self-pickling in the law could not actually be done all by oneself. Llewellyn, giving advice that would later be embraced in the fictional characters created by John Jay Osborn, Jr.,[462] explained that the study of law could really only be accomplished if students worked in groups. "In group work," he explained, "lies the deepening of thought. In group work lie ideas, cross-lights; dispute, and practice in dispute; cooperative thinking and practice in consultation; spur for the weary, pleasure for the strong. A threefold cord is not quickly broken: in group work lies salvation."[463] For

---

[458] See Chapter 13, *infra.*

[459] *Bramble Bush, supra* note 441, at 100 (emphasis in original).

[460] *Id.,* at 106.

[461] *Id.,* at 101.

[462] Chapter 13, *infra.*

[463] *Bramble Bush, supra* note 441, at 101.

Llewellyn, it was the law student's work with other law students that really delivered his or her legal education. As Llewellyn put it, "a school is not made up of faculty, and . . . a legal education is nine-tenths and upwards a product of the student body."[464]

But if Llewellyn advised his students temporarily to abjure common sense and ethics, he struggled to make sure that they would not give way to disillusion, which he regarded as a curse of his time, a curse whose lingering effects are still with us. In a chapter that explicitly invokes the mystic, Llewellyn suggested that there were two traps into which lawyers had a tendency to fall. One trap was the seeking after only the profits that law practice could bring, and the other, equally cynical and contemptible, was to commit oneself to an idealism that can never be fulfilled. What law students ought to do, Llewellyn explained, was to seek mastery of the law, and to understand how seeing reflected in the legal disputes the struggles of mankind could lend fulfillment and purpose to a life in the profession. Not idealism, exactly, though, perhaps, some of the zeal of idealism was required. Llewellyn's prescription for law students, was, instead of idealism, a realistic, objective, and holistic pursuit of the many-faceted truth of the human condition that study of the law can reveal.

In an extraordinary analogy, Llewellyn wrote that this path to fulfillment through legal practice was like the look of Gauguin's South Sea women. At first glance, he explained, they look as if they have no expectations from life, their "desire is empty, effort is illusion. Do what one will there will come disappointment." But look again, he wrote, "and see the power of living, the exuberance of life, driving on gloriously—while expecting nothing. There is the answer to our disillusion, in that old truth that neither

---

[464] *Id.*, at 137.

rainbow nor the pot of gold can be attained, nor would be worth the having if it were. But the search is good."[465] Just as Holmes could see in the whole of the law "echo[s] of the infinite,"[466] so Llewellyn, who, quotes a similar passage from Holmes in this chapter on why the law is worthwhile,[467] states that "As I watch the succession of the cases—moving, rising, taking form eternally—as I see the sweep of them entire, I find old formulae of tribute rising to my tongue: 'the full perfection of right reason'! The closer I can come to seeing law whole, the more nearly do I . . . find myself bordering on mysticism. There is such balance and such beauty and such consummate skill in this whole—seen whole; balance and beauty and skill beyond the little powers of the individual judges."[468]

The Bramble Bush, then, should be understood as an attempt by Llewellyn to preserve the humanity of his law students, and yet to inculcate law students in the legal philosophy for which he became famous, "legal realism." One of Llewellyn's most notable articles, explicating this philosophy (though he would not be inclined to over-dignify it by calling it a philosophy), was entitled "Some Realism About Realism,"[469] and it was an apologia of sorts for the kind of empirical research he and a number of colleagues at different law schools had undertaken. To a certain extent this aggregation of Llewellyn's fellow "legal realists" were following in the path of Roscoe Pound,[470] who had earlier undertaken a sociological study of law, and who, in

---

[465] *Id.*, at 133.

[466] Oliver Wendell Holmes, Jr., The Path of the Law, 10 Harv. L. Rev. 457, 478 (1897).

[467] *Bramble Bush, supra* note 441, at 132.

[468] *Id.*, at 131.

[469] Karl N. Llewellyn, Some Realism About Realism: Responding to Dean Pound, 44 Harv.L.Rev. 1122 (1931).

[470] See Chapter 7, *supra*.

professed contradistinction to Langdell,[471] had set out to see
what the law was actually doing, rather than what was set
out in the law books. This was also the aim of Llewellyn and
his fellow scholars, whom Llewellyn carefully described as
"not a group," but simply a cohort of frenzied researchers
pursuing different paths of empirical study, but united in
their zeal of discovery.[472]

Llewellyn cited the work of such scholars as Arthur
Corbin,[473] who spent about fifty years compiling a treatise
on contract law carefully illustrating where the ancient
legal doctrines had been modified through sensitive
treatment on the part of judges like Benjamin Cardozo, to
meet the actual needs of the marketplace. Corbin, who was
influential in the writing of the Restatement of Contracts
Law, drafted a famous section of that Restatement, Section
90, which provided, in extraordinarily-loose language, that
the formal requirements of contract doctrine were not
necessarily required to make a promise enforceable if
someone had "reasonably relied" on a promise, and the
enforcement of that promise were necessary to achieve
"justice." As Grant Gilmore later archly noted with regard
to Section 90, "no one had any idea what the damn thing
meant,"[474] but, as Gilmore explained, this "reliance"
principle bid fair to overtake the traditional and ancient
requirement set forth, among others, by Langdell and

---

[471] See Chapter 4, *supra*.

[472] *Some Realism*, note 469, *supra*, at 1256. ("A group philosophy or
program, a group credo of social welfare, these realists have not. They are not
a group.")

[473] Corbin's name appears 20 times in "Some Realism About Realism,"
supra note 469. His great work on the law of contract was Arthur L. Corbin,
Corbin on Contracts (originally published 1951 by West Publishing Company,
now available in a fifteen volume version edited by Joseph M. Perillo,
published by Lexis/Nexis), and published as a one-volume student hornbook in
1952, which is still an incisive guide to the legal doctrines.

[474] Grant Gilmore, The Death of Contract 64–65 (Ohio State University
Press, 1974).

Holmes, of "bargained for consideration" to support a promise.[475]

Llewellyn similarly noted the efforts of such men as Leon Green,[476] Dean, like Wigmore, of Northwestern University School of Law,[477] who sought to construct a new approach to the law of torts which focused on the facts of tort cases rather than the ancient principles of tort law.[478] Llewellyn himself was instrumental in drafting the Uniform Commercial Code, now enacted in all fifty states, an umbrella statute which dealt with sales contracts, bills and notes, bulk sales, and security interests, among other things, and, in clear distinction to the ancient common law rules regarding these topics, emphasized common sense, pragmatism, and the actual practice of American businesspersons. Thus, instead of the view condemned once in a famous Cardozo opinion, where "the precise word was the sovereign talisman" and "every slip was fatal,"[479] the UCC imposed a broad general obligation of "good faith," and "fair dealing," and, in effect, offered the courts the

---

[475] See generally *ibid*. This takeover of the law of promises by "reliance," substituting for "bargained for consideration" was the meaning of Gilmore's title the "death" of contract.

[476] Green's work is cited 13 times in *Some Realism About Realism, supra* note 449.

[477] For Wigmore see Chapter 6, *supra*.

[478] See, e.g., Henry H. Foster, Jr., Book Review [of CASES ON THE LAW OF TORTS, by Leon Green, Wex S. Malone, Willard H. Pedrick, and James A. Rahl, West Publishing Co., 1957], 18 La.L.Rev. 226 (1957). ("In 1931, Dean Leon Green published his Judicial Process in Tort Cases, and in 1939 his second edition appeared. If imitation is the sincerest form of flattery, Dean Green was quite churlish to prior compilers of torts materials. His materials expressed ingenuity and did not follow what had evolved to be the classical structure of torts casebooks. Adopting what has been called a functional perspective and viewing the subject matter from the eclectic approach of sociological jurisprudence, Dean Green pointed to the work environment of rule and doctrine. It was a unique collection of materials.") This functional casebook approach to the law of torts started by Green was followed by his student, my colleague, Marshall Shapo. See, e.g., Marshall Shapo, Cases and Materials on Tort and Compensation Law (West Publishing, 1976).

[479] Wood v. Lucy, Lady Duff-Gordon, 222 N.Y. 88, 91; 118 N.E. 214 (N.Y. 1917).

opportunity to remake the contracts of parties to conform with these newer principles, principles of justice akin to those of Restatement Section 90.[480]

A target of one of Llewellyn's fellow legal realists, Jerome Frank, was Roscoe Pound himself, whose writing Frank had mocked as indicated earlier, in his pungent book of applied psychology, *Law and the Modern Mind* (1930). Writing regarding Pound's claim that commercial law could be reduced to certain content, Frank asked, "are we not * * * listening to something like a small boy with a grown-up vocabulary talking of an ideal father?"[481] Pound appears not to have been amused, and as N.E.H. Hull reported, he wrote Llewellyn "I must confess I am troubled about Jerome Frank. When a man puts in quotation marks and attributes to a writer things which he not only never put in print any where, but goes contrary to what he has set in print repeatedly, it seems to me to go beyond the limits of permissible carelessness and to be incompatible, not merely

---

[480] The practical sensible approach of the UCC is summed up nicely on the website of one law firm, Fullerton & Knowles, active in practice in Virginia, Maryland, Pennsylvania, and the District of Columbia:

The UCC takes a very pragmatic and common sense approach to commercial transactions. It is usually not precise and does not provide exact rules. Many flexible terms are used, such as "reasonable" or "standards in the industry" or "commonly accepted practice." This can be frustrating in that the answers to a dispute are not always clear. A buyer can still argue about whether a seller took a "reasonable" approach. However, these terms do allow flexible and common sense solutions to practical problems.

The UCC has a philosophy of elastic performance to try and keep deals together. This philosophy frowns upon an "all or nothing" approach. The parties have to work together to keep things moving. For example, a buyer is generally not relieved of any further obligation if there are defects or delays in some deliveries. The seller will have a right to "cure" defects and continue deliveries. The buyer may be entitled to a credit for damages from the defects or delay, but the buyer must continue to take deliveries.

http://www.fullertonlaw.com/construction-law-survival-manual/uniform-commercial-code-sale-of-goods.html (accessed 13 February 2016).

[481] Frank, Law and the Modern Mind 306 (Brentano's 1930).

with scholarship but with the ordinary fair play of controversy."[482] Pound advised Llewellyn against any further association with Frank.[483] Pound liked Llewellyn,[484] who seems to have been quite a bit more housebroken than Frank, and either through some sort of discreet flattery,[485] or perhaps the most sincere form of flattery, imitation, Llewellyn might have eventually persuaded Pound that the efforts of the legal realists were simply outgrowths of the work of Pound himself.[486] Hull writes that "it would have been hard to separate the general tendency of Pound's views from that of Llewellyn's,"[487] and Llewellyn even suggested, in late 1931, that Pound ought to return to scholarship and give up Deaning. "Harvard may need a Dean," he wrote Pound, "but the law world at large needs the Sociological Jurisprudence."[488] In any event, Pound's successor, acting Dean Edmund Morgan, a friend of Llewellyn's, actually pressured the prestigious Harvard Law Review to publish Llewellyn's seminal piece introducing the legal realists to the rest of the academy and promoting their work.[489]

---

[482] N.E.H. Hull, *supra* note 436, at 197, quoting Pound to Llewellyn, March 21, 1931.

[483] *Ibid.*

[484] See, e.g., *id.*, at 197.

[485] Hull notes that "Whatever antipathy Pound had toward Frank, Llewellyn did not want to chance any rift between himself and the older man." *Ibid.*

[486] N.E. Hull notes that Yale's Dean, Charles E. Clark, a noted empiricist associated with the Legal Realists, had written Llewellyn of the legal realist movement that Pound "himself may almost be claimed to be the originator and certainly a foremost exponent." *Id.*, at 206, quoting from Clark to Llewellyn, Mar. 31, 1931. As Hull suggests of the realists, "they had gone to school on Pound's teachings." *Id.*, at 209.

[487] *Id.*, at 224.

[488] Llewellyn to Pound, November 25, 1931, quoted by Hull, *id.*, at 225.

[489] *Id.*, at 202, correcting an earlier impression that Pound himself had persuaded the editors of the Harvard Law Review to publish the piece. The piece in question was *Some Realism, supra* note 469.

Like Pound, Llewellyn took strands of his jurisprudence from many sources, and to use N.E.H. Hull's term in describing the two men, they were "bricoleurs," immensely practical men who used the tools and materials at hand to create new and useful constructs. For Hull, Llewellyn as a bricoleur was "not a devotee of social science, not a secret conservative defending custom against democratic regulation, not a theorist inspired by German neo-positivist philosophy," but rather was simply someone who "wanted a steady, pragmatic method to refashion and reform divorce, commercial law, and legal education."[490] As a man who made legal realism respectable, indeed who perhaps did more than anyone else to make it the dominant jurisprudence of the Warren Court and the American legal academy, it is hard to overestimate Llewellyn's importance. And yet, Llewellyn's mark on legal education is now more implemented than known. By contrast, the next figure we consider, Felix Frankfurter, is everywhere acknowledged as a titan, but his continuing influence seems steadily to diminish.

---

[490]   Hull, *supra* note 436, at 11–12.

CHAPTER 9

THE HARVARD SCHOOL OF REFLEXIVE JUDICIAL DEFERENCE

EARLY TO MID-TWENTIETH CENTURY

Felix Frankfurter
(Harvard, 1914–1917, 1920–1938; Oxford, 1933–1934)

■ ■ ■

Felix Frankfurter (1882–1965)
Harris & Ewing, 1939, Collection of the Supreme Court of the United States.

At Harvard Law School, where Frankfurter had taught in the teens, twenties and thirties, there was said to be, as late as the nineteen-seventies, an almost superstitious cult-like veneration of Felix Frankfurter. As one astute scholar noted in 1988, Frankfurter was habitually yoked with Holmes and Brandeis as "charter members of the Harvard school of reflexive judicial deference to majoritarian institutions."[491] To the same affect, Scott Turow, in his account of life as a first-year law student first published in 1977 explained, "Frankfurter, in truth, was a giant, but his opinions are all treated like biblical texts and his style of jurisprudence, now probably dated, is uncritically endorsed in most classrooms."[492] One Frankfurter biographer, who was then an assistant professor of government at Harvard, flatly stated that Frankfurter was "perhaps the most influential jurist of the twentieth century."[493]

There have been many books published on Frankfurter, although he has not been the most popular subject of recent scholarship, and it is likely that he is no longer the God-like figure at Harvard (or any other law school) that he was at one time. Still, in some ways he is an almost archetypical law professor, and is well worth examining. An early Jewish Justice, and, at one time a zealous Zionist, although a non-practicing member of his religion (which he regarded, apparently, as an accident of birth),[494] Frankfurter is a

---

[491] Robert A. Burt, Two Jewish Justices: Outcasts in the Promised Land 20 (California, 1988). The faint note of disdain in Burt's suggestion may be due to the fact that Burt was a *Yale* law professor, and also perhaps to Burt's belief that Brandeis had a different vision of the judicial role from that of Holmes and Frankfurter. See generally *id.*, at 20–26. Burt describes Frankfurter's jurisprudence as a "form of self-flagellation [which] is the critical test of a suitably detached judicial temperament" for adherents to the "Harvard school."

[492] Scott Turow, One L: The Turbulent True Story of a First Year at Harvard Law School 229 (Farrar Straus, Giroux, 2010 edition) (originally published 1977).

[493] H.N. Hirsch, The Enigma of Felix Frankfurter 3 (Basic Books, 1981). Professor Hirsh is now Professor of Politics and Comparative American Studies at Oberlin.

[494] Joseph P. Lash, From the Diaries of Felix Frankfurter with a Biographical Essay and Notes 89 (W.W. Norton, 1975). Lash notes that "He [Frankfurter] had left the synagogue at fifteen and never returned," and he wanted no rabbi at his funeral. *Ibid.* Frankfurter did say, though, near the end of his life, "I came into the world a Jew and although I did not live my life entirely as a Jew, I think it is fitting that I should leave as a Jew." This was his statement supporting his request that his friend, Professor Louis Henkin, an Orthodox Jew, speak at his funeral. *Id.* The "accident of birth" phrase is repeated also by Hirsh, *supra* note 493, at 23. ("Frankfurter regarded his

splendid example of the secularized Jewish law professor, now, perhaps, one of the dominant models in American Legal education.[495] Frankfurter's attitude toward the religion of his birth is a curious one. He appears to have wanted to succeed almost in clear spite of it. One of his biographers notes, for example, that Frankfurter chose, as his first job as a lawyer, employment in a firm that had never hired someone who was Jewish. Said Frankfurter, "I'd hear that they had never taken a Jew and wouldn't take a Jew. I decided that was the office I wanted to get into."[496] Frankfurter's religion of birth, while it was something he seems to have treated lightly at times, still had a profound effect on him. In his provocative psychological biography of Frankfurter, H.N. Hirsch observes that "Frankfurter was never able to shake his resentment at the degree to which he was excluded because he was a Jew, never able to overcome his ambivalence concerning his religion."[497]

Following a few months with a New York law firm, Frankfurter moved to the office of Henry L. Stimson, the

---

religion as a mere accident of birth, and was determined to succeed in the [Boston] Brahmin world.")

[495] Robert A. Burt, in his invaluable Two Jewish Justices, *supra* note 491, observes that "When I returned to Yale in 1976 as a law school faculty member, I was particularly struck by the fact that almost half my colleagues here were Jewish." Burt notes later in the book that "in 1970, 25 percent of the faculties in American law schools were Jews, while among 'elite' law schools Jews constituted 38 percent of the faculties." *Id.*, at 64. This contrasts notably with the fact that Frankfurter was the only Jew on the Harvard Law School faculty at the time of his appointment in 1914, and remained so until at least 1929. *Id.*, at 64. Burt also indicates that "By 1971, when the Harvard Law School appointed its first Jewish dean, there were Jews in the dean's chair at Yale, Columbia, Pennsylvania, Berkeley, and UCLA." *Id.*, at 65. Paul Carrington, one of the most astute critics of American legal education, in an article evaluating attempts to increase racial and gender diversity on law school faculties and in student bodies, throws off the remark that "Until Jewish culture . . . undergoes fundamental change there will be a disproportionate number of Jewish law teachers." Paul Carrington, Diversity, 1992 Utah L.Rev. 1105, 1154. On Carrington, see *infra*, Chapter 19.

[496] Lash, *supra* note 494, at 4.

[497] Hirsh, *supra* note 493, at 98.

United States Attorney for the Southern District of New York, who was in the process of gathering around him "the best young men out of the great firms and law schools, especially his own Harvard Law School," from which Frankfurter had graduated in 1906.[498] Three years later Frankfurter joined Stimson in private practice, then, in 1910, "when Stimson accepted the Republican nomination for Governor of New York, became his campaign assistant."[499] Stimson was defeated, but accepted an offer from President Taft to become Secretary of War, and brought Frankfurter to Washington in 1911 to serve him as Law Officer of the Bureau of Insular Affairs, with jurisdiction over Puerto Rico, the Panama Canal, the Philippines, Santo Domingo, Cuba, and Haiti.[500] Frankfurter continued to write speeches for Stimson, advised him on politics, and developed a social relationship with Justice Oliver Wendell Holmes, Jr.,[501] and had, as a housemate, Lord Eustace Percy, a young officer at the British Embassy. This, says one of his biographers, Joseph Lash, was the beginning of Frankfurter's strong Anglophilism.[502] More important, probably, was Frankfurter's association with Holmes, as Hirsch observes "Throughout his life Frankfurter's friendship with Holmes was his most cherished possession. It was Holmes who symbolized to Frankfurter the best of everything: the Brahmin establishment, achievement in the law, culture, learning."[503]

When Woodrow Wilson won the Presidential election in 1912, defeating Frankfurter's preferred candidate, the

---

[498] Lash, *supra* note 494, at 5.

[499] *Id.*, at 6.

[500] *Id.*, at 7.

[501] Hirsch suggests that "both Holmes and Brandeis more or less adopted" Frankfurter. Hirsch, *supra* note 493, at 31–32.

[502] Lash, *supra* note 494, at 8.

[503] Hirsch, *supra* note 493, at 32. On Holmes, see Chapter 5, *supra*.

progressive Teddy Roosevelt (and the Republican, Taft), Frankfurter stayed on for a while at the War Department to continue work on a water-power project,[504] but soon moved to join Roscoe Pound,[505] whom he had helped get to Harvard (from Northwestern) at the Law School, where he began his career as a Harvard Law Professor in the summer of 1914.[506] In that first year Frankfurter found time not only to teach his classes, but also to help found and do some writing for The New Republic, to get involved with Florence Kelly's National Consumers' League,[507] and to take over the pursuit of two pieces of litigation (involving minimum wages for women and maximum hours for men) on which Louis Brandeis had worked before he left to join the United States Supreme Court.[508]

Until about 1917, Frankfurter was not actually a Republican or Democrat, and while he was clearly a reformer, he was emphatically not a socialist.[509] Still, by 1916, Frankfurter, perhaps more influenced now by Brandeis, had decided that the candidate of the Democrats, Woodrow Wilson, had more appeal to him than the candidate of the Republicans, Charles Evans Hughes, whose party, Frankfurter had come to believe, was too associated with "big business," and insufficiently progressive.[510] With the beginning of World War I, Frankfurter returned to Washington to serve again in the War Department, in the Wilson administration.[511] This led to assignments in Europe, and to strengthening Frankfurter's association with Zionists such as Dr. Chaim

---

[504] Lash, *supra* note 494, at 9–10.

[505] See Chapter 7, *supra*.

[506] Lash, *supra* note 494, at 11–15.

[507] *Id.*, at 16–17.

[508] *Id.*, at 17–18.

[509] *Id.*, at 18–20.

[510] Hirsh, *supra* note 493, at 51.

[511] Lash, *supra* note 494, at 21.

Weizmann, although the efforts at that time to create a Jewish state in Palestine were not realized.[512] Back in the USA in the fall of 1917, Frankfurter became involved in labor mediation, acting on behalf of the Wilson administration to calm labor/management disputes that were disrupting wartime production. In that capacity he engaged in some actions that were clearly favorable to labor, and also befriended his fellow lawyer on what became the War Labor Policies Board, Franklin D. Roosevelt.[513] After the war, Frankfurter was at the Paris Peace conference, working toward the implementation of the British Balfour Declaration, creating a home for the Jews in Palestine. At that time highly committed to Zionism, Frankfurter was able to combine his passion for a homeland for the Jews with his Anglophilia, and he was able to spend some time with Balfour and other important English figures, who saw Zionism as compatible with the extension of the British Empire.[514]

Following his time in Paris, Frankfurter returned to Harvard. By then he had become something of a controversial figure, possibly because his Zionism spawned anti-Semitism, but soon the suggestion that Frankfurter was "dangerous" evaporated, as he became popular with students and colleagues, as he grew happier as a teacher, and as he became more mellow when he married the socially prominent (and non-Jewish) woman he had been courting for some time.[515] Still, during these early years at Harvard, Frankfurter did become involved with several of his colleagues in criticizing the government's anti-communist effort, its "war on the Reds," and Frankfurter served on the National Advisory Committee of the newly formed

---

[512]   *Id.*, at 21–22.

[513]   *Id.*, at 23–24.

[514]   *Id.*, at 27.

[515]   *Id.*, at 29–30.

American Civil Liberties Union.[516] He also continued to be an advocate for labor, and to write in The New Republic against the use of the labor injunction to prevent workers from striking.[517]

In the year 1924, Frankfurter backed the third-party Progressive candidate, Robert M. La Follette, for President, because of the Harvard professor's belief that "economic inequalities" were growing too great in the United States, the United States was employing "economic imperialism" against Latin America, and the Democratic party was relying to too great an extent on the "solid South." Frankfurter's belief was that La Follette represented the best hope for "the great interests of the workers and of agriculture," which is what he felt was most important to the country.[518] Whatever his progressive politics at the time, however, it is notable that Frankfurter's activities at Harvard also smacked of what can only be described as clear elitism. Joseph Lash writes that Frankfurter ignored his "mediocre" students, and that "He had time and patience only for the brilliant and the boys of old and wealthy families."[519] Frankfurter became a person who selected law clerks (or, as they were then known, "secretaries") for Supreme Court Justice Oliver Wendell Holmes, Jr., and then for Justices Brandeis and Benjamin Nathan Cardozo.

In the years before he was himself appointed to the Supreme Court, in 1939, Professor Frankfurter also acquired a reputation as a champion of civil rights, principally owing to his work on the Sacco-Vanzetti case, on behalf of the two Italian immigrant defendants, and in direct opposition to the then President of Harvard, A. Lawrence Lowell, who believed that the two defendants had

---

[516] *Id.*, at 31.

[517] *Id.*, at 32–22.

[518] *Id.*, at 35.

[519] *Id.*, at 35.

been properly convicted of murder. Lash hints that Lowell's opposition to Frankfurter's position in the case may have also had something to do with the two men's disagreements over Lowell's contemporary efforts to impose a "Jewish quota" on admissions to Harvard.[520] In any event, Frankfurter wrote an exhaustive attack on what he found to be improper procedures by the prosecutor in the case. The prosecutor's conduct was defended by no less a titan in the law of evidence than Dean John H. Wigmore[521] himself, who then was criticized by Frankfurter for failing adequately to acquaint himself with the record in the case. Lash suggests that Frankfurter had the better of the argument with Wigmore.[522] Despite Frankfurter's best efforts, however, following a report for the Massachusetts's governor, delivered by a commission chaired by Lowell, confirming the propriety of the conviction, the two defendants were executed. Frankfurter was reportedly devastated, as Lash reports, quoting Frankfurter's friend Learned Hand, he was "like a mad man. He was really beside himself."[523]

In 1928 Frankfurter began his voluminous correspondence with his former colleague on the War Labor Policies Board, Franklin Roosevelt, who had recently been elected governor of New York, and who began turning to the Harvard law professor for political advice.[524] Four years later, when FDR was about to be nominated as a Presidential candidate, Frankfurter turned down an appointment to the Supreme Judicial Court of Massachusetts, and FDR, who did not then know that Frankfurter would decline the Massachusetts nomination,

---

[520] *Id.*, at 37.

[521] See Chapter 6, *supra*, for Wigmore.

[522] Lash, *supra* note 494, at 38.

[523] *Id.*, at 39. See also, for Frankfurter's agonized belief that the two Italians were innocent and the victims of prejudice by Brahmins such as Lowell, Hirsch, *supra* note 493, at 90–94.

[524] Lash, *supra* note 494, at 40–41.

did tell him that he belonged on the United States Supreme Court.[525] It does appear that in 1932, as FDR prepared to run for President, his philosophy of gradualist pragmatism was mirrored by that of Frankfurter. Frankfurter wrote to the famous liberal journalist Walter Lippman, in April 1932, that he rejected any "comprehensive scheme of society, whether socialism or communism," or any other "full-blown new scheme" for the reorganization of the "Great Society."[526] In that same letter to Lippman, however, Frankfurter did suggest that he favored "gradual, successive . . . large modifications" that would "slowly evolve out of this profit-making society."[527] Once FDR was elected, he sought and received advice from Frankfurter, sometimes, apparently, even more than he could assimilate. At this point, another one of FDR's advisors, A.A. Berle, a Columbia law professor who had an even closer relationship to the new President-elect, but a prickly one with Frankfurter, notably said of him to FDR, that he had "considerable admiration of Felix Frankfurter's public career and an intense personal desire to see him shot."[528]

In March of 1932, FDR tried to persuade Frankfurter to accept appointment as Solicitor General (the federal government's top litigator, whose most notable assignment is to argue the government's cases in the United States Supreme Court), as a way of preparing him for an appointment to the Supreme Court itself, and as a means of overcoming resistance that might have been generated from nominating a man who was suspect because of his role as a professor, a partisan in the Sacco-Vanzetti matter, or his Jewish background.[529]   Frankfurter   declined   the

---

[525]   *Id.*, at 43.

[526]   *Id.*, at 44.

[527]   *Id.*, at 44–45.

[528]   *Id.*, at 46.

[529]   *Id.*, at 47. On the office of solicitor general see Lincoln Caplan, The Tenth Justice: The Solicitor General and the Rule of Law (Knopf, 1987).

appointment, but continued to serve as an informal advisor to FDR. His biographer H.N. Hirsch concludes that Frankfurter, by the middle of the thirties, was "perhaps the single most important nonelected official in national government," by virtue of his close relationship to FDR and "as the man who would supply scores of Harvard men for the growing [New Deal] federal bureaucracy."[530] Frankfurter actually spent much of the summer of 1935 living at the White House,[531] and, indeed, became so closely identified with the politics of the new administration that his Harvard colleague, Roscoe Pound, who had formerly been an enthusiastic backer of Frankfurter, became his critic, as did the pundit Walter Lippman.[532]

Frankfurter's lasting fame, according to Lash, is due to three factors—his work as an interpreter of the Court and the Constitution, his role as an advisor to FDR, and his "boys," or, as they were derisively known, Frankfurter's "Happy Hot Dogs,"[533] those students at Harvard law school who were his "disciples" and "protégées."[534] These included Thomas G. Corcoran (affectionately known as "Tommy the Cork"), who along with another former Frankfurter student, Benjamin Cohen, is credited with the drafting of the 1934 Securities and Exchange Act. Frankfurter, writes Lash, "was a one-man recruiting agency for the New Deal."[535]

Frankfurter's strong sympathy for FDR's New Deal led him to become alarmed at the United States Supreme Court's frustration of some of the New Deal efforts. The Court was acting pursuant to a belief that these legislative moves exceeded the Constitutional bounds, which, in the

---

[530] Hirsh, *supra* note 493, at 99.

[531] *Id.*, at 117.

[532] Lash, *supra* note 494, at 48–49. For Pound, see Chapter 7, *supra*.

[533] *Id.*, at 53.

[534] *Id.*, at 52.

[535] *Id.*, at 53.

view of a majority of the Court, limited Congressional lawmaking to the regulation of interstate commerce, and forbade the wholesale confiscation of property. Accordingly, Frankfurter, as did his mentor, Holmes, began to write, advocating a more flexible approach to the Constitution, one that could meet the changing needs of the times. Thus Frankfurter attacked the Court's *"Lochner-*era" jurisprudence, which forbade states from enacting minimum wage or maximum hours legislation because, according to the Court, it impinged on a purportedly constitutionally-guaranteed freedom of contract for employers and employees.[536] The Court had made use of that jurisprudence to throw out some early New Deal measures, in the great case of *Schechter Poultry Corp. v. United States* (1935).[537] Frankfurter blasted the Supreme Court as "A few, very few obstinate and blind men impervious to rational, disinterested argument [who] have written their narrow prejudices into the Fundamental Law of the land—for 30 years."[538]

Still, and running somewhat contrary to his defense of the New Deal, Frankfurter's scholarship eventually came to be praised for something else, his strong strain of belief in judicial restraint, and his admiration for the Constitutional scheme of separation of powers, where the Court does not impinge on the role of the Legislature or the Executive by making policy on its own initiative.[539] The lodestar of this part of Frankfurter's jurisprudence was the work of the great Harvard Constitutional theorist James Bradley

---

[536] See generally Lochner v. New York, 198 U.S. 45 (1905), and on the case see, in particular, the notable revisionist work, David E. Bernstein, Rehabilitating *Lochner*: Defending Individual Rights against Progressive Reform (Chicago, 2011).

[537] 295 U.S. 495 (1935).

[538] Felix Frankfurter to Marian Frankfurter, February, 1937, quoted by Hirsch, *supra* note 493, at 122.

[539] Lash, *supra* note 494, at 56.

Thayer,[540] who believed that the Court should restrain itself from overruling, on Constitutional grounds, " 'reasonable' policy decisions by popularly elected legislatures."[541] This latter strain, which made him an idol at Harvard, reflected Frankfurter's ultimate commitment to the rule of law as an unchanging guide to the securing of certainty and predictability in economic affairs. These inconsistent threads in Frankfurter's Constitutional analysis present something of a puzzle, and, while he was undoubtedly a great law professor, the fact that his thought simultaneously led in different directions may have contributed to the meme of the law professor as a person divided against him or herself. To hold, as Frankfurter did, these simultaneous understandings of a "living constitution" and "the rule of law," is not an easy undertaking.

Lash notes that Frankfurter appears to have counselled FDR to restrain himself from attacking the Court for frustrating the New Deal, and, instead, to consider spearheading a Constitutional Amendment "giving the national government adequate power to cope with national economic and industrial problems."[542] Relying on a Constitutional Amendment, of course, would have made it possible for Frankfurter to reconcile the rule of law and a living Constitution, but it was not to be. FDR brushed aside the Amendment proposal, as he blasted the Court for its "horse and buggy" view of the Constitution, and sought to increase the number of Supreme Court justices, to "pack the court," until it became more malleable to the New Deal's efforts. The "court packing plan," apparently opposed by

---

[540] See, e.g., James. B. Thayer, The Origin and Scope of the American Doctrine of Constitutional Law 7 Harv. L Rev. 129 (1893), and the symposium on the hundredth anniversary of that work in the Northwestern University Law Review, Volume 88 (1993).

[541] Hirsch, *supra* note 493, at 128.

[542] Lash, *supra* note 494, at 58.

Frankfurter,[543] on the grounds that it was too transparently a political attack on the judiciary, ultimately failed, but if FDR lost that battle he won the war by putting Justices, like Frankfurter, sympathetic to his ends, on the Court. And, indeed, while Frankfurter may have been initially against the "Court-packing" plan, he did suggest, after FDR put the plan forward, that the Court's decisions nullifying New Deal measures were "not defensible in the realm of reason nor justified by settled principles of Constitutional interpretation," and that it was necessary to do something "to save the Constitution from the Court, and the Court from itself."[544]

Quite possibly as a reward for his faithful service and advice, or, of course, equally possibly, because he was the best qualified person for the job, following the creation of a vacancy on the Court from the death of Benjamin Cardozo, in early 1939, FDR nominated Frankfurter.[545] There was some opposition to Frankfurter from those who wanted to see another Westerner on the court, and even from some wealthy Jews who feared a resurgence of Hitler-era anti-Semitism if another Jewish Justice (Brandeis still sat on the Court) was nominated, but it does appear that no one was regarded as better equipped to apply the Constitutional theories Roosevelt favored on the Court, and no one was in a better position to influence the Court for the future.[546] In Lash's words only a few "right-wing zealots" opposed Frankfurter's confirmation, on the grounds that he had "radical sympathies" because of his work in founding the ACLU and his work in the Sacco-Vanzetti case, although one Senator did demand to know if Frankfurter was a

---

[543] *Id.*, at 59.

[544] *Id.*, at 61 quoting from a letter from Frankfurter to FDR written February 9, 1937.

[545] *Id.*, at 63.

[546] *Id.*, at 64.

socialist like his friend Harold Laski. Frankfurter assured the senator he was not, and his nomination was unanimously confirmed.[547]

Still, the larger point reflected in this New Deal brouhaha was the duality in Frankfurter, indeed, perhaps Frankfurter's Constitutional schizophrenia, or at least his puzzling personality, that has been described as an "Enigma."[548] As suggested earlier, this is a complex state of mind, characteristic of the American Law Professor, that may, in part, explain some of the puzzlement with which the American law professor is viewed by those outside the academy. This duality manifests itself in several aspects of Frankfurter's career and thought.

Frankfurter's early politics were progressive, if not, at times, somewhat radical, but, as indicated in the beginning of this chapter, he is now best known for embodying, once he reached the United States Supreme Court, a jurisprudence of judicial restraint. Before he went on the Court, in a series of lectures on Justice Holmes, Frankfurter made clear that he viewed the judicial role as one that included great discretion. "[J]udges," he explained, "are not merely expert reporters of pre-existing law. Because of the free play of judgment allowed by the Constitution, judges inevitably fashion law." For Frankfurter, in his last year as a law professor, to understand the Court's interpretive, or perhaps legislative role, was really to understand something very important about American society: "[L]aw is one of the shaping forces of society. That is why to neglect the Supreme Court's role in our social and economic history

---

[547] *Id.*, at 65–66. See also Michael E. Parrish, The Hughes Court, in Paul Finkelman, ed., The Supreme Court: Controversies, Cases, and Characters from John Jay to John Roberts 682 (ABC–CLIO, 2014). ("Aside from a few cranky right-wing zealots who accused Frankfurter of being part of a vast communist conspiracy, his confirmation in the Senate came quickly on a voice vote in January 1939.")

[548] Hirsch, *supra* note 493.

is to omit vital factors of the story. The Supreme Court gives direction to economic forces, especially to the pace and the range of their incidence." In this connection, Frankfurter urged that John Chipman Gray got it right: "Whoever hath an absolute authority [like the United States Supreme Court] to interpret any written or spoken law, it is he who is truly the lawgiver to all intents and purposes, and not the person who first wrote or spoke them."[549] As a law professor, then, Frankfurter seemed to recognize a legislative role for the Court, and, thus, he was a critic of the Court's *Lochner*-era jurisprudence. Once he went on the Court, however, his perspective seems to have changed.

Quite intriguingly for someone who helped found the American Civil Liberties Union, he wrote opinions on the Supreme Court upholding the mandatory recitation of the pledge of allegiance, as he did, for example, in *Minersville School District v. Gobitis* (1940), over the objection of some Jehovah's witnesses. Frankfurter initially carried along with him some of his fellow liberals on the Court, Hugo Black, William O. Douglas, and Frank Murphy,[550] although he did so over a strong dissent by Justice Harlan F. Stone, and to the dismay of liberals off the Court, such as Howard Laski and even Eleanor Roosevelt.[551] Given Frankfurter's earlier clear liberalism, the *Gobitis* opinion seems a bit puzzling, although H.N. Hirsch is probably on the mark when he suggests that "Frankfurter was, in a very real sense, asking the Jehovah's Witnesses to make the same choice he himself had made—to accept the secular over the religious."[552]

---

[549] Felix Frankfurter, Mr. Justice Holmes and the Supreme Court 43 (Harvard, 2nd ed. 1961).

[550] Minersville School District v. Gobitis, 310 U.S. 586 (1940).

[551] Lash, *supra* note 494, at 69.

[552] Hirsch, *supra* note 493, at 148.

Whatever the cause, Frankfurter's opinion on the compelled Pledge of Allegiance to the flag as Constitutional law did not last long, and significantly, Black, Douglas, and Murphy[553] (who had concurred with Frankfurter in *Gobitis*) publicly indicated they had been wrong on the issue of compelling participation in the Pledge two years later.[554] Lash notes that Archibald MacLeish had "predicted that on the Bench Frankfurter would be an influence for permitting 'legislatures the widest latitude in framing economic measures altering property relations while sharply rejecting all attempts to curtail or restrict civil liberties,'" but this proved not exactly to be the case.[555] When, in 1943, in another flag-salute case, *West Virginia Board of Education v. Barnette* was decided, the majority repudiated Frankfurter's view, and Frankfurter dissented from the majority's decision that the state could not compel children to pledge alliance to the flag.[556]

The Court's *volte-face* on this issue, after only three years, has been called "one of the most abrupt reversals in its history."[557] Black, Douglas, and Murphy, who had been with Frankfurter in upholding the mandatory pledge in *Gobitis*, now condemned it, and, by implication, him. This was "a stinging personal rebuke" to Frankfurter, "a wholesale repudiation of his leadership,"[558] and he reacted strongly. Frankfurter's *Barnette* dissent is worth quoting from at some length, as it offers some poignant insights into both the judge and the man.[559] In Frankfurter's dissent in

---

[553] On Frankfurter's uneasy relationship with his fellow FDR appointees to the Court, see Noah Feldman, Scorpions: The Battles and Triumphs of FDR's Great Supreme Court Justices (Twelve, 2010).

[554] Lash, *supra* note 494, at 70.

[555] *Id.*, at 69.

[556] West Virginia Board of Education v. Barnette, 319 U.S. 624 (1943).

[557] Burt, *supra* note 491, at 43.

[558] *Id.*, at 48.

[559] Hirsch calls Frankfurter's *Barnette* dissent "a long, personal, emotional opinion, one that hardened Frankfurter's stand on the question of

Barnette, which Lash indicates "disturbed some of the
Justices who pleaded with him unsuccessfully to omit [some
of the personal statements in] it,"[560] in powerful language
that was to be frequently quoted as a statement of the
limitations on Justices' powers, and, contained the essence
of Frankfurter's later praised creed of judicial restraint,
Frankfurter wrote: "One who belongs to the most vilified
and persecuted minority in history, is not likely to be
insensible to the freedoms guaranteed by our
Constitution."[561] He continued:

> Were my purely personal attitude relevant, I
> should wholeheartedly associate myself with the
> general libertarian views in the Court's opinion,
> representing, as they do, the thought and action of
> a lifetime. But, as judges, we are neither Jew nor
> Gentile, neither Catholic nor agnostic. We owe
> equal attachment to the Constitution, and are
> equally bound by our judicial obligations.[562] . . . As
> a member of this Court, I am not justified in
> writing my private notions of policy into the
> Constitution, no matter how deeply I may cherish
> them or how mischievous I may deem their
> disregard. The duty of a judge who must decide
> which of two claims before the Court shall prevail,
> that of a State to enact and enforce laws within its
> general competence or that of an individual to
> refuse obedience because of the demands of his
> conscience, is not that of the ordinary person. It

---

judicial review and thereby set the tenor of his entire philosophy of law."
Hirsch, *supra* note 493, at 171.

[560] Burt, *supra* note 491, at 71.

[561] West Virginia Board of Education v. Barnette, 319 U.S. 624, 646
(1943) (Frankfurter, J. dissenting).

[562] These opening words of Frankfurter's dissent were described by Burt,
supra note 491, at 44, as "an extraordinary statement for the pages of the
United States Reports; nothing else in all those volumes, so far as I have read
in them, approaches this intense confessional tone."

> can never be emphasized too much that one's own
> opinion about the wisdom or evil of a law should be
> excluded altogether when one is doing one's duty
> on the bench. The only opinion . . . that is material
> is our opinion whether legislators could, in reason,
> have enacted such a law. . . . Most unwillingly,
> therefore, I must differ from my brethren with
> regard to legislation like this. I cannot bring my
> mind to believe that the "liberty" secured by the
> Due Process Clause gives this Court authority to
> deny to the State of West Virginia the attainment
> of that which we all recognize as a legitimate
> legislative end, namely, the promotion of good
> citizenship, by employment of the means here
> chosen.[563]

Frankfurter went on to remind his brethren that
Justice Stone (who was with the majority in *Barnette*), and
who had dissented from Frankfurter's majority opinion in
the early flag-salute case, *Gobitis*, had written that "the
only check upon our own exercise of power is our own sense
of self-restraint. For the removal of unwise laws from the
statute books, appeal lies not to the courts, but to the ballot
and to the processes of democratic government."[564]
Frankfurter then proceeded to explain more fully the
importance of this notion of "judicial self-restraint:"

> The admonition that judicial self-restraint alone
> limits arbitrary exercise of our authority is
> relevant every time we are asked to nullify
> legislation. The Constitution does not give us
> greater veto power when dealing with one phase of
> "liberty" than with another, or when dealing with
> grade school regulations than with college

---

[563] West Virginia Board of Education v. Barnette, 319 U.S., at 646–647
(Frankfurter, J., dissenting).

[564] Quoting from U.S. v. Butler, 297 U.S. 1, 79 (dissent).

regulations that offend conscience. . . . In neither situation is our function comparable to that of a legislature, or are we free to act as though we were a super-legislature. Judicial self-restraint is equally necessary whenever an exercise of political or legislative power is challenged. There is no warrant in the constitutional basis of this Court's authority for attributing different roles to it depending upon the nature of the challenge to the legislation. Our power does not vary according to the particular provision of the Bill of Rights which is invoked. The right not to have property taken without just compensation has, so far as the scope of judicial power is concerned, the same constitutional dignity as the right to be protected against unreasonable searches and seizures, and the latter has no less claim than freedom of the press or freedom of speech or religious freedom. In no instance is this Court the primary protector of the particular liberty that is invoked. . . .[565]

With these words, Frankfurter rejected the view of those of his purported fellow liberals who saw a profound difference between the rights of property (which the early New Deal court, in their view (in such cases as *Shechter*) had wrongly invoked in frustrating FDR's innovations), and civil rights, which they favored. For Frankfurter, now, every provision in the Constitution or Bill of Rights was equal, *and none permitted judges to innovate or legislate.* Invoking the authority of the Country's greatest judicial sage, deferred to both by him and by the liberals, Frankfurter went on to state:

When Mr. Justice Holmes, speaking for this Court, wrote that "it must be remembered that

---

[565] West Virginia Board of Education v. Barnette, 319 U.S., at 648–649 (Frankfurter, J., dissenting).

legislatures are ultimate guardians of the liberties
and welfare of the people in quite as great a degree
as the courts,"[566] he went to the very essence of our
constitutional system and the democratic
conception of our society. He did not mean that for
only some phases of civil government this Court
was not to supplant legislatures and sit in
judgment upon the right or wrong of a challenged
measure. He was stating the comprehensive
judicial duty and role of this Court in our
constitutional scheme whenever legislation is
sought to be nullified on any ground, namely, that
responsibility for legislation lies with legislatures,
answerable as they are directly to the people, and
this Court's only and very narrow function is to
determine whether, within the broad grant of
authority vested in legislatures, they have
exercised a judgment for which reasonable
justification can be offered.[567]

The Framers of the Constitution, Frankfurter continued,
"denied . . . legislative powers to the federal judiciary. They
chose instead to insulate the judiciary from the legislative
function. They did not grant to this Court supervision over
legislation."[568]

For Lash, this *Barnette* dissent seems to be a betrayal
of what Frankfurter maintained as a law professor, at least
insofar as the dissent expressed the view that property
rights are no less entitled to protection than civil rights.
This was, wrote Lash, "a departure from the view that he
had appeared to endorse in his lectures, that some rights
stood higher than others in the hierarchy of values to be

---

[566] Citing Missouri, K. & T. Ry. Co. v. May, 194 U.S. 267, 194 U.S. 270.

[567] West Virginia Board of Education v. Barnette, 319 U.S., at 649
(emphasis supplied) (Frankfurter, J., dissenting).

[568] *Id.*, at 650.

protected by The Court."[569] More important perhaps to Lash, was the fact that "In this writer's view this refinement uncoupled him from the locomotive of history."[570] Even more harshly, Lash stated that "Invoking the hallowed name of Holmes [Frankfurter] pushed the doctrine of judicial restraint to an extreme that violated the spirit of Holmes and separated him [Frankfurter] from the most innovative members of the court."[571]

Clearly, for example, Frankfurter was not the First Amendment absolutist his colleague Hugo Black was. Frankfurter thought that it was not the job of the Court regularly to second guess the weighing of the need for individual freedom against society's need for security and peace. For Black, apparently, the First Amendment required the court always to trump the legislative judgment where the legislature had failed to recognize what Black believed to be absolutely-secured First Amendment freedoms.[572] Here, of course, Lash, like most twentieth and twenty-first-century Constitutional commentators, indicates a preference for the view that the meaning and substance of the Constitution ought to change over time, and judicial innovators ought to be favored over conservatives. Lash is puzzled, apparently, why Frankfurter went in the direction he did. "We must ask why," says Lash. Lash seems to suggest that perhaps Frankfurter, as an outsider, and particularly a religious one, may have wanted to suggest that he could be trusted to uphold the values of the Christian majority of the nation.[573]

---

[569] Lash, *supra* note 494, at 73.

[570] *Id.*, at 73.

[571] *Id.*, at 73.

[572] *Id.*, at 78–79.

[573] *Id.*, at 73–74. For the theory that Frankfurter did, in fact, internalize the values of the "insiders," the Christian majority of the nation, or at least wanted to be perceived as upholding them, see, e.g., Burt, *supra* note 491, at 46–47. Burt sounds an intriguingly cautious note here, "as much as Frankfurter sought to portray himself in this insider's status, as much as he

Another biographer of Frankfurter, Robert A. Burt, expressly suggests that Frankfurter's voice eventually became that of "the quintessential insider."[574]

Another possibility, Lash suggests, is that Frankfurter's activities off the bench, and, in particular his somewhat controversial role as a close confident of Roosevelt, may have met any needs for the carrying out of Frankfurter's personal social or political preferences, presumably so that he could remain highly objective (restrained?) in his views of the law.[575] In any event, apparently, in what is a very balanced and thorough review of Frankfurter's life and jurisprudence, one has the very clear impression that Lash is still forced to regard Frankfurter as something of a failure, and his more single-minded colleague, Hugo Black, as a success. Writes Lash, "[W]here Black and Frankfurter diverged in regard to the Court's role as a guardian of individual rights and liberties, history has vindicated Black's absolutism and activism, for they served better to protect First Amendment liberties at a time when such protection was most needed, than did Frankfurter's doctrines of restraint and weighing of conflicting claims."[576] H.N. Hirsch, probably not going as far as Lash, but still believing that Frankfurter's jurisprudence never successfully reconciled "the contradiction in his own thoughts between his endorsement of judicial self-restraint and his belief in the existence of a hierarchy of Constitutional values," explains that Frankfurter was simply unable, unlike many twentieth-century liberals, to understand that it was appropriate for "maximum judicial

---

sought to persuade himself that he had attained it, I believe that it was never comfortably his." *Id.*, at 48.

[574] *Id.*, at 47.

[575] Lash, *supra* note 494, at 74–75.

[576] *Id.*, at 83. Lash does, however, make clear his approval of Frankfurter's stand in the *Brown* case in favor of the plaintiffs and against following the "separate but equal" doctrine of *Plessy v. Ferguson. Id.*, at 84.

self-restraint" to be applied and maximum latitude to be "given to the legislature in the field of economic policy, while close judicial scrutiny would be applied to the protection of civil liberties."[577]

Burt observes that "Frankfurter arrived with the expectation on all sides that he would become the intellectual and spiritual leader of the new Court that Franklin Roosevelt was reconstructing on the ruined battlements of the old."[578] This was not to be, however. Lash similarly notes how Frankfurter, used to being an intellectual leader in the law school environment, failed dismally to become the leader of his colleagues on the Court.[579] This may have been both because his fellow Justices didn't share his limited view of the judicial role, but also because of some disconcerting features of Frankfurter's personality which caused him to be excessively critical of his colleagues, and, indeed, to criticize them for the very conduct (for example extrajudicial dabbling in politics) in which he himself routinely engaged. Hirsch notes that Frankfurter offended both Black and Douglas, for example, because of his attitude that only "he [Frankfurter] held the doctrinal key to the legal universe."[580] Burt concludes that Frankfurter "was virtually consumed by a vitriolic anger toward his brethren,"[581] and further, perhaps going over the top just a bit, that "Frankfurter acted the leader abandoned by his followers, the lover spurned, the exile in his own country."[582]

---

[577] Hirsch, *supra* note 493, at 136–137.

[578] Burt, *supra* note 491, at 48.

[579] Lash, *supra* note 494, at 75–76. This is a major theme as well of Hirsch, *supra* note 493.

[580] Hirsch, *supra* note 493, at 141. On Frankfurter's relationship with his colleagues on the Court see also Feldman, *supra* note 553.

[581] Burt, *supra* note 491, at 48.

[582] *Id.*, at 49.

Was, then, Frankfurter a failure? Should he be admired, the way he was at Harvard in the 1970's? In his thoughtful study of Frankfurter and Brandeis, Robert Burt concludes that Frankfurter's "volubility," his "profusion of words," evident both in his judicial opinions and his activities as a law professor, and, before that, as a young man on the make, are the characteristics of a "parvenu,"[583] of a man self-consciously aware that he really doesn't belong where he is, and is engaged in an effort to disguise that fact by a blizzard of language. Burt goes further and suggests that "As he emphatically rejected any intimation that he remained an outsider, Frankfurter lost all sympathy for outsiders anywhere,"[584] and thus Frankfurter did not have the sympathy for racial and ethnic minorities which generally characterized the Warren Court.

There is no doubt that Frankfurter had some unusual, perhaps even repellant personal traits.[585] Burt writes that he exhibited "extraordinary vanity,"[586] and that his "conversations with other justices, as I read his version of them, were suffused with hectoring, condescending self-righteousness: only he [Frankfurter] understood the true issues at stake, only his motives were pure, only he embodied the noblest traditions of the Court. . . ."[587] David Dorsen, in his superb biography of Henry Friendly (who was something of a Frankfurter protégé) notes that Frankfurter

---

[583] Burt, *supra* note 491, at 91.

[584] *Id.*, at 123.

[585] On balance, though, Frankfurter appears to have been able to exercise considerable charm, and to have had a wide circle of admiring acquaintances. His wife is reported to have stated that "Felix has two hundred best friends." Burt, *supra* note 491, at 37, quoting from Lash, *supra* note 494, at 30. Frankfurter was reported by Isiah Berlin to have "had an uncommon capacity for melting reserve, breaking through inhibitions, and generally emancipating those with whom he came into contact." Burt, *supra* note 491, at 38, quoting from Isiah Berlin, Personal Impressions 85 (1981).

[586] Burt, *supra* note 491, at 51.

[587] *Id.*, at 52.

was "indefatigable but not always effective, partly because of the intensity of his approaches to people."[588] Burt speculates that Frankfurter's odd behavior is explained by "internal obstructions, a deep-rooted conception of himself that, much as he struggled against it, would not permit him to enter wholeheartedly into . . . insider's status." This, for Burt, explains his "self-defeating and isolating relations with his brethren, which obstructed his own explicitly chosen goals."[589] Worse, Burt ultimately concludes that in his zeal to demonstrate his qualifications as an "insider," the distance he had moved from arriving on American shores unable to speak a word of English to his status on the highest bench in the land, Frankfurter "lost an essential aspect of his judgmental capacity; he became too single-minded, an overeager apologist for the existing order. He embraced an attitude to America that provided no critical distance for him in reaching judgment on his contemporary society or on himself."[590]

One recent biographer of FDR, Conrad Black, appears, like others, to have been somewhat repulsed by what he took to be Frankfurter's sycophantic relationship with the President who appointed him to the Supreme Court,[591] and

---

[588] David M. Dorsen, Henry Friendly: Greatest Judge of His Era 73 (Harvard, 2012). Dorsen appears to subtly make the point that Frankfurter wanted Friendly to know that he—Frankfurter—had greased the skids (with Lyndon Johnson no less) to make Friendly's confirmation happen. *Id.*, at 77.

[589] Burt, *supra* note 491, at 53.

[590] *Id.*, at 60. Burt's extraordinary dual biography of Brandeis and Frankfurter reaches back to the ancient Jewish conflict between the Prophets and Priests of Israel. The Priests (Frankfurter is likened to one) emphasized order and hierarchy, the Prophets (like Brandeis) were the true champions of the law and the idealists who were sympathetic to the people. Burt implies about Frankfurter that like the Jewish priests of old he mistrusted the capacity of the people, instead "relying on ritual and demanding popular deference to [his] hierarchically superior status to secure obedience to [transcendent] norms." *Id.*, at 126.

[591] Black noted that FDR "preferred the somewhat pedantic but loyal Frankfurter to the opportunistic financier Bernard Baruch, but they were both useful and they were both rather obsequious to him." Conrad Black, Franklin

the flattery with which Frankfurter favored FDR (and several other of his idols)[592] is striking. For example, following an episode when the then New York Governor Roosevelt successfully garnered the resignation of a possibly corrupt Tammany politician, Frankfurter wrote to praise FDR's "complete vindication of your firmness, skill, and fairness as chief executive."[593] Joseph Lash, a somewhat sympathetic historian of Frankfurter's

---

Delano Roosevelt: Champion of Freedom 155 (Public Affairs, 2003). Black suggested further that "Roosevelt, though he could usually manage to disguise it, was not especially comfortable with leading academics unless they were completely subservient, like Frankfurter." *Id.*, at 317–318. Amplifying the point, Black stated that Frankfurter was "a pedantic courtier 'upon whom [Roosevelt] could always depend for instant laudatory reassurance,' " though Black does concede that Frankfurter "was also excessively intelligent, versatile, loyal to Roosevelt, possessed of generally excellent judgment, and ultimately an outstanding Supreme Court justice." *Id.*, at 338–339 (quoting Frank Freidel). Black hints at a duplicity or perhaps a self-delusion on Frankfurter's part: "Brandeis was also constantly giving advice to Frankfurter, who pipelined it on to Roosevelt, sometimes identifying the originating author and sometimes taking what he fancied to be the credit for himself," *id.*, at 412, and, to similar effect, "Frankfurter . . . straddled with the skill of the agile juridical politician that he was. . . ." *Id.*, at 413.

The "courtier" theme is also sounded by Lash, *supra* note 494, at 60–61, who notes that "FDR used men and women for *his* purposes, not theirs, but for someone like Frankfurter who needed the feeling that Roosevelt's countenance was not turned away from him, the exclusion [from the discussion on the Court-packing plan] must have been dismaying, and like courtiers usually, and there were elements of the courtier in Frankfurter's relationship to Roosevelt, the desire to be on the inside caused him to redouble his efforts to gain his principal's favor." (Emphasis in original). Hirsch concludes that "in their 722 pages of published correspondence, there is an almost unbelievable amount of flattery heaped on the president by Frankfurter." Hirsch, *supra* note 493, at 106.

[592] Hirsch points out that the "praise and flattery" that Frankfurter lavished on the "elderly Justice" Oliver Wendell Holmes, Jr. "almost have the tone of love letters." Hirsch, *supra* note 493, at 87. Hirsch could have omitted the "almost," as is strongly suggested by Frankfurter's phrases such as "You give me the exhilaration the life-intoxicated ferment that no other man does— and with you I feel the overtones and undertones which need no speech and have none." *Id.*, quoting Felix Frankfurter to Oliver Wendell Holmes, Jr., March 5, 1921.

[593] Lash, *supra* note 494, at 44.

activities[594] does suggest that Frankfurter's association with FDR "turned into hero worship, [and] carried with it some warping of judgment."[595] Lash notes Frankfurter's insight that both men and women "have to be told with great frequency that you love them," and indicates that the kind of flattery Frankfurter gave FDR was replicated in Frankfurter's perhaps overdone praise for Justice Stone of the Supreme Court, and Lash appears to imply that at least some of this lavish encomium may have been hypocritical.[596]

Frankfurter's possible duplicity has received great attention of late, and, for a while it appeared as if an entire cottage industry had grown up in the American Legal academy to attempt to determine whether Frankfurter was really loyal to the constitutional ideal of the rule of law,[597] or whether he was a shameless partisan in service to the goals of a transforming President. Frankfurter has even been accused of forging correspondence to promote his jurisprudential reviews, but this charge remains unproven.[598]

---

[594] Burt, on the other hand, does have some powerful reservations about Frankfurter and his personality. He reports, for example that Frankfurter, faced with a credible assertion of "Nazi genocide" of the Jews was unable to accept it because "My mind, my heart they are made in such a way that I cannot conceive it." Burt, *supra* note 491, at 102.

[595] Lash, *supra* note 494, at 49.

[596] *Id.*, at 49. Lash describes some of the letters to FDR as "courtier-like expressions" which are "melancholy testimony to an eagerness to please that went beyond loyalty." See also Hirsh, *supra* note 493, at 5, who notes that Frankfurter's correspondence with FDR "reveals a sycophantic flattery."

[597] Hirsch suggests that "When it suited his purposes, Frankfurter willingly abandoned his commitment to squeaky-clean legal procedures." Hirsch, *supra* note 493, at 80.

[598] See generally, for a discussion and refutation by the author of the Holmes Devise volume on the New Deal Court, on which Frankfurter sat, Richard D. Friedman, A Reaffirmation: The Authenticity of the Roberts Memorandum, or Felix the Non-Forger, 142 U.Pa. L.Rev. 1985 (1994).

There are elements of Frankfurter's work, then, or perhaps, to be more precise, his personality, that are puzzling. In his provocative psychological biography of Frankfurter, in much the manner as did Burt, H.N. Hirsch concludes that "we can understand him psychologically as representing a textbook case of a neurotic personality: someone whose self-image is overblown and yet, at the same time, essential to his sense of well-being."[599] Thus, Hirsch's explanation for Frankfurter's vitriol towards those who disagreed with him flows from this conception of Frankfurter's inflated self-image, "Frankfurter could not accept serious, sustained opposition in fields he considered his domain of expertise; he reacted to his opponents with vindictive hostility. Unconsciously, such hostility was a projection of his own self-doubt."[600] Hirsch appears to suggest that Frankfurter's personality defects, for example the fact that "he was above all, a snob,"[601] might not have hampered him while he was in the academy—which leads one to wonder whether a certain amount of neurosis might, indeed, be helpful to law professors—but that once he got on the Supreme Court Frankfurter's interactions with his colleagues, and, in particular, their failure to accept him as a leader of the Court, created "a serious challenge to his self-image," and his reaction adversely affected "both his relations with his colleagues and the content of his jurisprudence."[602]

On the Court, in government service, and even while in the academy, Hirsch tells us, when someone disagreed with him, Frankfurter's "response was to equate opposition to stupidity or self-seeking, and to seek vindication over his

---

[599]   Hirsch, *supra* note 493, at 3.

[600]   *Id.*, at 6.

[601]   *Id.*, at 90. Hirsch explains, "The Harvard Law School was the best law school; his friends were the wisest men, the best lawyers, the most charming people." *Ibid.*

[602]   *Id.*, at 6.

opponents."[603] Like others who manifested such a neurotic personality, apparently, Frankfurter came "to regard himself as a symbol of righteousness fighting against stupidity and prejudice."[604] So sure of Frankfurter's own abilities was he that he regarded himself, as do many law professors, perhaps, as "a symbol of reason and fairness."[605] Frankfurter seems to have seen the professional choices he made as the only appropriate ones, and, in particular, it was the duty of a person of integrity to spurn riches to serve the greater good. As Hirsch puts it "He was preoccupied with the idea that a lawyer faces a personal choice—he can either sell himself to the highest bidder . . . or he can shun money-making and devote himself to good causes, as he [Frankfurter] himself did."[606]

As one who saw his own motives as exceptionally pure and those of his adversaries less so, it is not surprising, as Hirsch notes, that Frankfurter could write to Learned Hand that the liberals on the Court, with whom he was increasingly to disagree,[607] had, as a "common denominator" in Frankfurter's words, "a self-willed self-righteous power-lust, conditioned by different causes, internal and external, undisciplined by adequate professional learning and cultivated understanding."[608] Of Black, Frankfurter wrote to Hand, "Hugo is a self-righteous, self-deluded part fanatic, part demagogue, who really disbelieves in law, [and] thinks it is essentially manipulation of language." Of his colleague Stanley Reed, Frankfurter wrote he "is largely vegetable—he has managed to give himself a nimbus of reasonableness but is

---

[603] *Id.*, at 60.

[604] *Id.*, at 62.

[605] *Id.*, at 66.

[606] *Id.*, at 81.

[607] See generally Feldman, *supra* note 553.

[608] Hirsch, *supra* note 493, at 181.

as unjudicial-minded, as flagrantly moved, at times, by irrelevant considerations for adjudication, as any [of the Justices]." Of William O. Douglas, he wrote that "Bill is the most cynical, shamelessly immoral character I've ever known."[609] By 1957, according to Hirsch, Frankfurter was even referring to the work of Chief Justice Earl Warren, as "dishonest nonsense."[610] Small wonder that Frankfurter found it increasingly difficult to get along with his colleagues.

In spite of all of this, and even though Frankfurter may have exhibited some of the same traits that Leon Panetta lamented in President Obama,[611] it is difficult not to regard Frankfurter with something of the same regard Turow says was bestowed on him at Harvard. Frankfurter may well have had some bizarre or perhaps neurotic personality traits, but his passion for the law, for the Supreme Court, and for Harvard seem to have partaken of the spiritual dimension that, if we take him at his word, religion may not have ultimately offered him. Echoing, perhaps, Blackstone's[612] and Wilson's[613] discovery of something divine in the common law, Frankfurter said of the Supreme Court, "Of all earthly institutions this Court comes nearest to having, for me, sacred aspects," and of the place where he taught and studied law, he wrote, "I have a quasi-religious feeling about the Harvard Law School."[614] His biographer, Robert Burt, writes that Frankfurter had similar feelings of adulation about America itself, and, of course, about Franklin Roosevelt. For Frankfurter, then, Holmes's Olympian detachment was not a possible posture, though

---

[609] *Id.*, at 182, quoting Frankfurter to Learned Hand, November 7, 1954.

[610] *Id.*, at 190.

[611] See the Introduction, *supra* note 1.

[612] See Chapter 1, *supra*.

[613] See Chapter 2, *supra*.

[614] Quoted in Burt, *supra* note 491, at 40.

the myth of the law professor above the world persists. For another law professor deeply immersed in his world, we turn to the fictional creation of C.P. Snow.

CHAPTER 10

THE LAW PROFESSOR
AS FICTIONAL MODERN
CAMBRIDGE DON AND DENIZEN
OF THE CORRIDORS OF POWER

EARLY TO LATE TWENTIETH CENTURY

Lewis Eliot
(Cambridge University)

■ ■ ■

With this chapter we take something of a departure from our usual concern, which is the actual lives of notable American law professors. Now we will consider perhaps the only fully-developed English fictional law professor, and soon we will encounter his analog among American law professors (Charles Kingsfield, of *The Paper Chase*).[615] Tocqueville famously described American lawyers (to their undying delight) as the only true aristocrats in America. He said they belonged to the people by birth, but to the aristocracy by habit and aspiration, and that, in effect, they made democracy in America work by tempering the passion and enthusiasms of the American people through their adherence to the conservative nature of legal forms. For Tocqueville, American lawyers countered the incessant popular clamor for the novel, with their almost

---

[615] See Chapter 13, *infra*.

superstitious veneration for order and the past.[616] One of the lessons to be learned by examining the career of American law professors is that what Tocqueville said about American lawyers, might, in general, be said even more strongly about the legal professoriate. They are the closest that one can come in America to a group that really does fancy itself a nobility charged with the task of remaking society in accordance with a set of values, originally traditional,[617] and now, perhaps, verging on the revolutionary.[618]

Be that as it may, when we encounter the fictional English law professor we're examining something quite different.[619] In his twentieth-century British milieu, there

---

[616] Alexis de Tocqueville's comments on American lawyers, and the manner in which they serve as a counterpoise to democracy are to be found in Book I, Chapter Sixteen of his Democracy in America (1831).

[617] For the traditionalists in the legal academy see, e.g., Chapter 1 (Blackstone), Chapter 2 (Wilson), Chapter 3 (Story), Chapter 9 (Frankfurter), Chapter 11 (Herbert Wechsler), Chapter 18 (Mary Ann Glendon), Chapter 19 (Paul Carrington), and Chapter 20 (Antonin Scalia).

[618] For the modern aspirations to the revolutionary in the American legal academy see Chapters 14 (Critical Legal Studies), 17 (Feminism), 21 (Critical Race Theory), and the Conclusion (Progressive politics).

[619] I ought to offer some explanation for why this chapter is the longest in the book, and, on the surface at least, the least relevant to explaining the American law professor. My excuses, such as they are, include the facts that this is the only extended fictional treatment of a British law professor, and that consideration of an English alternative (just as was true for Blackstone) illuminates the similarities and differences from the American, that the American legal profession used to think of itself as a profession of belles-lettres, and these novels of Snow's are beautifully written, and, selfishly, I wanted an excuse to read all eleven of them again. I also think that some of the characters in the series, most notably George Passant and Lewis Eliot are recognizable prototypes for some of the American law professors reviewed in this book. Thus Passant is much like the critical legal scholars (Chapter 14) and like President Obama (Chapter 23), while Eliot is a bit like Frankfurter (Chapter 9) and Paul Carrington (Chapter 19), and the fictional American law professor Charles Kingsfield (Chapter 13). See for yourself. I also think that Lewis's career as a civil servant, what we would regard as a bureaucrat, in England helps us understand the rise of the modern American Administrative state, a problem with which modern American law professors are increasingly coming to have to deal. Finally, I do believe that reading the series (and reading great fiction generally) is good for lawyers, because it inevitably and relatively painlessly

already is an hereditary aristocracy, and, indeed, a carefully calibrated social system relatively alien to the American experience. What's the role of a law professor (and a lawyer) there? This English legal academic, Lewis Eliot, is the creation of C.P. Snow, the brilliant English philosopher and scientist,[620] who popularized the term "The Two Cultures" to describe the difference in approach by humanists and scientists in the academy.[621] In his extraordinary eleven volume series, *Strangers and Brothers*, Snow tells the story of Eliot, a son of the lower middle class, who rises from humble provincial beginnings to become a barrister, then a law teacher at Cambridge, and also, eventually, a senior civil servant at Whitehall, who receives a Knighthood. This remarkable opus was one of the great literary achievements of the twentieth century, although it is relatively little known in America today. Anthony Burgess, the caustic and astute English critic of his fellow novelists, picked the series as one of the 99 best in English since 1939 (99, because, presumably, Burgess counted one of his own as one of 100, but falsely modestly refused to include it in his list).[622] Of these eleven works by C.P. Snow, Burgess indicated that they explored

> themes and locales never seen before (except perhaps in Trollope). Neglected since Snow's death [the series] deserves to be reconsidered as a highly serious attempt to depict the British class system

---

improves their writing, and teaches them more about themselves, the law, and the world. This chapter is intended as a guide and a summary to the eleven novels, but it contains many spoilers, and the intrepid reader may wish to tackle the eleven novels themselves, before this commentary.

[620] Charles Percy Snow, Baron Snow, Kt., CBE.

[621] C.P. Snow, The Two Cultures and the Scientific Revolution: The Rede Lecture (Cambridge, 1961). Available on the web at http://sciencepolicy. colorado.edu/students/envs_5110/snow_1959.pdf (accessed 9 March 2016).

[622] Anthony Burgess, Ninety-Nine Novels: The Best in English Since 1939 (Summit Books, 1984). Burgess's book is a splendid introduction to near-contemporary fiction. His eye is a very discriminating one.

and the distribution of power. The work has authority: it is not the dream of a slippered recluse but of a man actively involved in the practical mechanics of high policy making.[623]

Among those novels, *The Masters*[624] (about the selection of the master of a Cambridge college) and *The Affair*[625] (about academic fraud) are some of the best studies of the manner in which the academy resists integration with the broader society. Lewis Eliot is that rare creature (perhaps like Frankfurter[626]) who can straddle both domains, and the eleven English novels, perhaps, have something to say to us in a country where a law professor can become President.[627] Almost no American lawyers today read C.P. Snow (or much of any other fiction writer, for that matter), but Snow's grasp of university life, and his understanding of the workings of the "corridors of power"[628] (he is often credited with coining that phrase), and its lure for academics is simply unparalleled in modern literature.

As indicated, the eleven novels have many themes, spanning how life was lived by all classes and many professions in England during the twentieth century, but what one might describe as a major sub-theme surely is the role of the law professor and the role of the lawyer in twentieth-century England. While the protagonist of the series as a whole is clearly the eventual Cambridge external law lecturer[629] and senior civil servant Lewis Eliot, in the important first book, foreshadowing Eliot's later position,

---

[623] *Id.*, at 31.

[624] C.P. Snow, The Masters (Macmillan, 1951).

[625] C.P. Snow, The Affair (Macmillan, 1960).

[626] See Chapter 9, *supra*.

[627] On the views of our law professor President, see Chapter 23, *infra*.

[628] C.P. Snow, The Corridors of Power (Macmillan, 1964).

[629] Equivalent to an American Adjunct or "Part-Time" Professor, whose main occupational activities are conducted elsewhere.

there is a study of another external law lecturer, albeit one at a provincial technical college, George Passant (now the title of that volume,[630] it was originally simply called "Strangers and Brothers," the name of the whole series). Passant is Lewis Eliot's first law teacher, and Passant is a man of acute intelligence, but also strong passions and, at least when we are first introduced to him, powerful integrity. The novel, however, is also a study of fatal character flaws. This first novel, in drawing the portrait of Passant, sets up what will become an extraordinary contrast to the law professor Eliot will eventually become. There is a gorgeous irony in that Passant's inspiration and encouragement drives Eliot to sublime achievements, but the elements of Passant's character which make him a hero and superb mentor to his students hobble and, eventually destroy Passant's own personal ambitions.

Passant, while his avocation clearly is his connection with the provincial Technical College and Art School where he lectures, is doomed to a life as a law clerk in one of the town's modest office of solicitors.[631] According to Passant's account, at least, he does all the difficult intellectual legal analysis for the firm, but the firm's partners take the credit, refuse to advance him to partnership, and use him as essentially their wage slave. Passant tolerates this, because what he really wants is the stimulation of the young people he encounters at the College and Art School. He gathers about him a coterie of idealistic men and women, apparently in their late teens and early twenties, not all of whom are

---

[630] C.P. Snow, George Passant (Macmillan, 1940, originally published as "Strangers and Brothers").

[631] At this time the English legal profession was broadly divided into two classes, *solicitors* who did what we Americans would regard as office legal work, advising clients, and *barristers*, who argued cases in court. The barristers were clearly regarded as possessing a higher social status, but it was possible for solicitors to earn a quite decent living; somewhat less so their clerks, such as Passant, whose position as an articled clerk would be roughly comparable to that of an associate in an American law firm.

his students (at the two law lectures he delivers each week), but to whom he is devoted to an extent greater than advancing his own professional interests. Passant teaches law, and is capable of very astute analysis of legal doctrine, but, probably because the partners (owners) in his firm believe that all is not strictly above board in Passant's relationships with the female members of "the group" he mentors, they conclude that Passant is not worthy of the extraordinary trust that the status of partner demands, and thus he is condemned to the life of an articled clerk.

As the reader begins this first novel in the series this seems manifestly unjust, but as the work unfolds, it becomes evident that Passant has, indeed, been involved sexually with several females in "the group." When, finally, Passant's need for funds to support what becomes his sybaritic lifestyle, and, when, through a toxic combination of Passant's inadvertence, blind faith, self-indulgence, and self-delusion he is led into some shady business ventures, the reader's original sympathy for Passant starts to wane. As the climax of the book, there is an account of Passant's trial for obtaining money under false pretenses, which leads to the loss of his job at the Art School and Technical College. Passant (and two of his protégées) are found "not guilty" by the jury, but his reputation is severely damaged.

Passant's acquittal, which at least saves him from prison, is as a direct result of a brilliant defense carried on by the senior barrister in Lewis Eliot's chambers, one Herbert Getliffe. Getliffe understands Passant's wish to do good, and makes the jury see that Passant's efforts to inspire his students by offering them the freedom to develop themselves to the fullest are noble, but that weaknesses in Passant's philosophy led him to stretch that liberty to license. While the tactic of the prosecution was to suggest that the immoral character of Passant's liaisons should be taken as an indicator of his propensity to criminal conduct,

Getliffe (and, indeed the judge in the case) will have none of that. Still, the puzzle is why the clearly brilliant Passant should have found himself in such a set of circumstances, and why he turned out to be himself the predictable cause of his own downfall. This is illuminated in the peroration Getliffe gives to the jury. He first explains to the jury that Passant was a man with extraordinary talents who could, if he had wished, and if he had been more careful in his choice of colleagues, have risen to the top of law or any other profession. Instead, he deliberately chose to "waste" his life in pursuit of essentially sensual pleasure, and leading his group of young people to a life of "liberty." This, however, Getliffe argued, should not lead the jury to convict Passant of financial crimes for which there was very little evidence. Said Getliffe of Passant:

> He wanted to build a better world on the basis of this freedom of his; but it's fatal to build better worlds until you know what human beings are like and what you're like yourself. If you don't you're liable to build, not a better world, but a worse one; in fact you're liable to build a world for one purpose, and one only, that is just to suit your own private weaknesses. I'm certain that's exactly what Mr. Passant has done, and I'm certain that is exactly what all progressively minded people, if you'll let me call them that, are always likely to do unless they watch themselves. They usually happen to be much too arrogant to watch themselves.[632]

Getliffe goes on to suggest that the arrogance of such progressives flows, as it did in Passant's case, from the fact

---

[632] C.P. Snow, George Passant (originally "Strangers and Brothers") 307 (1940). Could what Getliffe says about those who seek to build a better world be applied to modern American legal progressives? See Chapters 14 and 23, and the Conclusion, *infra*.

that "He's never realized—though he's a clever man—that freedom without faith means nothing but self-indulgence."[633] Getliffe also states that "Freedom without faith has been fatal for Mr. Passant himself," and that, further, "Sometimes it seems to me that it will be fatal to most of his kind in this country and the world. Their idea of progress isn't just sterile, it carries the seed of its own decay."[634]

Attempting to explain how brilliant people—progressives—like Passant could lose faith, and be led to a life of self-indulgence, Getliffe blames the senseless carnage and destruction of World War I,[635] but he has posed the question that will dominate the next ten novels—is it possible in the twentieth century, after the betrayal by the leadership of the nations that led to the Great War, to build a true life of virtue and merit, and how can a law professor contribute to such an effort? One can see in George Passant, a progressive law professor of a type well known to contemporary America, indeed, one that we can see in the critical legal studies movement that we will soon encounter,[636] and one that, as we also will see, finds an example in President Obama.[637] How then, does the life of Lewis Eliot demonstrate that something else is possible?

In the next book we begin to learn two clear qualities of Lewis Eliot—his extraordinarily high intelligence and his extraordinary degree of empathy with his fellow human beings. This second book in the series, *The Light and the Dark*,[638] is essentially the story of Lewis's great friend, Roy Calvert. Roy's nature is reflected in the title to the book—

---

[633] C.P. Snow, George Passant, *supra* note 632, at 307.
[634] *Ibid.*
[635] *Id.*, at 308–309.
[636] See Chapter 14, *infra.*
[637] See Chapter 23, *infra.*
[638] C.P. Snow, The Light and the Dark (Faber, 1947).

he is brilliant, witty, charming, and sparkling, but, at the same time, he is frequently given to bouts of melancholy and feelings of despair. Lewis learns great life lessons from Roy, and loves him as he has loved few men, but Lewis knows, in the end, that there is little, even with Lewis's high degree of perception and feeling, that he (Lewis) can do to ease the pain that life brings for Roy. This pain is entirely spiritual and internal, as Roy leads a charmed life—he has great scholarly successes, wonderful love affairs, and many friends in England and abroad, but none of it really can stop Roy's agony. Roy desperately seeks a sense that he is not completely alone, and searches fruitlessly for a way to believe in God, but cannot find it.

This second book in the series is a psychological study of a tormented soul—Roy—but also suggests similarities in Lewis—who, we are told (without much elaboration) is trapped in an unhappy marriage with a psychologically disturbed woman who dies, without much comment, in the course of the narrative in this volume. Much of the book takes place in Cambridge, and Snow uses this book to draw a picture of the life of a Cambridge Don, which will be amplified in the famous fourth volume of the series.[639] Here Cambridge life is presented to show us another side of Lewis, the English law professor, an academic who can find appreciation not only for the scholarship of his friend Roy, an Orientalist, but also for the scientists and clergymen and others who are the other Dons on the College's faculty. This is not the story of a logic-chopping master of abstraction, as many American law professors will come to be, but of a sensitive man whose mind and heart are brimming with the

---

[639] C.P. Snow, *The Masters, supra* note 624. I am treating The Masters as the fourth volume, as it follows sequentially in time the third book in the series, though it was actually composed as the fifth book in the series and is often so described.

real complexities, ambiguities, and mysteries of flesh and blood.

In the course of this volume as well, which covers the period of the beginning of the Second World War, Lewis begins his career as a civil servant, in Whitehall,[640] contributing to the War effort, but also studying the ways of the bureaucracy. Lewis is being painted as increasingly omnicompetent in the ways of the world, and increasingly painfully aware of the ways of the heart as well.

One more extraordinary theme that weaves its way into this narrative of Cambridge college life is aristocracy, in the person of the Earl of Boscastle, of an ancient family with ties to Lewis's college. The Earl is about as pure an hereditary aristocrat as one can conceive, but for reasons that are slightly obscure, the Earl and his wife, the Countess Boscastle, adopt Roy and Lewis as part of their circle. Lewis seems oddly comfortable with them, and the Countess (in her time a great beauty, and, indeed, not originally an aristocrat herself) tells Lewis that he is fortunate to possess a self-confidence that few actual aristocrats can muster. The implication seems to be that Lewis, the law professor from a very modest background, has the potential for true greatness. The Countess helps Lewis along, with her gentle sarcastic wit, tries to teach him to dress and act appropriately, and is clearly doing what she can to propel him on and upward in the class-ridden England which still, to a certain extent, exists, though it is fast fading away in the modern world.

It is made clear that Lewis's politics, perhaps like those of the young Frankfurter,[641] are radical, but his original political sentiments seem to give way as he fits easily into

---

[640] Here used as a metonym for the British central governmental administration.

[641] See Chapter 9, *supra.* See also Chapter 14, *infra.*

the old somewhat aristocratic English academic and political order. The war goes on, however, the Earl loses his beloved son who dies heroically, and Roy, apparently with an obvious death wish, becomes a bomber pilot, and perishes as he is shot out of the sky. Lewis is despondent, as are the Boscastles, but Roy leaves behind a wife and young daughter, and Lewis somehow seems to suggest that just the fact that Roy lived brought something wonderful to him, Lewis. Roy died, in the end, Snow seems to suggest, without the consolation of hope,[642] but, somehow, Lewis clings to it, and it gives the title to the next book in the series.

The Third book, *Time of Hope*,[643] takes us back to Lewis's provincial childhood, and the events that set him on his path to become a barrister and a law professor. We meet his mother, who puts all her hopes for the future into Lewis, his father, who is a business failure, having gone bankrupt, and his strong-willed Aunt Milly, his father's sister. Aunt Milly believes Lewis to be possessed of only mediocre talents, but impresses on him the need for success, if only to wipe out the financial debts of his father. Curiously, Lewis rejects the love of his mother, and, essentially, strikes out on his own. By the sheer force of his extraordinary abilities, he wins a coveted studentship at the bar, and embarks on a career as a barrister, aided, in part, by his early law teacher, George.

At the bar, in London, Lewis quickly makes friends, and widens a circle of acquaintances who begin to funnel cases to him.[644] His future looks bright, and his hopes are

---

[642] "Hope," might well be seen as the major theme in C.P. Snow's work. See generally Nicolas Tredell, C.P. Snow: The Dynamics of Hope (Palgrave Macmillan, 2012).

[643] C.P. Snow, Time of Hope (Faber and Faber, 1949).

[644] Barristers are given cases ("briefs") to argue by solicitors, and barristers' professional success turns on their reputation among solicitors and, perhaps, among their solicitors' clients.

high, but there is one crippling handicap under which he suffers. He falls in love with Sheila Knight, the well-off daughter of a Vicar from their provincial home town. Sheila is utterly self-absorbed, clinically schizoid, and makes clear to Lewis that she doesn't love him, and never will. Somehow this just traps Lewis further, and, knowing that it will probably bring him deep unhappiness, and may even wreck his career, after Lewis drives away the only man Sheila says she ever actually loved, Lewis marries Sheila. Because Sheila requires constant attention and is utterly incapable of really caring about anyone except herself (and, indeed, as time goes on, becomes incapable of caring about herself either), Lewis's career suffers. Lewis sums up where he is, at age 28, "I had longed for a better world, and this was the summer of 1933. I had longed for fame: and I was a second-rate lawyer. I had longed for love; and I was bound for life to a woman who never had love for me and who had exhausted mine."[645] Accordingly, Lewis tells Sheila they must part, and she packs to go. Then, at the last minute, Lewis calls her back, and realizes that, no matter what, to cast her out would be worse than a life sentence of staying with her.

Time of Hope suggests that this man, Eliot, who will become a great man of affairs, and, perhaps, a great law Don, while he has superb intellectual abilities, and an uncanny ability to understand, explain, and charm his fellow humans, strangely does not yet possess what may be the most important and elusive human quality, the ability to carve out a life of happiness for himself. In *Time of Hope,* Lewis Eliot comes to grips with his own vanity and selfishness, but decides, ultimately, that he cannot cast aside his troubled wife, even if that's what it would take to ensure his career. In *Time of Hope,* Lewis has not yet become a law professor, but he is climbing the ladder of

---

[645] Time of Hope, *supra* note 643, at 393.

success in law; he decides to reject the easier, but less lucrative and less prestigious opportunity to become a solicitor. At that time the English legal profession was highly stratified, as indicated earlier, with solicitors being those who met with and advised clients on legal matters, and with barristers being elite members of the profession who were hired by solicitors (not clients directly) to argue cases in court.[646] It was from the ranks of barristers that King's Counsel were chosen (to assume responsibilities to represent the Crown in legal matters, and also to gain access to the most prestigious cases), and then from their ranks would come the judges. Lewis believes, at the end of *Time of Hope*, that he may follow this career path, but he doesn't know if his wife, Sheila, who requires much of his time, talent, and energy, will hold him fatally back. At the end of this book he has not yet realized that an academic career holds promise for him.

In the next book in the series, the most famous, *The Masters*,[647] Lewis has gained a position as a law don, at Cambridge, in an old and established college. *The Masters* is the fourth book in the series, and is the one that has achieved the most popular success, as it chronicles in precise detail how academic politics works. The purpose of the book might be to consider the truthfulness of the difficult to attribute quote that academic politics are the most vicious because the stakes are so small.[648] The subject is the election of a new master for Snow's unnamed Cambridge college (thought to be Christ's College, where Snow was himself a fellow). The selection of a new master is by vote of the 13 fellows of the college, each of whom has

---

[646] See note 644, *supra*.

[647] *The Masters*, *supra* note 624.

[648] The statement has been variously attributed to figures as diverse as Samuel Johnson, Henry Kissinger, and Jesse Unruh. See generally, Academic Politics Are So Vicious Because the Stakes Are So Small, Quote Investigator, http://quoteinvestigator.com/2013/08/18/acad-politics/ (accessed July 12, 2015).

one vote. The fellows range in age from early twenties to early eighties, and each has an equal say in who will become the new leader of the college. Lewis Eliot has been a fellow for three years, having joined the college in 1937 as a law teacher. He has secured his position with the help of Francis Getliffe, a gifted scientific fellow of the College, who is married to the sister of Lewis's great London friend, Charles March, who is the central figure in another volume. Francis Getliffe is the younger brother of Lewis's former employer, the barrister, Herbert Getliffe, whom we met in the first volume of the series.

There is some ambiguity about whether Lewis becomes an academic by virtue of his considerable talent, or simply because of his powerful connections. In any event, this book limns a law professor as an honest broker, as one of the few fellows capable of keeping a relatively cool head during tense times at the college. And, indeed, the book presents Lewis as possessing a remarkable ability to comfort his colleagues even in their extreme distress.[649] There are multiple fissures among the fellows, including a divide according to politics (the conservatives vs. the radicals) and one according to discipline (the scientists vs. the humanists). Curiously, Lewis, who is a radical, aligns himself with the conservative candidate for Master, because he has greater respect for his human qualities (empathy, self-criticism, subordination of his career interests to love), than the candidate of the radicals. Or perhaps Lewis, as a man of the law, has less sympathy for the radical candidate because that candidate is a rather dispassionate scientist, and not a careful student of the foibles of character.

The plot actually unfolds as if it were a thriller, with the puzzling question being who will win the election. At

---

[649] *The Masters, supra* note 624, at 326, where it is observed that Eliot has an ability to visit and cheer colleagues even when they are wretched with despair.

first it looks like there is a clear majority for Lewis's candidate, but then, as details of the personalities and personality problems of the thirteen fellows are revealed, alliances shift, and it remains uncertain until the end who will prevail. In the course of this struggle, several things about Lewis himself are revealed. One is that he left the bar because of the great pressure there (Eliot explains that he was brought "to the college when I decided that I did not want to go on competing all out at the Bar,")[650] and another is that he also joined the college to escape from his unhappy marriage (he lives essentially alone in Cambridge),[651] while his wife stays in their London home, to which Lewis returns for part of every week. Eliot is thus a law professor with divided loyalties—because he is, really, part-time (he spends part at the week at his firm of barristers) he cannot be considered for college offices. Still, he has full voting privileges as a fellow, and Snow makes it clear that Eliot's wisdom is given special deference by his colleagues (one credits Eliot with "astonishing judgment of men,"),[652] a wisdom which Eliot has acquired through suffering and self-doubt,[653] although Snow, himself a scientist, may have an ironic attitude toward his law professor subject. Indeed, the figure in the book who might well represent Snow himself, the radical candidate for master, the scientist, Crawford, is disliked by Eliot because "he once spoke of me as a barrister *manqué*."[654] Further, at one superb comic moment in the book, one of the senior fellows, an internationally famous dilettante of sorts, and an expert on the Icelandic sagas,

---

[650] *Id.*, at 57. For a similar move by the great American legal academic, Christopher Columbus Langdell, see Chapter 4, *supra*.

[651] *Id.*, at 177. ("When I was in distress, so that I wanted a refuge to hide in, Francis [Getliffe] had set to work to bring me to the college.")

[652] *Id.*, at 98.

[653] At one point he clearly indicates that he has known "what it is to have no use for yourself." *Id.*, at 217.

[654] *Id.*, at 301. *Manqué* is a French expression for having failed to become what one might have been.

who is just beginning to enter his dotage, has forgotten
Eliot's field, and asks him what he does. "Law," Eliot
replies. "I congratulate you," remarks the senior fellow, with
what must be mild disdain.[655] Even so, there is a realization
on the part of his college colleagues that the fact that Eliot
is a successful practicing barrister is good for their law
students,[656] so that Snow prefigures the eventual American
acknowledgement of the value of teaching aspiring lawyers
by clinical practitioners.[657]

Perhaps most important is a subtle underlying theme
of *The Masters*, the position, the eminence, and the social
duty of the fellows of the college, both in electing their
master, and in serving England. As the most respected
educators in the realm, they, according to Snow felt "a
profound comfort to be one of a society completely sure of
itself, completely certain of its values, completely without
misgivings about whether it was living a good life."[658] The
narrator (Eliot) states that he had "the luck to live
intimately among half a dozen different vocations," but in
words vaguely reminiscent of those of Duncan Kennedy that
were quoted in the Introduction, "Of all those I had the
chance to see, the college was the place where men lived the
least anxious, the most comforting, the freest lives."[659]

The Fifth book in the series, *The New Men*,[660] is an
extraordinary study both of interpersonal relationships and
of disciplinary contrasts. At one level it is a story of Lewis

---

[655] *Id.*, at 259.

[656] *Id.*, at 130.

[657] On the controversy over how law students should now be taught, see,
e.g., Chapter 4, examining Langdell's innovation of teaching lawyers by
academics rather than practitioners, and compare Chapters 14 (Critical Legal
Studies), and Chapter 19 (Paul Carrington), *infra*.

[658] *The Masters, supra* note 624, at 344.

[659] *Id.*, at 345. For Duncan Kennedy's words, see text accompanying note
4, *supra*.

[660] C.P. Snow, The New Men (Charles Scribner & Sons, 1954).

Eliot and his younger brother by nine years, Martin. Lewis had earlier been a law don, but is now a high official in a government ministry, as World War II begins to come to a close. Martin is a scientist, and has lived his life in Lewis's shadow, although Lewis has high hopes for him. "The New Men" of the title refers to the scientists, like Martin, who are laboring to produce an atomic bomb before the Germans, so that the apparently interminable and horrific ongoing war can be ended on terms favoring the allies. Martin, through Lewis's efforts, gets assigned to work on the atomic bomb project, at the government installation called "Barford," although both Lewis and Martin cannot believe that any decent government would ever use such an horrific weapon.

There is something of a curious naiveté about the scientists, particularly Lewis's old colleague from his days as a don, Walter Luke, a young idealist of dazzling talent. Luke, like the others, loves the purity of science, in particular its unvarnished search for truth, but the scientists' consciences are ripped asunder because they realize that, on their bomb project, they may be sowing the seeds of huge human destruction and disaster. Perhaps they trust themselves to be able to persuade their government not actually to use the bomb. To their dismay, however, before these English scientists are finished producing a workable atomic weapon, the Americans produce two, and proceed to drop one on Hiroshima and one on Nagasaki. Both Eliots and Walter Luke cannot believe any sane government can have participated in such human butcherage, even to end a war, and especially since they think the threat of the use of the bomb (after a suitable demonstration without human damage) should have been enough.

From another perspective, the book is about wartime affairs spiraling out of control. As a marvelously drawn minor character, the punctilious but superbly astute senior civil servant Hector Rose, puts it upon learning that the Americans are likely to drop an atomic bomb on the Japanese, "There are times when events . . . get too big for men."[661] The book then, is, to a certain extent, the old tale of man's inhumanity to man, but it is also about human failures of a different kind. The entire series is entitled *Strangers and Brothers*, and raised by this book is whether even brothers must, ultimately, remain strangers to one another. Lewis Eliot's brother Martin eventually turns down the extremely prestigious position of director of the bomb-producing project, at Barford, at that point the nation's most important scientific endeavor, the position that Lewis had encouraged him to accept, and one which would, quite simply, go far in fulfilling the ambitions that Lewis had for Martin, as his somewhat doting older brother. But Martin, unlike Lewis, wants only a quiet life in the academy, where he will not be faced with the participation in such a damnable activity as the manufacture of a nuclear arsenal. In a way, this is a repudiation of everything Lewis believes in, since he has left the rather more contemplative life of a law professor, for that of a man of affairs.

Martin finds happiness as a don, and Luke, accepting the position that Martin spurned, unexpectedly flourishes as a bureaucrat. A powerful subtheme in the book is the love affairs of the protagonists. Martin, against Lewis's advice, marries a gorgeous woman with a shady reputation, and, while Lewis tells him she'll ruin Martin's life (a woman, Sheila, Eliot's wife, has, as indicated, already done that to him—or so he thinks at this point), Martin's wife, Irene, resists temptation from an old lover, brings Martin happiness, and gives Luke a son whom they name, of course, "Lewis."

---

[661] *Id.*, at 148.

The New Men further paints the law professor Lewis Eliot, now the governmental functionary, as a deeper person than he outwardly seems. There are some odd characteristics that Lewis shares with his brother, Martin. "We were both," Lewis explains, "evasive, reticent men, who used irony to cheat out of its importance the moment in which we breathed. . . ."[662] One character in the book, comparing Lewis to Martin, says "I always thought you [Lewis] were more heavyweight than he [Martin] was—but that he was the finer man."[663] Luke calls Lewis a "wise old man,"[664] and a "cunning old dog,"[665] but as Lewis himself puts it, he was a "liberal minded man,"[666] and "I passed as a realistic man. In some senses it was true. But down at the springs of my life I hoped too easily and too much."[667] Just as Paul Carrington would later write that a law professor must harbor what Carrington called the essentially "romantic" hope to pass on to his or her students that the lash of power can be wielded with some restraint because of the rule of law,[668] so does Lewis Eliot harbor a similar essentially romantic hope that shows up in his relationship with his relatives and his colleagues. But *The New Men* leaves one wondering whether the job of a law professor is as noble as it ought to be. When Martin chooses an academic career over an important governmental position, Lewis muses that Martin's critics would say that his choice "had been stupid: he would stay there, doing his college teaching, without a realistic chance of achievement for the rest of his life."[669] Is Eliot telling us that perhaps to have chosen to

---

[662] *Id.*, at 269.

[663] *Id.*, at 226.

[664] *Id.*, at 55.

[665] *Id.*, at 160.

[666] *Id.*, at 259.

[667] *Id.*, at 45.

[668] See Chapter 19, *infra*.

[669] *The New Men*, *supra* note 660, at 279.

remain a law professor would have been equally "stupid?"
This is a question the rest of the novels implicitly address.

The pivotal sixth book in the Series, *Homecomings*,[670]
is quite a bit different from the rest. There is almost nothing
about Lewis's academic life, or even, really, his legal life.
Most of it takes place during and immediately after World
War II, and it is almost wholly about Lewis's personal life,
specifically his two marriages, and, more generally, how he
evolves as a person. He marries his first wife, Sheila, almost
on a whim, knowing that she is hopelessly neurotic and self-
centered, that she doesn't love him, and that she is
marrying him only because she sees no better alternative.
This is because of all the people she knows, she feels
comfortable only with Lewis. Sheila is the daughter of a
provincial parson and his rich wife, and she has very little
regard or connection with either parent. Her father, the
Vicar, is a vain hypochondriac, and while her mother tends
to her father's every complaint, there seems not much love
between mother and daughter. Whatever Sheila needs,
however, Lewis is unable to supply, probably because there
is simply something missing in Sheila herself, but also
possibly because a core of Lewis finds it impossible to open
up and simply accept love when it is offered.

Sheila believes that something in her head literally
snaps, and she determines, without telling Lewis, that she
can no longer go on. She deliberately overdoses on sleeping
pills, committing suicide when Lewis is spending the night
at his club, after a dinner with one of his civil servant
colleagues. Lewis is devastated, but now, for the first time
in years, is free of the need to care for Sheila and her moods,
and his career in the wartime civil service begins to take off.
One day, when Lewis is in hospital with lumbago, the same
colleague with whom he was out to dinner when Sheila died

---

[670] C.P. Snow, Homecoming[s] (Charles Scribner & Sons, 1956)
(originally published as "Homecoming," now appearing as "Homecomings.").

brings a guest to visit him, a lovely young woman named Margaret Davidson, the daughter of an immensely famous left-wing art critic, Austin Davidson. Margaret is everything Sheila wasn't—outgoing, self-confident, warm and caring, and, most importantly, comfortable in her own skin. Lewis falls in love, but, tragically, breaks up with Margaret when it becomes clear that he simply cannot overcome his reluctance to open up to other people, to let go his tight self-control, and actually to allow himself the relief of human vulnerability.

Margaret bounces back from the break-up with Lewis, marries a fine pediatrician, Geoffrey Hollis, and has a son, Maurice. Then, to the reader's great surprise, Lewis suddenly decides that he cannot live without Margaret, whom he has never stopped loving, and, somehow he convinces Margaret to divorce Geoffrey (who has never done her any wrong, but who is much less brilliant and interesting than Lewis), and marry him. Lewis convinces Margaret that he has learned from his mistakes, and assures her that he will be the more open, less reserved husband she has always wanted him to be. Influenced in part by Margaret's father, who explains that one can't help who one loves, they make a go of it, although (understandably) the spurned Geoffrey is somewhat embittered by the experience, and the new spouses are not without some residual guilt at the happiness they achieve, at Geoffrey's expense.

Lewis and Margaret even have a son together, whom they name Charles George Austin Eliot, after Lewis's friend Charles March, Lewis's friend George Passant, and Margaret's father. All is almost impossibly idyllic until their son develops what they believe is influenza, and is so diagnosed by Charles March, who is serving as his doctor. But March has misdiagnosed meningitis, and little Charles Eliot nearly dies, and is saved only when Geoffrey Hollis,

Margaret's divorced husband, is called in, who takes the appropriate steps and saves Lewis's and Margaret's child. The volume descends into pot-boiling melodrama at this point, but Snow is such a splendid writer that the reader doesn't really mind, as Lewis, fearing the death of his son, at first is inconsolable by Margaret and rejects her loving kindness, lapsing into his old walled-in self, but then, somehow, right before they learn that little Charles is going to make it back to health with no ill-effects, Lewis has an epiphany, the walls of his self-protection fall, and he is capable of finally opening his heart wholly to Margaret. For the first time in his life, it would seem, Lewis gains happiness and true love.

It might seem that this sixth novel has little to do with our study of law professors, but perhaps there is something to be learned here, that the kind of extraordinarily-focused absorption Lewis shows in everything he does detracts from his actual humanity. In simpler, stranger, less politically-correct times we used to tell law students that the law was a "jealous mistress," by which was meant that when you study, practice, and, it would seem, teach, law, virtually everything else fades in importance.[671] Perhaps C.P. Snow is reminding us that professional devotion is not all there is to human happiness, and something more (love(?) hope(?)) is needed. This may be something that the wisest law professors, such as Paul Carrington, understand,[672] though, perhaps, not all, and, until his time of crisis, this was not grasped by Lewis Eliot. But eventually it was, and like his creator, C.P. Snow, he moves on from a soul-crushing first

---

[671] See Karl Llewellyn's seeming acknowledgement of this in Chapter 8, *supra.*

[672] See Chapter 19, *infra.* See also the display of similar insight on the part of the Critical Legal Studies scholars, Chapter 14, *infra.*

marriage to something about as close to bliss as humans can achieve in his second.[673]

Homecomings is flush with intriguing secondary characters as well as the very clear delineation of the despair and triumphs of Lewis's first and second marriages. Sheila's and Margaret's fathers are contrasting studies in proper parenting, and Margaret's happily married, though childless, sister Helen is a great support to Margaret, while Sheila's status as an only child suggests another source of unhappiness for her. George Passant puts in a brief appearance, as he is hired for three years to work under Lewis at Whitehall, but the punctilious and super-competent civil servant Hector Rose believes George is too big risk to keep on permanently, and George is sent packing back to his provincial life. Here again, the law professor must learn to live in reduced circumstances, but curiously, just as Lewis learns to be happier, so does George, who leaves the ministry with his self-regard higher, even as he returns to professionally lower circumstances.

The Seventh book in the series, *The Conscience of the Rich*,[674] is also a bit of a departure from the others. The principal subjects are an extraordinarily-wealthy Anglo-Jewish banking family, the Marches, who bear a glancing relationship to the Rothschilds.[675] The book takes us back in time to the beginning of Lewis's legal career, the period shortly after the end of World War I, when Lewis meets the brilliant scion of the March family, Charles, who becomes

---

[673] For the manner in which Lewis Eliot's second and happier marriage does and does not correspond to Snow's own second and happier marriage (to the novelist Pamela Hansford), see generally John Halperin, C.P. Snow: An Oral Biography 247–269 (The Harvester Press, 1983) (A conversation with Lady Snow (Pamela Hansford Johnson), 22 February 1980).

[674] C.P. Snow, The Conscience of the Rich (Charles Scribner & Sons, 1958).

[675] See generally, Halperin, *supra* note 673, at 68–69, where it is indicated that the March family is based on an English Jewish family of merchant bankers and stock brokers with ties by marriage to the Rothschilds.

one of his best friends, in the course of studying to pass the
bar, and eventually to be taken into a barrister's chambers.
The family also intersects with Lewis's life as Charles's
sister, Katherine, marries Francis Getliffe (who is not
Jewish—and that fact is a cause of much concern to the
March family), a science don at the Cambridge college,
where, with his help, Lewis will eventually become a law
professor. Most of the book is devoted to the relationship
between Charles's father, Leonard, and his children,
Charles and Katherine. Leonard or "Mr. March," as he is
usually called, is one of Snow's great characters. He is
domineering and blustering, yet he regards himself as
something of a failure, because even though he manages
great wealth (mostly accumulated by earlier generations of
the family) he retires early, and spends his time presiding
over family gatherings and worrying about minute details
of catching trains and operating a London and a country
house.

In the book Leonard March is dealt two crippling blows.
One is when Katherine marries outside the faith, and the
other is when Charles decides to give up the practice of law,
and become a doctor. Strangely, it is the latter which cuts
far deeper, as it turns out that all of Leonard's frustrated
hopes for fame and success, now placed in Charles, will
never come to fruition. Leonard never matched the
accomplishment of his brother, Sir Philip March, a
Parliamentary Secretary, and candidate for a ministry, and
while Leonard loves his brother Philip (and the rest of his
family) this, nevertheless, smarts. (Much of this intriguing
novel is a study of envy, as well as a study of frustrated
love). Leonard finally grudgingly accepts the gentile Francis
as a valued member of the family, but somehow, perhaps
because it is too great a blow to his ego, he is never
reconciled to Charles's decision, which denies him the
realization of his hopes for his son.

Even more damaging to the father-son relationship is Charles's choice of wife, Ann Simon, who Jewish and is also rich, and devastatingly beautiful, but, somehow, a member of the Communist party, and a person committed to the eventual overthrow of the established order. It is Ann's politics which lead to a final breach between Charles and the rest of his family, when a party publication, *The Note*, moves ahead with an exposé on insider trading peripherally involving Sir Philip March and Francis's brother, Lewis's old chief, the irascible barrister, Herbert Getliffe. Ann indicates to Charles (through Lewis, when she is gravely ill, and confides in him) that if Charles wants it to happen, she will reveal information that will shut down *The Note* and stop the publication of the story damning to the March family.

In effect, Charles is forced to make a choice between furthering Ann's politics or protecting his family's reputation. A choice really between his father and his wife. Exercising the perhaps ironically-titled "Conscience of the Rich" (which Charles has already done by giving up a lucrative career at the bar and in affairs), he chooses his wife's interests over the rest of his family's, thus causing a permanent breach between himself, his father, and his sister Katherine. Mr. March and Katherine now refuse ever to see Charles again. His father, using the only means in his power, in a vain attempt to bring Charles to heel, cuts off his inheritance. Charles will now be a relatively poor man, but one clear in conscience, and one, Snow seems to suggest, at least partly owing to this fact, happy in his marriage and his career.

Lewis's role in this book is clearly peripheral, but from his early days at the bar, he is taken into the March's world, first simply as a friend of Charles (one of the few non-Jews (Francis is the other) drawn into the family fold), then later as a trusted advisor to both Leonard and Sir Phillip, as they unsuccessfully maneuver to avoid the taint of scandal. Charles is expelled from the family, but Lewis is invited to remain an occasional guest, and, except for friction with Francis when he and Lewis disagree over the choice of a master for their college, Lewis remains a close March family confidante and friend.

Precisely how *Conscience of the Rich* can be made to be seen as a parable of the life of a law professor is challenging, but perhaps it is something of a rumination on the connection of law professors with both wealth and morality, or as Snow calls it, in this volume, "conscience." Lewis is impressed with the opulence of the Marches, and also with the choice that Charles makes to favor his wife, Ann (whom Charles dearly loves), over his father. Lewis, after all, had an ambivalent relationship with his parents and brother, and is, at this time, locked in a marriage with the neurotic Sheila, whom he adores, but who gives him virtually no emotional support. Lewis is also on the left in politics (at this time against the fascists in Germany and in the Spanish Civil War, and, quite possibly, in favor of major change in the distribution of wealth and power in English society), and, to an extent, is living through Charles's family's activities, not only the attack on wealth, on the part of Ann, but the preservation of wealth on the part of the rest of the March family. This is a law professor divided against himself, displaying, perhaps, what Critical Legal Studies scholar Duncan Kennedy, will later call "the fundamental contradiction," a contradiction found in the very structure of the English Common Law and Blackstone's commentaries—a simultaneous commitment to individualism and altruism.[676] The choice of a Jewish family to demonstrate this contradiction and this agony of personal

---

[676] See generally Duncan Kennedy, The Structure of Blackstone's Commentaries, 28 Buffalo Law Review 205, 211–212 (1979) (Describing the "fundamental contradiction" as our need for others and our simultaneous need to be free from them).

choice is perhaps significant in light of the fact, as already observed, that for a time in the late twentieth century the American law professoriate was strikingly disproportionately Jewish.[677]

The Affair,[678] the eighth book in the series, though, like the others, a stand-alone novel, is a sequel to the fourth book, *The Masters*, which reveals what has happened to the principal characters of that book. Lewis Eliot, now a distinguished civil servant, returns to his Cambridge college, to help it extricate itself from a decision to terminate a young Fellow, Donald Howard, for scientific fraud. Howard's research conclusions, it appears, ultimately rest on data contained in a photograph that is proven to have been faked. Howard is, upon the College's learning of the fakery, sacked, but he maintains his innocence. Howard is not a likeable person (one of the Senior Fellows refers to him as "an unmitigated swine"),[679] and his communist and atheistic views don't help his relations with both the young and the older conservative and, in some cases, deeply religious, fellows. Still, some diligent research and thoughtful analysis, even by some of these more conservative fellows, including Francis Getliffe, and Lewis's brother Martin,[680] soon suggests that the falsified photograph may not have been produced by Howard, but rather by Howard's supervisor and mentor, a senior and exceptionally distinguished scholar.

The book, among its other many delights (like *The Masters*, it is a study in academic personalities, academic

---

[677] See note 495, *supra.*

[678] C.P. Snow, The Affair (Scribner's, 1960).

[679] *Id.*, at 19.

[680] Getliffe is now "Sir Francis" Getliffe, and Martin is well-ensconced among the movers and shakers of the College.

politics, and academic marriages[681]), is also a whodunit, with the reader left in doubt as to who is the actual miscreant, Howard or his mentor. As he did in *The Masters*, Snow demonstrates how coalitions and majorities are formed in an academic environment, and how class background, religion, and ideology may cause the Fellows to seek to shade the truth to be more in conformity with their prejudices. The principal theme of the book is justice, however, and to what extent academics ought to be able to put aside personal interest, prejudice, and ambition in order to achieve it.

Lewis Eliot, at the age of 48, who by now, though no longer a fellow, has gained the respect, if not necessarily the admiration, of the other fellows in the college,[682] and who, from humble provincial lower middle class beginnings, is now regarded as intensely clubbable,[683] is asked by the Master, Crawford, carefully to review the evidence against Howard, and to argue the case before the Court of Seniors (the oldest fellows, acting in a judicial capacity, to determine whether a wrong has been done against Howard, and whether he should be reinstated). Other members of the Court of Seniors are Arthur Brown, now the Senior Tutor and Lewis's onetime ally in his efforts to select a Master (ultimately unsuccessful), Nightingale, Lewis's old enemy (and a Fellow suspected of framing Howard), and Winslow, an undistinguished, somewhat embittered, but ultimately fair-minded man.

---

[681] It includes the intriguing suggestion (drawn from Snow's experience) that intellectuals are more interested in sex than are businessmen, though the latter think the former are less interested. *The Affair, supra* note 678, at 147.

[682] One of the younger Fellows describes Lewis as "frightfully important" and a "powerful and slightly sinister figure." *Id.*, at 4.

[683] The college Master, Crawford, with what appears to be pride, tells Lewis that he had "heard talk" of him at "the club," referring to the Athenaeum, on London's Pall Mall, the pinnacle of social academic achievement in his world. *Id.*, at 79.

Much of this volume, which could also be regarded as a courtroom drama, is taken up by the actual hearing before the Court of Seniors, when Lewis must match wits with Dawson-Hill, the superbly socially-connected, vain, and dashingly handsome barrister who achieved the success at the bar Lewis never managed, who views Lewis with mild disdain, but who fails to best him in the argument before the academics. Still, Dawson-Hill, towards the end of the book, performs a random act of kindness which suggests that he may be ultimately a finer and more generous man even than Lewis.

The book is about injustice, as well, and its title is drawn from the notorious Dreyfus affair,[684] but it is also a book about personal ambition, incivility and disloyalty, traits of profound importance for Lewis, and, by extension, for Snow. It is also about how academics are complex characters, with deeply ambivalent feelings, so that, for example, the rather selfish and despicable Howard, even though he may have been wronged by the college, still demonstrates a bit of selflessness and nobility as he refuses to air its dirty linen in public by taking his dispute to the law courts.[685] A strong subtheme, found in many of the other *Strangers and Brothers* novels as well, is the post-war replacement of the English world of class privilege and social stratification with an emerging new order based on intelligence and merit.[686] Snow (like Lewis Eliot) is not at all certain that something, however, is not being lost in the transition.

---

[684] As revealed by Snow in an "Author's Note," at the beginning of the book, which also makes clear that the theme of the book is "justice." Snow also indicates that "For the scientific fraud, I have drawn on the picturesque case of Rupp."

[685] *The Affair, supra* note 678, at 241–242.

[686] See, e.g., *id.*, at 78.

It is uncertain whether the lesson of the book is that ambition ought to be less important than other traits, and that, in particular, loyalty, civility, and tradition are more important than truth and justice, or if, instead, all of these features of personality and culture ultimately are essential and do all flow from the best of the English character. This English character does appear to be one for which justice is the most important of the virtues, it is a character Lewis Eliot aspires to, and, more often than not, demonstrates in this book. This presentation of Lewis Eliot is the law professor, like Kingsfield,[687] with professional flair, with Olympian detachment, but in Lewis's case, with unshakeable attachments to his college, his friends, and to his family. Lewis's devotion to justice, the foundation of law, is put to the test, as competing pressures of family, friendship, and politics play out in the course of the novel. *The Affair* is generally regarded as one of Snow's great successes, and the reader is dazzled by the fact that Snow, the author of the phrase "The Two Cultures,"[688] is able to illuminate, explicate, and criticize both the values of Snow's own culture, science, particularly the values of disinterested pursuit of knowledge and truth from that discipline, and the tenets of his law professor creation, Lewis's legal culture, with its values of tradition, order, morality and justice. Brilliantly, Snow shows how passion, politics, duplicity, self-interest and altruism, exist and are in tension in both cultures.

The Ninth book in the series, *The Corridors of Power*,[689] is the title that C.P. Snow contributed to the Anglo-American store of clichés, but as he acknowledges in an author's note, cliché or not, it does describe a reality of contemporary politics, and this novel is another case study

---

[687] See Chapter 13, *infra.*

[688] See note 621, *supra.*

[689] C.P. Snow, Corridors of Power (Scribner's, 1964).

in ambition. It is the story of a modern politician, the dashing Roger Quaife, who, when the book begins is "a youngish Conservative member who was beginning to be talked about." Quaife is handsome, substantial, a shrewd judge of character, and, in the course of the book, quickly rises to junior Minister status, and seems destined, eventually, for something even bigger, perhaps Prime Minister or, at least, Chancellor. Lewis Eliot clearly admires Roger, and soon becomes his confidante, or, perhaps, *eminence grise.* By now, the mid-fifties, Eliot has risen high in the Civil Service, and has received his knighthood, though he is still a rung below the supercilious and powerful uber-civil-servant, Hector Rose, whom Eliot continues somewhat to disdain, but with whom he must still do business, and to whom he accords a grudging respect, particularly as they find themselves allies (though not close friends) in the pursuit of Roger's eventual agenda.

This agenda, with which Lewis soon becomes quite publicly associated, is to dismantle Great Britain's nuclear arsenal, and, in the course of so doing, Quaife hopes, reduce the threat of nuclear proliferation, and thereby maximize the chances that humankind will escape a devastating nuclear holocaust. It is not the least accomplishment of the book that it effectively recalls a period both in Britain and the United States when it was believed the fate of humanity was hostage to nuclear weaponry, and that the globe could be incinerated by political mistakes at any time. Snow paints this attitude of Quaife's as exceptionally noble, particularly for a political conservative, and this particular politician's pursuit of nuclear disarmament as the epitome of moral courage and the enlightened use of stunning political talent. Lewis Eliot buys into it completely, and devotes himself to rallying the scientific, academic, social and political community behind Quaife.

This plot enables Snow to reprise his cast of Cambridge characters, particularly Walter Luke, Francis Getliffe, and Lewis's brother, Martin, all of whom join Lewis in his efforts, and stake their growing reputations on Quaife's policies and personality. And the repainting of the Cambridge world is not the only return to standard themes for Snow. What makes the book extraordinary, however, is that Quaife, presumably the epitome of political moral perfection, is, in his personal life, something quite a bit less. When the book begins Quaife is married to the dazzling, charming, and aristocratic Lady Caroline ("Caro"), and the handsome couple cut a fine figure in the salons of the hereditary aristocracy and the politically powerful, whose world is again nicely limned by Snow. Seemingly inexplicably, however, given the lineage, beauty, wit, intelligence, and indeed loyalty of his own wife, Caro, Quaife is revealed to be carrying on a love affair with Ellen Smith, the married wife of a high Tory Minister's nephew.

Just as Quaife's disarmament policy moves toward a crucial vote in the House of Commons, Ellen begins to get letters threatening to expose her affair with Roger and thus ruin him politically, letters presumably motivated by opponents of Roger's disarmament policy, quite possibly munitions manufacturers, who stand to lose fortunes if Roger is successful. This volume, like some of the others, again reads like a potboiler, as the reader is temporarily kept in the dark about what will happen to Roger, his marriage, his policy, and, indeed, the future of Great Britain. This ninth book is something of a masterpiece on many levels, among them Snow's dissection of how a politician becomes great, how his personality can magnify or diminish his ability to carry out policy, how marriages can endure, and the effect of sickness, health, thwarted ambition, and simple patriotism on the great and near-great. In the course of the narrative, Lewis Eliot loses one great friend, the ambitious Douglas Osbaldiston, who, though working for Roger, subtly sabotages him, while Lewis remains loyal to Quaife, even as Quaife and his policies politically and personally self-destruct. Roger, failing to achieve enough support for nuclear disarmament in a crucial vote in the House of Commons, tenders his resignation from the ministry, and, though he remains as a Conservative member of Parliament, it seems clear that Roger's once promising career is in tatters. Lewis Eliot, faithful to his friend Roger, and tarred by his association with Quaife's failed policy initiative, also resigns from the Civil Service, though Hector Rose persuades him to stay on for a few months, for appearance's sake.

Snow appears to make it clear that Quaife is a wise man, who recognizes that Britain's days as a Superpower are over, and its role in the world ought to be to demonstrate not the use of power, but rather moral superiority and foresight, but Quaife's fall is caused by the great number of British politicians (and their constituents) who simply don't get it. They refuse to face the reality of Britain's diminished world role, and they believe that they must maintain a nuclear arsenal to be regarded as an important nation with accordant influence. Snow hints, however, that Quaife's personal foibles and his affair with Ellen undercut his effectiveness, and may have imperiled civilization as well as his personal career. Lewis Eliot, the failed barrister, and now failed civil servant, remains faithful both to Roger and to Ellen whom Roger marries after he divorces Caro. He, like Lewis in his second marriage (and like Snow), enters into a conjugal relationship that is deeper and more satisfying. In one more irony, the industrialist super-tycoon Paul Lufkin, who once employed Lewis Eliot, and who backed Roger, even though Lufkin's own financial prospects were imperiled by Roger's disarmament policies, sees that Roger's blackmailer is professionally punished, and sees that Roger, though now bereft of Parliamentary influence, still collects two or three industrial directorships that provide Roger the means to carry on. Even so, Roger is now deprived of the aristocratic wealth and glamour which were his when he was married to his former wife, Caro. This might well be a statement by Snow that industrial power is now more prominent in Great Britain than politics or aristocracy. The last two books in the series, bringing the story to the last third of the twentieth century, continue this study of political, industrial, academic, and personal risk, reward, and punishment.

Francisco José de Goya y Lucientes,
"The Sleep of Reason Produces Monsters"
No. 43, from Los Caprichos (1798).
Google Art Project.jpg.

The tenth novel in the series, *The Sleep of Reason*,[690] is another departure for Snow, and, probably, the most disturbing of the eleven. The title is taken from a famous Goya engraving, "The sleep of reason Brings forth monsters." The picture (reproduced above) is of a sleeping gentleman (likely the artist himself), and, as he dreams, monstrous owls and bats hover menacingly about him. The question posed by the novel is whether men of reason, such as the law professor Lewis Eliot, can live their lives free

---

[690]   C.P. Snow, The Sleep of Reason (Scribner's, 1960).

from evil and darkness, and Snow's answer appears to be a reluctant, "No."

In a way, the book is a tale of two law professors, as Lewis is joined again by his former law teacher, George Passant, now retired, and living a somewhat reclusive life in their provincial home town. While George lives modestly, however, he has not abandoned his practice of cultivating the young, and encouraging them to live their lives free of the cant and restrictions of their elders. Snow broadly hints as well that George has continued to indulge his considerable libido by liaisons with younger women. The chief drama in the story is provided by George's niece Cora, and her friend Kitty Pateman, peripheral members of George's group of young acolytes. These two, Cora and Kitty, may or may not be involved in a lesbian romance. It is not their romance, however, which drives the plot, but rather their monstrous activities. They decide, for reasons that are never entirely clear, to kidnap, torture, and eventually murder an eight-year-old boy. Most of the book is consumed with the investigation and trial of the young women, and Lewis's and George's reaction to the proceedings.

In the course of their trial the women raise the relatively new English criminal defense of what we Americans would call "diminished capacity," hoping to convince the jury that while they did the horrid acts of which they are accused, at the time they lacked the responsibility for their own actions. The defense eventually fails, they are found guilty, and sentenced to life imprisonment (although it appears that they will probably serve for only about 10 years).

This book appears to contain the suggestion that George Passant's philosophy of liberty, which, we were reminded in the first volume, can lead to unprincipled license, has clearly done so in the activities of Cora and

Kitty. Upon the conviction of the girls, whom everyone in their home town appears to associate with George, Lewis's old mentor decides that he must leave England, and take up residence abroad, lest he be continually subject to ridicule and abuse for leading young people astray.

Snow appears to be suggesting that of the two, George, and Lewis, Lewis, because he has, throughout his life, tried to live closer to a code of personal responsibility, is the nobler individual, but it is the fate of Lewis, in the book, to be much less sure of himself, and to be drawn, strangely, to the horror of the trial, and the monstrous behavior of Cora and Kitty. Lewis rationalizes this by convincing himself that he is there to support his old mentor George, but Lewis shows up daily at the trial against the advice of his own son, Charles, who is just about to graduate from public (we Americans would say "prep" school), who believes that his father will tarnish his reputation by further association with George, and, by implication, with Cora and Kitty, the perpetrators of such horrific actions.

In addition to Lewis's usual examination of man's inhumanity to man (here the brutal acts of the young women), there is also a continuation of Snow's scrutiny of family life. Through the novel weaves the relationship of Lewis to his father, of Lewis to his son Charles and his step-son Maurice, and of Lewis to his brother Martin, and Martin to his son, originally named "Lewis," but who now calls himself "Pat." This is deep and convoluted stuff, and precisely what Snow is doing is elusive, but much of it, as in previous ruminations on Lewis, has to do with the extreme difficulty of giving and accepting love. In some relationships, such as that with his second wife, Margaret, this is easy for Lewis (though it was impossible with his first wife Sheila), but as the book unfolds, and as Snow parades characters from earlier novels almost in the manner of the last act of a Fellini film, we see how painful life can be for both Lewis, and for George. George never really accepts responsibility for his eccentricity (in an eerie parallel to the behavior of his niece and her likely lover who refuse to accept responsibility for the mayhem and horror they have perpetrated), while Lewis, if anything, takes on somewhat more responsibility than is his due.

This is evident when Lewis forces himself to visit Cora in her prison cell, offering his help, which is, more or less, refused. And it is even more evident when Lewis promises to be available to counsel Kitty Pateman's father, a monster himself (who may have spawned the monstrous aspects of his depraved daughter), who believes that the world has denied him the honors and advancement he believes he deserves, and who further believes that Lewis (though he has no influence or control that is relevant) somehow is frustrating Mr. Pateman's aims for his family. This includes not only his murderous daughter, but also a son tossed out of college for, of all things, fornication. Lewis helps the son find another college, but it's clear that the father has contaminated the son (as well as his daughter) with his dissatisfaction with the father's own lot in life.

A brief description doesn't really do justice to this book, which is an examination of the human condition similar to that undertaken by Balzac, to whose characters there are frequent references.[691] This is a novel of aspiration, ambition, and perversity, and yet, one which somehow still manages to affirm the goodness of life and the serendipity of events. In the book, Lewis is frustrated both by his

---

[691] Balzac's series of novels is known in French as *La Comédie humaine* (The Human Comedy), they depict French society, particularly that in Paris, from 1815 to 1848, following the restoration of the French Monarchy after the Revolution. The most famous is probably Honoré de Balzac, *Père Goriot* ("Father" or "Old Man" Goriot), written in 1835, which tells the story of an impecunious provincial, Eugène de Rastignac (whose ambition parallels that of Lewis Eliot) and a father, Goriot, who sacrifices to the point of destroying his finances to further the social pretensions of his daughters. Like *The Sleep of Reason*, *Père Goriot* is a tale of family relations gone sour.

relationship to his own father (with whom he has never been able successfully to connect), and by his inability to convince his nephew Pat (originally named "Lewis," but who now has rejected his uncle's name) to pay proper attention to a sweet village girl, Vickie, the daughter of the Vice-Chancellor of the local university on whose board Lewis serves. (Lewis was a student there when the local university was a provincial college). Vickie is herself loved unrequitedly by Francis Getliffe's son, who would be a much better match for her.

At the end of the book, in a series of strange turns, Lewis's father dies, but Lewis achieves some peace after he and his similarly-agnostic brother Martin arrange a proper parish church funeral for the old irascible man. The book ends with Martin announcing that Pat is engaged to marry Muriel, the daughter of Lewis's great and greatly troubled late friend, Roy Calvert, and that the marriage is to occur, among other reasons, because Muriel is pregnant with Pat's child. Martin is filled with joy, at the coming new generation, and Snow appears to imply that Lewis himself might be finding some solace.

The final novel in the series, the aptly-named *Last Things*,[692] is quite different from the penultimate book, which dealt with the darker aspects of humankind. *Last Things* is a rumination on the things we live for, and, in a sense, a final evaluation of many of the characters from the series. And yet, the metaphor of light and darkness, which glimmers in and out of the series, is still evident here. The event that starts the action in the book is Lewis Eliot's threatened loss of his eyesight, as one of his retinas detaches, and an operation fails to correct the condition. His treatments require Lewis to be temporarily blinded (by bandages) in both eyes, and he finds the temporary and

---

[692] C.P. Snow, Last Things (Scribner's, 1970).

perhaps permanent loss of sight, a life to be led in darkness, to be absolutely terrifying. Somehow it makes him face the possibility of death (the final "last thing?"), and he is plunged into a hopeless despair unlike anything he has ever experienced. And yet, strangely, when he doesn't die, and he lives through a night of sheer horror, hope creeps back in, and Lewis comes to face his past and future with a strange equanimity.

A second operation is a success, and while his sight is perhaps somewhat diminished, Lewis still has the use of his eyes, and can continue his activities, one of which, his writing, has begun to bring him into even more national prominence than his earlier receipt of a Knighthood. Sir Lewis now turns somewhat inward, to spend more time with the next generation, and, in particular, with his son with Margaret, Charles. Charles, like the young Lewis, is an idealist, and, while a huge academic success at Lewis's old Cambridge college (leaving the tantalizing question whether he will succeed his father as a fellow, and embark on a University career), Charles soon finds himself embroiled in the radical politics of the sixties, and equally embroiled in a relationship with Muriel, Roy Calvert's daughter, married in the last novel to Lewis's nephew, Pat. Muriel is one of the most enigmatic of Snow's women—she has her father's intellect and supreme self-possession, but she is spared Roy's terrible bipolarity. She is something of a beauty, and comfortably off as an heiress, with an elegant London townhouse. Curiously, Lewis finds her somewhat off-putting and scheming. She is several years older than Charles, and Lewis is not really sure his son's liaison with Muriel is wise, particularly since her politics might be even further to the left than that of his son.

In the course of a typical sixties take-over of university buildings at a London University, the student radicals are implicated in the disclosure of classified material regarding biological warfare. They, Charles among them, feel driven by their principles to reveal this governmental (in their eyes) misconduct, in an echo of Lewis's, Francis's, and Luke's opposition to the use of nuclear weaponry, in *The Corridors of Power* and *The New Men*. The purity of the students' idealism is contrasted in the book with the fact that their elders have been so apparently effectively co-opted by the system. Walter Luke and Francis Getliffe are in the House of Lords, and while they are men of the Labour party, they find themselves defending the government. Lewis turns down an appointment to the ministry (one also declined by Francis, but eventually accepted by Luke). Lewis thus manages to remain relatively untainted and finds himself in the unexpected role of advisor to his son, helping him to avoid disgrace that will short-circuit his son's promising career.

While all of this is going on, Lewis's beloved second wife's first son, Maurice, who stands for a sort of unselfish purity, for "goodness" in the last few books, who is unequipped for academic success, decides to devote himself to a career of serving the mentally disabled. Maurice marries Diana, a physically challenged and rather plain woman of exceptionally modest means (this, too, is presented as something of a noble self-sacrifice). Maurice's life is contrasted throughout the book with that of Martin's son Pat, a profligate, who squanders his talent in various schemes, and, as a result of his philandering, is divorced by Muriel. Pat also has a disconcerting (and disloyal) habit of leaking stories critical of his family to the newspapers, to Lewis and Margaret's distress.

As was true for *The Sleep of Reason*, this very brief summary of a part of the plot is inadequate to convey the rich texture of Snow's fiction, and his profound study not only of Lewis, but of a plethora of secondary and tertiary characters. There is also, woven within this texture, a fleeting commentary on other authors Russian, French, English, and even American who have explored the nuances of family life, a pantheon on which Snow has earned a distinguished place. Towards the very end of the book, Charles Eliot, perhaps prompted by a desire to live a life that will remove him from the shadow of his famous father, decides to leave Muriel and risk a career as a war correspondent. This is at first alarming to his mother and father, but, in the end, this gives his father, Lewis, not a little pride, and, even a touch of envy.

Lewis is then moved to ruminate on the three things he has wanted out of life since he was Charles's age, and growing up in a home where his mother had outsize ambitions for him. These three "hopes" as Lewis described them to "a girl who loved me a little," were "not to spend my life unknown: love: a better world."[693] In Charles's search for fame, his relationship with Muriel, and in his idealism, Lewis sees a three-fold mirror image of himself. The book ends, as Maurice and his wife Diana move to London, so that Margaret can assist with the birth of their daughter, who by all appearances is a healthy child. We don't learn what becomes of Charles, but in the last pages of this last volume, Lewis reaches a sort of accommodation with Muriel, who now trusts him to help keep open the possibility that she will get Charles back. We have the sense that Lewis himself, with a happy second marriage (to Margaret) with two loving sons, with a good relationship with his brother, Martin, albeit a shaky situation with his nephew, and with a solid career as a writer (and social critic), and creditable work as a law professor and a civil servant, has fully realized his three youthful hopes. The last book ends with the statement that Lewis now goes to sleep, not

---

[693] *Id.*, at 364.

focused on the end of his life, but rather "looking forward to tomorrow."[694]

Lewis Eliot's life in the academy not only shows the subtleties, the highs and the lows of academic personalities, but the novel series also reveals the personal intrigue and the occasional virtue of civil servants. Eliot's legal background apparently enables him to display a firm moral compass against which he measures his co-workers both in and out of the academy. Surrounded by the venal and the power hungry at Cambridge and at Whitehall, Eliot resists the temptation to corruption, and even though he reaches nearly the pinnacle of high government office, he spurns it, and seems fulfilled simply by virtue of his own virtue. Snow was not a lawyer, but, in the portrait that he draws of the law professor Lewis Eliot he brilliantly captured what Dean Carrington, criticizing Critical Legal Studies, was to call the "romantic" nature of the law.[695]

As indicated earlier, Snow is also famous for his writing that there were actually two academic cultures, one encompassing the hard sciences, such as physics, chemistry, biology, and astronomy (which were purportedly more objective because they dealt directly with the tangible facts of the real world) and the other encompassing the humanities and the softer "social sciences," including, for example, history, literature, and, perhaps, law. All of these social sciences formulated theories to categorize, regularize, and explain the workings of the real world, but none of them, really, could claim to prove their assertions by objective validation. Lewis Eliot's principal task may have been to bridge both cultures, and perhaps even to suggest how the law might function more objectively, if social scientists borrowed more from their colleagues in the hard

---

[694] *Id.*, at 380.
[695] See Chapter 19, *infra.*

sciences, just as Roscoe Pound,[696] and maybe even Wigmore[697] or Holmes,[698] believed.

That elusive notion, that the hard sciences can improve the law, probably has a lot to do with the current popularity of empirical studies in law schools. But still, the academic theories of such modern law professors as Barack Obama,[699] Bruce Ackerman,[700] and Cass Sunstein[701] may be more anchored in abstract and maybe even unprovable social science theories than they are in the realities of the hard sciences. For Snow, however, Lewis Eliot may have been a practical implementer of political and personal needs as much as he was a legal scientist. Snow's fictional English law professor was likely someone whose views were not that different from those, ultimately, of the greatest contemporary American legal academic pragmatist, Richard Posner.[702] The question of whether the law ought to be about implementing the pragmatic values of the judge or "neutral principles" of law, not really central to Snow, although perhaps touched upon by these novels, became in the American legal academy in the late nineteen-fifties, the most important jurisprudential issue, and it is the American argument for those "neutral principles" that we now examine.

---

[696] See Chapter 7, *supra.*
[697] See Chapter 6, *supra.*
[698] See Chapter 5, *supra.*
[699] See Chapter 23, *infra.*
[700] See Chapter 16, *infra.*
[701] See Chapter 22, *infra.*
[702] See Chapter 15, *infra.*

CHAPTER 11

ARE THERE NEUTRAL AND GENERAL PRINCIPLES OF CONSTITUTIONAL LAW?

MID-TWENTIETH CENTURY

Herbert Wechsler
(Columbia)

■ ■ ■

Herbert Wechsler (1909–2000)
Courtesy of Columbia Law School.

Herbert Wechsler co-wrote a brilliant casebook that is still one of the most important classroom texts on federal jurisdiction,[703] and he was reported to be one of the most outstanding law students at the Columbia University

---

[703] Hart & Wechsler, The Federal Courts and the Federal System (1953). The great federal judge, Henry Friendly, wrote of this text that it was "the most stimulating and exciting law book I had encountered since Wigmore's *Evidence*." Henry J. Friendly, In Praise of Herbert Wechsler, 78 Col. L. Rev. 974 (1978). For Wigmore, see Chapter 6, *supra*.

School of Law.[704] He served as the Editor-in-Chief of
Columbia's Law Review,[705] and later as the Director of the
American Law Institute.[706] He was, according to a
resolution passed by his colleagues at the Columbia Law
School, "the nation's most enduring theorist of law
reform."[707] This chapter though, will be devoted to a
consideration of Wechsler's writing, and while his law
school casebook on the federal courts was a monumental
achievement, for our purposes we can concentrate on one of
Wechsler's law review pieces. This work, which became one
of the most-frequently cited, and most controversial law
review articles in the twentieth century,[708] is *Toward
Neutral Principles of Constitutional Law.*[709]

  Neutral Principles was part of a dialogue that lasted for
several decades in the Holmes Lectures at Harvard Law

---

[704] One of Wechsler's Columbia law professors, Judge Harold Medina,
said of him, "[I]n my twenty-five years of teaching at Columbia Law School,
Herbert Wechsler was the most brilliant and stimulating of all my students."
Friendly, *supra* note 703, at 975 n.5.

[705] Resolution of the Faculty, May 12, 1978, reprinted in 78 Col.L.Rev.
947 (1978).

[706] *Id.*, at 948, the American Law Institute (ALI), is a highly-prestigious
association of judges, law professors, and lawyers who meet to suggest
revisions and commentaries on American public and private law. In particular,
the Institute promulgates "Restatements" of various doctrinal areas of the law
that attempt to summarize and regularize bodies of the common law.

[707] Resolution, *supra* note 705.

[708] Columbia Law Professor Kent Greenawalt said of this piece, in 1978,
that it "was almost certainly the most cited and most controversial discussion
of constitutional issues since World War II. . . ." Kent Greenawalt, The
Enduring Significance of Neutral Principles, 78 Col.L.Rev. 982 (1978). As late
as 2012, Wechsler's piece was reported to be the fifth most frequently cited law
review article of all time. Joe Palazzolo, "The Most Cited Law Review Articles
of All Time," The Wall Street Journal, Law Blog, June 1, 2012, http://blogs.wsj.
com/law/2012/06/01/the-most-cited-law-review-articles-of-all-time/ (accessed March
13, 2015).

[709] Herbert Wechsler, Toward Neutral Principles of Constitutional Law,
73 Harv. L.Rev. 1 (1959), reprinted in Herbert Wechsler, Principles, Politics,
and Fundamental Law 3 (Harvard, 1961).

School, evaluating the achievement of the Warren Court.[710] *Neutral Principles* is a tricky piece to classify. Legal Intellectual historian Herbert Hovenkamp has written that it was "intended both to defend and to limit the Supreme Court's counter-democratic decision in Brown v. *Board of Education.*"[711] Whatever the intention of the piece, however, it is difficult to over-estimate the impact of Wechsler's *Neutral Principles.* Henry Friendly, for example, stated in 1978 regarding the lecture that became *Neutral Principles,* "Professor Wechler's Holmes Lecture lifted the entire tone of scholarly constitutional discourse in our times."[712]

The decisions rendered by the United States Supreme Court, presided over by Chief Justice Earl Warren beginning in 1954, are some of the most dramatic developments in jurisprudence in the twentieth century. The Warren Court transformed the understanding of the Fourteenth Amendment to the Constitution, as a tool, through the incorporation doctrine, that could be used to give the federal courts supervision over matters of domestic policy that had heretofore been the exclusive province of the states.[713] These notable Warren Court decisions included,

---

[710] The Holmes Lectures, probably the most important ongoing lecture series in the American Legal Academy (of similar importance are the Storrs Lectures at Yale and the Rosenthal Lectures at Northwestern), are the result of a bequest to Harvard by Oliver Wendell Holmes, Jr. On Holmes, see Chapter 5, *supra.*

[711] Herbert Hovenkamp, The Opening of American Law: Neoclassical Legal Thought 1870–1970 307 (Oxford, 2015).

[712] Friendly, *supra* note 703, at 979. Friendly himself suggests that it "would be impossible to overstate what Professor Wechsler has contributed" to the activities of the American Law Institute, as executive director of the institute, tasked with the job of supervising its restatements of the law. *Id.,* at 980. Indeed, Friendly pulled out nearly all stops, explaining that Wechsler was "not simply a superb lawyer but a peerless man." *Id.,* at 981.

[713] The "incorporation doctrine" is the notion, expressed by a majority of the Supreme Court in several twentieth-century constitutional law decisions that the Fourteenth Amendment (which prohibits, in particular, actions by states that deprive citizens of the equal protection of the laws, due process, or

for example, the mandating of particular safeguards to protect criminal suspects from police over-reaching,[714] the redistricting of state legislatures so that only population could be a means of drawing boundaries,[715] the forbidding of mandatory Bible reading[716] and mandatory prayer in the public schools,[717] and the enforcement of racial integration in state educational and public recreational and

---

the privileges and immunities of United States citizenship) includes some or all of the safeguards provided for by the Bill of Rights (the first Ten Amendments) which nominally applied only against the federal government. The incorporation doctrine was once highly controversial, but now is pretty much accepted Constitutional law. Thus, for example, even though the First Amendment's explicit wording was that the federal legislature, "Congress," was to be restricted from infringing on freedom of speech and from interfering with the free exercise of religion and from making any law "regarding an establishment of religion," the Supreme Court, in the twentieth century, repeatedly declared that similar prohibitions ought to apply against State and local authorities as well. There have been many works exploring whether or not the framers of the Fourteenth Amendment did actually intend to "incorporate" the Bill of Rights against the state. For a recent provocative exploration of this question see Kurt T. Lash, The Fourteenth Amendment and the Privileges and Immunities of American Citizenship (Cambridge, 2014).

[714] See, e.g., Miranda v. Arizona, 384 U.S. 436 (1966) (holding that arrested suspects had to be informed of their constitutional rights, including a right to remain silent and to be assigned counsel, and that failure so to inform them might mean that any confessions obtained would be inadmissible), and Escobedo v. Illinois, 378 U.S. 478 (1964) (holding that criminal suspects have a right to counsel during police interrogations under the Sixth Amendment, and that the exclusionary rule (forbidding the use of evidence secured in violation of Constitutional rights) applied to the activities of state as well as federal officials), and Mapp v. Ohio, 367 U.S. 643 (1961) (earlier case indicating that evidence obtained in violation of the Fourth Amendment may not be used in state law criminal prosecutions in state courts, as well, as had previously been the law, in federal criminal law prosecutions in federal courts).

[715] See Baker v. Carr, 369 U.S. 186 (1962) (holding that the Court could review redistricting decisions by state officials), and Reynolds v. Sims, 377 U.S. 533 (1964) (holding that state legislative districts had to be roughly equal in population ("one man/one vote") in order to pass Constitutional muster).

[716] Abington School District v. Schempp, 374 U.S. 203 (1963) (school-sponsored Bible reading in public schools held to violate the First Amendment's establishment clause).

[717] Engel v. Vitale, 370 U.S. 421(1962) (holding that state officials who composed an official school prayer and encouraged its recitation in public schools violated the establishment clause).

transportation facilities.[718] No one in the nation really doubted that many of the members of the governments of the states, especially in matters of race, had discriminated against some of their people, but the Warren court's radical reorganization of state governments and practices was still unprecedented in our history, and was judicial legislation on a scale previously unforeseen.[719]

Wechsler was deeply disturbed by this development, and sought to articulate principles to restrain the judiciary,[720] while still allowing it to implement the values (e.g., against racial discrimination) that he thought were inherent in the Constitution. It is generally believed by Constitutional scholars that Wechsler's effort was a failure (albeit a noble one). Still, what Wechsler was trying to do was to preserve the rule of law in a time that he believed called for the Supreme Court creatively to implement longstanding Constitutional values. In some ways what Wechsler strived to achieve, insofar as he attempted to explain how the Court could conform to preexisting Constitutionally valid notions, was reminiscent of Langdell's efforts to find and promote the internal logic of the law,[721] and, two generations later, the same sort of jurisprudes who blasted Langdell had trouble with Wechsler.[722] What Wechsler started with his seminal law

---

[718] Brown v. Board of Education of Topeka, 347 U.S. 483 (1954) (Racial segregation in the public schools violated the Fourteenth Amendment's guarantee of the equal protection of the laws).

[719] For a fuller consideration of these developments, see, e.g., Stephen B. Presser, Recapturing the Constitution: Race, Religion, and Abortion Reconsidered (Regnery, 1994). See also, Matthew J. Franck, Against the Imperial Judiciary: The Supreme Court vs. the Sovereignty of the People (University Press of Kansas, 1996).

[720] For Felix Frankfurter's earlier efforts at such judicial restraint, see Chapter 9, *supra.*

[721] On Langdell see Chapter 4, *supra.*

[722] For a thoughtful description of the critics of Wechsler, and the suggestion, in particular, that Wechsler challenged the school of jurisprudence that sought to implement the ideas of Holmes and Pound calling for an activist

review article, based on his Holmes lecture responding to an earlier Holmes lecture by Learned Hand,[723] became an ongoing high-level debate about the nature of Constitutional law. This controversy continued with the 1968 Holmes lectures by Yale Law Professor Alexander Bickel and a 1971 law review article by United States Circuit Judge for the District of Columbia Circuit, Skelly Wright. These Holmes lectures, and the books and articles that resulted from them, are among the clearest and most provocative analysis of the extraordinary work of the Warren Court.[724]

Learned Hand, a judge on the United States Court of Appeals for the Second Circuit, in New York appears to be virtually universally recognized as one of the greatest American judges never to sit on the United States Supreme Court.[725] Like many conservatives from the bench and bar in the nineteen-fifties, Hand was deeply disconcerted by the

---

judiciary that would reformulate the law according to the social needs of the times, see, e.g., Anthony J. Sebok, Legal Positivism in American Jurisprudence 183 (1998). Sebok limns four critical responses. First, the "realist critics," who "rejected the concept of neutral principles in its entirety," second, the "internal critics," who simply argued that Wechsler had misunderstood the Warren Court's race cases, third, the "conservative critics," who transformed Wechsler's argument into an argument for "judicial restraint," and fourth, the "liberal critics," who attacked Wechsler based on their championing of the larger project of the Warren Court. *Ibid.*

[723] Friendly calls Wechsler's Holmes lecture, "a badly needed answer to the criticism [of the Warren Court] that Learned Hand had delivered from the same platform only a year before." Friendly, *supra* note 703, at 978.

[724] Hand's Holmes Lectures were published as Learned Hand, The Bill of Rights (Harvard, 1958), Wechsler's were later incorporated in a book, Herbert Wechsler, Principles, Politics, and Fundamental Law (Originally published by Harvard University Press in 1961, now available in a 2014 reprint from De Gruyter Company), Bickel's lectures were published as Alexander M. Bickel, The Supreme Court and the Idea of Progress (Yale, 1970, paperback edition 1978), and Skelly Wright's Law Review Article is J. Skelly Wright, Professor Bickel, The Scholarly Tradition, and the Supreme Court, 84 Harvard Law Review 769 (1971).

[725] See generally, Gerald Gunther, Learned Hand: The Man and the Judge (Oxford, 2010). As indicated earlier, the same is often also said about Henry Friendly.

pronouncements of the Supreme Court under Earl Warren. In a manner reminiscent of Sir William Blackstone's excoriation of the notion that judges should not make law,[726] Hand lashed out at the Warren Court Justices, whom he believed to be engaged in the wholesale reconstruction of Constitutional law, an effort that radically altered the meaning of that document. For the Justices to undertake such a task, Hand pleaded, was to take away from the American people their right to govern themselves. He argued that Justices should refrain, unless absolutely necessary, from overturning the acts of legislators or executives, since it was not the judge's job to change the law or to formulate policy. These tasks, Hand suggested, were for the more popularly-determined branches of the government, since ours, theoretically at least, was a republican form of government, one in which the people's elected representatives carried out their will, not one in which five unelected Ephors declared the law. Further, for Hand, it was the job of the Justices simply and sensibly to apply the original understanding of the United States Constitution, and not to improve upon it. Changes in constitutional law, Hand presumably maintained, should be effected, in accordance with the theory of popular sovereignty, by the Constitutionally-specified amendment process, and not by the Courts.[727]

This was too simple for Wechsler, for whom the judicial task involved more than slavishly following the understanding of the past. The great values embedded in the Constitution, Wechsler argued, did give the Justices

---

[726] See Chapter 1, *supra.*

[727] See generally, Learned Hand, The Bill of Rights, note 724, *supra.* The similarity of Hand's views on judicial restraint to Frankfurter's will be clear. See Chapter 9, *supra.* Hand added to Frankfurter's notion of "judicial restraint," however, the idea that Justices should interpret the Constitution only in accordance with its original understanding. On this notion see also the views of Justice Scalia, examined in Chapter 20, *infra.*

some license to implement those values in accordance with changes in American society. That license, however, could not authorize wholesale obliteration of other values in the document, and, thus, for example, the Constitution's value of equality could not simply be applied to trump its equally important value of freedom of association.[728]

Wechsler wrote at a time in American society when racial discrimination was still rampant, when the South still smarted from its treatment during the Civil War and Reconstruction, and when blacks in the South were widely perceived to be educated in public schools that were inferior to those available to whites. To the extent that Southern African-American children were deprived of the facilities necessary for a decent education, the injustice of the unequal situation was obvious, but, curiously, the United States Supreme Court, in its famous *Brown v. Board of Education* (1954) decision, the decision which found public school segregation by race to be unconstitutional,[729] grounded its conclusion of a Constitutional violation of equal protection not on a deprivation of equal educational facilities, but rather on the purported psychological damage done to black students by separating them from the whites. Said the Chief Justice in the key passage from the case, "To separate children from others of similar age and qualifications solely because of their race generates a feeling of inferiority as to their status in the community that may affect their hearts and minds in a way unlikely ever to be undone."[730]

---

[728] See generally Wechsler, *Neutral Principles, supra* note 709.

[729] Brown v. Board of Education, 347 U.S. 483 (1954).

[730] *Id.*, at 494. This was made even clearer in the Court's controversial Footnote 11, 347 U.S. 483, 495, n.11 (1954), where the Court observed that "Whatever may have been the extent of psychological knowledge at the time of *Plessy v. Ferguson* [the decision holding that "separate but equal" facilities were permissible in the provision of public transportation], this finding [that racial segregation is psychologically harmful to black children] is amply

Wechsler was one of the first to understand that the psychological underpinnings of *Brown* were weak, since segregation, at least insofar as it reduced racial tensions from forced association, could also foster a calmer environment more conducive to learning, and, indeed, segregated education might even (as some of its latter-day advocates have claimed) cultivate a sense of racial pride in African American children. Still, Wechsler understood that what the Court was actually pursuing was an assimilationist ideal for American society, much like that articulated only a few years later by Martin Luther King, Jr., that the color of a person's skin shouldn't matter, that the only important aspect of personhood was character.[731] But perhaps Wechsler also understood that America in the mid-twentieth century was not actually committed to that assimilationist ideal, and, perhaps never had been. Indeed, for Wechsler, even the Fourteenth Amendment itself could be read to preserve in the Constitution the ability of individuals to discriminate among persons with whom they chose to associate, on any basis they chose. For Wechsler, the Fourteenth Amendment, which provided that "no state" could deny its citizens the equal protection of the laws, meant, by implication, that while "no state" could

---

supported by modern authority." The text of Footnote 11 was "K. B. Clark, Effect of Prejudice and Discrimination on Personality Development (Midcentury White House Conference on Children and Youth, 1950); Witmer and Kotinsky, Personality in the Making (1952), c. VI; Deutscher and Chein, The Psychological Effects of Enforced Segregation: A Survey of Social Science Opinion, 26 J.Psychol. 259 (1948); Chein, What are the Psychological Effects of Segregation Under Conditions of Equal Facilities?, 3 Int. J. Opinion and Attitude Res. 229 (1949); Brameld, Educational Costs, in Discrimination and National Welfare (MacIver, ed., 1949), 44–48; Frazier, The Negro in the United States (1949), 674–681. And see generally Myrdal, An American Dilemma (1944)."

[731] From Martin Luther King's famous "I Have a Dream" speech, delivered 28 August 1963, at the Lincoln Memorial, Washington D.C. ("I have a dream that my four little children will one day live in a nation where they will not be judged by the color of their skin, but by the content of their character.")

discriminate on the basis of race, *any individual* was free to do so.

But, Wechsler recognized, in perhaps the most controversial part of his analysis, if individuals had a right to discriminate, *then it was the duty of American law to enforce that right.* This meant, for Wechsler, that there was a Constitutionally-guaranteed "freedom of association," which freedom permitted individuals to discriminate in their personal affairs, and even to associate with persons of whatever race they chose, excluding those with whom they did not wish to be associated. While this concept would, of course, be horrific to the politically correct of our era— remembering how a few years ago, Donald Sterling, because he did not wish his girlfriend to be seen with African Americans at basketball games was pushed out of owning his NBA franchise—it made sense to those, like Wechsler, living in an era where most Americans probably valued individual freedom more than racial equality.[732]

Thus it was that Wechsler could argue that the Supreme Court's decision in *Shelley v. Kraemer*,[733] in which the Court found a Fourteenth Amendment violation of equal protection when state courts enforced racially-restrictive

---

[732] On this purportedly constitutionally-protected value of freedom of association see generally, Ellen Frankel Paul, Fred D. Miller, Jr., and Jeffrey Paul, Freedom of Association (Cambridge University Press 2009), and my essay therein, Stephen B. Presser, Freedom of Association in Historical Perspective, originally published in 25 Social Philosophy and Policy 157 (2008). For Sterling's "rant" informing his African/American and Mexican girlfriend that he did not approve of her bringing African Americans to his basketball games, see, e.g., Brayden Goyette, LA Clippers Owner Donald Sterling's Racist Rant Caught On Tape: Report (UPDATES), Huffington Post, April 29, 2014, available on the web at http://www.huffingtonpost.com/2014/04/26/donald-sterling-racist_n_5218572.html (accessed 5 February 2016). For Mr. Sterling's loss of his NBA franchise, see, e.g., "Appeals court upholds $2 billion sale of Clippers," Associated Press, November 16, 2015, available on the web at http://espn.go.com/nba/story/_/id/14147968/donald-sterling-loses-appeal-reverse-2-billion-sale-los-angeles-clippers (accessed 5 February 2016).

[733] Shelley v. Kraemer, 334 U.S. 1 (1948).

residential covenants, made no sense, since by Wechsler's reading of the purported negative pregnant embedded in the Fourteenth Amendment, individuals were free to discriminate, and since Constitutionally preserved liberties ought to be preserved by the courts, it was the duty of the state and, presumably, even the federal courts, to enforce that discrimination.

The job of a court, for Wechsler, was to apply "neutral and general principles," which meant that the judge was *not* simply to pick the outcome he or she preferred and then implement it whether or not such an outcome was actually dictated by an unbiased (neutral) application of the existing law. Further, this "neutral" application of law was supposed to be stated in *general* terms enabling future judges to apply the same neutral principle to similar situations.[734] This, for Wechsler, as far as Constitutional law was concerned, was the essence of the rule of law itself.

It might be said, then, that Wechsler was the anti-Holmes. Unlike Holmes, Wechsler clearly did not believe that convenience or "policy" was the secret root which nourished judicial decision.[735] For Wechsler, it was not the job of the courts pragmatically to reformulate the law to make or to implement social policy, and thus his strong criticism of the Warren Court, even though he was at pains to show himself in sympathy with their liberal values, albeit not their iconoclastic methods. Wechsler couldn't bring himself, however, simply to embrace Hand's "original understanding" as a means of limiting the discretion of judges (a Constitutional hermeneutic that Supreme Court Associate Justice Antonin Scalia was later to champion as enthusiastically as Hand had done).[736] Apparently, unlike Scalia, Wechsler thought that, guided by Constitutional

---

[734] See generally, *Neutral Principles, supra* note 709.

[735] For Holmes, see Chapter 5, *supra*.

[736] For Scalia, see Chapter 20, *infra*.

values, there was some space in which judges could refit the document to meet the needs of the times, so that, perhaps, when all was said and done, Wechsler believed that the Constitution was a "living document." Still, when Wechsler tried to come to grips with the contrary principles he believed to be embedded in that document—for example, as already indicated, he believed that the Constitution embraced *both* the norm of equality (freedom from discrimination) *and* freedom of association—he was paralyzed. Perhaps this is why Wechsler's goal, to articulate neutral and general principles of Constitutional adjudication has come to be dismissed as utopian if not Panglossian.

Alexander Bickel, a Yale Law Professor, from the podium of the Holmes lectures about a decade after Wechsler spoke, taking a clear Holmesian turn, suggested that, when all was said and done, the work of the Warren Court will be judged by history, and the craftsmanship and the constitutional philosophy of the Court will be much less important than whether the policy aims of the Court accorded with the needs of the American people in the second half of the twentieth century. Bickel argued that the Warren Court's focus on centralization, equality, and legality were inconsistent with what Bickel believed the country desired, which was decentralization, diversity, and experimentation. The Warren Court's work, he argued (except for its advances in Criminal Procedure) was headed for irrelevance.[737]

Bickel's conclusion about the irrelevance of the Warren Court was sharply challenged by J. Skelly Wright, United States Circuit Judge for the District of Columbia Circuit, and a leading liberal on that important court. In a response to Bickel's Holmes lectures, which response Wright

---

[737] Alexander Bickel, The Supreme Court and the Idea of Progress (Yale, 1970).

published in the Harvard Law Review in 1971,[738] Wright suggested that Wechsler and Bickel, whom Wright labelled practitioners of the "scholarly tradition," were themselves sadly out of touch with the rising generation of law students, who found in the Warren Court inspiration and the articulation of the important American values "we all learned in high school." Rejecting what Wright apparently regarded as Bickel's amoral notion that history was to be the judge of the Warren Court, and rejecting what was for Wright an inappropriate focus on the craftsmanship of the Warren Court, Wright fully endorsed its work, and said that the decisions of the Warren Court ought, rather, to be judged by a standard of "goodness." For Wright, it met this standard, and, in particular, he praised the Warren Court for its progressive notions. Channeling Holmes, no doubt, Wright indicated that no Court could really articulate the kind of neutral and general principles Wechsler desired, that no Court ever had, and that if the Supreme Court had actually tried, they would have missed the vital opportunity they seized to lead the country in the direction the country needed to go. For Wright, Wechsler and Bickel were part of what he believed to be the discredited effort by conservatives begun by Edmund Burke, to turn back the clock and reverse the gains of the French Revolution.

Wright's law review article was a passionate performance, and a thorough result-oriented testimonial to the Warren Court. Wright's criticism of Wechsler's approach may not have been thoroughly fair, as Wechsler himself argued that he was not offering "a positive test, somehow injecting neutral principles with substance."[739] Wechsler's aim, as Laura Kalman has observed, was a much

---

[738] J. Skelly Wright, Professor Bickel, The Scholarly Tradition, and the Supreme Court, 84 Harvard Law Review 769 (1971).

[739] Laura Kalman, The Strange Career of Legal Liberalism 37 (Yale, 1996).

more modest one, not the setting forward of "a formula to guide or produce the decision of hard cases, but rather . . . a negative test, which would force the judge to ask himself, 'Would I reach the same result if the substantive interests were otherwise?' "[740]

Wechsler's "neutral principles" argument ultimately did not carry much weight with the majority of the Supreme Court. It is also not at all clear that his call for generality was one that could ever be successfully implemented. As one of his friendly critics, fellow Columbia Law Professor Kent Greenawalt, wrote, "The faculty of precise generalization is not a simple one to acquire and employ, even for able and experienced lawyers, and as the long history of criticism by other judges and academics evidences, no court escapes unscathed when its opinions are carefully dissected."[741] Moreover, one Warren Court historian, one closely associated with the critical legal studies school,[742] Morton Horwitz, citing the views of the "living Constitution's" most prominent exponent on the Warren Court, William Brennan, noted the ultimate futility of Wechsler's efforts:

> Reacting to the 'neutral principles' school of legal thought associated with [Felix] Frankfurter [and Wechsler], the Warren Court liberals understood that it was impossible not to incorporate one's deepest values into constitutional interpretation. In his later years, . . . Justice Brennan insisted that a 'balance of reason and passion' provided the best antidote to a kind of 'abstract rationality' that

---

[740] *Id.*, quoting Wechsler himself, as recorded in Norman Silber and Geoffrey Miller, Toward "Neutral Principles" in the Law: Selections from the Oral History of Herbert Wechsler, 93 Columbia Law Review 854, 925, 926–929 (1993). See *id.*, at 260 n.41.

[741] Kent Greenawalt, The Enduring Significance of Neutral Principles, 78 Col. Rev. 982, 1021 (1978).

[742] See Chapter 14, *infra.*

loses touch with 'the pulse of life beneath the official version of events.'[743]

But if Constitutional reason required passion to balance it,[744] and if abstract rationality was too divorced from judicial reality, how, then, to maintain the Constitutional ideal of the rule of law? One possibility was to suggest, as Ronald Dworkin did, that the problem, really, was more apparent than real, and that the Warren Court was not departing from the law at all, but was, instead, following something of a "higher law," a law of *principles* rather than *rules*, principles that flowed from the nature of the legal order itself.[745]

---

[743] Morton J. Horwitz, The Warren Court and the Pursuit of Justice 115 (Hill & Wang, 1998).

[744] For a provocative argument that at least since the time of Aeschylus the logic of the law needed to be supplemented with passion, see Paul Gewirtz, Aeschylus' Law, 101 Harvard Law Review 1043 (1988).

[745] In a way, this is what Horwitz seeks to do by suggesting that the Warren Court was explicating and articulating a view of democracy inherent in the Constitution that involved change over time as the culture shifted and as democracy came to require more social and political equality than that required at the Framers' time. See generally Horwitz, *supra* note 743.

CHAPTER 12

JUSTIFYING THE WARREN COURT

MID AND LATE TWENTIETH CENTURY, EARLY TWENTY-FIRST CENTURY

Ronald Dworkin
(NYU and Oxford)

■ ■ ■

Ronald Dworkin (1931–2013)
Taken at the Brooklyn Book Festival (2008) by David Shankbone.
Wikimedia Commons.

Ronald Dworkin's achievement was to defend the Warren Court through an appeal to something very much like "natural law." He was also notable as one of the few American law professors simultaneously to hold an appointment at a great English University, thus becoming something of an American Lewis Eliot.[746] Dworkin's

---

[746] For Lewis Eliot, see Chapter 10, *supra*.

English appointment was at Oxford,[747] and just as Blackstone trained a generation of English aristocrats at that university to implement Blackstone's notions of the English common law,[748] so it might be said that Dworkin's thought influenced a generation of English and American law students, law professors, and even judges, but in Dworkin's case, it was to implement a quite different style of legal exegesis. Blackstone believed that the judges' job was to follow the rules previously laid down, and, in a way, Dworkin conceived of the judicial task as similarly one of applying pre-existing law, although for Dworkin this pre-existing law consisted of *over-arching principles* inherent in the system of rules, and not necessarily any precise previously-articulated dictates. These *principles*, which, presumably, every sensible person would agree are inherent in the system of legal rules, include statements such as "no man may profit by his own wrong,"[749] or "everyone has the right to be treated with equal dignity and respect," and, as one commentator on Dworkin put it, "The origin of these principles lies not in the practical decision of some legislature or court but in a sense of appropriateness—often a sense of the moral appropriateness—developed in the legal profession and in the public during a considerable period of time."[750]

While Dworkin, who posited these purportedly clear pre-existing broad principles, could plausibly argue that his notion did not have judges actually making law, and thus

---

[747] "Oxford University, seeking the most incisive legal thinker it could find, appointed Dworkin, an American lawyer, to replace H.L.A. Hart as Professor of Jurisprudence." Marshall Cohen, "He'd Rather Have Rights," Book Review of Taking Rights Seriously by Ronald Dworkin [Harvard, 1977], New York Review of Books May 26, 1977 issue, available on the web at http://www.nybooks.com/articles/archives/1977/may/26/hed-rather-have-rights/ (accessed 11 March 2016).

[748] See Chapter 1, *supra*.

[749] See, e.g., Dworkin, Taking Rights Seriously, *supra* note 747, at 22, 46.

[750] Cohen, *supra* note 747.

his jurisprudence was consonant with our basic tradition that ours was a government of laws, not men, it was apparent, at least if one could take what the Warren Court did as an example, and an example of which Dworkin seemed to approve,[751] that Dworkin's jurisprudence gave considerable scope for judges to decide cases based on broad principles of *morality* rather than pre-existing rules of *law*. As Dworkin put it, summarizing his view of the Constitution:

> Our constitutional system rests on a particular moral theory, namely that men have moral rights against the state. The difficult clauses of the Bill of Rights, like the due process and equal protection clauses, must be understood as appealing to moral concepts rather than laying down particular conceptions; therefore a court that undertakes the burden of applying these clauses fully as law must be an activist court, in the sense that it must be prepared to frame and answer questions of political morality.[752]

Dworkin's approach all but sanctified what had been done by the Warren Court, which, of course, did believe that it was acting pursuant to morally appropriate principles—Earl Warren was famous, among other things, for disarming advocates who sought to argue their cases citing precedents or authorities by asking the simple question, "Yes, but is it fair?"[753] The Warren Court, and the theory

---

[751] Dworkin, Taking Rights Seriously, *supra* note 747, at 132 (indicating support for the Constitutional philosophy, "if not the particular decisions" of the Warren Court). For some discussion of those decisions see generally Chapter 11, *supra*.

[752] Dworkin, Taking Rights Seriously, *supra* note 747, at 147.

[753] See, e.g., "Earl Warren's Way: 'Is it Fair?' ", Time Magazine, July 22, 1974, at 66 (Obituary of Earl Warren) ("Warren's trademark on the bench was to interrupt a counsel's learned argument citing precedent and book with the simple, almost naïve question: 'Yes, but is it fair?' He believed that social justice was more important than legalisms: 'You sit up there and you see the

supporting it propounded by Dworkin, essentially opened the way for the achievement of the liberal, or, as we now call them, "progressive," political goals through the judiciary, such as, for example, the availability of abortion on demand,[754] the decriminalization of homosexuality,[755] and the sustaining of affirmative action.[756]

Dworkin's most impressive and influential work was probably his collection of essays originally published in elite law reviews and one journal of elite opinion, The New York Review of Books, gathered and published in 1977 as "Taking Rights Seriously."[757] Perhaps it is less than surprising that the reviewer for "Taking Rights Seriously" in the generally politically progressive New York Review of Books began his review by stating, "Ronald Dworkin's *Taking Rights Seriously* is the most important work in jurisprudence since H.L.A. Hart's *The Concept of Law* and, from a philosophical point of view at least, the most sophisticated contribution to that subject yet made by an American writer."[758] Two years

---

whole gamut of human nature. Even if the case being argued involves only a little fellow and $50, it involves justice. That's what is important.' "). A summary of the Time magazine article is available on the web, at http://content.time.com/time/magazine/article/0,9171,942946,00.html (accessed 7 August 2016).

[754] See, e.g., Roe v. Wade, 410 U.S. 113 (1973).

[755] Lawrence v. Texas, 539 U.S. 558 (2003).

[756] See, e.g., Grutter v. Bollinger, 539 U.S. 306 (2003).

[757] Ronald Dworkin, Taking Rights Seriously, *supra* note 747. It should be understood, however, that in his later work Dworkin did move beyond what might be described as the "political liberalism" which characterizes "Taking Rights Seriously," in order to argue that persons in society have *responsibilities* to themselves and each other, that should also be taken seriously. This might be most fully developed in Dworkin's later works, Justice for Hedgehogs (Harvard, 2011) and Life's Dominion (Knopf, 1993). See generally on this point, James E. Fleming, "Taking Responsibilities as well as Rights Seriously," 90 Boston University Law Review 839 (2010).

[758] Cohen, *supra* note 747. H.L.A. Hart became a Professor of Jurisprudence at Oxford University in 1952. The Concept of Law (Oxford, 1961) was his most famous book, and it set forth an essentially positivist conception of legal rules, suggesting that the legitimacy of such rules rested not on whether they agreed with substantive dictates of natural law, or

after Dworkin died, two Boston University law professors went even further, and suggested that "Dworkin is unmatched and unrivaled in legal philosophy and constitutional theory."[759]

Dworkin's notion that one ought to forswear rules for principles was hardly a new one, and, indeed, had been anticipated in America as early as 1908 by a man now generally regarded as a legal conservative, Roscoe Pound.[760] Still, Dworkin added a new spin to this old idea. Dworkin's legal philosophy, and, it would appear, his constitutional theory as well, heavily drew on the philosophy of John Rawls, the Harvard political philosopher,[761] who had worked out a system whereby the political goals of progressives seemed inherent in a purportedly objective theory of justice.[762] Rawls's argument in *A Theory of Justice*

"principles" of a kind suggested by Dworkin, but rather simply on their promulgation by a societally-approved lawmaker, such as a legislature. For a dazzling comparison between Dworkin's and Hart's jurisprudence, see Peter Gabel, Book Review [of Dworkin, *supra* note 747], 91 Harv.L.Rev. 302 (1977).

[759] James E. Fleming & Linda C, McClain, Dworkin's Perfectionism, Boston University School of Law, Public Law & Legal Theory Working Paper No. 15–45, at 1 (October, 2015). Available at http://www.bu.edu/law/files/2016/01/DworkinsPerfectionism.pdf (accessed 11 March 2016).

[760] See, e.g., Roscoe Pound, Mechanical Jurisprudence, 8 Col.L.Rev. 605, 622 n.69 ("To-day the principles are hidden by the mass of rules deduced from them, and, as these rules are laid down as and taken to be universal, not mere expressions for the time being of the principles, we have an administration of justice by rules rather than by principles. Legislative superseding of this mass of rules by well-chosen and carefully formulated principles seems to offer the surest relief.") To be sure, Pound was advocating use of "principles" by legislatures, while Dworkin was advocating use of "principles" by judges. For Pound, see Chapter 7, *supra*.

[761] See, in particular, Chapter Six of Taking Rights Seriously, *supra* note 747, at 150–183.

[762] For Rawls, see his massively-influential John Rawls, A Theory of Justice (Harvard, 1971). Rawls posited a "veil of ignorance," a hypothetical situation in which humans could meet, having no idea what position they would eventually assume in society, to be tasked with the formulation of optimal governing rules. *Mirabile dictu*, these more or less turned out to be the basic aims of liberal or progressive politicians in the late twentieth and early twenty-first century.

has been called by a leading intellectual historian of twentieth-century law, the "legal achievement" that "comes closest to matching the overwhelming impact of the most influential twentieth century school of legal thought, law and economics."[763]

As Dworkin summarizes Rawls's powerful argument, if the social contract were to be drawn up by rational men and women who were unaware of any particular pre-existing social position assigned to them, and were tasked with creating basic rules for governing society, even if they were to act only in their own self-interest:

> they will choose two principles of justice. These provide, roughly that every person must have the largest political liberty compatible with a like liberty for all, and that inequalities in power, wealth, and income, and other resources must not exist except insofar as they work to the absolute benefit of the worst-off members of society.[764]

These two "principles of justice" would seem to give considerable freedom to implement a regime which promoted individual desires, and, also, one that might well allow for great redistribution of resources, since the two principles seem to favor *equality* over *inequality*. For most of the late twentieth century, these liberal or progressive notions were nearly completely dominant in the American legal academy. In Rawls's conception, then, it might be accurate to suggest that these principles have the character of natural law—they are what rational men and women would objectively discern in the nature of society. Taken as

---

[763] Herbert Hovenkamp, The Opening of American Law: Neoclassical Legal Thought 1870–1970 319 (Oxford, 2015) (Hovenkamp writes that Rawls's "powerful anti-utilitarian argument for increasing expected welfare by improving the lot of the worst off was particularly influential in the 1980s and 1990s."). For Law and Economics, see Chapter 15, *infra*, on Richard Posner.

[764] Taking Rights Seriously, *supra* note 747, at 150.

a whole, then, what amounts to Dworkin's appeal to natural law for progressive ends furnishes a nice contrast with Blackstone's and Story's appeal to natural law for conservative ends,[765] and foreshadows, or perhaps complements, to an extent, what we will soon see as Richard Posner's appeal to a neutral economic natural law for pragmatic purposes.[766]

Instead, then, of examining the law as a series of concrete rules promulgated in detail by legislatures (the prevailing positivistic view of the law ostensibly maintained by such great legal positivists as Oliver Wendell Holmes, Jr.,[767] and H.L.A. Hart[768]), Dworkin argued that the essence of the judicial task was to discern the broader more abstract *principles* that were inherent in the system of legal rules, and to apply those principles in a manner that provided for the growth of the law to meet the needs of the times. As Dworkin later explained, commenting on the originalism and textualism of Justice Scalia,[769] Dworkin believed in a sort of "semantic-originalism," in which words used by legislatures or Constitutional conventions were "translated" in a "principled rather than a concrete and dated way."[770] By claiming that judges who applied principles were actually implementing content that was inherent in the already-existing rules (Constitution and statutes) Dworkin could plausibly argue that judges were not legislating, but were simply doing what was implied as the *intention* of the

---

[765] For Blackstone, see Chapter 1, *supra*, and for Story see Chapter 3, *supra*.

[766] See Chapter 15, *infra*.

[767] For Holmes, see Chapter 5, *supra*.

[768] For Hart, see H.L.A. Hart, The Concept of Law, discussed *supra* note 758.

[769] For Scalia, see Chapter 20, *infra*.

[770] Ronald Dworkin, Comment, in Antonin Scalia, A Matter of Interpretation: Federal Courts and The Law 120 (Princeton, 1997).

legislators (in statutes) or the American people (in the Constitution) themselves.

As Dworkin was later to explain it, "subject to the constraints of integrity which require judges to keep faith with past decision, 'The Constitution insists that our judges do their best collectively to construct, reinspect, and revise, generation by generation, the skeleton of freedom and equality of concern that its great clauses, in their majestic abstraction, command.' "[771] Indeed, for Dworkin, as one review of *Taking Rights Seriously* noted, "the courts must frame and answer the questions of political morality that the logic of the constitutional text demands. There is no alternative if we are to take constitutional rights seriously."[772] Or, as two quite sympathetic interpreters of Dworkin put it, "Dworkin's interpretive perfectionism takes the form of the 'moral reading' of the American Constitution: The Constitution embodies abstract moral principles rather than laying down particular historical conceptions, and interpreting and applying those principles require fresh judgments of political theory about how they are best understood."[773]

This "moral and principled reading of the Constitution," as Dworkin called it,[774] was, of course, precisely what the Warren Court purported to be doing, and was also inherent in what we might regard as some of the more legislative efforts of the Burger Court, such as *Roe v. Wade*.[775] Quite telling in this regard, and offering further

---

[771] *Id.*, at 122–123, quoting Ronald Dworkin, Life's Dominion, *supra* note 757, at 145 (1993).

[772] Cohen, *supra* note 747.

[773] Fleming and McClain, *supra* note 759, at 9.

[774] Dworkin, Comment, *supra* note 770, at 123.

[775] Roe v. Wade, 410 U.S. 113 (1973) is the decision in which the Supreme Court by a 7–2 vote found the right for a woman to secure an abortion before fetal viability to be a "fundamental right" protected by the Constitution, and thus not able to be regulated by the state unless the state could show a

support for the notion that Dworkin approved of the project of the Warren Court, was his defense of what the Court did in its most famous decision, *Brown v. Board of Education*,[776] when it declared that racial segregation in the public schools violated the Fourteenth Amendment's "equal protection" clause. Couching his defense of the Court in his version of the jurisprudence of "originalism," Dworkin wrote:

> Consider ... the *Brown* question: does the Fourteenth Amendment guarantee of "equal protection of the laws" forbid racial segregation in public schools? We know that the majority of the members of Congress who voted for that amendment did not expect or intend it to have that consequence: they themselves sustained racial segregation in the schools of the District of Columbia. So an expectation-originalist [presumably a person such as Justice Scalia] would

---

"compelling interest" for such regulation. *Roe*, as a blatant piece of judicial legislation, was subject to criticism from its issuance. As late as 2015, a prominent jurisprudential scholar, John Finnis, who held joint appointments at Oxford and Notre Dame, could write that "The Court's opinion was so ill reasoned that even the many constitutional law scholar[s] (including the most eminent) who strongly favoured a wholly permissive legal regime, regarded the decision as constitutionally disreputable, legally indefensible, and even as showing no sense of an obligation to be constitutionally sound in adjudication." John Finnis, Judicial Power: Past Present and Future, Oxford Legal Studies Research Paper No. 2/2016 Notre Dame Law School Legal Studies Research Paper No. 1604, at 10 (2015), available on the web, SSRN-id2710880.pdf (accessed 1 March 2016). Over time, the Justices seemed to back off from support for the decision. Finally, in Planned Parenthood v. Casey, 505 U.S. 833 (1992), in an opinion by a three-person plurality which purported to be following the principal holding of *Roe*, that there was a Constitutionally-protected right to secure an abortion before fetal viability, the Court retreated from the "fundamental right" and "compelling interest" language of *Roe*, and suggested that state regulation of abortion was permissible so long as an "undue burden" was not placed on a woman seeking to exercise her purported Constitutional right to terminate a pregnancy. For a comprehensive study of the Burger Court, see Michael J. Graetz and Linda Greenhouse, The Burger Court and the Rise of the Judicial Right (Simon & Schuster, 2016).

[776] Brown v. Board of Education of Topeka, 347 U.S. 483 (1954).

interpret the Fourteenth Amendment to permit segregation and would declare the Court's decision wrong. But there is no plausible interpretation of what these statesmen [who framed and enacted the Fourteenth Amendment] meant to *say* in laying down the language "equal protection of the laws," that entitles us to conclude that they *declared* segregation constitutional. On the contrary, as the Supreme Court held, the best understanding of their semantic intentions supposes that they meant to, and did, lay down a general principle of political morality which (it had become clear by 1954) condemns racial segregation. So on that ground, a semantic-originalist [a category in which Dworkin includes himself] would concur in the Court's decision.[777]

This jurisprudence, then, that advocated by Dworkin and employed by the Warren Court, was a means of virtually transforming the Constitution. Thus, in a similar manner as Dworkin approved of the expansion of the meaning of the principle of "equal protection of the laws" in *Brown* to prohibit racial segregation, the principle of the "Right of Privacy," for example, could be extended first, by the Warren Court to provide Constitutional protection for the practice of contraception,[778] and, eventually, in *Roe v. Wade*,[779] even for the decision to terminate a pregnancy.

In the work of Justice Anthony Kennedy, during the Chief Justiceships of William Rehnquist and John Roberts, Dworkin's type of jurisprudence was carried even further.

---

[777] Ronald Dworkin, Comment, *supra* note 770, at 115, 119 (footnote omitted, emphasis in original).

[778] Griswold v. Connecticut, 381 U.S. 479 (1965) (holding that Connecticut's anti-conception drug prohibition violated a "right to privacy," a right found in "penumbras" and "emanations" from other Constitutional provisions; more or less the precise methodology Dworkin advocated).

[779] Roe v. Wade, 410 U.S. 113 (1973).

Kennedy reformulated the "right of privacy" in his infamous "mystery passage," in which he declared that "At the heart of liberty is the right to define one's own concept of existence, of meaning, of the universe, and of the mystery of human life." He went on to add that "Belief about these matters could not define the attributes of personhood were they formed under the compulsion of the state."[780] While the meaning of these words is notoriously elusive, they appear to suggest that it should not be the business of the state to promote a particular philosophical worldview, much less to subscribe to any tenets of religion or morality. Kennedy's broad principle here, surely one that Dworkin would understand and embrace, is something more than traditional common law liberty as understood by Blackstone[781] and his successor law professors, and condones or prescribes a sort of radical individualism that, if taken to its logical ends, permits not only the legality of consensual homosexual relations, as Kennedy mandated in *Lawrence v. Texas*,[782] but also, it would seem, gay marriage,[783] assisted suicide, and, quite possibly, bigamy.

In a dense, but brilliant, explication of Dworkin's theory set forth in *Taking Rights Seriously*, Critical Legal Studies[784] scholar Peter Gabel explained that Dworkin was engaged, probably unconsciously, in an effort to justify the doctrinal departure of the courts, in an era that moved from early to late capitalism, from the common law and Constitutional law doctrines of the nineteenth century to those of the mid-twentieth century.[785] Just as Sir Edward

---

[780] Planned Parenthood of Southeastern Pennsylvania v. Casey, 505 U.S. 833, 852 (1992) (plurality opinion of Justices O'Connor, Kennedy, and Souter).

[781] See Chapter 1, *supra*.

[782] Lawrence v. Texas, 539 U.S. 558 (2003).

[783] As the Court, in an opinion written by Kennedy did eventually declare, by a 5–4 majority, in Obergefell v. Hodges, 576 U.S. ___ (2015).

[784] For Critical Legal Studies (CLS), see Chapter 14, *infra*.

[785] Peter Gabel, Book Review, *supra* note 758.

Coke, and later Blackstone, had justified the common law (which protected the interests of the great English landowning aristocracy) as dictated by the word of God Himself, and just as positivists such as H.L.A. Hart and Oliver Wendell Holmes, Jr., had justified traditional contract and Constitutional Law doctrines which promoted the free market and individualism in the era of laissez-faire capitalism, so Dworkin, suggested Gabel, was engaged in an effort to legitimate late twentieth-century law which had within it a redistributive and equitable dimension more suited to the modern welfare state or what Gabel called "late capitalism" or "pluralism."

Gabel found Dworkin's efforts essentially beside the point, since Gabel, as did some of his colleagues in the movement eventually known as Critical Legal Studies (CLS)[786] believed that it was time to move legal doctrines away from the traditional separation of public and private, and to create a legal system that could better ensure human happiness through the establishment of a form of decentralized socialism that had yet to appear in the modern world.[787] Gabel thus appeared to be arguing that it was time for law professors, like Dworkin, to stop being apologists for the established order, and, instead, to suggest means for the legal system actually to begin to meet what Gabel called "the true needs of the human heart."[788] This, was, of course, the ambitious project of CLS itself,[789] but for our purposes, at this point, it might be enough to suggest that with Dworkin's move to emphasize principles over rules, and to argue that when courts were engaged in that pursuit they were not engaging in legislation, but were seeking rather, to realize the aims of legislators and the

---

[786] See Chapter 14, *infra.*

[787] Gabel, *supra* note 758, at 315.

[788] *Id.*, at 314.

[789] See generally Chapter 14, *infra.*

American people themselves, it could be said that Dworkin, really, completed the enterprise which stymied Wechsler.[790] Untroubled by the apparent contradictions in Constitutional principles which bothered Wechsler, Dworkin somehow was able to order them in a manner that accorded with his essentially liberal or progressive notions, much in the manner as did the philosopher who inspired him, John Rawls.

Dworkin may well also deserve special attention as a notably successful and provocative law professor. There are "countless accounts of Dworkin's brilliance as a lecturer," and he was reported to speak "without notes and with great flair, making it all seem so graceful and effortless."[791] He inspired not only many students, but also many professors, who joined him in his effort "in defending a moral reading or philosophic approach to constitutional interpretation over and against all forms of originalism."[792] There was also, with Dworkin, a striking confidence that he was playing for the winning team, and that that team had been victorious from the beginning. It is also true that at the foundation of Dworkin's thought was the belief that it was possible to make statements about objective morality, and there is, in this foundation, a healthy skepticism about skepticism. As Dworkin put it at the end of a complex philosophical article:

> We want to live decent, worthwhile lives, lives we can look back on with pride not shame. We want our communities to be fair and good and our laws to be wise and just. These are enormously difficult goals, in part because the issues at stake are complex and puzzling. When are told that whatever convictions we do struggle to reach

---

[790] See Chapter 11, *supra.*

[791] Fleming and McClain, *supra* note 759, at 1.

[792] *Id.,* at 2–3.

cannot in any case be true or false, or objective, or part of what we know, or that they are just moves in a game of language, or just steam from the turbines of our emotions, or just experimental projects we should try for size, to see how we get on, or just invitations to thoughts that we might find diverting or amusing or less boring than the ways we used to think, we must reply that these denigrating suggestions are all false, just bad philosophy. But these are pointless, unprofitable, wearying interruptions, and we must hope that the leaden spirits of our age, which nurture them, soon lift.[793]

Referring to a group who lived in an age with, presumably, fewer "leaden spirits," the framers of our Constitution (whom originalists like Scalia have, of course, invoked to support their own views), Dworkin wrote that "Enlightenment statesmen were very unlikely to think that their own views represented the last word in moral progress. If they really were worried that future generations would protect rights less vigorously than they themselves did, they would have made plain that they intended to create a dated provision [instead of using broad and expansive language]."[794] Making light of Justice Scalia's worry that politicizing Supreme Court nominations would lead to Justices who would endanger the rights of individuals in order to pacify political majorities, Dworkin declared that "History disagrees. Justices whose methods seem closest to the moral reading of the Constitution have been champions, not enemies of individual rights, and as the political defeat of Robert Bork's nomination taught us,

[793] Ronald Dworkin, Objectivity and Truth: You'd Better Believe It, 25 Philosophy and Public Affairs 87, 139 (1996).

[794] Dworkin, Comment, *supra* note 770, at 124.

the people seem content not only with the moral reading but with its individualist implications."[795]

In this manner, Dworkin, the believer in an objective morality, could even identify himself with the view of "the people." And if Dworkin's confidence in his own views was impressive, even for a law professor, two of his admirers wrote that "We shall not look upon his like again. Ronald Dworkin made legal philosophy and constitutional theory the best they can be."[796] Even so, and while "Dworkin [eventually] rejected Rawls's political liberalism in favor of a comprehensive ethical liberalism," and while he "recognized considerable latitude for governmental encouragement of responsibility in the exercise of rights, he never fully developed a perfectionist theory of governmental responsibility to inculcate civic virtues."[797] Dworkin was a flesh and blood human being, but perhaps we might begin to test the thesis that he was as good as law professors get by comparing him to a fictional ideal, admittedly a contracts professor rather than a constitutional law professor, Charles Kingsfield.

---

[795] *Id.*, at 126–127.

[796] Fleming and McClain, *supra* note 759, at 3.

[797] *Id.*, at 4. For Fleming and McClain's effort to advance such a perfectionist theory, see James E. Fleming and Linda C. McClain, Ordered Liberty: Rights, Responsibilities, and Virtues (Harvard, 2013).

CHAPTER 13

THE AMERICAN LAW PROFESSOR AS ALOOF OLYMPIAN

MID TO LATE TWENTIETH CENTURY

Charles Kingsfield
(Harvard)

■ ■ ■

Professor Charles Kingsfield (of *The Paper Chase*)
As portrayed by John Houseman (1902–1988).
Original sketch by the author.

Charles Kingsfield, Professor of Law at Harvard, is, apparently, one of only two fictional teachers of law prominent in Anglo-American literature (C.P. Snow's Lewis Eliot is the other). Eliot, as we have seen,[798] is the law professor as Oxbridge don, as well as the law professor as man of affairs and astute friend, confident, husband and brother. Kingsfield shares some qualities with Eliot—abnormally high intelligence and cosmopolitan worldliness

---

[798] Chapter 10, *supra*.

for example, but there are profound differences. Eliot is painted as a uniquely sympathetic and empathetic human being, while Kingsfield is something of a moral monster. Kingsfield was created by John Jay Osborn, Jr., a 1970 graduate of the Harvard Law School, and a descendant of the First Chief Justice of the United States, John Jay.[799]

Osborn's character, Kingsfield, limned in the 1971 book,[800] the 1973 movie, and the TV series all called *The Paper Chase*, is notable for several intriguing idealized characteristics. One is Kingsfield's brutal use of the Socratic method, as an autocratic way for a teacher to maintain superiority over a student, as, perhaps, a patriarchal cudgel to beat lawyers-in-training into a form to meet the demands of an hierarchical and somewhat immoral and impersonal legal order.

Onetime Harvard Law School Dean, Robert C. Clark, blurbing on the back cover of the 40th anniversary edition of *The Paper Chase*,[801] called it "one of the most important books ever written about legal education in the United States," although he suggested that "Law schools have changed since John Osborn wrote this classic novel, but it is still valuable to reflect on his unforgettable portrait of the system from which we have progressed." To similar effect, Lawrence Tribe, himself one of the most famous liberal law professors in the late twentieth century (and, indeed, a mentor of President Obama,[802] who served Tribe as a research assistant), wrote, also blurbing the book, that *The Paper Chase* "is an iconic work that defines what legal education at its best used to teach and, more dramatically, what legal education at its worst used to be, ought not to

---

[799] See the Wikipedia entry for Osborn, https://en.wikipedia.org/wiki/John_Jay_Osborn,_Jr.

[800] John Jay Osborn, Jr., The Paper Chase (Houghton Mifflin, 1971).

[801] John Jay Osborn, Jr., The Paper Chase (Peninsula Road Press, 2012).

[802] See Chapter 23, *infra*.

have been, and, at least in some law schools—including
Harvard, thanks in no small part to John Osborn and his
influence—no longer is. I'm proud to have been one of John's
teachers, and not one of those (I hope) whom he used as his
images of how not to teach."

When the now famous novelist Scott Turow entered
Harvard Law School, in the fall of 1975, he appeared
convinced that "I will be certain that no matter what I do, I
will not do it well enough; and when I fail, I know that I will
burn with shame."[803] The myth of Kingsfield, and the
inevitable humiliation of students through the Socratic
method were, it would seem, well-established at the time.
There was considerable reality to that myth, at least at
some well-known law schools. Harvard in the late fifties and
early sixties, for Richard Posner,[804] appears to have been
rife with Kingsfieldian teaching. As Posner reports, "I loved
my first year at the Harvard Law School . . . in all its
brutishness. Harvard stacked its best teachers in the first
year and they were superb, though cold, demanding, and at
times nasty."[805] And, with regard to Harvard's great rival,
as Duncan Kennedy wrote in 1968, "Few will deny that the
atmosphere of the first year classroom [at Yale] is as heavy
with fear as it is tense with intellectual excitement. The
point here is more than that: students see professors as
people who want to hurt them; professors' actions often do
hurt them, deeply."[806] The sharp law professor put-down of
the overconfident law student in American law school lore

---

[803] Scott Turow, One L: The Turbulent True Story of a First Year at
Harvard Law School ix (Penguin books, 2010 edition, originally published by
Farrar Straus Giroux, 1977).

[804] See Chapter 15, *infra.*

[805] Quoted by Lincoln Caplan, Rhetoric & Law: The Double Life of
Richard Posner, America's most contentious legal reformer, Harvard Magazine
51 (January–February 2016).

[806] Duncan Kennedy, How the Law School Fails: A Polemic, 1 Yale L. Rev.
of Law and Social Action 71 (1970), available at http://digitalcommons.law.
yale.edu/yrlsa/vol1/iss1/7 (accessed January 10, 2015).

goes back a while. Northwestern Law School Dean and classroom martinet John Henry Wigmore's biographer quotes a 1922 letter to Wigmore from one of his students, recounting an episode in which Wigmore had disposed of a particularly garrulous and apparently clueless student by remarking, "Mr. _____, your verbosity exceeds your luminosity by a preponderance of magnanimity."[807]

Denying that one's law school was like that described in *The Paper Chase* seemed to be, to use Holmes's term, a "felt necessity" shortly after the appearance of the movie, in 1973, when, for example, The University of Chicago School of Law announced, "[T]he very mention of the Socratic Method strikes fear in the hearts of those considering attending law school. . . . [I]f anyone ever did teach a law school class like [John Houseman's portrayal of] Professor Kingsfield, no one at Chicago does today. Instead, our students discover quickly that the Socratic Method is a tool and a good one that is used to engage a large group of students in a discussion, while using probing questions to get at the heart of the subject matter". "The Socratic Method," Chicago's law school carefully explained, "is not used at Chicago to intimidate, nor to 'break down' new law students, but instead for the very reason Socrates developed it: to develop critical thinking skills in students and enable them to approach the law as intellectuals."[808]

For many entering law school in the Seventies and Eighties, however, the Kingsfieldian model still loomed large, and not just because of how it might frighten students, but also because of what it suggested about their

---

[807] Quoted in William R. Roalfe, John Henry Wigmore: Scholar and Reformer 54 (Northwestern University Press, 1977). For Wigmore, see Chapter 6, *supra*.

[808] "Prospective Students: Studying Law at Chicago: The Socratic Method". University of Chicago Law School. October 17, 1973. http://www.law.uchicago.edu/prospectives/lifeofthemind/socraticmethod, retrieved November 22, 2014.

law school professors. Thus, another characteristic of Osborn's fictional law professor is Kingsfield's remarkably austere and near Holmesian Olympian aloofness. Particularly as depicted in the movie, the nearly septuagenarian[809] but still vigorous and daunting Kingsfield, who speaks, like the late William Buckley, with a superbly aristocratically elegant Mid-Atlantic English accent, plays his role completely dead-pan, and, while he shows little discernable emotion, he appears, nevertheless, to display a diabolical delight in demonstrating the obviously inferior reasoning ability of his students. Both the book and the movie are gripping evocations of the first-year student experience at Harvard Law, but the movie, which nicely condenses and sharpens the action of the book, is virtually overpowering.[810]

In the movie's first scene in which we meet Kingsfield (played by John Houseman, in a role that won him an Academy Award), he is nattily attired in a three-piece suit and bow tie, his wiggly eyebrows probably his most prominent feature. Cold-calling on students, he so rattles the eager young law student protagonist, Mr. Hart (played by Timothy Bottoms) that after class Hart rushes to the lavatory and loses his breakfast. As the movie (and the book) move forward, however, Hart, an extraordinarily psychologically well-grounded Midwesterner (from Minnesota, and a graduate of the University of Minnesota),[811] improves his class performance in

---

[809] Kingsfield's age is not made clear in the movie, but the book states that "he was almost seventy years old." The Paper Chase, *supra* note 801, at 179.

[810] While not every critic embraced the movie, it seems notable that in 2006 the American Film Institute (AFI), listed it as one of the hundred "Most Inspiring Movies." It was number 91 on the list, ranking just above "Fame," and just below "Hotel Rwanda." http://www.afi.com/Docs/about/press/2006/100inspiring.pdf (accessed 7 August 2016).

[811] Osborn, the scion of an East Coast founding father, living in California, curiously lauds Hart's qualities as a Midwesterner. He has Hart's

Kingsfield's class, achieving the ability to answer Kingsfield's Socratic questions with precision and detail. Eventually, so Hart claims to his girlfriend (who, by coincidence, happens to be Kingsfield's daughter), Susan Fields (played in the movie by the almost ethereally lovely Lindsay Wagner), Hart actually gains the ability to think three questions ahead of where Kingsfield is going in class.

The thesis put forward a bit more succinctly in the movie than the book, is that Kingsfield, in using the Socratic method, is not really dabbling in evil at all, but rather is training his students to think for themselves, and training them as well never to be satisfied with the results they reach. "There are always more questions," Kingsfield explains. When the students come to him, Kingsfield maintains, their skulls are "full of mush," but when they leave him, they leave "thinking like a lawyer." This intriguing notion of what Kingsfield does, this somewhat positive or at least constructive vision of the law school Socratic method, is contrasted throughout the film with the experience that Hart has with Kingsfield's beautiful daughter—she continually urges him to be spontaneous, to explore, and to experience life, while, she implies, her father wrongly encourages him to analyze, to rationalize, and to compartmentalize. I suspect that the movie (and perhaps the book, too, although the movie is a bit more straightforward on this point) seeks to show that Hart is really in love both with Kingsfield and with his daughter. Hart is both absorbed by the law and entranced by the woman, and has a terrible time choosing between the two.[812]

---

girlfriend, Susan, say, "The law school wants you: the earnest ones. You've got class. The law school wants to suck out your Midwestern class." The Paper Chase, *supra* note 801, at 96.

[812] In one splendid passage in the book it is made clear how Kingsfield is seducing or overcoming Hart, "I sit in that damn [contracts] class. For days I sit there. Then I read his books in the library, and I abstract the cases he's

At one point, following Hart's excellent performance on the receiving end of the Socratic method, Kingsfield gives him the coveted assignment of helping to revise Kingsfield's treatise on Contracts, provided Hart completes his assignment over the weekend. In the movie, it is made clear that Hart was supposed to spend that weekend with Susan, at Massachusetts' glorious Cape Cod, but Hart blows off the daughter, to work on the father's law book, only to fail to complete the assignment on time. When Hart asks for an extension, he is told that the task has been assigned to someone else. This leads, in the movie, to a near nervous breakdown on Hart's part, but he pulls himself together, and even succeeds in getting back with Susan, and spending the postponed weekend at the Cape, where she tells him she's quite sick of hearing about her father.

It's not clear whether Susan really wishes to break with her law professor father, although it is strongly suggested in the movie that her mother, who is in a mental institution, and who is described as completely crazy, got that way, at least in part, because of her marriage to Kingsfield.[813] Still, Susan appears to glow, in the movie, when she describes to Hart that her father never misses the Harvard/Yale game (the two of them—Hart and Susan) are roaming around the Harvard football stadium at the time. She informs Hart that when she was a little girl she happily sat on her father's lap at The Game, with a President of the United States on one side of her father, and two Supreme Court Justices on the

chosen. I know everything about him. The stripe of his ties. How many suits he has. He's like the air or the wind, He's everywhere. You can say you don't care, but he's there anyway pounding his mind into mine. He screws around with my life." The Paper Chase, *supra* note 801, at 163.

[813] This is left undeveloped in the book, where the sole reference is Susan's statement that "As a matter of fact, she's blown her mind. She's in a mental hospital, crazy as hell." Susan adds, suggestively, "I'm not." The Paper Chase, *supra* note 801, at 45.

other.[814] To underscore the point of Kingsfield's connection to the high and mighty, or at least the famous and notable, in the movie, Hart has a tryst with Susan, at her father's house where he and Susan adjourn to Kingsfield's study, where Hart notes the pictures of Kingsfield with not only assorted Justices and Presidents, but also Ernest Hemingway, Adlai Stephenson, and Helen Keller[!]. Hart asks Susan what would Kingsfield say if he could see one of his students, Hart, in his underwear, with his daughter, in his study, and Susan remarks that he, Kingsfield, would want to see Hart "fondling his things."[815] This leaves ambiguous the precise relationship between Kingsfield and Hart, and it is further obscured by the fact that Kingsfield seems repeatedly to have trouble remembering Hart's name.

Even so, looking at the picture on the seating chart on the podium in front of him, when Hart is back in class, Kingsfield calls on Hart repeatedly, and, it appears to be hinted, Kingsfield may well know that Hart is sleeping with his daughter, and Kingsfield, it is implied, may not really want his daughter involved with law students. Kingsfield is, in the movie, representing his daughter in divorce proceedings against an earlier Kingsfield student,[816] and, when Kingsfield unexpectedly comes back home while his daughter and Hart are lolling about his place in the near-

---

[814] A similar point is made in the book, when it is noted that Kingsfield was on the 1929 Harvard Law Review (of which organization Barack Obama was later to be President and which journal Wigmore founded), with two future "Chief Justices" (presumably of the United States Supreme Court). The Paper Chase, *supra* note 801, at 53. For Barack Obama, see Chapter 23, *infra*, and for Wigmore, see Chapter 6, *supra*.

[815] The "fondling his things" line is in the book too, *id.*, at 53, although not the descriptions of the pictures of all of the notables named in the movie.

[816] In the movie Susan is in the process of getting a divorce from a law student, although in the book she has never married.

altogether,[817] Hart exits unceremoniously and purportedly anonymously by the back door (sans his clothes, which Susan brings to him as he waits in her car), and Kingsfield, realizing that Susan was with a man, remarks "I hope it wasn't a law student."

Hart is advised by his law student colleagues that the one thing that ought to be avoided if one wants academic success at Harvard Law—and it is hinted that such success, as indicated by high grades, is the only thing worth striving for at the school—is an entanglement with a woman. In the old days, as indicated earlier, we used to say that "the law is a jealous mistress," and this may be a modernized version of that notion.[818] A few of Hart's fellow first-year students fall by the wayside—one married student, Kevin Brooks, embarrassed by Kingsfield and, despite the fact that he has a photographic memory, unable effectively to analyze the importance of particular facts in cases, attempts suicide, and leaves the law school. Two other members of Hart's study group withdraw from the group as the interpersonal tensions become too intense, and Hart, and his best friend among his classmates, Ford (a graduate of Harvard College with an IQ of 191, and a scion of a family of multiple Harvard Law alumni, who, most of the movie, wears a bow tie much like Kingsfield's)[819] retreat to a hotel where they

---

[817] They are naked in the comparable scene in the book, The Paper Chase 53–54 (40th Anniversary edition, 2011), although in the book Kingsfield does not come unexpectedly home to surprise them.

[818] The book is more ambiguous on this point. Indeed, his classmate, Ford, who may or may not be the author's alter ego, advises Hart that the best thing he can do to survive the law school "mess," is "Find a good woman and hang on. Hang on like hell. I mean, throw yourself into the goddamned struggle like a maniac. Grab onto her boobs and don't let go." The Paper Chase, *supra* note 801, at 62.

[819] Ford is an intriguing character. Osborn himself was a graduate of Harvard College, and perhaps, as suggested in the prior note, Ford is his alter ego, although Osborn suggests in the preface to the 40th Anniversary edition of *The Paper Chase* that "Like Hart, I was an outsider. I grew up in California." *The Paper Chase*, *supra* note 801, Preface to the 40th Anniversary edition, 2011. While Ford in the movie seems to be the consummate elite Harvard

disturb the staff and hopelessly litter their room with law school notes and room service remains, while studying for their final exams.

At the end of his first year, Hart, primed and ready, takes his contracts exam, and encounters Kingsfield in an elevator. "I want to tell you that I truly enjoyed your class," says Hart. "That's fine, fine." replies Kingsfield, with sublime indifference. Hart then adds, dripping with what the movie maintains is Midwestern sincerity, "What I mean, is you really mean something to me and your class has really meant something to me." Kingsfield, staring at Hart as if he is encountering him for the first time, then says "What is your name?" Hart says, "Hart," and Kingsfield says "Thank you, Mr. Hart."[820]

Kingsfield then exits the elevator, turns his back to Hart, and begins to walk away, and then mutters to Hart, "Thank you very much." Hart promptly flees again to the Cape with Susan. Right before that happens, however, we are shown a shot of Kingsfield grading Hart's contracts exam, on which he affixes the grade, "A." It would seem that Hart has, in fact, won the Paper Chase. In the movie's climactic last scene, Hart, much like some self-satisfied reptile, is sunning on a rock, and Susan comes up to him to announce that she has just received notice from her father that her divorce is final, and that Hart has received his grades from the Law School (they are in an envelope which

---

College Student, always nattily attired very like Kingsfield himself, in the book Osborn writes that Ford is recognizable because in a sea of dressed-up law students he has "no sport coat, no tie." *Id.*, at 42.

[820] This curious final non-recognition scene is in the book as well, The Paper Chase, *supra* note 801, at 179, although it occurs not in an elevator, but outside the classroom building, Langdell Hall, which has a marvelous anthropomorphic brooding presence in the book. The failure to recognize scene is slightly more potent in the book because it follows an earlier scene (which takes place in the book in an elevator) when Kingsfield tells Hart (although without acknowledging his name) that "You. You did well in class today. Your mind seems to be getting sharper." *Id.*, at 140.

she hands him, helpfully labelled "Grades"). Hart makes a paper airplane out of the envelope, climbs up on some other, higher, rocks, and launches the grades (unopened) into the Atlantic.[821]

Probably based on at least one real-life Harvard Professor, Clark Byse,[822] Kingsfield stood for the unfeeling and, indeed, cruel, pedagogue both Ralph Nader[823] and later adherents of critical legal studies[824] were to rail against. If Byse was the model, he was said, by contemporary Harvard Law Students, to hold a heart of gold inside his crusty exterior, but the same could not be said of Kingsfield, who never loses his Olympian cool, nor ever betrays a tender feeling.

Another mythic characteristic was Kingsfield's status as an advisor to governments (like Lewis Eliot) and an influential scholar and public intellectual. Indeed, the movie notes that while Kingsfield has a treatise (presumably of professional interest to lawyers and law students) Kingsfield also has what might be a best-selling popular book, *Contracts in Everyday Life* [!], which has just been profiled in the then widely-circulated Life Magazine.[825] Thus Kingsfield exemplifies characteristics we

---

[821] For the similar scene in the book, see The Paper Chase, *supra* note 801, at 180.

[822] That would be my guess, as Byse's conduct of his contracts class to students entering the law school in 1968 (when I did) was quite similar to that portrayed by Houseman. Paul Carrington has suggested, however, that Kingsfield is patterned after a teacher, Edward "Bull" Warren, who had departed Harvard by the time Osborn was a student, but whose legend lingered. See generally, Paul Carrington, The Pedagogy of the Old Case Method: A Tribute to "Bull" Warren, 59 Journal of Legal Education 457, 462 (2010) (suggesting that Osborn used anecdotes about Warren that were still circulating at the time that Osborn (who was HLS Class of '70) was at the school).

[823] See *infra*, text accompanying note 841.

[824] See Chapter 14, *infra*.

[825] In the book Kingsfield is also the author of the casebook from which he teaches his first-years contracts. The Paper Chase, *supra* note 801, at 3.

have already observed in such figures as Joseph Story and Felix Frankfurter, although unlike Frankfurter, Kingsfield is an archtypical WASP. Kingsfield's creation probably owes little to Snow's Lewis Eliot, but Kingsfield shares Eliot's ability to move in different worlds and to hover above the law and government.

The Paper Chase, and the roughly contemporary *One L*, by Scott Turow,[826] did much to romanticize the Socratic method in general and Harvard Law School in particular, and may well have done quite a bit to suggest the preeminence of Harvard in legal education in the late twentieth century. Turow, who was later to gain extraordinary fame as the author of legal thrillers,[827] and who, during most of his fame as a novelist, simultaneously was a partner at a distinguished Chicago law firm, had been a creative writing instructor at Stanford before he attended Harvard Law School. His take on the law school and on the Socratic method, is grainier and more nuanced than is Osborn's,[828] although there are powerful similarities between the two books.

Turow explains in brilliant detail how first-year law students at Harvard are seduced by the language and promise of the law, and how most of the rest of their lives, while they are law students, withers away as they

---

[826] Scott Turow, One L: The Turbulent True Story of a First Year at Harvard Law School (Originally published 1977, republished, with an afterward, 2010). (Subsequent citations are to the Penguin Books 2010 edition).

[827] See, e.g., Scott Turow, Presumed Innocent (Farrar Straus & Giroux, 1987), Scott Turow, Innocent (Grand Central Publishing, 2010), and Scott Turow, Identical (Grand Central Publishing, 2013).

[828] In Turow's afterward to the 2010 reissue of his One L, Turow calls The Paper Chase "a well-known but far-fetched novel." Turow explains that before One L, "there was nothing from the ground level that offered a real-life recounting of what happened day by day to a person as she or he began learning the law." One L was written to fill this void. *One L, supra* note 826, at 272.

encounter their classes and professors.[829] Turow, however, is more skeptical of the wisdom of his professors than Hart was of Kingsfield, and Turow paints the law school experience with both a broader and a more detailed brush. One of Turow's creations, the pseudonymous young and glamorous professor "Nicky Morris," appears to be a Critical Legal Studies professor (likely modeled after the extraordinarily-charismatic Duncan Kennedy,[830] who taught at Harvard during the period Turow chronicled), who warns his students about the dehumanizing qualities of learning the law, but who, in the end, in the course of his sincere efforts to lessen the rigors and terrors of their legal education, inadvertently ramps up their anxiety levels and thus, ironically, terrorizes them even more.[831]

No one attempts mayhem or self-destruction in Turow's book, as one student did in Osborn's, but both works do indicate the possibility of intellectual burn-out, and the risk that the Socratic method, as practiced at Harvard in the late Sixties and Seventies, had the potential to stifle creativity, sensitivity, and humanity. Nevertheless, it is difficult to read these two books and not come away with at least some feeling that the pursuit of a law degree is an exciting intellectual odyssey, an enterprise overseen by heroic and

---

[829] It will be remembered that Llewellyn, *supra* Chapter 8, thought that was just fine.

[830] For Duncan Kennedy and Critical Legal Studies, see generally Chapter 14, *infra*. "Readers of the book [One L] familiar with Harvard Law School and the history of Turow's three years at HLS have deduced that Turow took [Arthur] Miller, whose civil procedure course he took, and assigned his fictional counterpart Perini to teach contracts, and he also took Duncan Kennedy, his contracts professor, and transformed him into the civil procedure professor Nicky 'Beat Nick' Morris." From the entry for "Arthur R. Miller," in Wikipedia, http://en.wikipedia.org/wiki/Arthur_R._Miller, accessed January 10, 2015.

[831] Turow, *supra* note 826, at 243–249. See also *id.*, at 204 for "Nicky Morris's" attempt to minimize the importance of law school grades, with regard to which, Turow indicates, "Though an admirable effort, Nicky's speech did little to relieve the prevalent anxieties."

admirable figures, and an undertaking that gives one the deeply satisfactory feeling of being "the living extension of tradition."[832]

In the Paper Chase book (and it is also reflected in the movie), John Jay Osborn, Jr. notes that the first-year law students divide up into three types.[833] The first group of students basically gives up, realizing that true distinction—making the Law Review—will elude them, and, as a result, they withdraw, and sit, anonymously, in the back of the classroom, failing to occupy the seats marked for them on the professor's seating chart. This means that they will not be called on, but it also means that they will be regarded by their colleagues as cowards. The second group sits in their assigned seats, and is brave enough to risk being called on, and will answer when interrogated. The second group lives in constant fear, but has more courage, and is thus more admirable, than the first group. The final group of the three actually raise their hands and volunteer. These, according to Osborn, are the men and women of pluck, who are recognized by their fellow students as those likely to succeed, and who even have the distinction of the professors actually learning their names.[834] One stirring chapter in the movie and the book is when Hart strives to join the third group and, at least temporarily, succeeds. The rise in his self-esteem and his influence among his fellows is considerable.

---

[832] This "living extension of tradition" line is uttered by Hart in the Paper Chase, *supra* note 801, at 152, and in the movie it appears in Kingsfield's own notes from his class on contracts with Samuel Williston, an actual early twentieth-century giant in the law of contracts.

[833] The Paper Chase, *supra* note 801, at 27–28.

[834] Osborn's view here may not be shared by all law students, of course. Both in my class in law school and in the classes that I teach, volunteers might be just as likely to be disdained rather than honored. Often labelled "gunners," these days, their fellows may see them as show-offs in love with the sound of their own voices, and some professors may regard them as distractions rather than as admirable participants in the learning experience.

Still, the risks of failing to achieve the polished performance a Kingsfield appears to demand are considerable, and, during my years at Harvard Law 1968–71 (at roughly the same time as Osborn, who was a class ahead of me), I knew plenty of students as affected by the Socratic method as was Osborn's character, Hart, and the members of his study group, and I actually had a classmate so driven to instability by the threat of failure, that he took his law school exams in Harvard's infirmary. Nevertheless, as *The Paper Chase* teaches, to succeed in Kingsfield's classroom or to ace his law exam was to boost one's ego nearly to Kingsfield's own superhuman proportions.

Somehow the lure of this kind of success was irresistible to thousands in the seventies and eighties. Scott Turow notes in the afterward to the 2010 reissue of *One L* that in the early seventies there was "a booming interest in the law," and that "between 1970 and 1974 law school applications had quadrupled."[835] Turow claims that his book was "the confession of an unabashed neurotic," and that "neither then [in the seventies], nor now [2010] is law school the same kind of crucible for most law students that it was for me."[836] Turow may not be correct on this point, and, indeed, my own feeling is that *The Paper Chase* and *One L* did much to make going to law school the default behavior for the best and the brightest of college graduates in the seventies and eighties.[837]

---

[835] One L, *supra* note 826, at 272. Turow suggests that much of this burgeoning interest in the law was as a result of Watergate and the lawyers who investigated and "sought to deliver justice to President Nixon's henchmen (many of them also lawyers)." *Id.*

[836] *Id.*, at 273. Adds Turow "As I sometimes joke, *One L* has provided law students for decades the reassurance that at least one person has gone through the whole experience feeling a lot crazier than they do."

[837] Turow candidly observes that "Some say reading about my excitement [about the first year of law school] drew them to law school. Others tell me that my tale of personal torment drove them away." *Id.*, at 274.

As jobs in law firms have become somewhat scarcer, the lure of law school has probably diminished, and it is most likely that at least some aspects of the Harvard Law School Osborn and Turow encountered are no more.[838] As Turow puts it, "Harvard ... is a kinder and gentler place, especially in the wake of the deanship of [now Supreme Court Justice] Elena Kagan, who worked a sea change by emphasizing that the students, not the faculty, deserved to be the first concern of the institution."[839] Even so, these two books, insofar as they glorified the American law professor as a mover and shaker and intellectual titan, may have contributed to popular culture an exaggerated notion of the wisdom of American law professors, an exaggerated notion that may have helped propel Barack Obama to the White House, and one that Secretary Panetta lamented.[840]

There is no doubt as well that Osborn's creation gave shape to something many law students despised. Thus, right before the time that Osborn was producing *The Paper Chase* and Turow was writing *One L*, there was underway a rear-guard action against Harvard and the Socratic method. This was fought in the work, among others, of Ralph Nader, who wrote a blistering essay against the kind of teaching done at Harvard (and most other law schools) at the time. His take on the classroom experience romanticized by Osborn and even Turow was rather different:

---

[838] At the time both Osborn and Turow were writing, Harvard was arguably at the very pinnacle of legal education, and the statistics suggested that its principal competitor at that time, Yale, did no better at recruiting the best students than did Harvard. By 2010 when Turow wrote his afterward to a reissue of *One L*, however, Yale was besting Harvard 9 to 1 in gaining students accepted at both places, in some years Stanford did better than Harvard, and other law schools, most notably NYU, Columbia, and the University of Chicago were giving Harvard a run for third place in success in enrolling students admitted to other top law schools. *Id.*, at 277–278.

[839] *Id.*, at 277.

[840] For Panetta's jibe, see the Introduction, *supra* note 1, and for President Obama, see Chapter 23, *infra*.

Harvard Law's most enduring contribution to legal education was the mixing of the case method of study with the Socratic method of teaching. Developed late in the nineteenth century under Dean Christopher Columbus Langdell, these techniques were tailor-made to transform intellectual arrogance into pedagogical systems that humbled the student into accepting its premises, levels of abstractions and choice of subjects. Law professors take delight in crushing egos in order to acculturate the students to what they called "legal reasoning" or "thinking like a lawyer." The process is a highly sophisticated form of mind control that trades off breadth of vision and factual inquiry for freedom to roam in an intellectual cage. The study of actual law cases— almost always at the appellate court level— combines with the Socratic questioning sequence in class to keep students continually on the defensive, while giving them the feeling that they are learning hard law. Inasmuch as the Socratic method is a game at which only one (the professor) can play, the students are conditioned to react to questions and issues which they have no role in forming or stimulating.[841]

Nader's argument was that Harvard Law produced docile automatons, fit only to practice law in the large law factories such as those of Wall Street, La Salle Street, and K Street. As far as Nader was concerned, the training at Harvard encouraged the budding lawyers to accept the law

---

[841] Ralph Nader, "Law Schools and Law Firms," The New Republic. Oct. 11, 1969. There seems to be a dawning awareness on the part of some legal academics, that the "legal mind" may need some correcting, some improvements in "mindfulness." See, e.g., Leonard L. Riskin, and Rachael Anne Wohl, Mindfulness in the Heat of Conflict: Taking Stock 20 Harv. Neg. L. Rev. 121 (2015).

as it was, and crushed any reforming zeal they might have brought originally to the study of law. For Nader, as for Bentham and Rantoul before him, what went on in the orthodox teaching and writing about the law was a defense of and a perpetuation of the established order, and a preparation of students for the assembly-line nature of Big Law practice. The idealized, hierarchical and patriarchal conception of the law which Kingsfield symbolizes, was also the subject of the powerful attack by Critical Legal Studies Scholars, Feminists, and Critical Race Theory scholars later in the twentieth and twenty-first centuries, as we will next see.

CHAPTER 14

CRITICAL LEGAL STUDIES: LAW AND THE MOVEMENT

LATE TWENTIETH CENTURY

Duncan Kennedy (Harvard)
Mark Tushnet (Wisconsin, Georgetown, Harvard)
Peter Gabel (New School)
Morton Horwitz (Harvard)
Robert Gordon (Buffalo, Wisconsin, Yale)
Roberto Unger (Harvard)

■ ■ ■

Duncan Kennedy (b. 1942), 1980
Photo by John Chapin.
Courtesy of Harvard Law School.

Mark Tushnet (b. 1945)
Photo by Rhoda Baer.
Courtesy of Professor Tushnet.

Peter Gabel (b. 1947)
Photo by Katherine Voutyras.
Courtesy of Mr. Gabel.

Morton Horwitz (b. 1938), 1979
Photo by John Chapin.
Courtesy of Harvard Law School.

Robert Gordon (b. 1945)
Photo by Harold Shapiro.
Courtesy of Yale Law School.

Roberto Unger (b. 1947)
Photo by Professor Unger.
Wikimedia Commons.

This chapter is a group biography within the overall structure of group biography. The Conference on Critical Legal Studies ("CCLS," "CLS," or "the Crits") was a remarkable development that emerged in American law schools in the late 70's and early 80's, spurred, in part by the Vietnam War and the Nixon imbroglio, and profoundly influenced by the thought of the Frankfurt School (Jurgen Habermas, Theodore Adorno, Herbert Marcuse etc.).[842] As Peter Gabel explains, "[T]he main factor was the Vietnam War and the growing awareness that dawned on millions of young people in particular that something insane was taking place, and it was taking place not because the war was in the economic interests of General Motors but because in some sense the whole world was out of its mind, out of touch with Being itself, living out scripts that rationalized the mass murder of millions of human beings."[843]

CLS was not always sympathetically received in some quarters of the law school professoriate. Thus, one critic suggested that "As refugees from the counterculture rebellion of the 1960s they [the Crits] introduced radical politics into what had been an insulated law academy. It was an elitist group teaching revolution at prestigious schools, affecting the proletariat look in class before getting in BMWs to drive home to enjoy a glass of wine and toast

---

[842] See generally, John Henry Schlegal, Notes Toward An Intimate, Opinionated, and Affectionate History of the Conference on Critical Legal Studies, 36 Stan.L.Rev. 391(1984), for the origin, development, and influences on CLS. Schlegal notes some of the antecedent events as "disillusion and hostility arising from the Vietnam War, Watergate, and nation's political shift to the right. Simultaneously came student clamor for relevance and clinical education and the assembly [on law school faculties] of a small but determined band of social science types dedicated to showing what was 'really' going on out there. . . ." Id., at 406.

[843] Peter Gabel, The Spiritual Foundation of Attachment to Hierarchy, in Duncan Kennedy, Legal Education and the Reproduction of Hierarchy: A Polemic Against the System 154, 156 (NYU Press, 2004).

the struggle against hierarchy and privilege."[844] This goes a bit too far, but in the late sixties and early seventies, in Cambridge, Massachusetts at least, there *was* a feeling in the air that revolution was around the corner, and it could be said that CLS was engaged in the formulation of a first draft of law for the second American Post-Revolutionary period that has yet to occur.[845]

One of the most perceptive analyses of CLS was offered in a Student Note in the Harvard Law Review, which quite properly linked CLS with American Legal Realism, suggesting, in short, that CLS perfected and completed what American Legal Realism had begun, but left unfinished. As suggested earlier, this Note indicated, "The Realist methodology was characterized by three tenets: an emphasis on study of the evolution of legal doctrine, a critical approach to use of formalistic reasoning, and a firm commitment to progressive law reform grounded in social scientific research."[846] And further, that "The work of the critical legal scholars can be understood as the maturation of these Realist methodologies—a maturation in which critical scholars explore incoherences at the level of social or political theory and critical scholarship is linked, not to

---

[844] Arthur Austin, The Top Ten Politically Correct Law Review Articles, 27 Fla.St.U.L.Rev. 233, 250 (1999).

[845] This must be offered with some hesitation; I once did hear one prominent CLS practitioner, in the early seventies, confidently (or, to be fair, perhaps it was only wistfully) talk of what would soon occur "after the revolution." At least one equally prominent figure in CLS, declared, when he was a law student at Yale in 1968, that "I do not think a revolutionary situation exists in the United Sates today, nor do I think such a situation likely in the near future." Duncan Kennedy, How the Law School Fails: A Polemic, 1 Yale L. Rev. of Law and Social Action 71 (1970), available at http://digitalcommons. law.yale.edu/yrlsa/vol1/iss1/7 (accessed January 10, 2015).

[846] Note, 'Round and 'Round the Bramble Bush: From Legal Realism to Critical Legal Scholarship, 95 Harv. L. Rev. 1669, 1671 (1982). For the earlier reference to this piece, see *supra* note 431 and accompanying text.

reformist policy programs, but to a radical political agenda."[847]

The members of CLS included among their number some of the most prominent law professors in the nineteen-eighties, with a powerful contingent at Harvard, regarded at the time as the "Rome" of Critical Legal Studies.[848] Some of the most notable professors associated with the movement included Duncan Kennedy, Morton Horwitz, and Roberto Unger, all three then at Harvard, Robert Gordon, at Wisconsin, and then Yale, Mark Tushnet, who taught at Wisconsin and Georgetown before moving eventually to Harvard, and Karl Klare, now the Matthews Distinguished University Professor of labor and employment law and legal theory at Northeastern University School of Law in Boston, Massachusetts.[849] The Emergence of CLS was, then, at the time it occurred, a rare instance of extremely left-wing academic thought appearing in the law schools, quite possibly because at the time it was exceptionally difficult to find teaching positions in the university departments of the arts and sciences (and those available paid poorly), but it was relatively easy for exceptionally bright students to end up teaching in the professional schools of law (where the salaries for professors were more substantial).

Explaining the powerful splash that CLS made at the top law schools is not easy, but some part, at least, was attributable to the sheer charisma of some of the CLS scholars. Kingsfield notwithstanding, charisma is not a quality associated frequently with law professors, but some CLS folks were the exception who proved the rule. The most

---

[847] *Id.*, at 1677.

[848] For the characterization of Harvard as the "Rome" of Critical Legal Studies, see, e.g., Laura Kalman, The Strange Career of Legal Liberalism 123 (1996). Professor Kalman has a fine discussion of CLS and the reaction to it from its conservative critics.

[849] For a discussion of these and other CLS Scholars, see *supra* note 846.

compelling of the group was probably Duncan Kennedy, an awesomely brilliant graduate of Yale Law School, who migrated to Harvard to teach, perhaps because he had alienated Yale by his acid criticism of that institution's law school.[850] Kennedy railed against what he perceived as "illegitimate hierarchies" in and out of the legal academy at Yale and elsewhere, and suggested, in tried and true fashion of some radicals, that committed young lawyers try to change their law firms from within by small upsetting gestures, like, for example, failing to wear a necktie at the law firm (it is rare, though not unheard of, to find a CLS scholar in a suit and tie, even when addressing a classroom). In a delightful and friendly critical work on CLS, Jack Schlegal, something of a CLS fellow traveler, characterized Duncan Kennedy as "a cross between Rasputin and Billy Graham. Machiavellian, and with a gift for blarney that would make the stone get up, walk over, and kiss him, he can work an audience or an individual with the seductiveness of a revivalist preacher, for Kennedy wants your soul."[851]

While much of the work of CLS was sophisticated in the extreme, it was still possible, given some remarks by some CLS scholars, to dismiss the movement as some sort of naïve quasi-communist conspiracy. The most notorious example might have been a couple of sentences written by one of CLS's founders and most prolific scholars, Mark Tushnet, who speculated about what he might do if he were a judge:

---

[850] See, e.g., Duncan Kennedy, How the Law School Fails: A Polemic, 1 Yale Rev. L. Soc. Action 71 (1970). This has been labelled Kennedy's "wonderfully jargoned, foul-tempered Polemic against the Yale Law School." Schlegal, *supra* note 842, at 393. Schlegal wrote, "Debarred it is said, from seeking a job at Yale because of the Polemic, Kennedy returned to Cambridge. . . ." *Ibid.* Kennedy is a graduate of Harvard College (class of 1964).

[851] Schlegal, *supra* note 842, at 392.

I am invariably asked, "Well, yes, but how would you decide the X case?" . . . My answer, in brief, is to make an explicitly political judgment: which result is, in the circumstances now existing, likely to advance the cause of socialism? Having decided that, I would write an opinion in some currently favored version of Grand Theory.[852]

These remarks were even thrown at Supreme Court nominee Elena Kagan (who was Dean of the Harvard Law School when Tushnet was hired there), to see if she agreed with them. She testified, "If Professor Tushnet meant that a judge should decide cases based on her own policy views about the best result, then I would characterize that approach as contrary to the rule of law." She was then asked "Would you endorse it? Why or why not?" And she replied, "No. Judges should decide cases based on legal sources, not on policy or political views." Her interlocutor, Senator Tom Coburn, then asked, "Do you agree with the views of the Critical Legal Studies movement?" Her answer: "No." She was, of course, confirmed.[853] Whether the now Justice Kagan continues to render rulings based only on "legal sources, not on policy or political views," can be left to the reader's determination.

In one of the most provocative and canonical pieces by a CLS scholar, Peter Gabel's review of a book by Ronald Dworkin,[854] noted briefly in Chapter 12, Gabel accused Dworkin of trying to romanticize and thus justify the legal

---

[852] Mark Tushnet, The Dilemmas of Liberal Constitutionalism, 42 Ohio St. L.J. 411, 424 (1981). See also, on Tushnet, *infra* note 1150.

[853] See generally "Kagan on Mark Tushnet and Harold Koh: Post Confirmation Hearing Responses to Senators Questions," July 10, 2010, a posting on the Constitutional Law Prof Blog site, http://lawprofessors.typepad.com/conlaw/2010/07/kagan-on-mark-tushnet-and-harold-koh-post-confirmation-hearing-responses-to-senators-questions.html (accessed January 9, 2015).

[854] Peter Gabel, Book Review (of Ronald Dworkin, Taking Rights Seriously (1977)), 91 Harv. L. Rev. 302 (1977).

system and the means of production of late capitalism, or as Gabel called it, "pluralism." In Gabel's view this was inappropriate because:

> In our world this production process operates very destructively, separating us from ourselves and from each other so efficiently that we forget what our true needs are by driving our memory of them into an oblivion which psychoanalysis calls "the unconscious." It is only by transforming these processes themselves rather than by tinkering with a legal system that legitimates them that we can create the possible conditions for a concrete justice—that is, the possible conditions for a living milieu in which human labor is a creative social activity, in which the production of material goods is purposefully designed to satisfy real human needs, and in which each person recognizes the other as "one-of-us" instead of "other-than-me" irrespective of sex or skin color. These possible conditions cannot emerge from the "free world" of an anarchic and exploitative market, nor from a state-bureaucratic socialism that simply reproduces the hierarchical structures of capitalist production techniques in another name. They can emerge only from an open and decentralized socialism that has yet to appear in developed form anywhere in the world.[855]

It is difficult not to have some sympathy with such a committed scholar who argues for what he believes is necessary to complete our real natures, what Gabel also characterized as the "true needs of the human heart as opposed to the distorted needs which have emerged from the operation of a market organized for profit,"[856] but the clear

---

[855] *Id.*, at 314–315 (footnotes omitted).
[856] *Id.*, at 314.

call for "an open and decentralized socialism that has yet to appear in developed form anywhere in the world," was not the typical thing one expected from American law professors, and alarmed some more conservative dwellers in the legal academy.

Still, it was hard not to be charmed by some of the rather romantic notions from at least some of the CLS scholars, particularly Kennedy and Gabel. In one of the more accessible CLS pieces, called by one critic, "an open window to CLS mentality,"[857] the first article in a symposium on CLS, published in the Stanford Law Review, there was a delightful dialogue between the two of them.[858] The repartee began with Kennedy lamenting to Gabel that "You are betraying our program by conceptualizing it. To accept or even sympathize with a statement like, 'The goal is to return to the unalienated situation. . . .'" To which Gabel apparently cut him off and corrected him, "Not that. We've never been there. The project is to realize the unalienated relatedness that is immanent within our alienated situation. I don't like 'goal' and we can't return to what hasn't yet been realized."[859] Rejecting Gabel's attempt at conceptualization, Kennedy suggested that "What I'm saying is, that that does not sound to me like an evocation which can fulfill the legitimate functions of communication, of language and knowledge, because it's abstract bullshit, whereas what we need is small-scale, microphenomenalogical evocation of real experiences in complex contextualized ways in which one makes it into doing it."[860] Explaining further, Kennedy and Gabel agreed that what they were seeking was something that they called

---

[857] Austin, *supra* note 844, at 250.

[858] Peter Gabel & Duncan Kennedy, Roll Over Beethoven, 36 Stan.L.Rev. 1 (1984).

[859] *Ibid.*

[860] *Id.*, at 3.

"intersubjective zap,"[861] and Kennedy then seemed to define that by saying "Let's just call it love. I mean we can call it love this week, and next week we'll call it community, and the week after that. . . ."[862]

Such an effort at establishing meaningful human contact is attractive, but other aspects of the dialogue between the two were disturbing. For example, there is Gabel's comment that "Of course I agree that there's no way to present anything like this, any knowledge any form of thought, that can't be taken over and falsified immediately, the same way that the appointment of Sandra Day O'Connor is an attempt to falsify the meaning of the women's movement."[863] Or Kennedy's lament that "So there's this conflict, which is, on the one hand, you want to get the best one you can; you want to be lucid; you want to be explicit; you want to get clear. But unfortunately the body snatchers are always nearby, and you wake up and they are all pods. The whole conceptual structure has been turned into a cluster of pods."[864]

The implication that all Republicans (or at least Republican Presidents) are probably corrupt and/or pod people does make it harder to take this analysis seriously (but then seriousness may not be what Kennedy and Gabel had in mind). It is also alarming when Kennedy repudiates a subtle concept that he advanced in his pathbreaking article on *Blackstone's Commentaries*, where he explored a "fundamental contradiction" in the law and in human relations which simultaneously sought to implement

---

[861] An elusive term which denoted deep and meaningful human contact, as Kennedy asked, "Why can't I call it just yearning? What's wrong with calling it intersubjective zap? Or making the kettle boil?" *Id.*, at 4.

[862] *Id.*, at 4.

[863] *Id.*, at 5.

[864] *Id.*, at 7. Kennedy is here referring to the movie, Invasion of the Body Snatchers. See, e.g., the riveting 1978 remake starring Jeff Goldblum and Geena Davis, which appeared six years before Gabel and Kennedy's article.

"altruism" and "individualism."[865] Fearing, apparently, that "the fundamental contradiction" could be put to bad use by pod people, Kennedy declared that the fundamental contradiction, which might have been a useful concept at one time for CLS, should now "be utterly extirpated and rooted out of our movement as an example of incorrect thought."[866] No party commissar could have put it better, but, of course, Kennedy may have been joking.

Even though they appear to be doing it, in the dialogue, both Gabel and Kennedy reject philosophizing, and seem to be striving for something more authentic, as Kennedy put it, "what I think we need to do is look for ways of talking, ways of responding, ways of doing things in which the goal is not convince people by Lucidity. It's not to grasp or control their minds by the explicitness and the beauty with which we get at the real structure of reality. But rather to operate in the interspace of artifacts, gestures, speeches and rhetoric, histrionics, drama, all very paradoxical, soap opera, pop culture, all that kind of stuff."[867] Or, as Gabel explained, "Trust among us may, although it hasn't yet occurred in human history, be creatable to the point at which the temptation to reject, objectify and misrecognize the other person is no longer a temptation, and it could still be the case that we could exist in time, negating and surpassing ourselves, but creating whatever we create in life through cooperation, love, mutual respect, mutual confirmation and so forth."[868]

The remarkable dialogue of "Roll Over Beethoven" is perplexing because while both are clearly committed to the CLS project, there seems to be a fundamental difference in

---

[865] See note 676, *supra,* and accompanying text. For Blackstone, see Chapter 1, *supra.*

[866] Gabel and Kennedy, *supra* note 858, at 18.

[867] *Id.,* at 9.

[868] *Id.,* at 20.

point of view between Gabel and Kennedy. As Kennedy described it "the gooey Pollyanna [Peter], who claims that everything can be made fine—and me [Duncan]—the dark, cynical meanie who wants to emphasize the down side of everything."[869] Perhaps what the Crits were really arguing for was something not all that different from the traditional aims of progressive theorists. As Gabel put it in one point of the dialogue, the people whom he taught at New College were "people who want to transform the society, to being about real equality, real democracy, shared control over the workplace, more love and connection—all of that."[870]

At least at one point some of the Crits (here Roberto Unger, Mark Tushnet and Peter Gabel are important) and their arguments against current legal hierarchies (Duncan Kennedy's critique of legal education especially)[871] served as a sort of antidote to the worship of figures like Charles Kingsfield.[872] As some of the Crits (here Bob Gordon is important) acknowledged, and as the Harvard Student Note celebrating their work made clear, their effort was really a reinvigoration of American Legal Realism, but their borrowing from Europe, their passion for social change, and the ecumenical nature of their endeavor (Roberto Unger was not only inspired by Marxism, but also by Catholic teaching) was appealing to many law students. Equally

---

[869] *Id.*, at 24.

[870] *Id.*, at 26.

[871] Published in book form as Duncan Kennedy, Legal Education and the Reproduction of Hierarchy: A Polemic Against the System (A Critical Edition, with an Introduction and Afterward by the Author, with Commentaries by Paul Carrington, Peter Gabel, Angela Harris and Donna Maeda, and Janet Halley, N.Y.U.Press 2004).

[872] See Chapter 13, *supra*. Indeed, there seems to be emerging in some of the latest scholarship from clinical law professors the idea that critical theory, of a kind that CLS was developing, can be of crucial importance even in the learning of techniques for transactional practice in business law clinics. See the notable recent article, Alina S. Ball, Disrupting Pedagogy: Incorporating Critical Legal Theory in Business Law Clinics, 22 Clinical Law Review 1 (2015).

appealing to some of them, perhaps, was the fact that the effort of CLS was also aimed at refuting the claims to objectivity and appropriateness of the then emerging school of law and economics.[873] At least some of the CLS scholars, if not the majority of them, might be described as seeking to "generate radical political alternatives to existing institutions and [to] challenge the legal culture with alternative theories suggesting that current orderings are neither necessary nor eternal."[874]

The Harvard Student Note on CLS said of the movement within the law schools, "Relentlessly iconoclastic, critical scholarship refuses to accept the legal, social or political suppositions of traditional academia."[875] It will not come as much of a surprise, then, to acknowledge that while some practitioners of CLS quite clearly were nobly attempting to reform the law from within, the total critique of purportedly illegitimate hierarchies, and the lambasting of the current legal profession for tunnel vision and for permitting the law to foster continued discrimination against the poor, the different, and the powerless, led some even liberal law professors to believe that there was something inappropriate about the presence of critical legal scholars in the legal academy. This led also, among some students and teachers, to a belief that the kind of scholarship in which the CLS scholars were engaged was of little use to lawyers. For many of their law school colleagues, it is difficult not to believe, the work of the Crits

---

[873] See, e.g., Note, *supra* note 846, at N.73 (noting that "the debunking of law and economics" was a "major effort of critical scholarship"). See also, in this connection, Morton J. Horwitz, Law and Economics: Science or Politics, 8 Hofstra Law Review 905 (1980) (The argument of a prominent CLS scholar that the efforts of the Law and Economics Scholars, and in particular, Richard Posner, are more about politics than about science). For Posner, see Chapter 15, *infra*.

[874] Note, *supra* note 846, at 1684. On this point see also Ball, *supra* note 872.

[875] *Id.*, at 1688. See also Ball, *supra* note 872.

was completely antithetical to the "treatise tradition," and was more fit for revolution than it was for the practice of law.

This was lamented and recognized by some of the more sensitive Crits, for example, the elegant Robert Gordon, who denounced the "rednecks" of the legal profession, which rednecks argued that the Crits had no place in law schools, and had an obligation to leave. For Gordon, the Crits were the most sensitive, the most honest, and the most reform-minded of the current crop of law professors, and the picture he painted of his CLS colleagues was an attractive one, indeed, one in keeping with the finest traditions of reform and service of the American Legal Profession.[876] Thus, while some professors found it difficult to distinguish among critical legal studies scholars, hard-core-Marxists and those advocating the overthrow of the United States Legal System by force and violence, some of the most brilliant law students were absolutely captivated, in the same manner that some professors, like Robert Gordon, were.

Is it more than a coincidence that Barack Obama went to the Harvard Law School at the period when CLS peaked? Could the President's very clear understanding that legal rules are malleable at the least, and likely to be ignored completely by those who have the power to do so, come from CLS?[877] Did Mark Tushnet, an extraordinarily brilliant and

---

[876] See the discussion of Gordon's dialogue with Paul Carrington, *infra*, Chapter 19.

[877] On the President and his beliefs, see Chapter 23, *infra*. Not just the President, but also his first Attorney General, Eric Holder, and by extension, the United States Department of Justice, may be influenced by CLS. This observation has begun to penetrate the mainstream (or at least the conservative part of the mainstream) media. See, e.g., Victor Davis Hansen, "Living Out Critical Legal Theory," The Corner, August 19, 2014 (National Review Online). ("So we live now, I think, in service to critical legal theory: Legal statutes are seen as constructs that legitimize the prejudices of the wealthy and the privileged of society. Our so-called legislatures and judiciaries

prolific CLS scholar, give away the game when he wrote in his infamous law review piece that his aim, if he were a judge would be to do what he could to advance socialism in this country? Is this where President Obama's purported Fabian Socialism comes from? Whatever its influence on the future President Obama, however, CLS became somewhat discredited after 1989, when decentralized socialism looked less attractive after the fall of the Berlin Wall, the collapse of the Soviet Union, and the triumph of free-market economics in the Balkans, but CLS's mantra that all law was essentially politics did receive some reinforcement after the *Bush v. Gore* decision in 2000, and prominent Crits still occupy senior teaching positions at Harvard and Yale, and several other law schools.

The CLS scholars recognized the clearly transformative character of American law, and implied that future transformations, to secure a more just legal system, were desirable. Perhaps the most prominent example of such scholars is the Harvard legal historian, Morton J. Horwitz. His 1977 book on the nineteenth century changes in private law, making just such an argument, *The Transformation of American Law 1780–1860*,[878] won the Bancroft prize, the

---

use the law as means of coercion to ensure their own position in a most unfair hierarchy. In response, the proverbial people, whether in Ferguson or at the border certainly, or, yes, at the Obama Department of Justice, have the moral right to ignore these constructs and instead to fashion their own sort of higher justice, which deserves to be canonized as legal and binding.") Accessed at http://www.nationalreview.com/corner/385718/living-out-critical-legal-theory-victor-davis-hanson, August 23, 2014. Hansen was commenting on Eric Holder's response to the events in Ferguson, Mo. in August 2014, when a white police officer killed an unarmed black teenager, and on the Obama administration's purported refusal to stem the tide of undocumented foreign national children flooding the nation's southern border. Whether Attorney General Holder was really influenced by CLS is simply speculative, however. Holder attended Columbia Law School, graduating in 1976, before CLS peaked in influence in the law schools, and Columbia, unlike Harvard, was not the "Rome" of CLS.

[878] Morton J. Horwitz, The Transformation of American Law 1780–1860 (Harvard, 1977). See also the later volume, Morton J. Horwitz, The

history fraternity's greatest honor. *Transformation*, surely one of the most important works in legal history in the twentieth century, may well have done more than any other work to bring the ideas of CLS quite close to the mainstream in the American legal academy, if not the academy generally. Moreover, several years after the perhaps illusory apparent decline of CLS, Horwitz published a much more accessible and passionate work on the Warren Court, again implying the contingency of law, this time Constitutional law, and showing how social forces could affect and change purportedly immutable law. The contrast Horwitz drew between two possible conceptions of Constitutional law is telling:

> If the Constitution outlines 'certain unalienable Rights' with which individuals are 'endowed by their Creator,' then one would expect a picture of historically fixed and unchanging constitutional rights. If, however, one expects legal principles to evolve over time depending on changing circumstances or changing moral and legal ideas, then we should avoid speaking of rights as if they are inherent in the nature of things, like the law of gravity. We should recognize instead that constitutional principles, like all legal principles, are inevitably created by judges in accordance with their conceptions of moral values and social needs.[879]

For Horwitz, the Warren court clearly embraced this latter, "living Constitution," view of Constitutional law, embodied in Warren's famous statement from *Brown v. Board of Education*, that one "can't turn back the clock," in

---

Transformation of American Law 1870–1960: The Crisis of Legal Orthodoxy (Oxford, 1992).

[879] Morton J. Horwitz, The Warren Court and the Pursuit of Justice 28–29 (1998).

Constitutional law to the time of the framers. Horwitz made this explicit when he discussed the Warren Court's transformation in the Constitutional law regarding reapportionment of state legislatures. The original Constitutional understanding, Horwitz made clear, was that bicameral legislatures, like the federal legislature itself, might have had one house constructed to reflect population, but a second house, like the United States Senate, might have reflected different traditional political subdivisions (or, as Thomas Jefferson had observed in his Notes on Virginia, some houses in state legislatures were designed to reflect property, rather than population).[880] The Warren Court, however, in its famous reapportionment decisions, such as *Reynolds v. Sims*, rejected this notion, allowing state legislatures to be reapportioned in all of their branches only on the basis of population, and claiming that this was dictated by the Fourteenth Amendment's Equal Protection clause. Wrote Horwitz, regarding this famous "one man one vote" standard for apportionment of state legislatures:

> . . . [T]he idea that equal protection meant that legislative districts in both houses [of state legislatures] should be required to contain equal populations was a dramatic rejection of the original constitutional understanding. It could only be justified on the grounds that democracy— the right to an equally effective vote—had evolved to become the foundational constitutional ideal. Such a view presupposed a 'living Constitution,' one that, in Chief Justice Marshall's words,

---

[880] Thomas Jefferson, Notes on the State of Virginia 149 (originally published 1787, available on the web in several places, among the best is http://www.thefederalistpapers.org/wp-content/uploads/2012/12/Thomas–Jefferson–Notes–On–The–State–Of–Virginia.pdf, accessed 15 March 2016). ("In some of the American States, the delegates and senators are so chosen, as that the first represent the persons, and the second the property of the State.")

changed and evolved over time, adapting to 'the various crises of human affairs.' Under such a view, the Court could legitimately generate new fundamental constitutional meanings.[881]

Conservatives, like Justice Scalia, would, of course, have dissented. Still, Horwitz's work on the Warren Court, presented in an extraordinarily readable and passionate short monograph, showed to legal and other audiences that transformation had been a characteristic of American law since the beginning, and continued, clearly, with the work of the Warren Court. Ultimately, however, the message of CLS was about more than past transformations, and was, really, the Thrasymachian insight that justifications for legal rules concealed their origin in raw assertions of power. Said Jack Schlegal, a friendly observer:

> Beyond its beginning [CLS] has only people, people sharing a common politics that convinces them that existing rules of law are not justifiable. If the liberal conceit continues to unravel, and all concerned become aware that the postulated dichotomy between the public sphere of politics and the private sphere of law is fraudulent—that, in a phrase, LAW IS POLITICS, pure and simple— then the movement and its visible organ [CLS] may be of some significance in the world. If not, if it remains a group of individuals providing each other with tremendous mutual support in a world seen to be basically hostile towards them, if it ends up only a "lonely hearts club for leftwing law professors," then it will still be important, maybe even more so.[882]

---

[881] Horwitz, Warren Court, *supra* note 879, at 85.
[882] Schlegal, *supra* note 842, at 410–411 (caps in original, footnotes omitted).

The Obama Presidency may be the unfolding of some of the ideas promoted by critical legal studies, in particular, that legal actors can reshape the institutions of the market economy and even of democracy itself. The Obama administration, in some ways, appears to be undertaking the transformation of American society through the use of the power of the central state. But if a President influenced by critical legal studies is employing executive power in a new and transformative manner, critical legal studies itself has not actually stood still, nor has it become as moribund as its critics might have assumed.

As late as 2015, in a new and expanded edition of his summary of the movement, its most provocative scholar, Roberto Unger, published *The Critical Legal Studies Movement: Another Time, A Greater Task*, in which he argued that, roughly forty years after its birth, Critical Legal Studies could still serve as an inspiration for radical reordering of American and world society. In a dense, but brilliant reexamination of CLS, Unger argued that "the potential of law and legal thought to inform the self-construction of society under democracy remains largely untapped."[883] Curiously, some at the elite reaches of the judiciary and the academy appear to have no interest in such an untapping. The man whom we will consider next, Richard Posner, wrote of CLS that they "exaggerated when they generalized their criticisms to all courts—exaggerated to a point at which they were seen as a residue of 1960's—style infantile leftism. Eventually they became a laughing-stock, imploded, and vanished with few traces."[884] What accounts for the deep difference in perception between

---

[883] Roberto M. Unger, The Critical Legal Studies Movement: Another Time, A Greater Task (Verso, 2015).

[884] Richard M. Posner, Divergent Paths: The Academy and the Judiciary 263–264 (2016). It is likely that the reports of CLS's death are greatly exaggerated. See, e.g., notes 883 and 872, *supra*.

Unger and Posner? Could it be that they actually live in different legal worlds?

CHAPTER 15

THE ECONOMIC APPROACH TO LAW

LATE TWENTIETH, EARLY TWENTY-FIRST CENTURY

Richard Posner
(Chicago)

■ ■ ■

Richard Posner (b. 1939)
Courtesy chambers of Judge Posner.

Profiled in the New Yorker[885] (a singular achievement for an American Law Professor), Posner was said in that profile to have a "freakish productivity," and to publish a book "every half hour."[886] It is true that he is the author of dozens of volumes, spanning topics from *Sex and Reason*[887]

---

[885] Larissa MacFarquhar, Profiles: The Bench Burner: How did a judge with such subversive ideas become a leading influence on American legal opinion?, The New Yorker, December 10, 2001, pages 78–89.

[886] *Id.*

[887] Richard A. Posner, Sex and Reason (Harvard, 1992).

to the Future of Capitalism.[888] According to the New Yorker, "He has written books about AIDS, law and literature, and the Clinton impeachment trial, and articles about pornography, Hegel, and medieval Iceland."[889] According to the Columbia Journalism Review in 2005, "Posner is the most prolific federal judge in American history. In addition to more than 2,200 published opinions, he's written thirty-eight books on a dizzying array of topics, from Monicagate to aging to intelligence reform, and more than 300 articles, op-ed pieces, reviews, and essays— including a recent blockbuster about the press."[890] By early 2016, the Harvard Magazine, in another admiring profile of Posner, could note that he had published 64 books since 1973, "counting each edition of several of his legal treatises."[891] That was apparently a publication record unmatched by any American Law Professor, and Posner was one of, if not the most, influential law professors of the late twentieth century. Well into the twenty-first, Posner could be said to be "the most influential American legal scholar during his almost half-century in the academy," as well as "the most cited legal scholar 'of all time' by a wide margin."[892] In 2001 Posner was "the jurist most often cited in scholarly articles—cited almost as much as the next two, Ronald Dworkin[893] and Oliver Wendell Holmes, Jr.[894] added

---

[888] Richard A. Posner, The Crisis of Capitalist Democracy (Harvard, 2011).

[889] MacFarquhar, *supra* note 885.

[890] John Giuffo, Judging Richard: One of America's most influential judges seems to take a dim view of journalism, but the record reveals a more complicated case, Columbia Journalism Review, November 10, 2005, available at http://www.law.uchicago.edu/news/posner111005 (accessed September 17, 2015).

[891] Lincoln Caplan, "Rhetoric and Law: The double life of Richard Posner, America's most contentious legal reformer," Harvard Magazine 49, 50 (January–February 2016).

[892] *Id.*, at 50, quoting Fred Shapiro, a librarian at Yale Law School.

[893] See Chapter 12, *supra*.

[894] See Chapter 5, *supra*.

together."[895] The New Yorker labelled him "the most mercilessly seditious legal theorist of his generation."[896]

Posner is not simply famous as a law professor, but has also been an enormously important federal judge.[897] "He has been among the country's most influential judges in shaping other court decisions, measured by the number of times other judges have cited his judicial opinions."[898] Indeed, Henry Friendly, the most famous federal lower court judge of *his* era wrote to Posner to say that he believed that Posner was "the best judge in the country."[899]

Posner is generally credited with the invention or at least the popularization of Law and Economics,[900] the jurisprudential strain within American Legal Education that argued that American law in general, and the American common law in particular, was best understood as the application of cost-benefit analysis to social problems, in a search for the best means of wealth maximization or

---

[895]   MacFarquhar, *supra* note 885, at 78.

[896]   *Ibid.*

[897]   Henry Friendly and Richard Posner "have been cited by name by the U.S. Supreme Court, the U.S. Courts of Appeals, and the U.S. Districts[sic] Court more often by far than any other circuit court judges." William Domnarski, The Correspondence of Henry Friendly and Richard A. Posner 1982–86, 51 Am.J.Leg.Hist. 395, n.2 (2011). Posner "is the most influential circuit court judge of his" generation. *Ibid.* Posner took his seat as a federal judge at the age of 43, and continued to teach at the University of Chicago throughout his tenure on the bench, with the title of Senior Lecturer in Law.

[898]   Caplan, *supra* note 891, at 50.

[899]   Domnarski, *supra* note 897, at 400, quoting Henry Friendly to Richard Posner, September 19, 1984.

[900]   Lincoln Caplan writes that Posner built on "the work of Nobel Prize-winning economists Gary Becker, Ronald Coase, and George Stigler, the economist Aaron Director, and the legal scholar Guido Calabresi," and "did more than anyone else to promote the approach called 'law and economics.'" Caplan, *supra* note 891, at 52. For the seminal importance of Coase, see, e.g., Elizabeth Hoffman and Matthew Spitzer, "The Enduring Power of Coase," 54 Journal of Law and Economics 563 (2011). Available at: http://chicago unbound.uchicago.edu/jle/vol54/iss5/18.

efficiency.[901] As late as 2016 it could be said that law and economics, "remains the most influential movement in the law since the 1930's."[902] Posner's 1972 *Economic Analysis of Law*[903] was "published when he was only 34 years old," and "changed the way that law was understood."[904] In this work "Posner included lengthy sections on the common law, family law, regulation, corporate and securities law, tax and wealth distribution, constitutional law, and federalism."[905] Posner's essential thesis in the book was that "economic efficiency is the most defensible goal for legal rules. Redistribution may be appropriate too, but it should be explicit and direct rather than disguised by costly regulations or subsidies."[906] This mode of thought, sometimes called "The Chicago School," because so many practitioners of law and economics have worked at the University of Chicago, is known for its relentless and perhaps even bloodless analysis of law and policy according to costs and benefits.

A central tenet of this approach to jurisprudence is that the common law judges, presumably both in England and America, have taken advantage of the flexibility offered by the system of following precedents and turning them in new directions, pragmatically to create new applications of legal

---

[901] Herbert Hovenkamp, The Opening of American Law: Neoclassical Legal Thought 1870–1970 118–119 (Oxford, 2015) makes clear that neither Ronald Coase, Richard Posner, nor Guido Calabresi (the three most important scholars who influenced the forming of the intellectual school that became law and economics) "single-handedly invented law and economics," and as Hovenkamp's book shows "Economic analysis of law" was well developed long before these three. *Id.*, at 318. Still, Hovenkamp concedes Posner's powerful expansion of "the domain of law and economics to nearly every legal area." *Id.*, at 319.

[902] Caplan, *supra* note 891, at 52.

[903] Richard A. Posner, Economic Analysis of Law (Little Brown, 1972).

[904] Domnarski, *supra* note 897, at 397. The book is currently in its 9th edition.

[905] Hovenkamp, *supra* note 901, at 319.

[906] *Id.*, at 319.

rules that encouraged economic development, maximization of wealth, and sensible efficiency. As Posner put it in a June 13, 1983 letter to Henry Friendly, "[I]n my scholarly writing I espoused the view, which I continue to believe, that the common law represents a more or less consistent body of principles, many of them explicable in terms of simple economic theory."[907] As the *New Yorker* explained, "In hearing a case, [Posner] doesn't first inquire into the constricting dictates of precedent; instead, he comes up with what strikes him as a sensible solution, then looks to see whether precedent excludes it."[908]

Posner's approach, now proceeding under the rubric of "legal pragmatism," or a "practical and instrumental" approach to deciding cases, was summarized by one of the country's outstanding legal journalists, Lincoln Caplan, as

> "*forward-looking*, valuing continuity with the past only so far as such continuity can help us cope with the problems of the present and of the future;" "*empirical*" focused on facts; "*skeptical*," doubtful that any decision legal or otherwise represents "the final truth about anything" because frames of reference change over time; and "*antidogmatic*" committed to "freedom of inquiry" and "a diversity of inquirers"—in other words to the "*experimental*"—because progress comes through changes in frames of reference over time "the replacement of one perspective or world view with another."[909]

A jurisprudence focused on "forward looking," "empirical" analysis, which is "skeptical," "antidogmatic," and "experimental," is, of course, one fraught with judicial

---

[907] Quoted in Domnarski, *supra* note 897, at 405.

[908] MacFarquhar, *supra* note 885, at 78.

[909] Caplan, *supra* note 891, at 50 (the italics were said by Caplan to be Posner's).

discretion and uncertainty. This sort of jurisprudence, then, comes about as close as anything can to justifying the role of judges (as, it is true, they have been sometimes at common law) as creators and shapers of the law, and as such, presents a direct challenge to the notion that there is a clearly-established rule of law that ought to govern human actions in general and the decisions of judges in particular. America's most brilliant legal scholar, Richard Posner, then, appears to have little faith in the most traditional of American notions, that ours is a government of laws, not men.

And if common law judges have great discretion, for Posner judges on the United States Supreme Court have even more. In a recent op-ed piece in the Washington Post, Posner stated that "the Supreme Court is not an ordinary court but a political court, or more precisely a politicized court, which is to say a court strongly influenced in making its decisions by the political beliefs of the judges." For Posner, given the uncertainty in the meaning of Constitutional language, and the failure to anticipate what the future would hold by the Constitution's framers, discretion for Supreme Court justices was inevitable, and while they might utter "official" or "self-protective" claims that "the law made me do it," this was and is not the case.[910]

Earlier, before he embraced "pragmatism," and while he was still closely identified with "law and economics" and its adherents at the University of Chicago, Posner was described as having "the most magnificent and chilly mind in this realm," and one article in the New York Times Sunday magazine claimed that Posner once was able, on the basis of empirical survey data, to use "projections to price

---

[910] Richard A. Posner, The Supreme Court is a political court, Republicans' actions are proof, The Washington Post, March 9, 2016, available on the web at https://www.washingtonpost.com/opinions/the-supreme-court-is-a-political-court-republicans-actions-are-proof/2016/03/09/4c851860–e142–11e5–8d98–4b3d9215ade1_story.html (accessed 4 April 2016).

the benefit of preventing the extinction of the human race at $600 trillion."[911] Law and Economics' obvious debt to Oliver Wendell Holmes, Jr. is underscored by the fact that Posner edited a collection of Holmes's writings,[912] Holmes is Posner's "hero,"[913] and Holmes's influence can be discerned in much of Posner's scholarship, as indicated earlier.

Posner began his scholarly career as a darling of the Right (in 1981, he was a Reagan appointee to the United States Court of Appeals for the Seventh Circuit, which sits in Chicago), but his latest scholarship, his espousing "legal pragmatism," leans more toward the center or even the left, as he has increasingly become both a pragmatist and a libertarian. He was an early champion of the Common Law, but his latest writing begins to question, to a certain extent, the free market, and Posner's work is a sign, perhaps, that even the most brilliant of legal scholars cannot help but exhibit some indecision in the early twenty-first century. Whatever the beliefs of the early Posner, by the time he considered the impeachment of President William Jefferson Clinton by the House of Representatives in late 1998, and the Senate Trial in which the President prevailed, Posner's pragmatism had begun to look distinctly post-modern, as his thought seemed to reflect the profound difficulty of achieving an objective view of law, politics, or, indeed, reality.[914] Thus, he wrote of that "Affair of State," that

---

[911] Benjamin Wallis Wells, "Cass Sunstein Wants to Nudge Us," New York Times Magazine, May 13, 2010, available on the web at http://www.ny times.com/2010/05/16/magazine/16Sunstein-t.html?pagewanted=all&_r=0 (accessed February 28, 2015).

[912] Richard A. Posner, ed., The Essential Holmes: Selections from the Letters, Speeches, Judicial Opinions, and Other Writings of Oliver Wendell Holmes, Jr. (Chicago, 1992).

[913] MacFarquhar, *supra* note 885, at 88.

[914] For a similar observation on the content of the currently trendy "postmodern" thought, see, e.g., Charles L. Barzun, Jerome Frank, Lon Fuller, and a Romantic Pragmatism, University of Virginia School of Law, Public Law and Legal Theory Research Paper Series 2016–6, January 2016, at 20, and

> [I]n one [of the two possible 'narratives'], a reckless, lawless immoral President commits a series of crimes in order to conceal a tawdry and shameful affair, crimes compounded by a campaign of public lying and slanders. A prosecutor could easily draw up a thirty-count indictment against the President. In the other narrative, the confluence of a stupid law (the independent counsel law), a marginal lawsuit begotten and nursed by political partisanship, a naïve and imprudent judicial decision by the Supreme Court in that suit, and the irresistible human impulse to conceal one's sexual improprieties, allows a trivial sexual escapade (what Clinton and Lewinsky called 'fooling around' or 'messing around') to balloon into a grotesque and gratuitous constitutional drama. The problem is that both narratives are correct.[915]

Critical Legal Studies, explored in the previous chapter, has been seen by some as a long overdue reaction to the purportedly, market-oriented atomistic and somewhat impersonal aspects of Posnerian law and economics.[916] The article that put Posner on the map of provocative legal scholars, and that may have helped lead

---

n.96. ("If it is impossible to observe pure 'facts' about the world, then it would seem we have reason to distrust *all* knowledge claims and view them instead as merely the product of political, economic, social, racial, ideological—or simply arbitrary—interests, and hence irrational (or at least epistemically unjustified). This is, of course, precisely the kind of conclusion some have interpreted 'postmodernists' as endorsing.' ") (emphasis in original)

[915] Richard Posner, An Affair of State: The Investigation, Impeachment and Trial of President Clinton 92 (Harvard, 1999).

[916] For an important critical legal studies' scholar's critique of Law and Economics as politics rather than science, see Morton J. Horwitz, "Law and Economics: Science or Politics?," 8 Hofstra Law Review 905 (1980). For a suggestion that microeconomic analysis may overly simplify the complexity of legal issues, see, e.g., Ronald J. Allen, Complexity, the Generation of Legal Knowledge, and the Future of Litigation, 60 UCLA L. Rev. 1384 (2013).

to antipathy toward the law and economics movement by many in the academy, was called "Killing or Wounding to Protect a Property Interest,"[917] and in it, Posner, drawing on clear, albeit neglected, case law, established that while judges and lawyers steadfastly maintained that human life was the highest value, the actual result of court decisions was, in some instances, to privilege the use of deadly force to defend private property, for example, by setting "spring guns" to kill or wound an unauthorized intruder when one was unable to defend one's valuable property oneself. Posner pointed out other significant areas in which the law appeared to favor property use over human life, such as, for instance, allowing automobiles when there was clearly going to be some loss of life as a byproduct of driving, or allowing the construction of skyscrapers, when there was inevitably going to be some loss of life from hazardous construction.

Some saw in this kind of Posnerian analysis a bloodless regard for the established order, and a naked assertion of the primacy of economic goals over redistributional ones, and this sort of criticism consistently dogged what soon came to be known as "law and economics," with Posner as its chief advocate. As Lincoln Caplan described it, Posner was blasted "for favoring efficiency and individual liberty at the expense of equality, fairness, and justice."[918] Part of this adverse reaction might be explained by the fact that Posner "began propounding the conservative economics of the Chicago School in the late nineteen-sixties, when the legal academy was almost entirely left of center; for this reason he became the object of furious criticism even before he published his more outré theories."[919] Posner himself, in a

---

[917] Richard A. Posner, Killing or Wounding to Protect a Property Interest, 14 J.L. & Econ. 201 (1971).

[918] Caplan, *supra* note 891, at 52.

[919] MacFarquhar, *supra* note 885, at 78.

letter to Henry Friendly in 1984, when Posner may have been under consideration for the United States Supreme Court (he was never so elevated), indicates that "I have become an object of mysterious fascination to a segment of the press, which is doing a pretty good job of portraying me as a weirdo on the basis of some of my pre-judicial academic writing (misrepresented) and a handful of my opinions (misunderstood)."[920]

It does appear that there are personal elements about Posner which might lead to mischaracterization. The New Yorker reported that "he has about him the distant omniscient, ectoplasmic air of the butler in a haunted house."[921] "Posner's pugnacity and impatience, his willingness to confront bureaucracy with practicality, and his tendency to catch people off guard are attributes for which he has become known,"[922] and not always admired. Posner appears to admit that "I have exactly the same personality as my cat. . . . I am cold, furtive, callous, snobbish, selfish, and playful, but with a streak of cruelty." Among the lawyers who appear before him, apparently, "Posner has a reputation . . . for being harsh but not nasty." "Posner takes the Michael Corleone approach. . . . It's business, not personal."[923]

Moreover, some of Posner's writing *is* provocative, to say the very least. He once suggested that "the current adoption system be replaced by a free market in babies, which, he maintained, by offering financial incentives to biological mothers, would make both would-be parents and

---

[920] Richard Posner to Henry Friendly, December 26, 1984, quoted in Domnarski, *supra* note 897, at 411.

[921] MacFarquhar, *supra* note 885, at 78.

[922] Giuffo, *supra* note 890.

[923] MacFarquhar, *supra* note 885, at 81.

potential sellers better off."[924] In that suggestion, of course, the notion of the commodification of human life, which was hinted at in "Killing or Wounding to Protect a Property Interest,"[925] fully flowers.

Still, the criticism of law and economics as inhumane is not wholly fair to Posner, who understands that society is still at least somewhat committed to caring for the sick and infirm (indeed, he suggested that one of the costs of permitting spring guns was injury to burglars who, if impecunious, would have to rely on the provision of health care by the public).[926] Still, Posner frankly acknowledged, in at least some of his early work, that law and economics had nothing to say about the proper distribution of goods in society, and it was clear that a profound regard for private property and individual human liberty was central to Posnerian thought, while some of his critics seemed clearly to favor redistribution, if not socialism.[927]

Posner was unfazed by the critics of law and economics. Noticing that many of those critics sought to undermine the economically-oriented worldview of him and his cohorts, Posner suggested that, for his money, so to speak, economists still had the best grasp of reality of any of the social scientists, and that the approach of legal sociologists, legal anthropologists, and legal psychologists—to pick but a few of the subspecialties that attacked law and economics— were deeply flawed. Indeed, Posner asserted that, when all was said and done, the economists were not only

---

[924] *Id.*, at 81. The article in question was Richard Posner and Elisabeth M. Landes, "The Economics of the Baby Shortage," 7 J. Leg.Stud. 323 (1978).

[925] *Supra* note 917.

[926] For this suggestion, see *Killing or Wounding, supra* note 917.

[927] For one of the most famous critiques of Posner, while still recognizing his aims and strengths as an analyst, see Arthur Allen Leff, "Economic Analysis of Law: Some Realism about Nominalism." 60 Va, L.Rev. 451 (1974).

methodologically superior, but smarter.[928] It was, accordingly, no surprise that Posner's personal popularity sometimes seemed low in the academy. Nevertheless, Posner's influence, particularly on the judiciary, should not be minimized. As one appreciation recently put it "Posner . . . has continued our tradition of great judges."[929] In this he was like Henry Friendly, the two of them were judges who could resist the "increasingly politicized, bureaucratized, and specialized" nature and the increasing workloads of the Federal bench, which combined to deprive "more and more judges of time for reflection, discussion, and outside reading," which Posner himself once said "bode ill for the continuation of our tradition of great judges."[930] It could also be said, by one of the most astute critics of twentieth-century legal thought that "An important key to the success of [Posner's] work, and to the law and economics movement generally, has been an ability to marshal its insights into a positive and evolving program for legal reconstruction, something that other twentieth-century critiques including Legal Realism and Critical Legal Studies were never able to accomplish."[931]

More, there is about Posner a sense of the absurd that is, still, quite charming. Thus, for example, when he and his wife, Charlene (Radcliffe, class of 1960), lived in Washington, "they owned a Norwegian elkhound of servile disposition, poignantly misnamed 'Fang.' "[932] Posner effects something that may well be genuine modesty. He began at

---

[928] See, e.g., Richard A. Posner, "The Economic Approach to Law," 53 Tex.L.Rev. 757 (1975) (responding to critics such as Leff).

[929] Domnarski, *supra* note 897, at 416. Mr. Domnarski recently published the first full-length biography of Posner, William Domnarski, Richard Posner (Oxford, 2016).

[930] Richard A. Posner, "In Memoriam: Henry J. Friendly," 99 Harv. L. Rev. 1724, 1725 (1986), quoted in Domnarski, *supra* note 897, at 416.

[931] Hovenkamp, *supra* note 901, at 319.

[932] MacFarquhar, *supra* note 885, at 82.

Yale College at the age of 16, where he was elected to Phi Beta Kappa as a junior, and graduated *summa cum laude* in English.[933] At Harvard Law School he became the President of the Harvard Law Review [as did Barack Obama],[934] and in 1962, he was awarded the Fay diploma, which goes to the student with the highest combined grade point average during the three years of law school.[935] Posner still claims that "I'm not any kind of genius or anything."[936] This may be simply incorrect. "Norman Dorsen, a former president of the American Civil Liberties Union and a longtime New York University law professor who helped write the petitioner's brief in *Roe v. Wade*," appears to dissent. Dorsen reports on the views of Justice William Brennan for whom Posner clerked on the United States Supreme Court. "Brennan was a friend of mine," indicates Dorsen, "and he said to me once that he only met two geniuses in all his years. One was Justice William O. Douglas, and the other was Dick Posner." Dorsen adds "Brennan wouldn't have used the word genius lightly."[937] Philip Elman, a member of the Federal Trade Commission, for whom Posner worked following his Brennan clerkship, referred to Posner as "my genius assistant."[938]

Posner does affect some elements of misanthropy, as when he explained to the writer of his *New Yorker* Profile that "People don't say interesting things. . . . A lot of socializing is just dull—I'd rather read [write?] a book."[939] Still, as one of his sharpest critics, Arthur Allen Leff, understood,[940] Posner has a fundamental devotion to

---

[933] Caplan, *supra* note 891, at 51.

[934] See Chapter 23, *infra*.

[935] *Id.*, at 51.

[936] MacFarquhar, *supra* note 885, at 83.

[937] Quotations are from Giuffo, *supra* note 890.

[938] Caplan, *supra* note 891, at 51.

[939] MacFarquhar, *supra* note 885, at 83.

[940] See note 927, *supra*.

human freedom. He believes that "[A] person is responsible for his own life. External forces and events are just the raw materials out of which we make a life, and we have no right to blame anyone else for the result because it was ours to make or muff. This is a philosophy, or a psychology, basically optimistic, cheerful, and forward-looking, of self-assertion, of liberation from oppressive frameworks such as that created by religion or other dogmas."[941] This isn't really the common lawyers' natural law view of a Blackstone[942] or a Story,[943] but it is not an unattractive one.

Even so, the free-wheeling nature of Posner's jurisprudence has to give any conservative a bit of pause. Posner flatly rejects the views of Justices such as Antonin Scalia[944] or Clarence Thomas, who believe in originalism,[945] the notion that the Constitution should be interpreted according to its understanding at the time it was ratified. While Scalia has famously suggested that eighteenth-century dictionaries be turned to in order to establish the meaning of the Constitution, for Posner "The Constitution is just authorization to the Supreme Court and the lower courts to create a body of common law, which we call 'constitutional.' "[946] What Posner recently wrote of Henry Friendly could be seen to apply to Posner himself:

---

[941] MacFarquhar, *supra* note 885, at 86.

[942] Chapter 1, *supra.*

[943] Chapter 3, *supra.*

[944] Chapter 20, *infra.*

[945] See, e.g., Steven G. Calabresi, Originalism: A Quarter Century of Debate (Regnery, 2007). See also, for a spirited debate between a non-originalist and an originalist, Robert W. Bennett and Lawrence B. Solum, Constitutional Originalism: A Debate (Cornell University Press, 2011), and see, for a rejection of "originalism," and a scholarly defense of the notion of a "Living Constitution," David A. Strauss, The Living Constitution (Oxford, 2010).

[946] Caplan, *supra* note 891, at 50, quoting from Posner's latest (at this writing) book, Divergent Paths: The Academy and the Judiciary (Harvard University Press, 2016).

He tempered academic brilliance with massive common sense. . . . He saw cases not as intellectual puzzles to be solved but as practical disputes to be resolved sensibly and humanely. He bent his powerful legal intelligence to the service of shaping legal doctrine to the enablement of sensible results in individual cases. The aim was to improve the law—American law is in constant need of improvement, in fact is a mess to a degree that only insiders can appreciate—without unduly perturbing the doctrinal and institutional framework that provides necessary stability and continuity.[947]

If the entire federal judiciary were composed of Richard Posners (or Henry Friendlys) this might not be problematic, but, as indicated earlier, what Posner appears to believe is that the judicial task is ultimately legislative. This is, to put it bluntly, at odds with our tradition. As one of Posner's most distinguished critics, the law and literature scholar, James Boyd White, wrote of Posner, his pragmatism "misunderstands the nature of both law and democracy, including the obligation—moral, political, and legal—to respect the authority of legal texts and the fundamental principle of separation of powers.' "[948]

Still, for all his accomplishments, and for all his ultimately undeniable genius, there is, in Posner's candor, something very appealing, indeed. He holds back not at all. He was recently quoted as declaring "I think today's Supreme Court is extremely mediocre."[949] In his opinions, Posner has said, he tries to be "practical and candid," and "to avoid 'solemnity and pomposity,'" and, as Lincoln

---

[947] Richard A. Posner, Forward, to David M. Dorsen, Henry Friendly: Greatest Judge of His Era xiii (Harvard, 2012).

[948] Quoted in Caplan, *supra* note 891, at 51.

[949] *Id.*, at 53.

Caplan observed, "He generally succeeds."[950] Indeed, Caplan went further and declared that Posner's opinions "are crisply written tightly organized, and brightly argued. They are easy to follow and a pleasure to read."[951] That could be said of very, very few appellate judges. "I do try to be candid; I try not to hide my reasoning," Posner told one reporter, "I don't think my opinions really read like the opinions of other judges. Most judicial opinions have a lot of hot air in them."[952]

And if Posner feels free to criticize his fellow judges and even the Justices of the Supreme Court, he is even more critical of his academic colleagues. In a book-length attack about their shortcomings he published in 2016, he condemns what he regards as the "legal culture" they promote, which for him can be seen to be "reflecting the standpatism, the backward-looking focus that is endemic to the judiciary."[953] Rather than praising the nobility or the aspirations of the law, as would a Blackstone, a Story, a Langdell,[954] a Frankfurter[955], or even a Dworkin,[956] Posner appears to believe that there is something deeply missing in the law, which belies its frequent claims to be scientific, solid, objective, accurate or reliable. "[L]aw," Posner explains, "like literary criticism with which it is sometimes compared, and politics which it resembles (while resenting the comparison), and moral philosophy (which could be thought a branch of politics), does not have solid foundations." Instead, "It is ultimately a collection of rules and procedures, highly malleable, often antiquated, often

---

[950] *Id.*, at 55.

[951] *Ibid.*

[952] Giuffo, *supra* note 890.

[953] Richard A. Posner: Divergent Paths: The Academy and the Judiciary 370 (Harvard 2016).

[954] Chapter 4, *supra.*

[955] Chapter 9, *supra.*

[956] Chapter 12, *supra.*

contestable, often internally conflicted, for managing social conflict—a set of aging, blunt tools."[957] True it may be, then, that while Posner might well be Llewellyn's[958] ideal legal realist judge, Posner is not a champion of the rule of law or a government of laws, not men, but still Posner and his jurisprudence are something a bit different from the bloviating superiority of the kind of law professor Duncan Kennedy seemed to scorn. Let's turn, then, to two law professors from Kennedy's alma mater, Yale.

---

[957]　Posner, *supra* note 953, at 376.

[958]　On Llewellyn, see Chapter 8, *supra*.

CHAPTER 16

POPULAR CONSTITUTIONALISM AND THE UNWRITTEN CONSTITUTION

LATE TWENTIETH, EARLY TWENTY-FIRST CENTURY

Bruce Ackerman (Yale Law School)
Akhil Amar (Yale Law School)

■ ■ ■

Bruce Ackerman (b. 1943)
Photograph by Harold Shapiro.
Courtesy Yale Law School.

Akhil Reed Amar (b. 1958)
Photograph by Harold Shapiro.
Courtesy Yale Law School.

As Duncan Kennedy[959] may have understood (since that's where he went to law school), for the Platonic Form of a modern legal academic, nothing can quite compare to a Yale law professor, and there is an impressive audacity to the Constitutional theories of Bruce Ackerman and Akhil Amar, two of the most highly-regarded contemporary Yale

---

[959] See notes 4, 806, 850, and 871 *supra*, and accompanying text.

law professors. The two have put forth a theory of the Constitution in which its meaning can be amended not just through the procedure in Article V (which generally calls for the concurrence of two-thirds of the members of both houses of Congress and three quarters of the state legislatures),[960] but simply through great popular movements, as supposedly occurred at the time of the New Deal, and, later, at the time of the Warren Court.

For Ackerman, who began to set forth the full articulation of this theory in his remarkable We The People: Foundations (1991)[961] there are two kinds of political eras. One is an era of "ordinary" politics, when accepted norms are followed, and the rule of law is applied as it was in the past. Occasionally, however, there are "Constitutional moments," extraordinary times, when the American people (in whose interest, of course, the Constitution is supposed to operate), take it upon themselves, through widespread political expression, to alter the meaning of the document. A "Constitutional moment" is actually a series of events which could be a multistep, multiyear process, "which includes a series of public debates, political fights, elections, and court battles."[962] Evidence of such "Constitutional moments" might be found in "a piece of constitutional text,

---

[960] United States Constitution, Amendment V. For the use of the article V amendatory process see, e.g., Thomas E. Brennan, The Article V Amendatory Constitutional Convention: Keeping the Republic in the Twenty-First Century (Lexington Books, 2014), and David E. Kyvig, Explicit and Authentic Acts: Amending the U.S. Constitution, 1776–2015 (Kansas, Reprint ed., 2016).

[961] Ackerman's work is to be completed as a four-volume exegesis. So far three volumes have appeared. We the People, Volume 1: Foundations (Harvard, 1991), We the People, Volume 2: Transformations (Harvard, 1998), and We the People, Volume 3: The Civil Rights Revolution (Harvard, 2014). The final volume, We the People, Volume 4: Interpretations, will set forth Ackerman's "full-blown theory of constitutional interpretation." Tom Donnelly, Book Review [of Ackerman's Volume 3]: Judicial Popular Constitutionalism, 30 Constitutional Commentary 546 (2015).

[962] Donnelly, *supra* note 961, at 544.

a transformative Supreme Court decision, a landmark statute, or an important political speech."[963] Such "Constitutional moments" have included upheavals such as the Jacksonian Era, the Civil War Era and Reconstruction, and the Great Depression. As a sympathetic critic put it, "Bruce Ackerman's big idea is that popular sovereignty is (and ought to be) the driver of constitutional change within our system."[964] As that critic, Tom Donnelly, explained, elaborating on Ackerman's work:

> In Ackerman's view, American history teaches a simple, but profound lesson. When the American people speak, our tradition permits them to shatter conventional legal barriers and change our constitutional baselines—whether by establishing a new constitution (e.g. the Founding), re-founding our republic through transformative amendments (e.g. Reconstruction), or reshaping foundational ideas without altering the words of the Constitution (e.g. the New Deal).[965]

Pursuant to this theory, courts ought to follow the understanding of the people whether it flows from "the constitutional text that *they* ratify, the constitutional revolutionaries that *they* endorse, [or] the new constitutional understandings that *they* reach."[966]

Lest the notion of popular constitutionalism seem too free-floating, its most thoughtful advocates may seek to limit the reach of the theory. Thus, Tom Donnelley argues that popular constitutionalism should only be used by the

---

[963] *Id.*, at 547.

[964] *Id.*, at 543.

[965] *Id.*, at 543–544. For Donnelly's embrace of Ackerman's project, see, e.g., *id.*, at 546: "Ackerman gets the big things right. Constitutional change ought to be driven by the American people. Courts ought to be bound by genuine acts of popular sovereignty even if they don't satisfy Article V."

[966] *Id.*, at 550 (emphasis in original).

judiciary as a rule of Constitutional construction, "whenever the Constitution's text is vague or irreducibly ambiguous."[967] When, by contrast, "the semantic meaning of the Constitution's text is clear, it ought to control even the committed popular constitutionalist."[968] This is a laudable conservative notion, but, nevertheless, for Donnelly, when the Constitution's text's meaning is "unclear and the American people have reached a considered judgment about how best to give that text life, the popular constitutionalist should grant considerable weight to that judgment as a default rule."[969] Given the ordinary malleability of words, this gives considerable discretion, to say the least, to amend the Constitution outside of Article V.

This discretion appears to be whole-heartedly embraced by Bruce Ackerman. Indeed, much in the manner as did Ronald Dworkin,[970] then, Ackerman conveniently described what he believed to be an actually-existing system of Constitutional Law change which seemed to support the activities and policies he favored. He created, then, an intriguing extra-legal defense of the actions both of the New Deal Court and of the Warren Court, as well. Ackerman's notions, which came to be embodied in the work of several scholars proceeding under the banner of "Popular Constitutionalism,"[971] offered a means of supporting, in the

---

[967] *Id.*, at 550.

[968] *Id.*, at 551.

[969] *Ibid.*

[970] See Chapter 12, *supra.*

[971] Apparently Ackerman himself is not "generally labeled a popular constitutionalist," but Ackerman "was an important forerunner of the movement, urging scholars to look outside both the courts and the formal constraints of Article V to find the real story of Constitutional change in the United States." Tom Donnelly, *supra* note 961, at 541. For two leading articulations of the theory of popular constitutionalism see Larry D. Kramer, The People Themselves: Popular Constitutionalism and Judicial Review (Oxford, 2004) (Donnelly calls Kramer the "Founding Father" of Popular Constitutionalism, Donnelly, *supra* note 961, at 549) and Richard Parker, Here

purported name of popular sovereignty, what would otherwise have to be regarded as egregious departures by the Hughes, Warren, and Burger courts from previously-prevailing orthodox Constitutional interpretation. According to this approach "questions of constitutional interpretation" are "authoritatively settled only by 'the people' " and, as indicated, it is the job of even the Supreme Court to "yield to" the judgment of the people "about what the Constitution means."[972]

Popular Constitutionalism claims legitimacy through the theory of popular sovereignty, which, after all, is the only legitimate American Constitutional philosophy, since we have neither a monarchy nor an hereditary aristocracy, nor, of course, do we have an established religious hierarchy. In the words of Richard Parker, "After all, democracy—its aspirations, its operation, its dangers—is what, most fundamentally, our Constitution is *about*."[973] Parker notes that "To be sure, affirmation of majority rule has long been a staple of talk about constitutional law, but the power of its simple claim has been sucked out of it. Restoration of that power is the aim of a Populist reorientation of constitutional discourse"[974] Nevertheless, it is striking that much of "popular constitutionalism," including Ackerman's view (and Dworkin's) is clearly consistent with the politics of the Democratic party in the late twentieth- and twenty-first century, and this also reflects a near-consensus in the elite legal academy.

---

the People Rule: A Constitutional Populist Manifesto (Harvard, 1994). For an intriguing and sophisticated argument that the advocates of popular constitutionalism have failed to understand the subtle interplay of democracy and constitutionalism in our tradition, see Martin H. Redish, The Paradox of American Constitutionalism: The Role of an Independent Judiciary in a Democratic Society (Stanford University Press, forthcoming, 2017).

[972] The quotes appear in Donnelly, *supra* note 961, at 549–550, but are from the work of Larry Kramer.

[973] Parker, *supra* note 971, at 4 (emphasis in original).

[974] *Id.*, at 97.

Northwestern Law Professor James Lindgren reported that "In the 2010s, the dominant group in law teaching remains Democrats, both male and female. Democrats make up nearly 82 percent of law professors."[975]

Quite possibly the most ambitious undertaking regarding popular Constitutionalism besides Ackerman's massive four-volume effort, is Akhil Amar's provocative book, published in 2012, *America's Unwritten Constitution*.[976] Amar, in a manner that distinguishes him from many law professors, has the gift of being able to write books which can be understood by a lay audience.[977] In a project somewhat similar to that undertaken by Dworkin,[978] Amar is prepared to justify judicial decisions which have departed from the text of the Constitution, in order to implement "principles" such as "separation of powers," "checks and balances," and the "rule of law," which are "part of America's working constitutional system—part of America's *unwritten* Constitution."[979] For Amar, then, "The eight thousand words of America's written Constitution

---

[975] See, e.g., Kate Hardiman, Law schools dominated by Democrat professors, research finds, The College Fix, August 31, 2015, http://www.the collegefix.com/post/24015/ (accessed 8 February 2016). An updated version of Lindgren's study concluded that "The data show that in 1997 women and minorities were underrepresented compared to some populations, but Republicans and Christians were usually more underrepresented. For example, by the late 1990s, the proportion of the U.S. population that was neither Republican nor Christian was only 9%, but the majority of law professors (51%) was drawn from that small minority." James Lindgren, Measuring Diversity: Law Faculties in 1997 and 2013 (Abstract and Author's Note). Lindgren's paper is Northwestern Law & Econ Research Paper No. 15–07, Northwestern Public Law Research Paper No. 15–17 (2015), and available on the web, at http://papers.ssrn.com/sol3/papers.cfm?abstract_id=2581675 (accessed 8 February 2016).

[976] Akhil Reed Amar, America's Unwritten Constitution: The Precedents and Principles We Live By (Basic Books, 2012).

[977] See, e.g., Akhil Reed Amar, America's Constitution: A Biography (New York: Random House 2006), a quite accessible introduction to the topics of Constitutional law and Constitutional history.

[978] See Chapter 12, *supra*.

[979] Amar, *supra* note 976, at ix.

only *begin* to map out the basic ground rules that actually govern our land."[980] Pursuant to his theory, Amar boldly declares that "Since the written Constitution does not come with a complete set of instructions about how it should be construed, we must go beyond the text to make sense of the text."[981]

Since many words are inherently ambiguous, perhaps it must be conceded that some principles of interpretation are needed to make sense of the document,[982] but how, then, are these principles of interpretation to be selected, and how might they be used to constrain the powers of government (in order to secure the rights of the people), which, after all, is supposed to be the purpose of the document? Once we start venturing beyond the text, in Amar's words, how do we know that we are still subject to some restraints? How do we prevent an invocation of the "unwritten constitution" to be anything other than arbitrary? Amar is not insensitive to this problem. He recognizes, at least, that "America's unwritten Constitution could never properly ignore the written Constitution, which is itself an integral part of the American experience [!]"[983] For textualists such as Scalia,[984] however, there may be small comfort in this concession on Amar's part, for Amar makes clear that in order to do "justice" to the text of the Constitution, we must recognize and approve of "various extratextual practices and precedents," which have grown up as a result of "textual portals" which are "welcoming us to journey beyond the Constitution's text." Among these are the mention of "unenumerated rights" in the Ninth Amendment, and

---

[980] *Ibid.* (emphasis supplied).

[981] *Id.*, at x.

[982] See generally Antonin Scalia, A Matter of Interpretation: Federal Courts and the Law (Princeton, 1997), and Antonin Scalia and Bryan A. Garner, Reading Law: The Interpretation of Legal Texts (West, 2012).

[983] Amar, *supra* note 976, at xi.

[984] For Scalia, see Chapter 20, *infra*.

apparently, many other such "portals" which have resulted in the treatment of "many of our Constitution's most important topics, from federalism, congressional practice, executive power, and judicial review to race relations, women's rights, popular constitutionalism, criminal procedure, voting rights, and the amendment process."[985]

Amar believes that we have never completely abandoned the British notion that "the traditions, practices, understandings, principles and institutions that collectively structure the basic British system of government and way of life" are a binding "Constitution," though an "unwritten" one.[986] Similarly, for Amar, the "judicial opinions, executive practices, legislative enactments and American traditions" constitute a source of an "unwritten" but still binding Constitution for America which supplements, or perhaps it would be correct to say, to do "justice" to Amar, *implements* our written Constitution.[987] Amar seems to imply, however, that some of these "unwritten" practices applied by Justices have, instead of doing "justice" to the written Constitution (as Amar understands it), "have done violence to the text." Amar indicates that he believes that these latter pernicious practices have "faded away,"[988] but unless Amar is simply prepared to accept the Panglossion notion that we have reached a point where we are now at the best of all possible worlds of implementing an unwritten Constitution, Amar needs to make clear just how we discern appropriate parts of an unwritten Constitution which do "justice" to the written document and do not do "violence" to it. It would be one thing, of course, simply to turn to history to reveal a purportedly clear "original understanding" of the document, as textualists such as Scalia and originalists such as

---

[985] Amar, *supra* note 976, at xi.

[986] *Id.*, at xii.

[987] *Id.*, at xiii.

[988] *Id.*, at xi.

Clarence Thomas are inclined to do, but this is not, strictly speaking, Amar's method, although he does depend, to a great extent, upon our history. For Amar, though, history is not, as it is for Scalia and Thomas, a means of restricting Constitutional meaning, instead, apparently, history reveals broad trends offering an opportunity for expansive Constitutional interpretation.

Thus, summarizing his argument in an "Afterward," Amar maintains that there are three other "useful" understandings of America's Constitution that ought to supplement its text. First, says Amar, "America's 'constitution' encompasses cherished principles of higher law that are widely understood to limit American government officials, even if these specific principles do not appear explicitly in the terse [constitutional] text."[989] Second, "America's 'constitution' comprises the practices, protocols, procedures, and principles that constitute the government." Such practices and protocols apparently include federalism, separation of powers, and "America's two-party duopoly."[990] Third, "America's unwritten 'constitution' should also be understood to encompass the basic tools and techniques by which faithful interpreters tease out the substantive meaning of the written Constitution and unwritten rights and structures."[991]

Amar's task, he assures us, is to undertake to bridge the gap between "textualists," and "living constitutionalists," the "deep divide in our current constitutional culture," and by doing so to further our understanding that "Like the Chinese symbols yin and yang, America's written Constitution and America's unwritten Constitution form two halves of one whole, with

---

[989]   *Id.*, at 481.
[990]   *Ibid.*
[991]   *Ibid.*

each half gesturing toward the other."[992] When that becomes clear, Amar appears to assure us, we will understand, in a lovely rhetorical echo of Jefferson's first inaugural address, that "We are all textualists; we are all living constitutionalists."[993] But would we all be willing, as Amar is, to accept his notion of "faithful interpreters" who have been able to "tease out the substantive meaning of the written Constitution and unwritten rights and structures," or is this one more defense of an elite ivy-league argument?

If, then, Amar is to be successful in this endeavor, he must demonstrate that we would all be willing to accept what he labels the "unwritten" Constitution. This is not likely to be the case. For example, he begins his articulation by claiming that there are certain restrictions on American governments that predate the Bill of Rights, and the explicit enumeration of rights in the First Amendment, and that we ought to recognize

> America's preeminent right, the freedom of speech. Textually this freedom appears in the First Amendment, but if everything depended solely on this explicit patch of constitutional text, which became part of the Constitution in 1791, then the First Congress in 1789 and 1790 would have been free to pass censorship laws had it so chosen. But surely the First Congress had no such power. And surely states have never had proper authority to shut down political discourse, even though the First Amendment does not expressly limit states. The robust wide-open, and uninhibited freedom of American citizens to express their political opinions is a basic feature of America's unwritten

---

[992] *Id.*, at xiii.

[993] *Id.*, at xiii. See Thomas Jefferson, First Inaugural Address, March 4, 1801, available at http://avalon.law.yale.edu/19th_century/jefinau1.asp. ("We are all Republicans, we are all Federalists.")

Constitution that predates and outshines the First
Amendment. Or so I claim.[994]

And so he does, but is this reliance on anything other than
the charismatic assertion of a brilliant Yale law school
professor, the kind that Duncan Kennedy contemplated?[995]

"The terse text [of the written Constitution]," Amar
explains "is inextricably intertwined with the implicit
principles, the ordaining deeds, the lived customs, the
landmark cases, the unifying symbols, the legitimating
democratic theories, the institutional settlements, the
framework statutes, the two-party ground rules, the
appeals to conscience, the state-constitutional counterparts,
and the unfinished agenda items that form much of
America's unwritten Constitution."[996] And Amar's
"unwritten constitution" does not spring only from
American experience. "international norms and ideals," he
explains "are key features of America's unwritten
Constitution to the extent they have in fact been widely
embraced by the American people and have thereby woven
themselves into the fabric of America's lived experience or
America's symbols, or to the extent that these foreign ideals
and norms have touched the conscience of Americans."[997]
This is surely eloquence, and it is just as surely "popular
constitutionalism," but is it also unbridled license to make
of the Constitution anything a gifted Yale Law Professor
might want it to be?

One reviewer of *An Unwritten Constitution*, leading
libertarian Georgetown Law Professor Randy Barnett,
writing in The Wall Street Journal, wondered whether
there really were restraints on Amar's permissible

---

[994] *Id.,* at xv.

[995] For Kennedy's thoughts on Yale law professors, see notes 4, 806, 850,
and 871 *supra,* and accompanying text.

[996] Amar, *supra* note 976, at 479.

[997] *Id.,* at 482.

amending of the Constitution by extra-constitutional means. Asking whether Amar's theory actually amounted to what has at times been advanced as the "living constitution" notion—that the document ought to be altered by judicial decision as the needs of the times changed, Barnett wrote that, in effect, while Amar maintained that judicial decisions that clearly flew in the face of the meaning of the written text were impermissible, still Amar went on to "advocate an exception that is big enough to drive a living constitution through." Barnett stated that " 'An erroneous precedent that improperly deviates from the written Constitution may in some circumstances stand,' [Amar] tells us, 'if the precedent is later championed not merely by the court, but also by the people.' 'When the citizenry has widely and enthusiastically embraced an erroneous precedent,' [writes Amar] the courts may 'view this precedent as sufficiently ratified by the American people so as to insulate it from judicial overruling.' When this happens, according to Mr. Amar, the erroneous precedent becomes part of America's unwritten Constitution."[998] This is the same Amendment outside Article V that Amar's colleague and mentor Bruce Ackerman advocated. Barnett concluded, "Despite Mr. Amar's best attempts to convince us otherwise, the danger of the unwritten Constitution remains. The label elevates non-constitutional authorities to a stature equal to, or even greater than, that of the written Constitution. Where Mr. Amar cannot make the written Constitution say what he wants, he can simply appeal to the unwritten Constitution to say the rest. And, judging from this book, the unwritten Constitution just

---

[998] Randy Barnett, The Mirage of Progressive Originalism: A new legal theory attempts—and fails—to unite leftist politics with constitutional fidelity, The Wall Street Journal, September 7, 2012, available on the web at http://www.wsj.com/articles/SB10000872396390444914904577619763983330558 (accessed 3 January 2016).

happens to agree with everything Akhil Reed Amar believes is right and good."[999] Just so.

This problem of untrammeled discretion on the judiciary's part, is, of course, the difficulty that all proponents of "the living constitution," or, if we like, "popular constitutionalism," face. A fine summary of this difficulty was recently offered by Tom Donnelly, who recognized the problem of how judges applying "popular constitutionalism" are supposed to understand the purportedly expressed voice of the people. With commendable understatement, he suggested that while the general notion of interpreting an ambiguous constitutional text according to the expressed popular will is easy enough to state, "the practical challenges of applying it are considerable." Donnelly continued:

> Public ignorance runs high, and public consensus is rare. And even when such a consensus is possible, how should we define it? Should we look to polling data, the political rhetoric of our major parties, social movement activism, the laws on the books, recent election returns, or some other talismanic source? Should we require evidence of super-majority support for a given position or a mere majority? Should our approach differ for different constitutional provisions, and when, if ever, should public consensus yield to an individual interpreter's own sense of fairness and good social policy? And finally, are judges even competent to decipher the public's constitutional views in the first place, or should we simply call upon them to refer to the elected branches as the

---

[999] Ibid. For Professor Barnett's take on interpreting the Constitution and what should be done with it, see, e.g., Randy E. Barnett, Our Republican Constitution: Securing the Liberty and Sovereignty of We the People (Broadside Books, 2016), and Randy E. Barnett, Restoring the Lost Constitution: The Presumption of Liberty (Princeton, 2003).

soundest way of combating judicial supremacy and respecting popular sovereignty?[1000]

Donnelly confessed that "These are vexing questions,"[1001] but chose not to offer answers to them. Perhaps there are no such answers, given popular constitutionalism's inevitably open-ended character.

Beginning about twenty-five years ago, some Americans were seeking a "Flag Protection Amendment,"[1002] which would have permitted Congress to pass legislation prohibiting the physical desecration of the flag of the United States, thus reversing the United States Supreme Court decision in *Texas v. Johnson*,[1003] which had held that flag-burning was constitutionally-protected speech. The Amendment had great popular support, sometimes running as high as 80% of the people surveyed.[1004] Still, at that time, there were those who claimed that such an Amendment would have been an unconstitutional and impermissible Amendment, because of the kind of inherent freedom of expression which, for example, Amar here posits.[1005] In a similar fashion, Tom Donnelley believes that "there may be certain constitutional provisions worth excluding from popular constitutional analysis—in particular, minority-protective provisions like the First Amendment."[1006] But, how, then, can we know

---

[1000] Donnelly, *supra* note 961, at 551–552.

[1001] *Id.*, at 552.

[1002] See generally Robert Justin Goldstein, Saving "Old Glory": The History of the American Flag Desecration Controversy (Westview Press, 1994).

[1003] Texas v. Johnson, 491 U.S. 397 (1989).

[1004] Disclosure. I was, at the time, employed as a consultant by a group advocating the passage of the Amendment, the Citizens Flag Alliance. See generally, http://www.citizensflagalliance.org/ (accessed 13 March 2016).

[1005] See text accompanying note 994, *supra*. For a skeptical approach to "Freedom of Expression," and a claim that it is not a basic human right, see Larry Alexander, Is There a Right of Freedom of Expression? (Cambridge, 2005).

[1006] Donnely, *supra* note 961, at 552.

which parts of the Constitution are subject to amendment through popular constitutionalism, and which are not? How can we be certain of the scope and content of the extra-constitutional principles, the "unwritten" constitution that Amar claims exists?

There may not be an answer to such questions, but one prominent judge, Richard Posner (see the preceding chapter) doesn't believe they matter at all. Indeed, in an extraordinary recent book, *Divergent Paths: The Academy and the Judiciary*,[1007] Posner argues generally that what concerns the academy and what concerns the judges have little in common. For Posner, his fellow academics, particularly Constitutional scholars, are airy theorists, while judges, as far as he is concerned, are practical problem-solvers who ought to be unconcerned with doctrinal or historical niceties. In a broad-ranging blast, Posner states flatly that judges, and, in particular Supreme Court Justices, "are not 'philosophical.' They do not engage with abstruse issues of 'meaning.' They do not read H.L.A. Hart or Ronald Dworkin, or the flights of fancy of such current constitutional gurus as Laurence Tribe and Akhil Amar."[1008] If these Constitutional scholars have little of worth to contribute, who does? Perhaps the feminists, whom we next consider.

[1007] Richard A. Posner, Divergent Paths: The Academy and the Judiciary (Harvard, 2016).

[1008] *Id.*, at 277. Note 23 on that page of Posner's book cites as such a "flight of fancy," *Amar's Unwritten Constitution, supra* note 976, which is excoriated (along with Laurence Tribe, The Invisible Constitution (Oxford, 2008)) yet again at Posner, *supra* note 1007, at 320.

CHAPTER 17

TOWARDS A FEMINIST CRITIQUE OF LAW

LATE TWENTIETH, EARLY TWENTY-FIRST CENTURY

Catharine MacKinnon
(Michigan)

■ ■ ■

Catharine MacKinnon (b. 1946)
Courtesy University of Michigan Law School.

The daughter of one of the most conservative judges to sit on the United States Court of Appeals for the District of Columbia Circuit,[1009] Catharine A. MacKinnon became the most visible and brilliant radical feminist theorist teaching

---

[1009] George E. MacKinnon, who served on the United States Court of Appeals for the District of Columbia Circuit from 1969 to 1995. Judge MacKinnon was said to have been described by an unnamed "Washington Lawyer," as "so far right he makes Goldwater look like George McGovern." Donald Dale Jackson, Judges: An Inside View of the Agonies and Excesses of an American Elite 313 (Atheneum, 1974).

in a law school, and one of the most influential scholars transforming constitutional interpretation and legislation along feminist lines. Few law professors have evoked as strong feelings as MacKinnon does. In a powerful appreciation of MacKinnon by a feminist periodical, it was stated that "Everywhere that MacKinnon has taught, she has stirred strong feelings in students and faculty—it seems that no one's support or opposition has been lukewarm. In 1983, after she taught a 5-week course at Harvard, women students organized to have her appointed to the faculty. During the long, drawn-out battle, Dean James Vorenberg told students, 'I never want to hear that woman's name again.' "[1010] This account continued, "Most recently, MacKinnon's own alma mater, Yale Law School, gave her an icy welcome as a visiting law professor. Yale Professor Geoffrey Hazard accused MacKinnon of having no 'genuine comprehension of the law.' "[1011] What could have prompted

---

[1010] Professor MacKinnon, Off our Backs, Vol. 19, No. 4 (April 1989), p. 4.

[1011] *Ibid.* Hazard's view was not shared by all at Yale, to say the least. See, e.g., the following summary of MacKinnon's work published on the web in Broad Recognition: A Feminist Magazine at Yale:

> MacKinnon is the, still living, inventor of American sexual harassment law, in both education and employment. Indeed, "sexual harassment" was a legal theory she introduced to the nation in her 1979 book, The Sexual Harassment of Working Women, and has since elaborated in numerous Supreme Court cases. She also won a verdict of $735 million in the New York case Kadic v. Karadzic (2000), thereby establishing that rape could legally constitute an act of genocide. She is one of the most cited legal scholars in all history; she is the most cited woman.

Chase Olivarius-McAllister, Older Man, Younger Woman, originally published in Reflections on Coeducation: A Critical History of Women at Yale (2010) in honor of the 40th anniversary of coeducation at Yale College, available on the web at http://www.broadrecognitionyale.com/2010/10/25/older-man-younger-woman/ (accessed 12 August 2016). This piece makes clear that MacKinnon has been extraordinarily successful as a practicing lawyer as well as a scholar. It should also be noted that characterizing MacKinnon as a "feminist", as I do, and as the piece from Broad Recognition does, may not fairly reflect MacKinnon's current perspective, which might better be described as one broadly advocating "substantive equality," rather than simply, as done here,

this kind of reaction from (apparently exclusively male) law professors? What does it tell us about the nature of the American law professoriate, and about feminism?

The occasionally acerbic and frequently brilliant Richard Posner[1012] admires MacKinnon, in spite of disagreeing with her politics, regarding her, like Martin Luther King as a "moral entrepreneur" a person "who, through sheer charisma and rhetorical force," is able to "sweep people headlong out of their accustomed inertia and inspire new moralities altogether."[1013] Whatever the then Dean Vorenberg's reaction to MacKinnon, his successors in Harvard's Deanship apparently happily presided over MacKinnon's continuing appointment as James Barr Ames Visiting Professor of Law at Harvard, and her permanent position is as Elizabeth Long Professor of Law at the University of Michigan School of Law, whose website accurately reports that she is "among the most widely cited legal scholars in the English language."[1014]

---

using her as an exemplar of dominance feminism. For MacKinnon's current work, see, e.g., her casebook, Sex Equality (Foundation Press, 2016).

[1012] See Chapter 15, *supra*.

[1013] Quoted by Larissa MacFarquhar, Profiles: The Bench Burner: How did a judge with such subversive ideas become a leading influence on American legal opinion?, The New Yorker, December 10, 2001, at 84.

[1014] http://www.law.umich.edu/FacultyBio/Pages/FacultyBio.aspx?FacID =CAMTWO (accessed October 30, 2014). This is borne out by many studies, see, e.g., a 2009 survey by Brian Leiter, Karl Llewellyn Professor of Jurisprudence at the University of Chicago School of Law, probably the man most knowledgeable about academic reputations in the law school world, who ranks MacKinnon at Number 18, among the most important legal thinkers in American Law of the past century (ranking available on the web at http:// leiterlawschool.typepad.com/leiter/2009/05/the-most-important-legal-thinkers -in-american-law-of-the-past-century.html) (accessed 12 August 2016) (Others on that list included in this book are Holmes (#1), Posner (#2), Dworkin (#3), Llewellyn (#7), Scalia (#10), Sunstein (#11), Frankfurter (#19), Pound (#20), Ackerman (#21), Wechsler (#22), and Wigmore (#24)), Fred R. Shapiro, The Most Cited Legal Scholars, 29 Journal of Legal Studies 409, 421, 424 (2000) (ranking MacKinnon among the 32 most highly cited legal scholars of all time), and Fred R. Shapiro, The Most Cited Legal Books Published Since 1978, 29

As noted by Cass Sunstein,[1015] in an absorbing review of a book of MacKinnon's speeches,[1016] feminist theory might be divided into at least three strands. The first of these Sunstein labels "difference theory," which is something of a misnomer, as the core tenet of that theory appears to be that the law should not treat women differently from men, as, pursuant to that theory, the Fourteenth Amendment's Constitutional mandate of equal protection of the laws demands equal treatment for both sexes.[1017] This philosophy is said to be adhered to by perhaps the leading women's rights organization, the National Organization for Women (NOW), and was the inspiration for the so-called Equal Rights Amendment or ERA, the key provision of which was that "Equality of rights under the law shall not be denied or abridged by the United States or by any state on account of sex."[1018]

One of the puzzles of the late twentieth and early twenty-first century is why the Equal Rights Amendment, as it was called—the prime proposal of the "difference" feminist theorists—failed to garner the requisite number of state legislatures to become an Amendment to the Constitution, even though it had repeatedly easily achieved the required two-thirds super-majorities in the Congress. MacKinnon, similarly, states that "Why an explicit guarantee of women's equality was rejected as part of the

---

Journal of Legal Studies 397 (2000) (Three of MacKinnon's books ranked #4, #8, and #20).

[1015] See Chapter 22, *infra.*

[1016] Cass Sunstein, Book Review: Feminism and Legal Theory (A review of Catharine MacKinnon, Feminism Unmodified: Discourses on Life and Law (Harvard, 1987)), 101 Harv. L. Rev. 826 (1988).

[1017] See U.S. Constitution, Amendment Fourteen. (Providing *inter alia* that "No state shall make or enforce any law which shall abridge the privileges or immunities of citizens of the United States; nor shall any state deprive any person of life, liberty, or property, without due process of law; nor deny to any person within its jurisdiction the equal protection of the laws.")

[1018] See, e.g., The ERA: A Brief Introduction, http://www.equalrights amendment.org/overview.htm (accessed October 30, 2014).

constituting document of the United States is a good
question, one it takes some courage to ask."[1019] She adds
that "It is hard for women to face the fact that we live in a
country that rejects our equality."[1020] The suggestion was
often made that the fears of unisex bathrooms or compelling
women to assume combat roles in the military[1021] scuttled
the Amendment, but MacKinnon raises the darker
possibility that the male legislators who ultimately killed
the ERA did so because "they might have had a real stake
in sex-discrimination—an economic, social, psychological,
institutional, and sexual stake, the more determinative to
the degree that it may be nonconscious."[1022]

It may well be, though, that the ERA is no longer
necessary, because the United States Supreme Court,
ignoring the legislative history of the Fourteenth
Amendment, has now decided, by a 7–1 majority, to read
the equal protection clause as if it guaranteed what the ERA
proposed. Thus, in *U.S. v. Virginia* (1996),[1023] the Court
held that the state of Virginia could not continue to operate
the Virginia Military Institute (VMI) as an all-male
institution, because to deny women admission to VMI
violated the Amendment's equal protection clause. Whether or
not the ERA could ever pass in the United States, it is now clear,
as Justice Ginsburg wrote for the majority in the VMI case, that
"neither federal nor state government acts compatibly with

[1019] Catharine A. MacKinnon, "Unthinking ERA Thinking" in Catharine
A. MacKinnon, Women's Lives: Men's Laws 13 (Harvard, 2005) reprinting
Catherine A. MacKinnon, Book Review [Jane Mansbridge, Why We Lost the
ERA (1986)], 54 U.Chi.L.Rev. 759 (1987).

[1020] *Ibid.*

[1021] See, e.g., James C. Clark, Fear of Unisex Bathrooms Doomed ERA,
Orlando Sentinel, April 28, 1991. Available on the web at http://articles.
orlandosentinel.com/1991–04–28/news/9104280615_1_equal-rights-amend
ment-senate-the-amendment-two-votes (accessed 22 February 2016).

[1022] Women's Lives, *supra* note 1019, at 15.

[1023] 518 U.S. 515 (1996). Justice Thomas recused himself from the case
because his son was attending VMI at the time. Justice Scalia was the lone
dissenter.

the equal protection principle when a law or official policy denies to women, simply because they are women, full citizenship stature-equal opportunity to aspire, achieve, participate in and contribute to society based on their individual talents and capacities."[1024] It would appear, then, that at least one strand of feminist theory has achieved something close to its goal, if persuading a majority of the Supreme Court can be taken as success. MacKinnon would be unlikely to accept this rather sanguine analysis, as she indicates that simply achieving a "women's auxiliary of the Equal Protection Clause," would not do much to reduce "the social institutionalization of practices through which women are violated, abused, exploited, and patronized by men *socially*—in collaboration with the state. . . ."[1025]

"Difference" (or, if you like, "equality") theory, however, is only one approach to feminism. More intriguing and, perhaps, more controversial, is "different voice" theory, generally associated with the work of Carol Gilligan, who asserted that there are distinctly male and female social behaviors associated with problem solving, and, in particular, while men have an "ethic of justice," with clear winners and losers, women favor an "ethic of care," which leads to attempting to resolve conflict situations in a manner in which everyone is better off, and that these patterns hold from childhood into adulthood.[1026] Gilligan's conclusion, it might be said, is that men and women are hard-wired to be different, and that, generally speaking, men and women seek different things in social interaction.

[1024] 518 U.S., at 532.

[1025] MacKinnon, *supra* note 1019, at 17 (emphasis in original). For MacKinnon's powerful argument that the ERA is still necessary, in order for the United States to come closer to achieving real equality for all its citizens, see Catharine A. MacKinnon, Toward a Renewed Equal Rights Amendment: Now More than Ever, 37 Harvard Journal of Law & Gender 569 (2013–2014).

[1026] Carol Gilligan, In a Different Voice: Psychological Theory and Women's Development (Harvard, 1982).

"Different voice" theory may have achieved some impact on the legal system, as some safety regulations do recognize, for example, that women of child-bearing age need special protection, and pregnancy leave ought to be something available to women because of the unique status of women as child-bearers. Moreover, the movement for "comparable worth,"[1027] does suggest that different jobs preferred differently by the sexes (for example males tend disproportionately to be truck drivers and women tend disproportionally to be personal assistants or caretakers) ought to be paid the same because they are of "comparable worth" to society. Pursuant to this notion, the purported genetic differences that cause men to prefer one set of jobs and women another should not work to their economic disadvantage. The recognition of different manners of dispute resolution, involving arbitration, mediation, and settlement, all in the ascendance in the twentieth and twenty-first centuries, may also be something of an acceptance of the insights of "different voice" theory. Still, in our generally "politically correct" times, there is resistance to a theory based on the assertion of immutable biological differences, and thus there is something of a conflict between "difference" theory (which would treat all equally) and "different voice" theory, which would not.

And, indeed, there is a third strand of feminist theory that rejects at least some of the conclusions of both "difference" and "different voice" theory. This is what might be labeled the "dominance" theory of feminism. Catherine MacKinnon was its most prominent practitioner, but several other feminists have contributed to this strain of thought, including, at least, Andrea Dworkin,[1028] and

---

[1027] See, e.g., Paula England, Comparable Worth: Theories and Evidence (Aldine Transaction, 1992).

[1028] See, e.g., Andrea Dworkin, Pornography: Men Possessing Women (Putnam, 1981) and Andrea Dworkin, Intercourse (Free Press, 1987).

Kathryn Abrams.[1029] The central insight of the dominance feminists is that current American society is a patriarchy designed to allow and perpetuate the subordination of women to men, and that women cannot achieve equality in society until this dominance is halted.[1030] Dominance feminism, then, is impatient with the notion of mere or formal "equality" as a standard for treating women in society, because the currently existing conditions for men, in the view of dominance feminists, are imbued with structures that subordinate women. Accordingly, MacKinnon condemns the "substantive misogyny of liberal neutrality."[1031] As she explains, "tolerance is the solution liberalism offers. A very substantive sexual blackmail lies at the heart of this liberal tolerance."[1032] Or, as MacKinnon puts it, with great eloquence, "anyone with an ounce of political analysis should know that freedom before equality, freedom before justice, will only further liberate the power of the powerful and will never free what is most in need of expression."[1033]

Dominance feminism may well be the most radical strand of this inherently radical school of thought, and, in contrast to the language of the ERA, the "dominance" feminists might, accordingly, suggest a Constitutional Amendment that would simply provide, "The Dominance of Men over Women is hereby abolished." If the ERA couldn't make it through the state legislatures, it would seem that such a Dominance Amendment's chances of passage are not

---

[1029] See, e.g., Kathryn Abrams, Songs of Innocence and Experience: Dominance Feminism in the University, 103 Yale L. J. 1553 (1994), and Kathryn Abrams, Sex Wars Redux: Agency and Coercion in Feminist Legal Theory, 95 Col. L. Rev. 304 (1995).

[1030] See, e.g., Catherine A. MacKinnon, Feminism Unmodified: Discourses on Life and Law 2 (Harvard, 1987). ("We need to know more about how women respond and experience being second class. . . .")

[1031] *Id.*, at 15.

[1032] *Ibid.*

[1033] *Ibid.*

great. Moreover, there is a set of attitudes embodied in nineteenth-century American law some of which still linger, that would clearly be overturned by such an Amendment.

Consider, for example, one of the most famous nineteenth-century utterances regarding the role of women in society. Mr. Justice Bradley, joining in the Court's decision that the state of Illinois could limit the practice of law to the male sex, stated that "[t]he natural and proper timidity and delicacy which belongs to the female sex evidently unfits it for many of the occupations of civil life. . . . The paramount destiny and mission of women are to fulfill the noble and benign offices of wife and mother. This is the law of the Creator."[1034]

It does appear, however, that even "dominance" feminism has begun to make inroads into orthodox Constitutional jurisprudence. Thus, in the 1992 important decision, *Planned Parenthood v. Casey*,[1035] for example, the United States Supreme Court's holding that a woman need not notify her husband before seeking an abortion was expressly linked to a repudiation of the Court's nineteenth-century observation that a woman's place was in the home, as wife and mother, and to a recognition that the days in which the husband could control his wife's acts were over.[1036]

[1034] Bradwell v. Illinois, 83 U.S. 130, 142 (1873). Whatever the validity of Mr. Justice Bradley's sentiments in 1873, in 1872 Illinois passed legislation making it possible for women to be admitted to the bar. See, e.g., "First Women Lawyers," an article on the web on the site of the Women's Bar Association of Illinois, https://wbaillinois.org/first-100-years/ (accessed 12 August 2016).

[1035] Planned Parenthood v. Casey, 505 U.S. 833 (1992).

[1036] 505 U.S., at 897 (Plurality opinion of O'Connor, Kennedy, and Souter). ("Only one generation has passed since this Court observed that "woman is still regarded as the center of home and family life," with attendant "special responsibilities" that precluded full and independent legal status under the Constitution. Hoyt v. Florida, 368 U.S. 57, 62 (1961). These views, of course, are no longer consistent with our understanding of the family, the individual, or the Constitution.")

There are some challenging aspects to feminist theory, and one of the most prominent is its core tenet that gender or sexuality is "socially constructed." Some of MacKinnon's thought, as is true for some critical legal scholars,[1037] is difficult for one new to the discourse. Consider, for example, some words from the Introduction to what is probably MacKinnon's best-known book, a compilation of her speeches, *Feminism Unmodified: Discourses on Life and Law* (1987)[1038]:

> ... Women get their class status through their sexual relations with men of particular classes; perhaps their racial status, also no less real for being vicarious, similarly derives from racial hierarchies among men. From these and other examples, gender in this country appears partly to comprise the meaning of, as well as bisect, race and class, even as race and class specificities make up, as well as cross-cut, gender. A general theory of social inequality is prefigured, if inchoately, in these connections.[1039]

Still, this passage does manage to make reasonably clear that, for MacKinnon, and for other dominance theorists, all aspects of gender appear to be a product of existing institutions in society, but this view fails to take into account the obvious biological differences between men and women, and the intractability of gender characteristics that the "different voice" feminists appear to understand.

[1037] See Chapter 14, *supra*.

[1038] *Supra* note 1030.

[1039] Feminism Unmodified, *supra* note 1030, at 2–3. These words of MacKinnon's summarize a major trend in current thinking about equality, that is termed "intersectionality." See, e.g., Kimberle Crenshaw, "Demarginalizing the Intersection of Race and Sex: A Black Feminist Critique of Antidiscrimination Doctrine, Feminist Theory and Antiracist Politics," 1989 University of Chicago Legal Forum, available on the web http://chicagoun bound.uchicago.edu/uclf/vol1989/iss1/8 (accessed 12 August 2016).

But if some of MacKinnon's thought is problematic, much is not, and there is still blazing insight that she displays. When she seeks to simplify, she can shine. For example, she boils her definition of feminism down to the simple thought that it can be "a tacit belief that women are human beings in truth but not in social reality."[1040] She is particularly provocative and brilliant in exploring the connection between what she regards as a pernicious social construction of gender and pornography, insofar as pornography is part of the active practice of the subjugation of women to men. In a powerful summary of this part of her thought, she explains:

> . . . [P]ornography makes inequality into sex, which makes it enjoyable, and into gender, which makes it seem natural. By packaging the resulting product as pictures and words, pornography turns gendered and sexualized inequality into 'speech' which has made it a right. Thus does pornography, cloaked as the essence of nature and the index of freedom, turn the inequality between women and men into those twin icons of male supremacy, sex and speech, and a practice of sex discrimination [MacKinnon argues that pornography is a form of sex discrimination] into a legal entitlement.[1041]

As Sunstein correctly observes, this aspect of MacKinnon's thought is cogent and persuasive, and thinking about the effect of pornography on women and on our conception of the appropriate gender roles and sex makes one look at many features of modern society and iconography quite differently. As Sunstein puts it, "Sexualized violence toward women is pervasive in advertising, popular culture, and everyday life. It is difficult to see much of popular culture—

[1040] Feminism Unmodified, *supra* note 1030, at 216.
[1041] *Id.*, at 3.

and some high art as well—in quite the same way after reading *Feminism Unmodified.*"[1042]

None of this is to say, however, that Feminist thought is not without its difficulties, and even among feminists. It is, perhaps, not surprising that "dominance" feminism is in tension with "different voice" feminism, because the "dominance" theorists are concerned that purported biological differences might serve as a pretext for the subordination of women. MacKinnon is particularly critical of "construing gender as a difference," because this "obscures and legitimizes the way gender is imposed by force. . . . The idea of gender difference helps keep the reality of male dominance in place."[1043] Or, as she passionately explains, "Differences are inequality's *post hoc* excuse, its conclusory artifact, its outcome presented as its origin, the damage that is pointed to as the justification for doing the damage after the damage has been done, the distinctions that perception is socially organized to notice because inequality gives them consequences for social power."[1044] Gender, then, in this view, is a suspect and possibly pernicious social construct. As MacKinnon explains, "One of the most deceptive antifeminisms in society, scholarship, politics, and law is the persistent treatment of gender as if it truly is a question of difference, rather than treating the gender difference as a construct of the difference gender makes."[1045]

And when MacKinnon writes of the reality of male dominance and male abuse of women it is powerful, disturbing, and impossible to ignore. The reality she

---

[1042] Sunstein, book review, *supra* note 1016, 101 Harv.L.Rev., at 848.

[1043] Feminism Unmodified, *supra* note 1030, at 3. Indeed, there is a wonderful and telling barb aimed by MacKinnon at some of her sister academic feminists, "As male academics have been able to afford to talk in ways that mean nothing, so also women. . . ." *Id.*, at 5.

[1044] *Id.*, at 8.

[1045] *Id.*, at 8–9.

describes for many women is one of horror. "Just to get through another day, women must spent an incredible amount of time, life, and energy cowed, fearful, and colonized, trying to figure out how not to be next on the list. . . . To be about to be raped is to be gender female in the process of going about life as usual."[1046] Thus, she notes that "feminism is built on believing women's accounts of sexual use and abuse by men. The pervasiveness of male sexual violence against women is therefore not denied, minimized, trivialized, eroticized, or accepted as marginal or episodic or placed to one side while more important matters are discussed. The fact that only 7.8 percent of women in the United States have not been sexually assaulted or harassed in their lifetime is not considered inconsequential or isolated."[1047] This is an extraordinary assertion. If it is true, it is staggering, and there is resistance to accepting this as a reflection of reality. Thus, there is some suggestion in the literature critical of feminism that some of the empirical claims made by dominance feminists, in particular, regarding the incidence of rape that occurs in America,[1048] may not be accurate, but there is empirical evidence that supports the views of MacKinnon and others, and the dominance and other feminists have clearly had a profound influence on law students and legal education. Even if there is some disagreement over the statistics of the claims of male abuse, there is surely enough reality to warrant concern, and, as indicated, this concern has begun to shape and influence what is done by courts, including the Supreme Court of the United States.

[1046] *Id.*, at 7.

[1047] *Id.*, at 5.

[1048] See generally Edward Greer, The Truth Behind Legal Dominance Feminism's "Two Percent False Rape Claim" Figure, 33 Loyola of Los Angeles Law Review 947 (2000), and sources there cited, particularly footnote 3, at 947–948.

As indicated earlier, the understanding of many, if not most of the feminist legal scholars is a radical one, as it calls for a fundamental restructuring of American society, and, perhaps, a fundamental redistribution of wealth, or at least power. MacKinnon's approach may even call into question the prevalent practice of heterosexual behavior. "It may be worth considering," she writes, "that heterosexuality, the predominant social arrangement that fuses this sexuality of abuse and objectification with gender in intercourse, with attendant trauma, torture, and dehumanization, organizes women's pleasure so as to give us a stake in our own subordination."[1049]

As part of her evaluation of misconceptions about sexuality that are harmful to women MacKinnon has also mounted an impressive critique of Freudian psychology, and, in particular, Freud's reversal of his original understanding that women's claims of childhood sexual abuse were real. "Finally," she writes, "the truth about women's lives did not matter to Freud. And neither the truth about women's lives nor the truth about Freud now appears to matter to the Freudians."[1050] For MacKinnon, Freudian psychology (which she argues fails to understand the reality actually affecting women) is but another in the many ways in which men seek to further their desires in general and the oppression of women in particular. As she explains, "Freud and his contemporaries appear to have shared a mass sexual hallucination that became a theory that became a practice that became a scientific truth because men wanted it that way."[1051]

All of this is a grim view of reality indeed, and one that would inevitably argue for a radical cure. As MacKinnon

---

[1049] Feminism Unmodified, *supra* note 1030, at 7.

[1050] Chapter 19, Sex, Lies, and Psychotherapy, in Women's Lives: Men's Laws, *supra* note 1019, at 253.

[1051] *Id.*, at 254.

states, advising those who would come to grips with our current situation of female inequality, "Be more radical than anyone has ever been about the unknown, because what has never been asked is probably what we most need to know."[1052] Occasionally it is difficult to know whether MacKinnon's radicalism is as much for dramatic effect as it is for seeking serious change. For example, in describing the content of her 1987 book of essays, and the ideas presented, she states, advising her reader, "Try thinking without apology with what you know from being victimized," and that "These are largely new conceptual problems, but this is not primarily a conceptual program. This may be what is most new about it. If it does not track bloody footprints across your desk, it is probably not about women."[1053] Sometimes the metaphors are not easy to follow or accept, as, for example, "If what turns you on is not your bottom line, and if you understand that pornography literally means what it says, you might conclude that sexuality has become the fascism of contemporary America and we are moving into the last days of Weimar."[1054]

This apocalyptic view may not be easy to accept, and not all women, even in the legal academy, appear to be leaving bloody footprints. MacKinnon's is not, then, the only possible view of reality, though it does merit serious attention, and it is undeniable that MacKinnon's views have had an impact as powerful probably as that of any contemporary law professor,[1055] over several decades,

---

[1052] Feminism Unmodified, *supra* note 1030, at 9.

[1053] *Id.*, at 9.

[1054] *Id.*, at 15.

[1055] Mark Tushnet, the most prolific and one of the most visible of the Critical Legal Scholars [See Chapter 14, *supra*], in a blurb on the back cover of the paperback edition of MacKinnon's Women's Lives: Men's Law's (2007), is recorded as stating that "Histories of American law in the late twentieth century will discuss the contributions of only two or three people who made major contributions to the law as scholars, not judges. Richard Posner [See Chapter 15] is one, Catharine MacKinnon is another." The quotation came

"From statutory law in the 1970's, to constitutional law in the 1980's, to international law in the 1990's and beyond. . . ."[1056] Even so, it is, perhaps, possible to be a woman and even a conservative legal scholar in the academy, and while they are rare, they can be important, provocative, and influential, as well, although perhaps addressing very different issues, with very different solutions for our current dilemmas. One such scholar is Mary Ann Glendon.

from Tushnet's book review of the hardback volume of Women's Lives, published in the American Lawyer.

[1056] Catharine A. MacKinnon, Women's Lives: Men's Laws v (Harvard University Press, 2005).

CHAPTER 18

AGAINST THE IMPOVERISHMENT OF LEGAL DISCOURSE

LATE TWENTIETH, EARLY TWENTY-FIRST CENTURY

Mary Ann Glendon
(Harvard)

■ ■ ■

Mary Ann Glendon (b. 1938)
Courtesy of the photographer, Tanit Sakakini.

Mary Ann Glendon is a truly rare commodity in the law professoriate—a conservative Christian woman. While it is true that there are some signs that this is beginning dramatically to change; traditionally, law professors, especially at the elite law schools, have been almost exclusively male, and, in the last few decades, they have tended to be overwhelmingly liberal or progressive in their politics, and with some exceptions, not ostensibly Christian in their thought. More, and increasingly, as noted earlier,

347

law professors, especially at the elite institutions, have tended to be Jewish.[1057]

Glendon, then, offers a different perspective because of her personal ascriptive qualities, but she is also unique in her distinction among law professors as having been a former Ambassador of the United States to the Holy See (The Vatican). She has continued her association with the Vatican, and, at one time was the highest ranking woman in the service of that religious polity. At this writing (June 2015), she is the Learned Hand Professor of Law at Harvard University and a member of the Board of Supervisors of the Vatican Bank, after having served on a commission appointed by Pope Francis to make recommendations for the Bank's reform. She is the former President of the Pontifical Academy of Social Sciences and serves as Vice-Chair of the U.S. Commission on International Religious Freedom. Glendon is a member of the prestigious American Academy of Arts and Sciences, one of the highest honors an American academic can obtain, she is a member of the International Academy of Comparative Law, and is a past president of the UNESCO-sponsored International Association of Legal Science. Few legal, or for that matter, any other species of American academics have a more stellar resume. Her Catholic faith is as important to her as was Roberto Unger's to him, but where Unger appeared to write legal scholarship in a revolutionary vein, as a Critical Legal Studies Scholar,[1058] Glendon writes in a manner to preserve traditional values, and, indeed, has taken pains to show that some purportedly progressive Constitutional doctrines have gone too far.

She is the sole author of many important and critically acclaimed books, among them The New Family and the New

---

[1057] See, e.g., note 495, *supra*.
[1058] For Critical Legal Studies, see Chapter 14, *supra*.

Property (1981),[1059] Abortion and Divorce in Western Law (1987),[1060] The Transformation of Family Law (1989),[1061] Rights Talk: The Impoverishment of Political Discourse (1991),[1062] A Nation Under Lawyers (1996),[1063] A World Made New: Eleanor Roosevelt and the Universal Declaration of Human Rights (2001),[1064] and, most recently, The Forum and the Tower: How Scholars and Politicians Have Imagined the World, from Plato to Eleanor Roosevelt (2011).[1065]

In her 1991 book, *Rights Talk*, perhaps the clearest and most complete statement of her key jurisprudential notions, and which will receive the most attention here, Glendon laments the sad state into which American political discourse has fallen, and, in particular, the concomitant "Cynicism, indifference, and ignorance concerning government" which she found to be "pervasive" in this country.[1066] A profound symptom and a partial cause for what she calls "the impoverishment of our political discourse," Glendon argues, is an "intemperate rhetoric of personal liberty" or "rights talk" which has all but eliminated the "sense of personal responsibility and of civic

---

[1059] Mary Ann Glendon, The New Family and the New Property (Butterworths, 1981).

[1060] Mary Ann Glendon, Abortion and Divorce in Western Law: American Failures, European Challenges (Harvard, 1987).

[1061] Mary Ann Glendon, The Transformation of Family Law: State, Law, and Family in the United States and Western Europe (Chicago, 1989).

[1062] Mary Ann Glendon, Rights Talk: The Impoverishment of Political Discourse (Free Press, 1991).

[1063] Mary Ann Glendon, A Nation Under Lawyers: How the Crisis in the Legal Profession Is Transforming American Society (Harvard, 1996).

[1064] A World Made New: Eleanor Roosevelt and the Universal Declaration of Human Rights (Random House, 2001).

[1065] Mary Ann Glendon, The Forum and the Tower: How Scholars and Politicians Have Imagined the World, from Plato to Eleanor Roosevelt (Oxford, 2011).

[1066] Glendon, *Rights Talk*, *supra* note 1062, at ix.

obligation,"[1067] which used to prevail in our republic, and, indeed, as we have already seen in the work of law professors such as James Wilson[1068] and Joseph Story,[1069] was essential to those who wrote and first interpreted our Constitution. For Glendon it is not so much that there is anything really wrong with the notion of "rights," it's just that the "new version of rights discourse," now prevalent in America, has pushed out other, older, and more sensible versions. For Glendon, "legal speech," the vernacular of the law that is experienced by Americans, is now saturated with a new kind of "rights talk," that is "a good deal more morally neutral, adversarial, and rights-oriented" than it was in the early nineteenth century.[1070] The new version, in Glendon's words, is characterized by "starkness and simplicity," by "its prodigality in bestowing the rights label, its legalistic character, its exaggerated absoluteness, its hyperindividualism, its insularity, and its silence with respect to personal, civic, and collective responsibilities."[1071]

A telling example of what Glendon meant was given early in her book, reporting on the response of one member of the American Legion, who was asked to defend his group's opposition to the United States Supreme Court's surprising 1989 decision that flag-burning was speech protected by the First Amendment to the Constitution.[1072] He was asked by a TV network interviewer, Jane Pauley, what the flag symbolized for the American Legion, and all he could think of to say was "It stands for the fact that this is a country where we have the right to do what we want," which, as Glendon points out, was to "espouse a principle

---

[1067] *Id.*, at x.

[1068] See Chapter 2, *supra.*

[1069] See Chapter 3, *supra.*

[1070] Glendon, *Rights Talk, supra* note 1062, at 3.

[1071] *Id.*, at x.

[1072] Texas v. Johnson, 491 U.S. 397 (1989).

that would have sanctioned the very act he despised."[1073] Glendon appears to understand that the Legionnaire, who could feel deeply that the flag represented the selfless sacrifice of the men and women who have fought and died for our freedoms, who could sense that for him the flag was an object of actual sacred veneration, and that for him and many like him (as recently as the 1990's, a majority of Americans voiced their approval of an Amendment to forbid the physical desecration of the flag) there was a belief that there was a societal need for some such deference to tradition, sacrifice, and altruism which might actually trump an individual's desire to desecrate such a venerated object. For Americans devoted to absolute rights, and all they represented in the last part of the twentieth century, however, to articulate or even understand such a view was almost impossible. It was some sign of the power of this "rights talk," particularly among law professors, that when the American Legion sought to find academics to support their quest for a "flag-protection" Amendment, few responded.[1074]

What gives *Rights Talk* extraordinary power, and Glendon's argument in the book extraordinary nuance and depth, is her comparison of America with other countries, and her impressive appreciation for both our and other cultures. Glendon is one of the country's leading legal comparativists, and is also the co-author of a leading casebook on comparative law, now in its fourth edition,[1075]

[1073] *Rights Talk, supra* note 1062, at 8.

[1074] Richard Parker of Harvard, Robert Nagel of Colorado, and I were among the very few. Our colleagues regarded us as misguided, to put it kindly. Parker's views have already been noted in Chapter 16, *supra*. For Nagel see, e.g., his excellent screed on contemporary legal education and the damage it has wrought, Robert Nagel, Unrestrained: Judicial Excess and the Mind of the American Lawyer (Transaction, 2008).

[1075] Mary Ann Glendon, Paolo Carozza, and Colin Picker, Comparative Legal Traditions, Text, Materials and Cases on Western Law (West Academic Publishing, 4th ed. 2014). See also, Mary Ann Glendon, Paolo Carozza, and

one of several such co-authored works on international law and comparative topics. In *Rights Talk*, Glendon sought to understand what it was that gave Americans an unrealistic absolute conception of rights, and how it could be that our current culture fails so dramatically to understand that with rights come responsibilities, and that, ultimately, for a society successfully to meet the real needs of its citizens, the exercise of rights has to be tempered with social duties.

In a dazzling display of learning, Glendon demonstrates in *Rights Talk* that, while Americans adopted the Lockean[1076] and Blackstonian[1077] absolute conceptions of property rights as the basis for our society's legal paradigm, European systems, particularly those of France and Germany, were more influenced by Jean-Jacques Rousseau, whose *Social Contract*[1078] stressed the contingent nature of property rights, and the limits placed upon them by other social concerns, such as securing the welfare of all. She is even able to demonstrate that by the twentieth century, while the Blackstonian absolutism (though transferred from classical property rights to the purported "right of privacy") still prevailed in America, in other common law countries, most notably Canada and the United Kingdom, milder conceptions of rights flourished, along with a greater emphasis on community and a lesser emphasis on individualism. Glendon was part of a growing awareness of, as she labelled it "the impoverishment" of

---

Colin Picker, Comparative Legal Traditions in a Nutshell (West, 3d ed. 2008) (Concise introduction to the topic).

[1076] See John Locke, Two Treatises of Government: In the Former, The False Principles, and Foundation of Sir Robert Filmer, and His Followers, Are Detected and Overthrown. The Latter Is an Essay Concerning The True Original, Extent, and End of Civil Government (Awnsham Churchill, originally published 1689, dated 1690).

[1077] On Blackstone, see Chapter 1, *supra.*

[1078] *Jean-Jacques Rousseau, Of the Social Contract, or Principles of Political Right (In the original French, Du contrat social ou Principes du droit politique)* (originally published, Marc Michel Rey, 1762).

American political discourse's emphasizing "rights." This growing awareness often proceeded under the rubric of "Communitarianism," and thus it is not surprising that one of the country's leading communitarian theorists, Amitai Etzioni,[1079] contributed a blurb to *Rights Talk*, in which he stated "If you are going to read only one book in preparation for the '90's, make it this one."

Glendon shows, in her marvelous chapter in *Rights Talk*, "The Lone Rights Bearer,"[1080] that the American legal notion that Constitutional rights (such as the right to privacy) attach only to the individual, is flawed. It stands in stark contrast to the European ideal that the individual exists in a web of relationships to other individuals in society, particularly other members of the individual's family, to which members duties are owed, and for which members society should aid the individual in carrying out his or her responsibilities. We Americans have, according to Glendon, embraced a version of the individualistic theories of John Stuart Mill, whose seminal *On Liberty*[1081] set forth the great principle that individuals should be free to engage in whatever activities they choose, so long as they do not harm other individuals. Glendon makes clear that Mill advanced that principle not really so that everyone could do precisely as he or she pleased, but in order for society itself to profit from the creativity of individual geniuses, and so that civilization would not descend into complete mediocrity. We Americans, however, forgot this frankly elitist and communitarian aspect of Mill, and simply embraced an unthinking individualism that resulted both in a plethora of protected individual rights, and a misunderstanding of what was necessary really to enable

---

[1079] See, e.g., Amitai Etzioni, ed., The Essential Communitarian Reader (Rowman & Littlefield, 1998).

[1080] Rights Talk, *supra* note 1062, Chapter 3, 47–75.

[1081] John Stuart Mill, On Liberty (originally published 1859, by John W. Parker & Son).

the enjoyment of rights, a sensitivity to the fact that individuals have to exist with other individuals in society.[1082] Europeans, she suggests, more influenced by Rousseau and his followers, such as Immanuel Kant,[1083] understand that humans in society owe duties to each other, and the exercise of those duties responsibly, is the best means to further human flourishing.

Glendon is also clear that the American tradition of attempting to divorce law from morality, a tradition perhaps best exemplified by Holmes's notorious "bad man" theory of the law referred to earlier,[1084] leads us to forget that for real human flourishing it is impossible to separate the duties we owe each other from the individual freedom our Constitution guarantees to us. Worse, our focus on the Constitution, and the Supreme Court's failure to articulate constitutionally-based duties as well as rights, leads Americans (obsessed with the Constitution) not to realize that other elements of our tradition, exemplified by state and local statutes and regulations, do, in fact, impose social duties, and go far toward meeting our social needs. While Glendon also demonstrates that European nations do a better job, in their foundational documents, of emphasizing the duties of citizens and of the polity itself, her review of state laws and state agency administration is also a powerful corrective to the tendency of American lawyers (and most American law professors) to study and reflect on

---

[1082] For the earliest and still most powerful sustained critique of Mill, arguing that liberty can only be secured if it is recognized that it must be undergirded by law and morality, see James Fitzjames Stephen, Liberty, Equality Fraternity (1874). Available on the web in an edition published by the liberty fund, http://oll.libertyfund.org/titles/572 (accessed 15 March 2016).

[1083] See, e.g., Immanuel Kant, Groundwork for the Metaphysics of Morals, edited and translated by Allen W. Wood (Yale, 2002, originally published 1785).

[1084] On Holmes, see Chapter 5, *supra.*

federal constitutional law rather than the actual workings of the state and local governments.[1085]

Glendon realizes that moving beyond individual rights as the nearly exclusive focus of the law and society will require a reinvigoration of "intermediate associations" between the individual and the state. Glendon indicates that these associations are the "seedbeds of civic virtue,"[1086] and include, among others, families, neighborhoods, and religious associations.[1087] The problem of wiping out communities through "urban renewal" is a familiar one, and dates back to the 1950's and 1960's, but Glendon is particularly searing and astute when she suggests that this was the destruction of "irreplaceable social networks in the name of a cramped (and frequently mistaken) vision of progress."[1088] As Glendon puts it, "A kind of blind spot seems to float across our political vision where the communal and social, as distinct from individual or strictly economic, dimensions of a problem are concerned."[1089] In her Chapter 5 of *Rights Talk*, "The Missing Dimension of Sociality,"[1090] Glendon ruefully notes that at the time of the Founding, the Framers took for granted that "families, custom, religion, and convention [would] preserve and promote the virtues required by our experiment in ordered liberty," but the erosion of those institutions and their laudable functions has been all but ignored by our policy-

---

[1085] For Glendon's comparison of the work of state and local governments to the European experience, and for the Supreme Court's failure adequately to take account of what the state and local governments do, because of the Court's related failure to emphasize individual duties and collective social responsibility, see her Chapter 4, "The Missing Language of Social Responsibility," *Rights Talk, supra* note 1062, at 76–108.

[1086] *Id.*, at 109.

[1087] *Id.*

[1088] *Id.*, at 111.

[1089] *Id.*, at 112.

[1090] Chapter 5 is pages 109–144 of *Rights Talk, supra* note 1062.

makers and legislators.[1091] She quotes Emile Durkheim's observation that these intermediate associations, what Durkheim called "secondary groups," prevent the disintegration of civil society, and, ultimately, are necessary to the maintenance of the nation itself.[1092]

Thus, Glendon explains, when American society and American courts in particular ceased thinking of the family—one of these "secondary groups"—as an institution needing to be preserved in its traditional role, and began thinking of the family only as a group of autonomous individuals whose individual rights took precedence over their collective duties, it's no surprise that divorce proliferated, the number of children born out of wedlock increased, child support became more difficult for many single parents, juvenile delinquency increased, and pressure mounted on the government to provide for what breadwinners within families had formerly done.[1093] Sadly, as she observes, American policy-makers have been afraid to address the issue of what happens to individual character and virtue when the family disintegrates, and what that disintegration, in turn, does to American society generally. The family, for Glendon, is the place where "citizens acquire the capacity to care about the common good," where "people learn to view others with respect and concern, rather than to regard them as objects, means, or obstacles," and where boys and girls "develop the healthy independence of mind and self-confidence that enable men and women to participate effectively in government and to exercise

---

[1091] *Id.*, at 116.

[1092] *Id.*, at 118–119. Many of these "secondary groups" we would now regard as charitable organizations, or "non-profits," such as hospitals, private schools, community, trade or professional organizations, colleges, universities, and the like. For an argument that there is an increasing legal recognition of small groups in the polity which recognition could contribute to the furthering of democracy and efficiency, see Nadav Shoked, The New Local, 100 Va. L.Rev. 1323 (2014).

[1093] See, e.g., Glendon, *supra* note 1062, at 122–127.

responsible leadership."[1094] As broken families proliferate, these vital functions of this vital intermediate association deteriorate. Accordingly, Glendon suggests that instead of reinforcing those legal and political attitudes that have rent families asunder, we ought to undertake governmental policies not necessarily to try to restore only the traditional model of the two-parent family, but to ease the burden on single parents, and to take other steps to reinforce the roles of family and community in building more virtuous citizens. Summarizing her critique of the ascendant "rights-talk" in the late twentieth century, Glendon declares that "The paradox of liberalism seems to be that the strong state, the free market, and a vital civil society are all potential threats to individual citizens and to each other, yet a serious weakness in any one of them puts the entire democratic enterprise in jeopardy."[1095] In our time, Glendon argues, the weakness is in "a vital civil society," and to recover from that weakness, it may be necessary to create programs that strengthen the role not only of families, but also "religious, charitable, and other voluntary associations."[1096]

In the penultimate chapter of *Rights Talk*, Chapter 6, "Rights Insularity,"[1097] Glendon, drawing on her knowledge as a comparativist, suggests that American courts could learn from European judges how better to conceptualize "rights," as not absolute, but as subject to modification in the interests of the community. Glendon, in a manner reminiscent of Herbert Wechsler,[1098] calls for our judges to engage in the resolution of disputes over rights by reference to clearly articulated principles, although, like Wechsler, Glendon appears to realize that this involves difficult

---

[1094] *Id.*, at 129.

[1095] *Id.*, at 138.

[1096] *Id.*, at 141.

[1097] *Id.*, at 145–170.

[1098] See Chapter 11, *supra*.

choices between competing values. Moreover, her study of European judges has convinced her that "Like many great judges in the [Anglo-American] common-law tradition, the members of the European Court have realized that there can be no watertight separation between law and morality, or between public and private."[1099]

Her final chapter, "Refining the Rhetoric of Rights," is her attempt to come to grips with the difficulty that "our rights-laden public discourse easily accommodates the economic, the immediate, and the personal dimensions of a problem, while it regularly neglects the moral, the long-term, and the social implications."[1100] In this final chapter, Glendon sounds a communitarian, or perhaps a traditional conservative note, as she indicates that "the new rhetoric of rights is less about human dignity and freedom than about insistent, unending desires. Its legitimation of individual and group egoism is in flat opposition to the great purposes set forth in the Preamble to the Constitution: 'to form a more perfect Union, establish Justice, promote the general Welfare, and secure the Blessings of Liberty to ourselves and our Posterity.' "[1101] Moreover, she acknowledges that "the possibility must be reckoned with that our shallow rights talk is a faithful reflection of what our culture has become."[1102] Glendon suggests that women, those who have traditionally "taken primary responsibility for the transmission of family lore and for the moral education of children," may play an important role in saving our legal and general culture from the woes that she limns.[1103] Glendon ought to be regarded, then, as an important feminist scholar, as she recognizes the unique and

---

[1099] Glendon, *Rights Talk, supra* note 1062, at 157.

[1100] *Id.,* at 171.

[1101] *Id.,* at 171–172.

[1102] *Id.,* at 172.

[1103] *Id.,* at 174.

important aspect of our culture that women and women's work illustrates. Some of the feminist scholars we examine here, women such as Catherine MacKinnon[1104] and Patricia Williams,[1105] have produced work with as many radical implications as did the Critical Legal Scholars.[1106] Still, a reading of Glendon's articles and books points one in quite a different conservative direction, as *Rights Talk* makes clear.

Just as Glendon calls for a recognition of the important mediating role for women in American society and law, she recalls to our understanding that for all its creation of pernicious "Rights Talk," the "dominant ethos of the legal profession is still one where civility and adequately complex speech are the order of the day, and where nuance and subtlety are expected to the degree required by the subject under discussion," so that compromise and settlement, planning and the conferral of reciprocal benefit can still be the most important things lawyers can do, thus facilitating relationships rather than adversarial conflict.[1107] *Rights Talk* ends with a powerful suggestion that "The greatest hope for renewal, perhaps, lies in the American political tradition itself, in its time-honored ideals of tolerance, respect for others, public deliberation, individual freedom and responsibility, and the mandate for self-restraint implicit in the rule of law."[1108] Thus Glendon is able to place her hope for moving beyond "Rights Talk," in an American renewal of political discourse uniquely furthered by "the variety of our racial and ethnic groups, the opportunities for innovation and experimentation inherent in our sort of federalism, our neighborliness, our stubborn religiosity, and

---

[1104] See Chapter 17, *supra.*

[1105] See Chapter 21, *infra.*

[1106] See Chapter 14, *supra.*

[1107] *Rights Talk, supra* note 1062, at 175–176.

[1108] *Id.,* at 176.

even, within bounds, our attachment to a gambling, risk-taking, profit-making economy." Still, she warns that this renewal will only happen if Americans in politics and the press "have the will, ability, courage, and imagination necessary" for such an effort.[1109]

Not surprisingly for a scholar who understands that individualism is not all there is, and that for true human flourishing it is imperative to cultivate intermediate associations, those that mediate between the individual and the state, Glendon has devoted much of her scholarship, unlike many of the scholars treated here, to legal issues involving the family. Generally speaking, the most prestige in the American Legal Academy is accorded to those who work in Constitutional Law, Antitrust, Securities Regulation, and other fields of interest to an elite financial and political community. Issues of Family law, including marriage, divorce, child custody, and adoption have not, usually, been the areas of concern to those most prominent in the elite law schools. But here, as well, Glendon is exceptional. She has written some of the most penetrating and brilliant examinations of divorce, and abortion, and, again, has been unique in the manner in which she has compared and contrasted the American experience with that of other nations, a manner that underscores many of the suggestions offered in *Rights Talk.*

While *Rights Talk* might well be regarded as her masterpiece, it was nicely foreshadowed by her important Abortion and Divorce in Western Law (1987),[1110] which she delivered in one of the pre-eminent legal lecture series, Northwestern University School of Law's Julius Rosenthal Foundation Lectures, in 1986. *Rights Talk* clearly drew from Glendon's work in both family law and in comparative law, and *Abortion and Divorce in Western Law*, as the name

---

[1109] *Id.*, at 183.

[1110] *Supra* note 1060.

implies, is a comparative study of how these two topics are treated both in the United States and in other Western Countries. In this provocative series of lectures, Glendon argues that the United States is "at the extreme end of the spectrum when cross-national comparisons are made" with regard to selected aspects of divorce and abortion. With regard to abortion, "Not only do we [in America] have less regulation of abortion in the interest of the fetus than any other Western nation, but we provide less public support for maternity and child raising."[1111]

Moreover, according to Glendon, "Only in America has a vast profit-making industry grown up around abortion."[1112] Equally alarming, for Glendon, is the fact that "to a greater extent than in any other country, our courts have shut down the legislative process of bargaining, education, and persuasion on the abortion issue." She believes that we should reexamine our absolutist position on abortion, to take the issue away from the courts and return it to public discussion and to the legislatures, and seek to move closer to a European model, in order to preserve freedom of choice to terminate pregnancies in the early months of fetal gestation, but after that to have increasing respect for the human life of the fetus, and, further, that we should do more, as Europeans do, both to encourage the possibility of adoption and also to provide assistance to mothers in raising their children. As she sums it up, "Our law stresses autonomy, separation, and isolation in the war of all against all, in contrast to Sweden where the laws emphasize sex equality and social solidarity, West Germany where the message is pro-life and social solidarity, and France where equality, life, and solidarity are all sought to be promoted."[1113] We should recognize, she claims,

---

[1111] *Abortion and Divorce, supra* note 1060, at 2.

[1112] *Id.,* at 20.

[1113] *Id.,* at 58.

in company with feminists that we recently considered, such as Carole Gilligan and Catherine MacKinnon,[1114] that the women affected by abortion policy have their own distinctive approach to law, one that rejects domination over women by predominately male judges or legislatures, and also emphasizes relationships over rights.[1115]

Similarly, with regard to divorce, Glendon notes, "Divorce is as readily available in most American states as it is anywhere, but we have been less diligent than most other countries in seeking to mitigate the economic causalities of divorce through public assistance or enforcement of private support obligations."[1116] And it is not just the practical failure to support divorced spouses and minor children that is problematic with modern American "no-fault" divorce law as Glendon understands it. In a manner quite similar to what she was later to do in *Rights Talk*, Glendon suggests how modern American divorce law reflects dangerous trends in modern American values. "The no-fault terminology," she explains, "fit[s] neatly into an increasingly popular mode of discourse in which values are treated as a matter of taste, feelings of guilt are regarded as unhealthy, and an individual's primary responsibility is assumed to be to himself."[1117] Even worse, as she shows, "The American story about marriage, as told in the law and in much popular literature, goes something like this: Marriage is a relationship that exits primarily for the fulfillment of the individual spouses. If it ceases to perform this function, no one is to blame and either spouse may terminate it at will."[1118] This makes marriage about simply "self-fulfillment," and this is in stark contrast with an

---

[1114] See Chapter 17, *supra*.

[1115] *Abortion and Divorce, supra* note 1060, at 50–58.

[1116] *Ibid.*

[1117] *Id.*, at 108.

[1118] *Ibid.*

earlier common law conception of marriage which recognized that it included irrevocable duties of care, loyalty, and support not only to one's spouse, but to God, and, really, to the community as well.[1119] Glendon, perhaps reflecting feminist sympathies, makes quite clear that the effect of current American divorce practices, possibly owing to the fact that most American judges who dictate them are males who have relatively little sense of what is involved in child rearing, is to impose greater financial and other burdens on the custodial parent in divorces involving minor children, and these custodial parents are much more likely to be female than male.[1120] Accordingly, Glendon proposes reforming American divorce law to treat families with minor children differently from those divorces involving childless couples; a simple, but wise reform, and one routinely incorporated in European nations. While there are stop-gap measures such as these that might alleviate problems for some families involved in divorce, however, what is most impressive about Glendon's volume is her overall conclusions about the difference between American and European practice.

Glendon's strong suggestion, then, is that the effort in last few decades of the twentieth century, to enable easier access to abortion and divorce for American women,

---

[1119] For this nineteenth-century approach to law and the family, see, e.g., Stephen B. Presser, and Jamil S. Zainaldin, Law and Jurisprudence in American History 682–768 (West, 8th ed. 2013).

[1120] See, e.g., Corie Lynn Rosen, Men v. Women: Who Does Better in a Divorce? https://www.legalzoom.com/articles/men-v-women-who-does-better-in-a-divorce (Dec. 2009, accessed 15 March 2016). ("Women are typically awarded custody of the children. Because our predominant social values suggest that children are best situated with their mothers, women often do the lion's share of child rearing in divorced families, even in shared custody cases. . . . Since mothers usually take some time away from their careers, and since women still earn slightly less than men, it is fair to say that most women, even prior to divorce, have lower earning power than their male spouses. . . . The problem of lower earning power is exacerbated by child care responsibilities.")

prompted by an ideology, or perhaps a psychology of "individual self-fulfillment," may have had some pernicious side-effects in undermining both respect for the sacredness of human life, and the sanctity and cohesiveness of the American family. Just as she argued in *Rights Talk*, her work on Abortion and Divorce reminds us that an ideal legal system would not simply focus on highly individualistic rights in, as she put it—a war of all against all,[1121] but, rather, Americans ought to learn from Europeans that an ideal legal system ought to encourage community, solidarity, and social flourishing. In some ways, this is the same message that we encountered in Critical Legal Studies,[1122] and, indeed, a message similar to that of other feminist scholars, but with Glendon it has a strongly conservative rather than a strongly progressive coloration. Glendon's similarity to these other modern legal philosophies is also evident in the manner that she borrows from other areas of intellectual experience, most notably the thought of the great social thinkers from Greece and from the European enlightenment. In *Abortion and Divorce in Western Law*, she nicely uses Plato, Rousseau, and a later French thinker, Tocqueville, to illuminate the recent American experience.

Glendon, as indicated, makes a few practical suggestions, but it is equally striking that she suggests that if a true transformation of American law is to take place it will take more than just the lawyers to effect it. Quoting Plato, she closes her book by indicating that "there are times when we need enchantments, inspiration, or poetry as much as we need philosophy."[1123] Let's turn then, to a law

---

[1121] *Abortion and Divorce, supra* note 1060, at 58.

[1122] See Chapter 14, *supra*.

[1123] *Id.*, at 142, referring to "Plato, Phaedo 78a; and The Laws, 951." *Id.*, at 190, n.87. In the first dialogue Plato has Socrates extolling the virtues of a "singer of charms" to sooth the fears of children, and in the second (apparently a reference to Book 12 of The Laws) Plato is suggesting the value of challenging

professor who once borrowed from Mark Twain, one of the
great American enchanters, to try to teach a lesson about
legal pedagogy.

existing laws by comparing the experience of other peoples, and in one
memorable passage, "Amongst the mass of men there always exist—albeit in
small numbers—men that are divinely inspired; intercourse with such men is
of the greatest value, and they spring up in badly-governed States just as much
as in those that are well governed. In search of these men it is always right for
one who dwells in a well-ordered State to go forth on a voyage of enquiry by
land and sea. . . ." Translation by R.G. Bury. Cambridge, MA, Harvard
University Press; London, William Heinemann Ltd. 1967 & 1968.

CHAPTER 19

THE LAWYER AS ROMANTIC

LATE TWENTIETH, EARLY TWENTY-FIRST CENTURY

Paul Carrington
(Duke)

■ ■ ■

Paul Carrington (b. 1931)
Photograph courtesy Duke University.

For many years, Paul Carrington was the Dean of Duke Law School (1978–1988), and in and out of the Deanship he has been a thoughtful critic of American legal education. His biography is somewhat different from most of the law professors discussed here in that Carrington has never had tenure at a Northeastern or Ivy League institution, or one on the West Coast.[1124] Still, he has a law degree from

---

[1124] Carrington probably could have had such a post had he desired one. Carrington was a visiting professor at the University of California at Los Angeles in 1975 and at the University of California at Berkeley (Boalt Hall) in 1988.

Harvard (class of 1955), so that he is familiar with the legal culture that dominates these pages. Even so, unlike many of those we have considered, before he became a law professor, he served for two years (1955–57) in the United States Army, and his teaching career exposed him to a wide variety of institutions. According to his web biography at Duke, "He has been a member of the law faculties at Wyoming, Indiana, Ohio State, Michigan, and Duke. He has held visiting appointments at ten other American law schools (including Southern Methodist University and the University of Texas) and has taught in five foreign universities."[1125] Carrington has a substantial body of scholarship, but it is his work as a law reformer, and, simultaneously, conservative legal critic, that serves to make him particularly distinctive.

With regard to his legal reformation efforts, as Duke's website summarizes, "He first initiated efforts to secure enactment of the Uniform Commercial Code in Wyoming; it was enacted in that state in 1960, one of the earliest enactments of that legislation. In 1967–1969, he directed the American Bar Foundation study of the United States Courts of Appeal. In 1969–1971, he directed a study of legal education for the Association of American Law Schools. In 1970–1973, he served as an elected trustee of the Ann Arbor Board of Education. In 1973–1975, he served the Federal Judicial Center as vice chair of the Advisory Council on Appellate Justice, organizing the 1975 national conference on that subject. In 1976–1978, he directed a program of law reform for the Supreme Court of Michigan."[1126]

Impressive as all of these efforts were, we are particularly concerned with his work on the study of legal education for the Association of American Law Schools (AALS), which produced, in 1971, a document that came to

[1125] https://law.duke.edu/fac/carrington/ (accessed September 25, 2015).
[1126] *Ibid.*

be called "The Carrington Report."[1127] While the Report
came to be widely circulated, and while it was relatively
widely discussed, it is noteworthy that its more interesting
recommendations were not widely implemented, although
periodic attempts to do so have occurred. For example, as
one sympathetic reader of the report, Robert A. Gorman,
explained, it proposed for law schools,

> a multi-track system with the typical student
> qualifying for graduation after two years; the
> return to the law school for further training after a
> period in practice; the development of first-year
> courses cutting across traditional course lines and
> integrating social-science method and concerns
> about professional responsibility; the broadening
> of the students' information base in the second
> year through electronic technology; and the
> training in different skills through intensive and
> diversified seminar work.[1128]

Gorman's observations were made in 1982, and have been
repeated in the 34 years since, with relatively little
effect,[1129] although a very few law schools, Northwestern
among them,[1130] have experimented with a two-year law

[1127] Paul D. Carrington, Training for the Public Professions of Law, 1971,
reprinted as Report of the Curriculum Study Project Committee (The
Carrington Report), 1971 A.A.L.S.Proc. Part One 15–22, 44–5–; Reprinted in
Herbert L. Packer and Thomas Ehrlich, New Directions in Legal Education: A
Report Prepared for the Carnegie Commission on Higher Education, 1972,
app. A. at 93.

[1128] Robert A. Gorman, *Legal Education at the End of the Century: An
Introduction*, 32 J. LEGAL EDUC. 315, 317 (1982). Gorman said of the
Carrington Report that it was the "single most thoughtful, provocative, and
constructive document" in the legal education literature of the 1970's. *Id.*, at
317.

[1129] Ten years out Gorman reported that Carrington's ideas had "little
discernable impact on curriculum development." *Id.*, at 317.

[1130] From 2009 to 2015, Northwestern offered a general two-year
"Accelerated JD Program," in which the normal three-year curriculum was
compressed into two years, in particular by adding summer components.
Demand for the program did not meet original expectations, and solicitation of

degree, and, as indicated, even the current President of the United States, Barack Obama, has expressed agreement with the notion. Nevertheless, there is great professional reluctance to abandon that third year of law school, although there are some indications that New York is flirting with the idea of admitting students to the bar after only two years of law school, and there is at last some feeling that those holding out for continuing the third year of law school ought to have the burden of proving it is necessary.[1131]

To this day, however, the traditional first-year law program consisting primarily of discrete common law doctrinal courses in traditional subjects such as contracts, torts, property, criminal law, constitutional law, and civil procedure, and the second and third year composed of optional specialized classes building on these traditional subjects, such as business associations, evidence, taxation, intellectual property, antitrust, or trusts and estates, predominates. For better or for worse, in most law schools, the names of the courses at least, bear a strong resemblance to those that were offered fifty years ago, although, of course, the doctrinal content of the courses has changed as courts and legislation have altered them. More law professors lecture now than they did in the era of Kingsfield

---

applications for the program was indefinitely suspended in October of 2015. See generally announcement by Dean Daniel B. Rodriquez, October 2, 2015, available on the web at http://www.law.northwestern.edu/about/news/news display.cfm?ID=761 (accessed 26 January 2016).

[1131] See, e.g., Samuel Estreicher, The Roosevelt-Cardozo Way: The Case for Bar Eligibility After Two Years of Law School, 15 N.Y.U. J. Legis. & Pub. Pol'y 599 (2012), and Daniel B. Rodriguez and Samuel Estreicher, Make Law Schools Earn A Third Year, The New York Times, A27, Jan. 17, 2013. See also Jonathan Lippman, The State of the Judiciary 2014: Vision and Action in Our Modern Courts, 3 (2014). (Discussing a proposal under which third year law students can take the New York state bar exam in February of their third year in return for devoting their last semester of law school to providing legal services to the indigent, "under the supervision of a legal services provider, law firm, or corporation in partnership with their law school.")

(in the sixties and seventies and early eighties, when the Socratic method still prevailed),[1132] and a few intrepid law professors have begun to explore the connections between social science research and the law, but their inroads into the curriculum are limited, though social science approaches now dominate the law reviews.

It might be said, however, that the principal difficulty with late twentieth-century law training, which the Carrington Report highlighted, was its abstract nature, and the failure of American law schools to take seriously their obligation actually to train lawyers for the practice of law, a complaint about legal education that has not ceased in the ensuing four decades.[1133] While President Obama and others have observed the obvious redundancy in the third year of legal education, with the exception of a few law schools who have emphasized clinical training preparation for the actual practice of law in the third year, it is astonishing how virtually every law school has successfully clung to the three-year required program, in which students are engaged in discrete doctrinal courses through all three years of law school, courses that actually do little to prepare them for what they will encounter when they begin serving the needs of clients. It is this divorce from the needs of the real world, of course, that Leon Panetta was echoing in his criticism of President Obama,[1134] and this is something that the legal academy finds it difficult, if not impossible, to shed.

Writing in a letter to the Editor to the Texas Bar Journal in 2013, Carrington expressed extreme frustration with his fellow law school teachers and administrators for their longstanding refusal to recognize the superfluity of the

---

[1132] For the fictional law professor Charles Kingsfield, the creation of the author John Jay Osborn, Jr., see Chapter 13, *supra*.

[1133] See, e.g., Harry Edwards, *supra* note 11.

[1134] See note 1, *supra*, and accompanying text.

third year of law school. The creation of that third year, by nineteenth-century legal administrators, such as those at Harvard[1135] came about, Carrington lamented, "not [because of concern] for the competence of lawyers but [rather because of a felt need for advancing] the status of our profession." This might have made some sense when most lawyers did not have four years of college behind them as well, but given the extraordinary rise in the costs of professional education, and, in particular, the astronomical burden now placed on law students from student loans, "[r]equiring three years made more sense in 1963 [when expenses were less] than it does now. . . . If our profession wishes to remain open to members who come from impecunious families, it must face the reality that three years of law school is unnecessary."[1136] For Carrington, the third year never really made sense in terms of the needs of practice. As he put it:

> The three-year degree was fashioned at Harvard in 1870 to elevate the social status of those holding Harvard Law degrees. Many Harvard students looked at the third-year curriculum and left without a degree. Harvard understood that great lawyering does not require prolonged formal education. It awarded an honorary Ph.D. to Thomas Cooley [A great Michigan Supreme Court Justice, and a particular hero of Carringon's],[1137] who had a year of elementary school and a year in a law office before moving to Michigan at the age

---

[1135] On this nineteenth-century innovation at Harvard, see, e.g., Chapter 4, *supra*, on Langdell, and sources there cited.

[1136] Paul D. Carrington, Letter to the Editor, Texas Bar Journal, May 2013, http://mydigimag.rrd.com/article/Letters+to+the+Editor/1386205/0/article.html (accessed September 26, 2015).

[1137] See, e.g., Paul D. Carrington, The Constitutional Law Scholarship of Thomas McIntyre Cooley, 41 Am. J. Legal Hist. 368 (1997); Paul D. Carrington, Law as "The Common Thoughts of Men": The Law—Teaching and Judging of Thomas McIntyre Cooley, 49 Stan. L. Rev. 495 (1997).

of nineteen and hanging out his shingle. He moved on to be the Michigan Supreme Court clerk, then its chief justice, then the founding dean of the University of Michigan Law School, then the author of the leading works on constitutional law and on torts, the president of the American Bar Association, and the designer and founding chair of the Interstate Commerce Commission regulating the nation's railroads. Cooley "read the law" and became perhaps the best lawyer in America.[1138]

Further, Carrington noted, "Benjamin Cardozo and Henry Stimson, two of the wisest and best 20th century lawyers, skipped the third year, took the New York Bar Examination, and become famous for their good professional judgment."[1139]

Making clear that the bar and the law schools were losing touch with the need to keep the profession democratic, and noting the ironic effect of the federal government's meddling in the area, Carrington concluded:

The price of all higher education in the United States increased as a consequence of the 1965 federal law guaranteeing the repayment of loans to students. In real dollars, taking account of inflation, the price of higher education is now about five times what it was when that law was enacted. The money is spent on elevated academic salaries, extended administrative services, and reduced ratios of students to teachers at all levels. "Higher" education keeps getting higher in price. . . . As a result of this elevation of the price, the requirement of three years is increasingly

---

[1138] Carrington, Constitutional Law Scholarship, *supra* note 1137.
[1139] *Ibid.*

discriminatory. The offspring of working class families often leave law school with substantial debts that they cannot repay from their earnings as rookie lawyers. For many, their prospective careers are ruined.[1140]

Only a thoughtful law professor who had served as an administrator and a thorough student of the profession could be such an effective critic of higher education in general and of law school in particular, but it was not simply from his concern with the practical needs of law students that Carrington acquired a reputation as one of the most interesting, and, in some ways, notorious commentators on legal education. Carrington's work, particularly his historical study of the profession of law teaching, reveals a profound concern with not only the practical training of lawyers, but also their moral and ethical contributions to legal practice and to the rule of law. For Carrington, it was much more important for a lawyer to really care what the law was about than to have pursued a particular three-year course of study. Thus, as Carrington made clear in a 2013 piece, his models for great lawyers and great law teachers, in particular the eighteenth- and nineteenth-century titans, George Wythe, Thomas Jefferson, Henry Clay, and Thomas Cooley, became great lawyers from spending time with other great lawyers and reading on their own, though they never attended anything we would recognize as a law school.[1141]

Quite possibly as important for legal education as the Carrington Report was a controversy in which Carrington

---

[1140] *Ibid.*

[1141] See generally, Paul D. Carrington, Founding Legal Education in America, 40 Pepperdine L. Rev. 343 (2013); Paul D. Carrington, "Legal Education for the People's Populism and Civic Virtue," 43 U. Kan. L. Rev. 1 (1994); Paul D. Carrington, Teaching Law and Virtue at Transylvania University: The George Wythe Tradition in the Antebellum Years, 41 Mercer L. Rev. 673, 678 (1990).

became embroiled in 1984, at the apex of the influence of Critical Legal Studies[1142] in American law schools. Deeply disturbed by the implications of what Carrington believed to be the CLS scholars' skeptical legal ideology, and as concerned at that time for the inculcation of virtue in lawyers as he was later in 2013, Carrington suggested that the practitioners of CLS ought to leave law schools, perhaps for other havens in the University (presumably the departments of sociology or political science). After all, Carrington argued (perhaps inaptly), would you want atheists teaching in Divinity Schools? This led to a spirited exchange of published pieces with Robert Gordon (of Yale) who defended the Crits' commitment to the rule of law.

What began this exchange was a remarkable short piece written by Carrington, and published in the *Journal of Law and Education*, a periodical pretty much read only by law professors. Ostensibly an appreciation of Mark Twain's *Life on the Mississippi*, and, in particular, of Twain's understanding of professional education, this short essay, "Of Law and the River,"[1143] sought to demonstrate that the education of River Boat pilots in Twain's era was actually quite similar to the education of lawyers in late twentieth-century America. Both professions used an arcane terminology, both professions had, in some cases, virtual life or death responsibility for those who depended on them, and both professions, according to Carrington, ought to be engaged in inculcating in their novices the key virtues of courage and wisdom. More, both professions, Carrington seemed to suggest, ought to be fostering an unqualified love of their subject matter, and, quite possibly, an ultimately uncritical embrace of its accepted values. Without such an uncritical acceptance, without what

---

[1142] See Chapter 14, *supra*, for Critical Legal Studies.

[1143] Paul D. Carrington, Of Law and the River, 34 Journal of Legal Education 222 (1984).

Carrington called a "faith" and a "romantic innocence" in the values of their craft and its importance in restraining arbitrary power, legal practitioners were headed for failure, and possibly even nihilism or despair.

It became clear that what Carrington was up to in drawing the analogy between law students and cub pilots was to launch an extraordinary and not particularly thinly veiled attack on Critical Legal Studies.[1144] Railing at a group that he called "legal nihilists," Carrington suggested that if law professors had lost their sense of faith in the law and its ability to restrain "the lash of power," they should leave the legal academy, perhaps for other jobs in the university. Carrington argued that "legal nihilist" teachers would disable their students from doing the law's work, and would, instead turn them away from the seeking of justice, and toward "bribery or intimidation,"[1145] the last thing the law needed.

Robert Gordon, a prominent figure in Critical Legal Studies, responded to Carrington,[1146] whose earlier "Carrington Report,"[1147] the critique of contemporary legal education, Gordon called a work of "stunning grace," but he accused Carrington of hanging out with the "rednecks" of the legal academy, and of behaving in the same manner as

---

[1144] There is, however, a theme in Carrington's criticism of legal education which is an implied critique of the legal profession, and, in particular, its recent transformation from something once rather like a calling, to simply another business devoted to making money. On this trend see also Harry T. Edwards, *supra* note 11.

[1145] Carrington, Of Law and the River, *supra* note 1143, at 227.

[1146] For Gordon's initial reply to Carrington, see Robert W. Gordon to Paul D. Carrington, "Of Law and the River," and Of Nihilism and Academic Freedom, 35 J.Legal Ed. 1 (1985). For Carrington's response to Gordon's criticism, see Paul D. Carrington to Robert Gordon, 35 J.Legal Ed. 9 (1985), and for Gordon's rejoinder to Carrington's response, see Robert W. Gordon to Paul D. Carrington, 35 J.Legal Ed. 13 (1985). Their dialogue appears in an edited version in Stephen B. Presser & Jamil S. Zainaldin, Law and Jurisprudence in American History 1212–1238 (West, 8th ed. 2013).

[1147] Note 1127, *supra*.

the members of the House Un-American Activities Committee, in the nineteen-fifties, when they engaged in "Red-baiting."[1148] There was some truth in what Gordon said, and there were surely members of the legal academy, as indicated earlier (and this included at least one of my senior colleagues at Northwestern) who, at the time Gordon and Carrington were carrying on their debate, found it difficult to distinguish among Marxists, Critical Legal Studies Scholars, and those who advocated the overthrow of the United States Government by force and violence. A few Critical Legal Studies scholars did find it difficult to secure permanent jobs at American law schools,[1149] and, while some of the most prominent among them ended up at schools like Harvard and Yale, this might have been the exception rather than the rule.

Still, whatever the early hostility to the crits, and whatever the troubles of a few of them in gaining tenure at their law schools, the fact that Gordon got it at Yale, and that Mark Tushnet (who, as indicated earlier, once claimed that were he a judge his aim would be to do whatever was necessary to advance socialism),[1150] Morton Horwitz,

---

[1148] Presser & Zainaldin, *supra* note 1146, at 1228.

[1149] For the suggestion that critical legal studies scholars were denied tenure at Harvard owing to their adherence to the movement (though Harvard Law School's Dean denied it) see Jennifer A. Kingston, Week in Review: Harvard Tenure Battle Puts 'Critical Legal Studies' on Trial, New York Times, August 30, 1987, available on the web, at http://www.nytimes.com/1987/08/30/weekinreview/harvard-tenure-battle-puts-critical-legal-studies-on-trial.html (accessed 25 January 2016). For the earlier observation about some professors' confusion about CLS and the overthrow of the U.S. government, see text following note 876, *supra*.

[1150] Mark Tushnet, "The Dilemmas of Liberal Constitutionalism," 42 Ohio State Law Journal 411, 424 (1981). See text accompanying note 852, *supra*. Since that time Tushnet, now the William Nelson Cromwell Professor of Law at Harvard, and probably the most prolific of the Critical Legal Studies scholars, and the man generally credited with a major role in the founding of that movement, has written a series of exceptionally sophisticated descriptive and prescriptive analyses of Constitutional law. See, e.g., Mark Tushnet, Red, White and Blue: A Critical Analysis of Constitutional Thinking (Kansas, Revised edition 2015); Why the Constitution Matters (Yale 2011) and The

Duncan Kennedy, and Roberto Unger achieved it at Harvard, does cause one to wonder whether there isn't something to be gained in the elite reaches of the academy by leaning far to the left. When the Berlin Wall fell in 1989, and when Critical Legal Studies seeming call for a decentralized and humanistic socialism that had yet to appear anywhere in the world seemed to be falling on deaf ears, its appeal waned a bit. Still, in 2000, when *Bush v. Gore* convinced a gaggle of more than 400 law professors that the Supreme Court majority ruled for Bush simply because they were Republicans, CLS's message that law was essentially politics once again had some resonance.[1151]

More provocatively, as suggested earlier, one is led to wonder whether CLS's mantra that all law is politics might have shaped the education of Barack Obama when he was at Harvard Law in the mid-eighties.[1152] Finally, one might be concerned that the elite law schools, such as Harvard, may have veered off in the wrong direction as early as Langdell. This is what, apparently, Carrington came to believe. Thus, in 1990, a bit after the *contretemps* with Gordon, Carrington blasted the prominence of legal education as practiced particularly in the Northeast and on the West Coast. Law schools there, Carrington argued, had come to underrate the "vision of Jefferson, Kent, Wilson,

---

Constitution of the United States: A Contextual Analysis (Bloomsbury, 2nd ed. 2015).

[1151] See generally Presser & Zainaldin, *supra* note 1146, at 1382 (Noting Yale Law Professor Jack Balkin, ruminating on the result in *Bush v. Gore*, where he declared that "the big winners . . . were American Legal Realism and Critical Legal Studies.").

[1152] On Barack Obama, see Chapter 23, *infra*. On the CLS claim that "law is politics," see, e.g., Mark V. Tushnet, Critical Legal Studies: A Political History, 100 Yale L.J. 1515, 1517 (1991) (Acknowledging that there is a "proposition common to most [CLS] authors that law is politics . . . when one understands the moral, epistemological, and empirical assumptions embedded in any particular legal claim, one will see that those assumptions operate in the particular setting in which the legal claim is made to advance the interests of some identifiable political grouping." (footnote omitted)).

Wythe, Tucker, Clay and others," the vision that lawyers could be virtuous leaders of American society. Carrington (whose career teaching, as indicated earlier, was primarily devoted to the South and the Midwest), was trying to recall the profession of law teaching to its better nature. He tried to be encouraging, in particular by still maintaining that though it was accompanied by "[l]ittle celebration" there was still an abiding sense, dwelling in every law school in America, that law ought to be taught as public virtue.[1153]

The threats to Carrington's concept of "public virtue" or "romantic" faith in the law remain strong, however, and, in an even more powerful act of protest, Carrington, in the fall of 1992, lamented one more wrong turn in legal education, the push for "diversity" in the recruitment of students and faculty in the law schools. His polemic on this topic, published in the Utah Law Review,[1154] as relevant now as it was twenty four years ago, explained that "*Diversity!* has become the *nom de guerre* of an aggressive movement among law students and teachers, and some other members of American academic institutions. Although miniature in the numbers it commands," he stated, "the style of the movement threatens to harm relations and institutions. It promises benefits to few. Despite *Diversity!*'s proclaimed connection with the civil rights movement, its premises and aims conflict with those of that movement."[1155] His

---

[1153] Paul D. Carrington, The Revolutionary Idea of University Legal Education, 31 Wm. & Mary L. Rev. 527, 574 (1990).

[1154] Paul D. Carrington, *Diversity!,* 1992 Utah L.Rev. 1105.

[1155] *Ibid.* (Emphasis in original). "Nom de guerre," French for "war name" refers to the moniker one adopts the better to fight battles or advance a cause. One of the more notable uses of such *noms de guerre* appears among Palestinians, as for example, Yasser Arafat, who adopted the nom de guerre "Abu Ammar." Both "Abu Ammar" and Yasser were in homage to an early companion of the Prophet Muhammed, Ammar ibn Yasir. For Ammar ibn Yasir, see, e.g., Abdul Aziz Ash-Shanawi, The Ministers Around the Prophet 115–128 (Darussalam, 2004).

"polemic",[1156] Carrington, explained, was "written to encourage resistance among those who care about the law and the institutions of law teaching, and to encourage opposition by those who care about civil rights."[1157] Mincing no words, Carrington declared that the current push for "race consciousness" in the law schools was a "fraud."

This was because rather than advocating "race consciousness," in order eventually to achieve "uncoerced race-conscious selection of law students and teachers in the exercise of professional educational judgment to enhance the quality of the intellectual life of institutions of higher learning,"[1158] as proponents of diversity such as Supreme Court Justice Lewis Powell writing in the *Bakke* case had urged,[1159] its proponents in the law schools were after something quite different. "What the *Diversity!* movement seeks," claimed Carrington, "is a payment made by educational institutions, at the expense of individuals seeking admission or employment, to compensate members of groups said to be disadvantaged by historic injustices to their ancestors."[1160] "The movement," Carrington continued, "also seeks to hold educators accountable to persons outside their institutions, in order to ensure faithful payment of such compensation and thereby diminishes academic freedom."[1161]

In this extraordinary and clearly intentionally controversial piece, then, Carrington appeared to be claiming that those leading the push for "diversity" in the law schools, and perhaps their allies in critical legal

---

[1156] For the labelling of the article as a "polemic" see Carrington, *supra* note 1154, footnote "a."

[1157] *Id.*, at 1105.

[1158] *Id.*, at 1106.

[1159] Regents of the University of California v. Bakke, 438 U.S. 265, 269–324 (1978) (Powell, J.).

[1160] *Ibid.*

[1161] *Ibid.*

studies,[1162] were practitioners of "a pathology of divisive intolerance,"[1163] and were really seeking racial reparations,[1164] possibly through the essentially clandestine application of racial quotas,[1165] pursuant to "the

---

[1162] *Diversity!* includes a blast at Duncan Kennedy, *id.*, at 1113–1114 ("More than a few of the advocates of *Diversity!* share Duncan Kennedy's belief that 'guilt, anger, mistrust, cynicism, and bitter conflict' are useful instruments of politics. Perhaps reasonable minds can differ as to whether mistrust, anger, and bitter conflict are effective politics, but they are precisely the conditions that legal institutions in every culture aim to relieve or prevent, and they are conditions that American civil rights law aims to dissolve." Citations omitted. Here Carrington appeared to be implying that Kennedy's politics were inconsistent with Carrington's beliefs about what a law professor ought to be doing.) For further criticism of critical legal studies in Carrington's piece, see *id.*, text accompanying notes 21–22. For Kennedy, see Chapter 14, *supra.*

[1163] *Diversity!*, supra note 1154, at 1115.

[1164] See *id.*, at 1155–1165, addressing the irrationality of such reparations, or, to put it more neutrally, such a compensation scheme based on past injustice. Carrington is particularly witty and biting, or perhaps simply ironic, when he suggests that because women in an earlier era were responsible for the passing on of past mores and attitudes, one of which was that women ought primarily to be interested in being mothers and homemakers, the wrongs of these women might require compensation for men:

> Much of the gender-role disadvantage experienced by women was caused by other women, who raised their daughters to be mothers instead of lawyers. How would one divide responsibility between men and women for the existence of mores that governed the lives of both? If, as many believe, mothers have largely controlled the moral development of American children, then it is women, not men, who bear the primary responsibility for our present moral defects. The logic of compensation would dictate a preference for men in order to punish women for their grandmothers' moral failings.

Id., at 1159–1160 (footnotes omitted). Compare the views of Catherine MacKinnon and Patricia Williams, Chapter 17, *supra* and Chapter 21, *infra.*

[1165] *Id.*, at 1107 ("The difference between affirmative action and quota is not always easy to discern, but it is quite real. The critical difference is between voluntary and involuntary race or gender consciousness. Where such consciousness is compelled, it becomes necessary to measure compliance. A quota is the necessary consequence. Quota is therefore an apt word to describe any program of regulation that requires admissions officers or academic employers to attain demographic goals, whether those goals are fixed explicitly or implicitly. It is precisely such regulation that the advocates of *Diversity!* seek to impose.") On quotas "to compensate existing persons for injustices experienced by their forbears," see *id.*, at 1119.

larger objective" of "Politically Correct
multiculturalism."[1166] While Carrington himself
championed and lauded what he regarded as the
"extraordinary" and "stunning" increases in minority and
female teachers and students of law, particularly in the
middle decades of the twentieth century,[1167] he believed
that the proponents of "*Diversity!*" were threatening the
ideals Carrington cherished of the law professor as a
"teacher, scholar, and public citizen"[1168] and of law as a
discipline that reflected disinterested virtue,[1169] the
"transcendent interests and values of the [legal]

[1166] *Id.*, at 1110. On Carrington's appropriate disdain for misconceived
multiculturalism, and, in particular the criticism of American law as
"Eurocentric," see *id.*, at 1114. ("Alas, insofar as it is politically incorrect to
purvey 'Eurocentric' ideas, all law teachers are doomed in the same way that
a sushi chef is doomed to express Asian influence on our cuisine.")

[1167] See, e.g., *id.*, at 1126–1127.

[1168] *Id.*, at 1148.

[1169] See *id.*, at 1202. ("When cast as a regulatory command, a *Diversity!*
standard has the effect of preventing law teachers from accepting, on their
own, a public responsibility for the selection of students to whom they propose
to share a sense of public duty and for the selection of their colleagues. In this
respect, mandatory *Diversity!* is a misappropriation of moral worth,
transferring that responsibility from teachers to a remote corporate
institution.") See also *id.*, at 1148, suggesting that professors should exhibit
"traits of public virtue or good citizenship," and that these traits are not "linked
to race or gender." See also *id.*, at 1151, calling "inclusiveness" virtuous in the
classical sense, because "Its aim is to save the whole, to strengthen the bonds
between factions by assuring that the institutions of the law are effectively
shared." See also *id.*, at 1152, where it is suggested that law teachers who hold
politically significant offices and share their political influence "with people
having different perspectives can be a manifestation of republican virtue." See
also *id.*, at 1178, "it is the historic mission of law teaching to nourish students'
concern for the general public interest so that if as graduates they are cast in
public roles, they will practice public virtue."

culture,"[1170] "civility and self-discipline,"[1171] "meritocratic educational practices,"[1172] a "shared public interest,"[1173] and academic freedom,[1174] as well as leaving law schools

---

[1170] See, e.g., *id.*, at 1111–1112. ("At least since Roman times, law has been employed to celebrate and reinforce the capacity of professionals to make disinterested decisions and to give disinterested advice. Effective participation in legal work requires not only a sensitivity to subcultural interests and values, but also to the transcendent interests and values of the culture as a whole. This generalized sensitivity ought to inform judicial decisions and the professional judgment of those who are advocates, or who counsel others about the likely results of legal disputes. There is but one Supreme Court of the United States and only one set of subordinate institutions, complex though they are. There is but one Constitution and one set of subordinate legal texts, profuse though they are. All of these are written in one language, indeterminate though it often is. There is, in short, but one legal culture. Those who participate in it must to some extent subordinate their subculturally derived impulses.")

[1171] *Id.*, at 1118.

[1172] *Id.*, at 1128–1129 (Implicitly praising the University of California educational system for meritocratic and non-discriminatory practices in the years before the 1980's, *id.*, at 1134 (noting that one of the costs of a quota system which Carrington suggested California was moving toward would be that "The superior minority and women students whose academic achievements were authentic by meritocratic standards would bear the cost of this diminution in the value of their credentials."), and also *id.*, at 1135 (expressing the fear that support and enthusiasm for the California public university system, and the efforts of students seeking admission might decline if there was a realization that "college and graduate or professional school admission [w]as a racial lottery rather than a reward for academic achievement.") See also *id.*, at 1153, suggesting that hiring less qualified teachers on a racial or gender basis can harm their students and future clients of those students. See also *id.*, at 1170. ("The founders of most public universities gained support for their ideas by advocating the importance of meritocracy as the instrument of social mobility.")

[1173] *Id.*, at 1113.

[1174] Carrington here is concerned with the possibility that if law school faculties are now told the sort of persons that they must hire and the kind of students they must admit, or risk losing accreditation, it may not be long before other politically popular goals will lead to a further erosion of self-determination on the part of law school faculties. *Id.*, at 1203. ("If the Regents of the University of California or the Association of American Law Schools are this day bent on imposing a benign demographic policy on law faculties, one may be sure that the next social cause to attract their eye will be different, and perhaps displeasing to those presently concerned about our demographics.")

and their faculties open to charges of unconstitutional discrimination.[1175]

In his *Law and the River,* Carrington championed the virtue of "courage" among law students and professors, and in his writing such as *"Diversity!,"* and his brave attack on the political correctness of his era,[1176] Carrington practiced what he preached. A similarly courageous boldness can be found in the next legal scholar we consider, Antonin Scalia.

[1175] *Ibid.* See also *id.,* at 1136–1146 for an elaboration of the Constitutional problems in a quota system. For the continuing Constitutional battle over this issue, see Fisher v. Texas, ___ U.S. ___ (2016), and, in particular, Justice Scalia's comments at the oral argument in that case, discussed *infra,* Chapter 20.

[1176] Carrington acknowledged that he was fighting the "politically correct," in *Diversity!, id.,* at 1109. Carrington called "political correctness," the "parent chic ideology" of *"Diversity!" Id.,* at 1110. For a summary of what the politically correct were seeking, and the relevant literature, see, e.g., *id.,* at 1110, n.12, singling out, as "full-length treatments," Dinesh D'Souza, Illiberal Education: The Politics of Race and Sex on Campus (Free Press, 1991) and Roger Kimball, Tenured Radicals: How Politics has Corrupted Our Higher Education (Harper Collins, 1990).

CHAPTER 20

TOWARDS ORIGINALISM AND TEXTUALISM

LATE TWENTIETH CENTURY

Antonin Scalia
(University of Virginia, 1967–1971;
Chicago, 1977–1982; Georgetown and
Stanford, 1977, 1980–1981)

■ ■ ■

Antonin Scalia (1936–2016)
Steve Petteway, Collection of the Supreme Court of the United States.

Antonin Scalia, a 1960 *magna cum laude* graduate of the Harvard Law School and a Notes Editor for the Harvard Law Review, taught for a while both at the University of Virginia and at the University of Chicago, visited for a time at Georgetown University in 1977, and then had a visiting year at Georgetown and Stanford (1980–81), and thus qualifies as a law professor. He was, of course, best known as the most visible member of the United States Supreme Court. He died in 2016, when he was the senior Associate

Justice, having been appointed by Ronald Reagan in 1986. Remarkably, at the time of Scalia's nomination, the Republicans controlled the Senate, and Scalia's appointment sailed through the Senate Judiciary committee by a vote of 18 to 0, and then through the full Senate by an incredible vote of 98–0. This may have been a tribute to the man's unique jurisprudential qualities, or may simply be due to a realization that it was politically incumbent on the Senators not to stand in the way of the first Italian-American nominated to the Court. Scalia's easy time before the Senate stands in marked contrast to the political and judicial disaster that was President Reagan's nomination of Robert Bork. By that time, 1987, the Republicans had lost control of the Senate, and laying the groundwork for the verb "To Bork," meaning unjustly, elaborately and systematically to smear a nominee, the Democrats turned the hearings for Bork into a full-throated assault on conservative theories of Constitutional interpretation.[1177]

Whatever the current tendency to politicize Supreme Court nominations, and to attack any judicial theories that might cut back on the interpretations Democrats favor, it is clear that the once uncontroversial Scalia is now best known for his bold conservative jurisprudence displayed on the Supreme Court.[1178] He was regarded as the most visible champion of the notion that the only acceptable Constitutional hermeneutic is a jurisprudence of "original understanding" or "plain meaning." Versions of this judicial philosophy have gone by a number of different names, including *textualism, originalism,* and *traditionalism,* but

---

[1177] For Bork's account of his confirmation battle see his bestseller, Robert H. Bork, The Tempting of America (Free Press, 1990).

[1178] But see the extraordinary forthcoming new book by David Dorsen, The Unexpected Scalia: Liberal Opinions from a Conservative Justice (Cambridge, 2017), which argues powerfully that Scalia ought to be recognized as a major contributor to liberal legal thought.

they all seem to boil down to the same thing. That thing is an attempt to return American Constitutional jurisprudence to the conception articulated by Hamilton in Federalist 78, where the role of the judiciary is to interpret, not to make, the law. It is an attempt to recapture Hamilton's expressed notion, borrowed from Montesquieu, that

> though individual oppression may now and then proceed from the courts of justice, the general liberty of the people can never be endangered from that quarter; I mean so long as the judiciary remains truly distinct from both the Legislature and the Executive. For I agree, that "there is no liberty, if the power of judging be not separated from the legislative and executive powers."[1179]

Scalia was thus a scornful opponent, generally speaking, of the dominant theory in the American legal academy, the theory generally embraced for decades by the Democrat members of the Senate, that the Constitution is a "living document" (as it was understood, for example, by most of the Court under Earl Warren; and as it is still understood by most American Constitutional Law professors).

Scalia's jurisprudence was not completely consistent on that point, as he allowed for change in the meaning, for example, of the First and Fourth Amendments. He was a staunch defender of the First Amendment, and was the fifth vote on the court for the majority in *Texas v. Johnson*,[1180] which held, to the dismay of some patriotic conservatives, that flag burning could not be prohibited because it was protected "speech." This reportedly led to a firestorm of criticism from conservatives, but also led Scalia's wife

---

[1179] Alexander Hamilton, James Madison, John Jay, The Federalist Papers 434 (Clinton Rossiter, ed., New Introduction and Notes by Charles R. Kesler, 1999) (citing Montesquieu, Spirit of Laws, Volume I, p. 181).

[1180] Texas v. Johnson, 491 U.S. 397 (1989).

somewhat derisively to greet him in the morning by singing "it's a grand old flag."[1181] Scalia has also been notable for his belief that new forms of electronic surveillance need to be subjected to the traditional constitutional requirements of probable cause and search warrants before they can be employed, which, in those decisions, generally put him in the company of the court's liberals.[1182]

On other constitutional issues, however, the ones that subjected him to criticism from those on the left, most notably the right of privacy in general, but especially abortion, he was the most visible defender of the view that there is no textual basis for Constitutional protection. "We should get out of this area," Scalia wrote, "where we have no right to be, and where we do neither ourselves nor the country any good by remaining[,]"[1183] and leave the choice of how to formulate the law of privacy and the law of abortion to the state legislatures.

Not for Scalia, then, the essentially legislative role praised by Ronald Dworkin.[1184] Scalia's dissents in abortion cases were unrelenting in his criticism of his colleagues who fashioned, in his opinion, arbitrary rules to preempt state or federal legislatures from regulating the practice. Scalia was particularly withering in his attacks on his former colleague, Sandra Day O'Connor, whose "undue burden"

[1181] See, e.g., Nina Totenberg, Justice Scalia, the Great Dissenter, Opens Up, NPR, April 28, 1988, updated May 8, 2008, available on the web at http://www.npr.org/templates/story/story.php?storyId=89986017 (accessed 19 March 2016).

[1182] See, e.g., United States v. Jones, 132 S. Ct. 945, 565 U.S. ___ (2012), where Scalia wrote the opinion for the majority, holding that law enforcement officials' placing a Global Positioning System (GPS) tracking device on a vehicle of a suspected drug-trafficker to monitor the vehicle's movements constituted a search under the Fourth Amendment. See also Dorsen, note 1178, *supra*.

[1183] Planned Parenthood v. Casey, 505 U.S. 833, 1002 (1992) (Scalia, J., dissenting).

[1184] See Chapter 12.

standard in abortion cases Scalia derided as completely incoherent and unworkable.[1185] Even more striking was Scalia's blasting of his colleagues', particularly Anthony Kennedy's, majority in *Lawrence v. Texas*, which majority, Scalia claimed, had "signed on to the so-called homosexual agenda" in deciding that consenting homosexual acts may not be subjected to criminal penalties.[1186] And, still more biting, was Scalia's dissent in *Obergefell v. Hodges* (2015), the decision that declared, based on the same sort of "liberty" analysis the Court displayed in *Planned Parenthood v. Casey*, that each state was compelled to grant rights to same-sex couples to marry.

Mocking Justice Kennedy's language which Kennedy employed in writing for the Court in *Obergefell*, where Kennedy had suggested that (1) because the right to marry was a "fundamental" one, and (2) because the Constitution's "due process" clause guaranteed fundamental liberties, then (3) same-sex couples should be free to marry, Scalia said of the majority's decision, "The opinion is couched in a style that is as pretentious as its content is egotistic. It is one thing for separate concurring or dissenting opinions to contain extravagances, even silly extravagances, of thought

---

[1185] See, e.g., Scalia's dissent in Planned Parenthood v. Casey, *supra* note 1183, at 988 ("The 'undue burden' standard is not at all the generally applicable principle the joint opinion pretends it to be; rather, it is a unique concept created specially for these cases, to preserve some judicial foothold in this ill-gotten territory") or *id.,* at 992. ("The inherently standardless nature of this [undue burden] inquiry invites the district judge to give effect to his personal preferences about abortion. By finding and relying upon the right facts, he can invalidate, it would seem, almost any abortion restriction that strikes him as 'undue'—subject, of course, to the possibility of being reversed by a court of appeals or Supreme Court that is as unconstrained in reviewing his decision as he was in making it.")

[1186] Lawrence v. Texas, 539 U.S. 558, 602 (2003) (Scalia, J. dissenting). ("Today's opinion is the product of a Court, which is the product of a law-profession culture, that has largely signed on to the so-called homosexual agenda, by which I mean the agenda promoted by some homosexual activists directed at eliminating the moral opprobrium that has traditionally attached to homosexual conduct.")

and expression; it is something else for the official opinion of the Court to do so." Scalia then noted that "If, even as the price to be paid for a fifth vote, I ever joined an opinion for the Court that began [as Kennedy's did]: 'The Constitution promises liberty to all within its reach, a liberty that includes certain specific rights that allow persons, within a lawful realm, to define and express their identity,' I would hide my head in a bag. The Supreme Court of the United States has descended from the disciplined legal reasoning of John Marshall and Joseph Story[1187] to the mystical aphorisms of the fortune cookie."[1188]

All of this rhetorical flair gave Scalia the greatest prominence as an exemplar of the view that judges should *interpret* rather than *make* law. As Scalia explained in a cogent slim volume in 1997, "[M]any believe that [The Constitution] is, in effect a charter for judges to develop an evolving common law of freedom of speech, of privacy rights, and the like. I think that is wrong—indeed, . . . I think it frustrates the whole purpose of a written constitution."[1189] After the record of the Warren and Burger Courts, it is, of course, a nice question whether this view, that judges should not make law, any longer accurately reflects reality, but there is no doubt that Scalia's views have traditionally been embraced by Republican candidates seeking to win the Presidency, such as the successful candidate (although perhaps due to the intervention of a Supreme Court majority that included Scalia),[1190] George W. Bush, and the unsuccessful John McCain and Mitt Romney.

[1187] On Story, see Chapter 3, *supra*.

[1188] Obergefell v. Hodges, 135 S. Ct. 2584, 2630 n.22 (Scalia, J. dissenting, lambasting language from Justice Kennedy for the majority, to be found at 135 S.Ct., at 2593).

[1189] Antonin Scalia, A Matter of Interpretation: Federal Courts and the Law 13 (1997).

[1190] See generally Bush v. Gore, 531 U.S. 98 (2000).

It may not go too far to suggest that Scalia himself made something of a political (or at least a cultural) crusade in promoting his views, and, repeatedly over the three decades that he was on the bench, he had actually gone on tour, to give speeches and promote his jurisprudential views. He was widely recognized as a gifted and witty lecturer. As indicated already, he was a writer of extraordinary flair, and he had been described as "The Rock Star of One First Street."[1191] The prolific and incisive judicial commentator, George Washington University Law Professor Jonathan Turley, suggested that Scalia was the nation's first "celebrity justice."[1192] Along with his close friend (and frequent judicial adversary) Ruth Bader Ginsburg, Scalia even became the subject of a one-act opera.[1193] Possessed of an almost irresistible personal Mediterranean charm, Scalia appeared born to do television interviews, something which before him was virtually

---

[1191] See, e.g., the extraordinary website, "Underneath Their Robes," for October 4, 2004, a posting by "Article III Groupie," who describes herself as "a federal judicial starf**ker." http://underneaththeirrobes.blogs.com/main/2004/10/_article_iii_gr.html (accessed 12 January 2016) ("Naughty Nino! He goes on tour, playing to packed houses, and those who don't get in to see him are crestfallen. He thinks orgies 'ought to be encouraged.' He has groupies (in addition to the undersigned), as well as a fan club. The conclusion is inevitable: Justice Scalia is a rock star!") The term "Rock Star of One First Street" appears on the "Underneath Their Robes" website for October 24, 2016 (http://under neaththeirrobes.blogs.com/main/2004/10/utr_news_and_vi.html, accessed 12 January 2016), and is used as well by Bruce Allen Murphy as the title of one of his chapters in his book on Scalia, Scalia: A Court of One (Simon & Schuster, 2014).

[1192] Jonathan Turley, "Justice Scalia is a political star—and that's bad for the Supreme Court," The Washington Post, Friday January 21, 2011 ("Scalia is the first real celebrity justice. When he appears at conservative events, supporters line up to greet a man who seems more oracle than orator. They are drawn not just to his originalist views but to the sense that he is a purist on a court of relativists.") Available at www.washingtonpost.com/wp-dyn/content/article/2011/01/21/AR2011012102923.html (accessed 12 January 2016).

[1193] The opera, Scalia/Ginsberg, by Derrick Wang, is about "law, music, and the power of friendship in a divided world." It had its world premiere in 2015. Justice Ginsburg attended and said, "I had a wonderful time. I loved every minute of it." http://www.derrickwang.com/scalia-ginsburg/ (accessed 30 January 2016).

unheard of for a sitting Justice. Scalia co-wrote one important dense treatise, setting forth a defense of the Hamiltonian and the Blackstonian view that judges should find and not make the law, and on his book tour for this volume (written with noted legal lexicographer Bryan Garner),[1194] seeing Scalia on TV talk shows was a surprisingly frequent phenomenon.

In his recently published provocative judicial biography of Scalia,[1195] Bruce Allen Murphy argues that Scalia was something of a failure, as it was hoped, when he was placed on the Court, that he could be a consensus builder, and lay the foundation for a Supreme Court majority who could consistently defend conservative values, and, thus, serve as an intellectual counterweight to such earlier liberal consensus-builders as Earl Warren and William Brennan. Scalia did not succeed in this, Murphy argued, because of his acerbic personality, his love of the cutting comment from the bench, and his inability to compromise. Murphy's view reflects the standard liberal critique of Scalia, and illustrates to what extent judging is now perceived as political log-rolling.

Murphy believed that Scalia too often let his Republican partisanship get the better of him, as, for example, Murphy argues happened with *Bush v. Gore*.[1196] There is some basis, perhaps, for Murphy's belief given that Scalia was a friend of Bush's Vice President, Dick Cheney, with whom Scalia had gone duck hunting, and who was the defendant (in his official capacity) in a lawsuit that came before Scalia's Court from which Scalia refused to recuse himself. Because there are grounds for suggesting that

---

[1194] Antonin Scalia and Bryan A. Garner, Reading Law: The Interpretation of Legal Texts (West, 2012). On Blackstone, see Chapter 1, *supra*.

[1195] Murphy, *supra* note 1191.

[1196] *Supra* note 1190.

Scalia's friendship with Cheney should have no effect on a decision regarding Cheney's official functioning, Scalia may well have been within his rights so to refuse to recuse himself, but since recusal sometimes ought to be done where there is an appearance of impropriety even if there is no actual misconduct, Murphy (and others) have argued that Scalia unnecessarily and unwisely subjected himself and his court to public opprobrium.

It isn't clear whether this reflects most badly on Scalia or his critics. In the time of Justice Story there may have been no controversy caused by the fact that Story was not only a law professor and a bank President at the same time that he was a Justice,[1197] but, quite possibly to a greater degree than Scalia, Story may have been on intimate terms with the great figures of politics of his time, and of course, so was the hallowed and venerated Felix Frankfurter in his.[1198] In ours, sadly, it may now be impossible for a liberal critic of Scalia, such as Murphy, to understand what Scalia was trying to do with his jurisprudence, and for such a critic not to attribute nefarious motivations to him.

In the late twentieth and early twenty-first centuries, perhaps for the first time, politics and constitutional interpretation became intertwined in a manner that is now all but impossible to separate, and, again for the first time, our two leading political parties divided over Constitutional hermeneutics. This seems to have been brought to a head during the administration of George W. Bush, when it looked as if he might succeed in packing the lower federal courts with conservative nominees, and thus reverse the tendency of those courts, established during the administrations of Democrats, to implement and expand

---

[1197] For Story, see Chapter 3, *supra.*
[1198] See Chapter 9, *supra.*

the principles embodied in the Warren and Burger Court's decisions.

Searching for a way to prevent what might have become a roll back of those decisions, and advised by two prominent liberal law professors and an activist lawyer, during a period during George W. Bush's Presidency, when the Democrats controlled the Senate, New York's Senator Charles Schumer held hearings on what he called "judicial ideology." He invited witnesses who suggested that what was needed on the federal bench was a "balance" between judicial ideologies, thus, presumably, requiring that the Senate refuse to confirm too many judges manifesting only one "ideology." This was a splendid way of suggesting that the belief of Republican Justices such as Scalia, that the judiciary should restrain itself from creating new rights under a "living constitution," was just one of two equally valid approaches to conduct on the bench. For Schumer, the conservative ideal manifested by Scalia, that judicial discretion should be minimized, was just one "ideology." In order to maintain "balance" on the bench, Schumer urged, if a conservative was confirmed, that ought to be "balanced" by the appointment of someone who believed in the living constitution, or, presumably, a nominee more acceptable to the Democrats who wanted to preserve the legacy of the Warren Court or *Roe v. Wade*. Schumer even argued that nominees to the Court had the burden of persuading the Senate that their ideology would not upset what Schumer seemed to believe was a delicate "balance" of ideologies on the courts. This was a far cry from the view that had generally prevailed in the twentieth century, or at least before the Bork nomination, that the burden was on the Senate clearly to demonstrate that the person nominated to the Court by the President was unqualified for the job, if anyone sought to challenge the nomination.[1199]

For someone like Scalia, who believed that a conservative approach to judging was the only appropriate way to preserve the rule of law, Schumer's idea of ideological "balance" on the bench makes no sense. If one believes, as did Scalia, that Hamilton and Montesquieu got it right, and that the tasks of legislating and judging are distinct and should not be combined, lest judges become tyrants, usurping the people's right to be represented through the legislature, then what Schumer was advocating flew in the face of our traditions, and was like asking that there be a balance on the bench between "right" and "wrong." Scalia's traditional view on this point was strikingly similar to that articulated by Learned Hand a generation before—that the job of a Justice is to interpret the law, not to make it, and that it ought to be the task of Constitutional and legal theory to guide the judge in refusing to be a legislator.[1200]

Scalia's teaching and judging was also notable for his rejection of "legislative history" as a means of

---

[1199] For further details on the hearings on judicial ideology see *infra*, Chapter 22, considering Cass Sunstein's role in these hearings. For some rumination on the problem of "judicial ideology," see, e.g., Stephen B. Presser, Should Ideology of Judicial Nominees Matter?: Is the Senate's Current Reconsideration of the Confirmation Process Justified? 6 Texas Review of Law & Politics 245 (2001), Stephen B. Presser, Testimony on judicial ideology before the Senate Subcommittee on the Constitution, 50 Drake Law Review 453 (2002), and Stephen B. Presser, Judicial Ideology and the Survival of the Rule of Law: A Field Guide to the Current Political War over the Judiciary, 39 Loyola University (Chicago) Law Journal 427 (2008).

[1200] For the suggestion that Scalia's efforts to articulate this view were misguided, and that, indeed, "The claim that judicial interpretation is a rigorous analytical process, comparable to syllogistic deduction, or at least to skilled translation of technical materials from a foreign language, and so really does generate demonstrably correct answers to even the most difficult-seeming questions that arise in litigation is fatuous," see Richard M. Posner, Divergent Paths: The Academy and The Judiciary 101 (Harvard, 2016). For Posner's views in general see Chapter 15, *supra*.

interpretation. He argued powerfully for the proposition (put forth earlier, indeed, by Rufus Peckham[1201]) that since legislators might have different things in mind when supporting particular bills, it makes sense only to rely on the language they agreed on—what Scalia calls "plain meaning," and what has also been referred to as "textualism."

Scalia also become famous (or notorious, depending on your point of view) for his rejection of the "living constitution" theory favored by progressives. That theory, Scalia argued persuasively, was simply a license for judicial legislation. Similarly, Scalia rejected the use of foreign jurisprudence in the interpretation of American law, preferring only to rely on domestic understanding and tradition. This put him at odds, for example, with his colleagues Anthony Kennedy and Elena Kagan (another former law professor) who have publicly taken the position that American Constitutional law ought to develop in tandem with changes in international Human Rights jurisprudence.[1202]

There was a brief flurry of speculation when Chief Justice William Rehnquist died in 2005, that Scalia might be nominated to succeed him, but, in his Scalia biography, Bruce Murphy argued that Scalia had alienated too many of his colleagues for that to have happened. Indeed, Murphy

---

[1201] In the famous antitrust case, United States v. Trans-Missouri Freight Association, 166 U.S. 290, 318–319 (1898). ("[D]ebates in congress," Peckham wrote, "are not appropriate sources of information from which to discover the meaning of the language of a statute passed by that body.... [T]he result being that the only proper way to construe a legislative act is from the language used in the act, and, upon occasion, by a resort to the history of the times when it was passed.")

[1202] See, e.g., Ben Johnson, Foreign Law: Coming Soon to a Supreme Court Near You, May 24, 2010, The Right's Writer: Commentary by Ben Johnson, http://therightswriter.com/2010/05/foreign-law-coming-soon-to-a-supreme-court-near-you/ (accessed 19 March 2016) (Arguing that Kagan, Kennedy and others are inclined to borrow jurisprudence from other countries).

claims that Scalia's outspokenness, his tendency to push the envelope on judicial ethics and, indeed what Murphy claims is Scalia's penchant for creating conflict rather than avoiding it, made him "the poster child for misbehavior and controversy on the United States Supreme Court."[1203]

There was no doubt that Scalia was outspoken, and probably no doubt that he reveled in the attention he received, although it is, of course, impossible to know whether that flowed from a desire to create conflict as Murphy asserted, or, if one wanted to be more charitable, a sincere passion on Scalia's part to correct prior errors, and return Constitutional jurisprudence to that of an earlier era. Murphy was, however, on to something when he referred to Scalia as a "poster child," since an inordinate amount of attention was often placed by the press on what Scalia had to say. A fascinating case in point was the brouhaha created in late 2015 over questions Scalia asked in the oral argument of *Fisher v. Texas*, a case brought to determine if the University of Texas's affirmative action policies violated the Fourteenth Amendment.

Some of the information in *amicus* briefs for the case suggested that affirmative action, insofar as it resulted in the admission of minorities with lower academic qualifications than other students, created a situation where those students so admitted were more inclined to academic failure, thus resulting in frustration and harm to the very people affirmative action was designed to help. This, the so-called "Mismatch" theory, was the argument made in a number of academic studies, most notably those reported by Richard Sander and Stuart Taylor.[1204] In brief, their contention was that some minority students,

---

[1203] Murphy, *supra* note 1191, at 360.

[1204] See generally, Richard Sander and Stuart Taylor, Jr., Mismatch: How Affirmative Action Hurts Students It's Intended to Help, and Why Universities Won't Admit It (Basic Books, 2012).

particularly blacks and Hispanics, might do better in less challenging academic environments, where their academic qualifications were the same as their fellow students, rather than admitting them to elite universities where they would be at the low end of prior academic achievement (at least as measured by grades and standardized test scores) and where competition might relegate them to the bottom of their classes. It has been a not generally well-known, but undeniable, fact that particularly for more elite institutions of higher learning, admitted minority students have had dramatically lower grades and standardized test scores than their non-minority fellow students.

Scalia was certainly aware of these facts (which, while rarely made public, are no secret to those who have been associated with academic life for the last few decades). Accordingly, at the recent oral argument before the Supreme Court, at which the contributions of affirmative action to the academic goal of "diversity" were at issue, Scalia sought, presumably, to invoke and pursue Sander and Taylor's analysis, in order to determine whether the purported benefits of affirmative action were outweighed by the costs to students so admitted. Thus, perhaps a bit inartfully, Scalia addressed the lawyers arguing the Constitutionality of Texas's affirmative action plan. "There are those who contend that it does not benefit African-Americans to get them into the University of Texas where they do not do well, as opposed to having them go to a less-advanced school, a slower-track school where they do well," Scalia stated. He then went on, "One of the briefs [presumably the one citing the research of Sanders and Taylor] pointed out that most of the black scientists in this country don't come from [elite] schools like the University of Texas," rather "they come from lesser schools where they do not feel that they're being pushed ahead in classes that are too fast for them." Scalia then indicated his view that if the University of Texas were forbidden from having race-conscious affirmative action programs it might have fewer African Americans, but, he suggested, "Maybe it ought to have fewer. And maybe some—you know, when you take more, the number of blacks, really competent blacks admitted to lesser schools, turns out to be less."[1205]

Scalia's questions ought to strike an objective observer as an honest attempt to come to grips with a difficult social problem, but they caused a firestorm. According to *The Week* magazine, Steve Nelson of the Huffington Post stated that Scalia's "bigoted remarks" were "simply astonishing" and echoed "the separate but equal' standard established by his 19th century predecessors on the court."[1206] Senate Minority Leader Harry Reid, in a moment of what may have been unintentional irony given his thoughtlessly inappropriate remarks once directed at Justice Clarence Thomas,[1207] excoriated Justice Scalia on the Senate floor,

---

[1205] The materials in quotes are taken from the Supreme Court transcript of the arguments in the case, as reported by CNN. They are available at http://www.cnn.com/2015/12/11/politics/supreme-court-antonin-scalia-african-americans-audio/ (accessed 8 January 2016).

[1206] Controversy of the Week: Affirmative action: should blacks go to 'lesser' colleges?, The Week, December 25, 2016, at 3.

[1207] When the Rehnquist vacancy as Chief Justice opened up on the Court, Reid made clear his view that "Scalia" was "one smart guy" and that while he disagreed with his opinions he might be able to vote to confirm him as Chief Justice, but this would not be true for Clarence Thomas, because, according to Senator Reid, "I think that he has been an embarrassment to the Supreme Court," and "I think that his opinions are poorly written. I just don't think that he's done a good job as a Supreme Court justice." Reid cited no evidence to support those propositions, and it was widely assumed that Reid may have been jumping to a conclusion based on Thomas's race. For Reid's remarks about Scalia and Thomas, see, e.g., http://www.cnn.com/2004/ALLPOLITICS/12/05/judges.reid.frist/ (accessed 8 January 2016), and for the assertion that Reid's remarks about Thomas may have suggested prejudice, see, e.g., the report of Jan Crawford, following an interview with Thomas:

In an interview in 2008, I asked Thomas why people continue to embrace this grossly false storyline—why they sell him short, understate his intellect—and why they persistently believe he merely has "followed" Scalia, when in fact there's absolutely no basis for that.

stating that "It is deeply disturbing to hear a Supreme Court justice endorse racist ideas from the bench."[1208]

Even in the liberal legal community, however, Scalia had his defenders. One of the most thoughtful analyses came from Geoffrey Stone, a former law school Dean and provost at the University of Chicago (who was once Scalia's colleague at Chicago):

> Although I often disagree with Justice Scalia, and although I emphatically disagree with him about the constitutionality of affirmative action, the outrage and condemnation sparked by this comment [in the oral argument in the *Fisher* case] is completely unwarranted. Justice Scalia's comment, which asked about the merits of an argument frequently made against affirmative action, and which was made specifically in briefs before the Supreme Court in this very case, was perfectly appropriate. As is often the case, Justice Scalia might have helped himself by framing his comment in a more sensitive manner. But the plain and simple fact is that his question gave the attorney for the University of Texas an

---

"Give me a break. I mean this is part of the—you know, the black guy is supposed to follow somebody white. We know that," Thomas told me. "Come on, we know the story behind that. I mean there's no need to sort of tip-toe around that. . . . The story line was that, well I couldn't be doing this myself, he must be doing it for me because I'm black. That's obvious. Again, I go back to my point. Who were the real bigots? It's obvious." But why no uproar, I asked. Why no outcry? "People feel free to say about me what they think about lots of blacks," Thomas told me. "Because of the heterodox views I've taken, they have license to say it about me with impunity." Or put another way: In Harry Reid's worldview, Clarence Thomas isn't the "right" kind of black guy.

The materials in quotations are from Justice Thomas. Chicago Tribune and CBS reporter Jan Crawford's report on her interview with Thomas can be found at http://www.cbsnews.com/news/racism-doesnt-always-have-a-southern-drawl/ (accessed 8 January 2016).

[1208] Quoted in The Week, *supra* note 1206.

opportunity to respond to one of the central arguments made against the constitutionality of affirmative action. . . .

In the affirmative action context, as in the other settings, this raises the question whether the college is exploiting the students for its own ends—to achieve diversity—at the expense of the students' own best interests. Put simply, is a student better off graduating in, say, the bottom 20 percent of a first tier college or in the top 20 percent of a second tier college?

Stone went on to add, that "In the Supreme Court's view, it is unconstitutional for public institutions of higher education to take race into account in making admissions decisions unless they have a compelling interest for doing so. Even the possibility that the mismatch theory is correct, at least for some students, might be sufficient, under that standard, to invalidate affirmative action programs. That is [in Stone's view] bad constitutional law, but as long as it is the law of the land it is perfectly appropriate and sensible for a justice to ask about this." Stone concluded, reprimanding Scalia's critics, "It is time that we stopped condemning each other for asking hard questions, however much we might not like them."[1209] Stone made clear that he didn't necessarily subscribe to the "mismatch" theory either, but he understood that this was a subject on which social scientists could differ, and Scalia's query was not the act of a racist, but rather of a jurist seeking to arrive at the right answer to a Constitutional question. And Stone is not the only liberal who has written in defense of Scalia. In an important book soon to be published, in fact, David Dorsen, the author of an acclaimed biography of Henry Friendly,[1210] argues that Scalia himself ought to be recognized as the author of some important liberal opinions.[1211]

Still, many of Scalia's liberal critics, such as Murphy,[1212] had a difficult time seeing Scalia as anything but a partisan, and a self-defeating one at that. But as even Murphy himself concedes, Scalia may have been aiming to influence the future as well as his own time, and Scalia could build a plausible case that the values of his jurisprudence (and, unlike Holmes, Scalia had values in his jurisprudence),[1213] adherence to the rule of law and limiting legislation to the elected representatives of the sovereign people, were what made America great. Murphy paints a portrait of Scalia as something of a jurisprudential failure, but the Federalist Society, a group of lawyers and law students that Scalia helped found, a group now numbering in the thousands, promulgates Scalia's ideas of limited Constitutional government, the primacy of the states as law makers, and the clear separation of the legislative, executive and judicial powers. The Federalist Society's strong organizational and lobbying efforts have had an impact in the selection of federal judges, and in shaping the media's view of the judicial task.

If Scalia's opinions and his arguments with his colleagues have not yet carried the day on the Court, they may yet with a Federalist Society-influenced group of future Justices. One of the founders of the Federalist Society, a former Scalia clerk, Northwestern University Law Professor Steven Calabresi, wrote, following Scalia's

---

[1210] Henry Friendly, Greatest Judge of His Era (Belknap Press of Harvard University, 2012). Richard Posner wrote in the introduction to this volume that "we learn more about the American judiciary at its best than we can learn from any other biography—not only more, but an immense amount." *Id.*, at xi.

[1211] Dorsen, *supra* note 1178.

[1212] *Supra* note 1191.

[1213] On Holmes, see Chapter 5, *supra*.

untimely death, that Scalia was "the most important justice in American history—greater than former Chief Justice John Marshall himself. Justice Scalia believed in following the law and in textualism. And he never misconstrued federal statutes to reach constitutional issues he wanted to decide the way Chief Justice Marshall did in famous cases like *Marbury v. Madison* and in *Gibbons v. Ogden.*"[1214] Perhaps not everyone would share Professor Calabresi's belief that Scalia was greater than Marshall, but he was undeniably a great Justice, and a great law professor. He was the late twentieth and early twenty-first century's greatest judicial traditionalist, and perhaps its greatest champion of the rule of law. If Scalia was a traditionalist, however, it's important to understand that that's not all there was to jurisprudence in the early twenty-first century. The "Living Constitution" theory was still held, probably by a huge majority of American academics, and a majority of American judges. Critical Legal Studies,[1215] and related theories still had some influence, and, in particular, there was another important approach that went by the name of Critical Race Theory. It is to that theory, and one of its most prominent expositors, that we next turn.

[1214] Steven G. Calabresi, Scalia Towered Over John Marshall: Supreme Court Justice reshaped a misguided legal culture, USA Today, February 24, 2016, available on the web at http://www.usatoday.com/story/opinion/2016/02/13/scalia-text-legacy-clerk-steven-calabresi-column/80349810/ (accessed 19 March 2016). On the Federalist Society, see also note 1355, *infra*, and accompanying text.

[1215] See Chapter 14, *supra*.

CHAPTER 21

CRITICAL RACE THEORY

LATE TWENTIETH, EARLY TWENTY-FIRST CENTURY

Patricia J. Williams
(Columbia)

■ ■ ■

Patricia J. Williams (b. 1951)
Photo by David Shankbone, 2007 Brooklyn Book Festival.
Wikimedia Commons.

Patricia Williams is the James L. Dohr Professor of Law at Columbia University School of Law. She is one of the most distinguished and celebrated African-American law professors. Upon granting her one of its fellowships (the so-called "genius grant") in 2000, the MacArthur Foundation recognized Williams for having created "a new form of legal writing and scholarship that integrates personal narrative, critical and literary theory, traditional legal doctrine, and empirical and sociological research."[1216]

Williams's most notable book, published in 1991, was *The Alchemy of Race and Rights.* As her publisher, the Harvard University Press, touted, "From its very first lines, *Alchemy* announced itself as a deeply personal work, braver and far more vulnerable than most anything else on a university press's law list:

> Since subject position is everything in my analysis of the law, you deserve to know that it's a bad morning. I am very depressed. It always takes a while to sort out what's wrong, but it usually starts with some kind of perfectly irrational thought such as: I hate being a lawyer.

"That very incongruence [the description from her publisher continued]—the disconnect between Williams's writing and the impersonal analysis that would generally be expected from the work of a law professor—reflects the ideas of the book itself, run through with defiance of society's need to limit by categorization."[1217]

Here, then, is something different for a law professor—overt loathing of the law, and a narrative approach that is undeniably powerful, but often obscure—as complex and contradictory, perhaps as the variety of human existence itself. It might even be appropriate to describe Williams as "an anti-law professor." She is a woman of paradox. In her most famous essay (reprinted as the last chapter of *Alchemy*) she tells the story of her great-great-grandmother who was purchased as an eleven-year-old by a white lawyer named Austin Miller who immediately impregnated her.

[1216] Harvard University Press Blog, 27 February 2013, http://harvardpress. typepad.com/hup_publicity/2013/02/honoring-the-work-of-patricia-williams.html (accessed 24 October 2014).

[1217] Ibid.

"While I don't remember what I was told about Austin Miller before I decided to go to law school," she writes, "I do remember that just before my first day of class my mother said, in a voice full of secretive reassurance, 'The Millers were lawyers, so you have it in your blood.' "[1218]

Williams was an early proponent of "story-telling"[1219] as a means of teaching law. For her it was a deeply personal means of reflecting upon her experiences as an African-American woman in the academy and in the legal system. Catharine MacKinnon[1220] has given an excellent explanation of the felt need for "story-telling" as a means of understanding and suggesting changes in our legal system. "Story-telling entered legal discussion," MacKinnon suggests, when some scholars realized

> that the analytic-argumentative engine [of the law] has been running on particulars that have not been particular enough, and on submerged or entirely absent specifics. Legislation has been predicated on too many elided voices as the common law has marched majestically past unbridgeable cases. In the relative absence of women, children, people of color, and working

---

[1218] *Id.*, quoting from Patricia Williams, The Alchemy of Race and Rights: Diary of a Law Professor 216 (Harvard, 1991).

[1219] On "legal storytelling," a controversial and exciting relatively recent development in legal scholarship, see, e.g., Nancy Levitt, Legal Storytelling: The Theory and the Practice—Reflective Writing Across the Curriculum, 15 The Journal of the Legal Writing Institute 259 (2009), Peter Brooks & Paul Gewirtz eds., Law's Stories: Narrative and Rhetoric in the Law 232 (Yale U. Press 1996), Daniel A. Farber & Suzanna Sherry, Telling Stories Out of School: An Essay on Legal Narratives, 45 Stan. L. Rev. 807 (1993), and Richard Delgado, Storytelling for Oppositionists and Others: A Plea for Narrative, 87 Mich. L. Rev. 2411 (1989).

[1220] See Chapter 17, *supra.*

people, the legal mill has been grinding a grist that is too thin to begin with.[1221]

For Professor Williams, "story telling" was a means, not just to approach criticism of American law, but also of reflecting on the human condition. Thus, for Williams, her story-telling occasionally verges on, if it does not pass, the point of poetry rather than prose.[1222] For example, in the last chapter of *Alchemy*, where she is engaging in some ruminations about her love/hate relationship with the law of contracts, and her rage at too often being dismissed as of little consequence because she is black and a woman, Williams borrows from a practice of her godmother. This extraordinary woman, Williams's mother's cousin, Marjorie, had been a dark-skinned child, but had a light-skinned black mother. Marjorie's mother gave Marjorie up to some of Williams's other female relatives, in order more easily to "pass," and, eventually, to marry a rich white man. Marjorie used to entertain and soothe the future law professor, the young Patricia Williams, she reports, by telling her tales of polar bears. The crucial paragraph:

> My mother's cousin Marjorie was a storyteller. From time to time I would press [Marjorie] to tell me the details of her youth, and she would tell me instead about a child who wandered into a world of polar bears, who was prayed over by polar bears, and was in the end eaten. The child's life was not in vain because the polar bears had been made holy by its suffering. The child had been a test, a message from god for polar bears. In the polar-bear universe, she would tell me, the primary object of

---

[1221] Catharine A. MacKinnon, "Law's Stories as Reality and Politics," in Catharine A. MacKinnon, Women's Lives: Men's Laws 58 (Harvard, 2005).

[1222] Similarly, MacKinnon observed that "Storytelling has opened up legal discussion, giving it sweep of gesture, depth, ambiguity, connection, vaulting it toward literature." *Id.*, at 61.

creation was polar bears, and the rest of the living world was fashioned to serve polar bears. The clouds took their shape from polar bears, trees were designed to give shelter and shade to polar bears, and humans were ideally designed to provide polar bears with meat.[1223]

The polar bears, it would seem, are metaphors for white people, or, perhaps, for the impersonal rules of the law, and the bears could be expected to think nothing of devouring Ms. Williams, who proceeds, right after thus relating Marjorie's story of the bears, to confess that "There are moments in my life when I feel as though a part of me is missing. There are days when I feel so invisible that I can't remember what day of the week it is, when I feel so manipulated that I can't remember my own name, when I feel so lost and angry that I can't speak a civil word to the people who love me best."[1224] The polar bears (or the discomforts of being a law professor?) then, are relentless in their ceaseless stalking of Professor Williams.

And yet, a few pages later in this quite magnificent (if careening and dizzying chapter), Williams extravagantly praises, and then laments, the bears, when she recounts a recent episode involving real New York polar bears who attacked a young black child. "In reality," she tells us, "it was a lovely polar bear afternoon. The gentle force of the earth. A wide wilderness of the islands. A conspiracy of polar bears lost in timeless forgetting. A gentleness of polar bears, a fruitfulness of polar bears, a silent black-eyed interest of polar bears, a bristled expectancy of polar bears. With the wisdom of innocence, a child threw stones at the

---

[1223] *Alchemy, supra* note 1218, at 228.
[1224] *Ibid.*

polar bears."[1225] The bears maul and kill the child, and the bears are subsequently put down by the authorities.[1226]

Apparently Williams was not the only radical law professor disturbed by this episode. She reports that "In the plenary session of the national meeting of the Law and Society Association, the keynote speaker unpacked the whole incident," involving the actual bears, and the eleven-year-old child victim of the bears. The child's "Hispanic-welfare-black-widow-of-an-alcoholic mother," as Ms. Williams called her, brought suit,[1227] and this incident, writes Professor Williams, quoting the Law and Society Association speaker, was "a veritable laboratory of emergent rights discourse. Just seeing that these complex levels of meaning exist, she exulted, should advance the discourse significantly." This does bring us into a universe of "discourse" rather different from an ordinary contracts class, and a deeply troubling one.

Alchemy closes with another puzzling paean to polar bears, who are invoked after Professor Williams relates an unhappy incident when she was physically shoved aside by an unruly group of participants in a Dartmouth summer basketball camp, a camp she pungently describes as "about two hundred prepubescent males. . .[,] an all-white, very expensive, affirmative-action program for the street-deprived." She encountered "about a hundred" of these "street-deprived" white youths, in groups of about 25, who jostled, smacked, and pushed her off the sidewalk into the gutter. She yells at them, "Don't I exist for you? See me! And deflect, godammit!"[1228] Puzzled by this "crazed black person"[1229] whom they had previously ignored, the wealthy

[1225] *Id.*, at 234.
[1226] *Ibid.*
[1227] *Id.*, at 235.
[1228] *Ibid.*
[1229] *Ibid.*

white prepubescents give Williams a "wide berth."[1230] She reports:

> I pursued my way, manumitted back into silence. I put distance between them and me, gave myself over to polar-bear musings. I allowed myself to be watched over by bear spirits. Clean white wind and strong bear smells. The shadowed amnesia; the absence of being; the presence of polar bears. White wilderness of icy meateaters heavy with remembrance; leaden with undoing; shaggy with the effort of hunting for silence; frozen in a web of intention and intuition. A lunacy of polar bears. A pride of polar bears. A consistency of polar bears. In those meandering pastel polar-bear moments, I found cool fragments of white-fur invisibility. Solid, black-gummed, intent, observant. Hungry and patient, impassive and exquisitely timed. The brilliant bursts of exclusive territoriality. A complexity of messages implied in our being.[1231]

This passage ends the main text of her book. This is undeniably beautiful, suggestive and lyrical stuff, although the stream of consciousness is more suggestive than explanatory, but perhaps that is Ms. Williams's aim. And she is not alone in this sort of writing. Professor Williams is a leading figure in the Critical Race Theory (CRT) movement,[1232] which is something of a successor to CLS, and which school of thought, as the name implies, explores the effects of race on law. Ms. Williams writes a column for the Nation magazine (the country's leading progressive, or maybe even radical, publication), under what may now be

---

[1230] *Ibid.*

[1231] *Id.*, at 236.

[1232] See generally, Kimberle Crenshaw et al. eds., Critical Race Theory: The Key Writings that Formed the Movement (The New Press, 1996).

seen to be the unsurprising title of "Diary of a Mad Law Professor." The "Mad" elusively denotes either anger or insanity, and perhaps further indicates, for Ms. Williams, some core ambivalence about herself and her role in the academy.

"Scarcely fifteen years old," Touro College law professor Daniel Subotnik wrote in 1998, "Critical Race Theory ('CRT') has generated a passion among its adherents, mostly minority academics, that has already fueled at least a dozen books, probably 250 law review articles and a half-dozen conferences. And though the academy, along with the country, has moved somewhat to the right in recent years, this shift has neither shaken the faith of CRT's advocates ('CRATs') nor diminished its drawing power."[1233] "If anything," Subotnik concluded, "the movement seems stronger than ever."[1234] The central message of critical race theory "is not simply that minorities are being treated unfairly, or even that individuals out there are in pain—assertions for which there are data to serve as grist for the academic mill—but that the minority scholar himself or herself hurts and hurts badly."[1235] Subotnik continues, "Virtually all of Critical Race thought is marked by deep discontent with liberalism," and also by a deep discontent with "a system of civil rights litigation and activism, faith in the legal system, and hope for progress...."[1236] Sometimes, then, what hope that is left, as in the work of Ms. Williams, is sadly tinged with despair.

In an analysis of CRT scholars which is quite applicable to Williams, two other commentators, Peter Goodrich and

---

[1233] Daniel Subotnik, What's Wrong With Critical Race Theory? Reopening the Case for Middle Class Values, 7 Cornell J.L. & Pub. Pol'y 681–682 (1998).

[1234] *Id.*, at 682.

[1235] *Id.*, at 693.

[1236] *Id.*, at 683.

Linda Mills, state that Critical Race Theory "has been defined historically in terms of voice and resistance, silence and exclusion. It dates back in this form to the 1980s, and it is written in large part from the perspective of the minority students who left the classroom so as to dramatize and confront the pattern of discrimination and exclusion."[1237] Angela P. Harris, now the University of California at Davis Distinguished Professor of Law, Boochever and Bird Endowed Chair for the Study and Teaching of Freedom of Equality, and Director, Aoki Center for Critical Race and Nation Studies, writes, in a forward to *Critical Race Theory: An Introduction* (2nd ed.), that when she was a first-year law student, in 1983, at the University of Chicago School of Law, in her entering class of 180 students, there were only 4 African-Americans, one Asian-American, and two Latinos. Moreover, "All of our professors were white, and all but two were male. Even more disorienting, however, than mere demographics was the fact that the lively discourse on racial-ethnic relations, both domestic and international [which she had experienced a year earlier as a graduate student in social science at the University of Chicago] was gone." "None of my professors," she explains, "talked about race or ethnicity; it was apparently irrelevant to the law. None of my professors talked about feminism or the concerns of women either."[1238] At that time, in 1983, Professor Harris notes, "there seemed to be no critical literature on race and the law."[1239] "We finished our legal educations," she reports, "never having found a place where the sophisticated discourse of racial

---

[1237] Peter Goodrich and Linda Mills, The Law of White Spaces: Race, Culture, and Legal Education, 51 J, Legal Educ. 15, 16–17 (2001).

[1238] Angela Harris, Forward to Richard Delgado and Jean Stefanic, Critical Race Theory: An Introduction xv–xvi (2nd ed. N.Y.U Press 2012).

[1239] *Id.*, at xvi.

critique in which we lived our everyday lives could enter the legal canon."[1240]

This has begun to change, and now, as might be implied from Professor Harris's *Forward* and Professor Williams's work, and as Goodrich and Mills suggest, "much of the success of critical race theory as a political movement has been derived from its vehement assertion of outsider identities and narratives."[1241] They continue:

> Critical race theory grew out of the civil rights movement and was from its origins a political movement. In the terms used by Derrick Bell in his casebook Race, Racism, and American Law,[1242] the movement was about consciousness of race in the analysis and teaching of law. Race consciousness implied activism and, wherever necessary, confrontation with authority. A significant aspect of the authority that Bell sought to challenge was that of the academic hierarchy and its assertions both of excellence and of knowledge as attributes of an elite white norm. It was on this issue that he resigned from Harvard Law School, and on this issue that he took his distance from the political quietism of the [Critical Legal Studies scholars].[1243]

Professor Harris indicates that three years after she received her law degree, in 1989, she had become a first year law teacher and attended "the first-ever workshop" on CRT, held at the St. Benedict Center in Madison, Wisconsin. There she was made aware of a community of scholars addressing the topics she had found missing in her law

---

[1240] *Id.*, at xvii.

[1241] Goodrich and Mills, *supra* note 1237, at 17.

[1242] Derrick A. Bell, Race, Racism, and American Law (6th ed., Aspen, 2008).

[1243] Goodrich and Mills, *supra* note 1237, at 18–19.

school. She was introduced to the work of "some of the people who, by then, had begun to be recognized across the nation as major intellectual figures: Derrick Bell, Kimberle Crenshaw, Richard Delgado, Mari Matsuda, [and] Patricia Williams."[1244]

Specifically considering Patricia Williams, another observer, Nikol G. Alexander-Floyd, notes "Williams's approach (what she calls 'a model of inductive empiricism, borrowed from—and parodying—systems analysis') . . . integrates insights from the humanities and social sciences as well as the law and engages individuals in the production of legal reasoning and knowledge; moreover, it uses various types of stories and personal encounters to make the experience of legal 'others' comprehensible."[1245] Thus, Professor Williams, as is true of "Many critical race theorists . . . employ[s] irony, storytelling, and the relaying of personal experiences in an effort to affront and expose the law's false presentation of itself as linear, objective, unyielding, and timeless. As black feminist legal theorist Patricia J. Williams observes,"[1246] writes Alexander-Floyd, "Legal writing presumes a methodology that is highly stylized, precedential, and based on deductive reasoning. Most scholarship in law is rather like the 'old math': static, stable, formal—rationalism walled against chaos."[1247]

But CRT strives to be something different. In an intriguingly titled book chapter, " 'Where By the Way, is This Train Going?': A Case for Black (Cultural) Studies,"[1248] Mae Gwendolyn Henderson, professor of English at the

---

[1244] Harris, *Forward, supra* note 1238, at xvii.

[1245] Nikol G. Alexander-Floyd, *Critical Race Black Feminism: A "Jurisprudence of Resistance" and the Transformation of the Academy*, 35 Signs 810, 813 (2010).

[1246] *Id.*, at 812–813.

[1247] *Id.*, at 813.

[1248] Amritjit Singh and Peter Schmidt, eds., Postcolonial Theory and the United States: Race, Ethnicity, and Literature 95 (2000).

University of North Carolina at Chapel Hill, helps us situate Professor Williams's writing in the broader current field of "Cultural Studies." Ms. Henderson writes that "cultural studies has privileged the study of vernacular and mass culture." She continues: "cultural studies redefines the boundaries delineating traditional disciplinarities. It has shifted, redrawn, and sometimes even dissolved the lines demarcating conventional disciplinary borders by engaging in institutional and ideological analyses. The mode of inquiry in cultural studies entails an examination of material and concrete cultural practices in the context of conditions of their production and reception."[1249]

Or, as Ms. Williams herself explains in the first essay in *Alchemy*:

> On the one hand, my writing has been staked out as the exclusive interdisciplinary property of constitutional law, contract, African-American history, feminist jurisprudence, political science, and rhetoric. At the same time, my work has been described as a 'sophisticated frontal assault' on laissez-faire's most sacred sanctums, as 'new-age performance art,' and as 'anecdotal individualism.' In other words, to speak as black, female, *and* [a] commercial lawyer has rendered me simultaneously universal, trendy, and marginal.[1250]

Ms. Williams, then, and other writers of cultural studies or CRT, such as Richard Delgado and William Eskridge,[1251] are examining, exploring, and implementing

---

[1249] *Id.*, at 96.

[1250] *Alchemy, supra* note 1218, at 6–7. On Feminist Jurisprudence generally, see, e.g., Cynthia Grant Bowman, Laura Rosenbury, Deborah Tuerkheimer, and Kimberly A. Yuracko, Feminist Jurisprudence: Cases and Materials (West Publishing, 4th ed. 2010).

[1251] See, e.g., Richard Delgado, The Rodrigo Chronicles: Conversations About America and Race (NYU Press, 1995), Richard Delgado and Jean

identity politics in the legal academy. While not generally known to the general American public, the work of these theorists in law school and out on legal issues involving race, gender, sexuality, and ethnicity has exerted a powerful influence. Thus, "[N]ot only race-crits but also queer-crits, LatCrits, and critical race feminists [now] seek to reveal and challenge the practices of subordination facilitated and permitted by legal discourse and legal institutions."[1252] Indeed, as even Justice Scalia had observed, such works of cultural advocacy have been important in shaping the view of a majority of the United States Supreme Court.[1253]

Williams indicates that her piece, "On being the Object of Property," is "her favorite" of "all the essays she has written,"[1254] and it provides a clear look at how she contemplates the law and life in the contemporary United States. In the course of that essay, which examines the manner in which the institution of slavery affected African-Americans, Williams states that "In my search for roots, I must assume not just as history but as an ongoing psychological force, that, in the eyes of white culture, irrationality, lack of control, and ugliness signify not just

---

Stefancic, Critical Race Theory: An Introduction (NYU Press, 2nd ed. 2012), William N. Eskridge Jr., Gaylaw: Challenging the Apartheid of the Closet (Harvard, 1999).

[1252] Angela Harris, *Forward*, to Delgado and Stefanic, *supra* note 1238, at xviii.

[1253] Lawrence v. Texas, 539 U.S. 558, 602 (2003) (Scalia, J. dissenting).

[1254] Charles H. Rowell and Patricia J. Williams, An Interview with Patricia J. Williams, Callaloo, Vol. 19, No. 4 (Autumn 1996), 823–834, *available at* http://www.jstor.org/stable/3299116, at 833. The essay, which appears as the concluding chapter in *The Alchemy of Race and Rights*, has been called, by her publisher, "Williams's most noted piece, a work still equal parts moving and challenging after all these years." Harvard Blog, *supra* note 1216.

the whole slave personality, not just the whole black personality, but me."[1255]

Not surprisingly, Williams appears to have some ambivalence, then, about both the law and the teaching of it. With regard to the law of contracts, she writes,

> Contract law reduces life to a fairy tale. The four corners of the agreement become parent. Performance is the equivalent of obedience to the parent. Obedience is dutifully passive. Passivity is valued as good contract-socialized behavior; activity is caged in retrospective hypotheses about states of mind at the magic moment of contracting. Individuals are judged by the contract unfolding rather than by the actors acting autonomously. Nonperformance is disobedience; disobedience is active; activity becomes evil in contrast to the childlike passivity of contract conformity."[1256]

It is challenging to unpack this, but it certainly suggests that the enterprise of entering into agreements and relying on their enforceability, the essence of the law of contract, is rather a dehumanizing experience, as far as Ms. Williams is concerned.

If the same can be said for the view of many of the practitioners of critical legal studies, critical race theory, and for legal story-tellers generally, that is, if their undeniable descriptive power (and even poetry) is debilitating and bewildering, it is no wonder that the popular image of law professors, as articulated by Secretary Panetta,[1257] suggests some law professors' inability to make a meaningful contribution to achievement, policy execution, or even discourse. The poetry, subtlety and humor of law

---

[1255] *Alchemy, supra* note 1218, at 221.

[1256] *Id.*, at 12.

[1257] See note 1, *supra*, and accompanying text.

professors, unfortunately, often escapes their students as well. Perhaps this happens to Patricia Williams. As the Harvard University Press reported, in a piece celebrating a symposium honoring Williams's work, referring to her book, *Alchemy*:

> Fittingly, *Alchemy* ends with "A Word on Categories,"[1258] in which Williams notes that her editor here at HUP was "waging something of a struggle" with the Library of Congress about how the book was to be categorized for cataloging purposes. "The librarians think 'Afro-Americans— Civil Rights' and 'Law Teachers' would be nice. I told my editor to hold out for 'Autobiography,' 'Fiction,' 'Gender Studies,' and 'Medieval Medicine.' "[1259]

Whether or not Williams's work is debilitating, her vision is an evocative one, and a legal academy bereft of a poetic sensitivity such as hers would be a much duller one,[1260] and, it must be admitted, there are plenty of other law professors supremely devoted to the practical, or so, at least it would seem. One such was Richard Posner.[1261] Another is Cass Sunstein.

[1258] Alchemy, *supra* note 1218, at 256–257.

[1259] Honoring the work of Patricia Williams, Harvard University Press Blog, 27 February 2013, http://harvardpress.typepad.com/hup_publicity/2013/02/honoring-the-work-of-patricia-williams.html (accessed 19 January 2016).

[1260] On the need for a poetic vision in legal scholarship see, e.g., the words of Mary Ann Glendon quoted in Chapter 18, *supra* "there are times when we need enchantments, inspiration, or poetry as much as we need philosophy" text accompanying note 1123, and see also Charles L. Barzun, "Jerome Frank, Lon Fuller, and a Romantic Pragmatism," University of Virginia School of Law, Public Law and Legal Theory Research Paper Series 2016–6, January 2016, at 22–23. (Quoting the purportedly radical realist Jerome Frank as believing that we need judges "with a touch in them of the qualities which make poets, who will administer justice as an art." We should, therefore, Frank believed, "encourage, not discountenance, imagination, intuition, insight." Barzun quotes Frank, Law and the Modern Mind, *supra* note 481, at 181.)

[1261] See Chapter 15, *supra*.

CHAPTER 22

CHANGING THE LEGAL FABRIC OF THE NATIONAL GOVERNMENT TOWARDS LIBERTARIAN PATERNALISM

LATE TWENTIETH, EARLY TWENTY-FIRST CENTURY

Cass Sunstein
(Chicago; now Harvard)

■ ■ ■

Cass Sunstein (b. 1954)
Photograph by Phil Farnsworth.
Courtesy Harvard Law School.

By 2014, "Cass Sunstein had written 28 books plus 15 books coauthored with others, around 500 scholarly articles, and hundreds of journalistic articles for *The New York Review of Books*, *The New York Times*, *The New Republic*, *The American Prospect*, *Bloomberg View*, and many other outlets."[1262] Sunstein taught for many years at the University of Chicago, and is now Walmsley University Professor at Harvard. The author of a profile of Sunstein in the New York Times wrote, in words that help to understand law professors in general and former University of Chicago colleagues Richard Posner, Barack Obama and Sunstein that:

> The professors in Hyde Park [the site of the University of Chicago School of Law] believe in something called the University of Chicago mind. It runs cold and analytical when the rest of the culture runs hot. Chicago scholars tend to be social scientists at heart, contrarian but empirical, following evidence to logical extremes. They are centrally interested not in what it is like to be an individual within society but in how society washes over individuals, making and remaking them. During the campaign, when his former Chicago colleagues were asked to detail Barack Obama's intellectual evolution, many of them described him in these terms. But they knew Obama, at best, only partly exhibited this tradition. His friend Cass Sunstein, who is certainly the most productive and probably the most influential liberal legal scholar of his generation, inherited it in full. "Cass has," says Saul Levmore, a former dean of the [University of Chicago] law school, "the quintessential University of Chicago habit of mind."[1263]

[1262] Lincoln Caplan, The Legal Olympian: Cass Sunstein and the modern regulatory state, 117 Harvard Magazine 43, 47 (January–February 2015).

[1263] Benjamin Wallis Wells, "Cass Sunstein Wants to Nudge Us," New York Times Magazine, May 13, 2010, available on the web at http://www.ny times.com/2010/05/16/magazine/16Sunstein-t.html?pagewanted=all&_r=0 (accessed February 28, 2015). Wells observes in his admiring portrait of Sunstein that "when other academics talk about [Sunstein's] mind, they do so

Immediately prior to his return to the legal academy, Sunstein served in the administration of Barack Obama, as head, from 2009 to 2012, of the White House Office of Information and Regulatory Affairs (OIRA), an office that Sunstein describes as "the cockpit of the regulatory state," with responsibility for ensuring that the benefits of particular regulations outweighed their costs.[1264] For much of that time Sunstein's extraordinarily prolific output and his outspoken public demeanor made him one of the most visible law professors in the country, and there was much speculation that when the Democrats regained the Presidency Sunstein would be nominated to the Supreme Court. Curiously, this didn't happen, even though Sunstein was reportedly a close friend and advisor of President Obama.

Perhaps Sunstein somehow became too politically radioactive, as some conservatives believed he stood for everything they were against in the Obama administration. Glen Beck, for example, repeatedly called Sunstein "the most dangerous man in America" and claimed that "Sunstein wants to control you. . . . He's helping the government control you."[1265] In person, Sunstein hardly seems dangerous, and, as one laudatory recent article accurately observes "Sunstein comes across as a brainy and cheerful technocrat, practiced at thinking about the

---

in the way people talk about the ballet, as something precious that ought to be preserved." *Ibid.*

[1264] Caplan, *supra* note 1262, at 43. It has been recently suggested that this office has come to be also a means of maintaining control of the regulatory state by lawyers. Thus, in an important book on the American regulatory state, the author, Daniel Ernst, maintains that OIRA is "a principal conduit of economic expertise and presidential control, [which] remains under lawyerly hegemony," as "[s]even of OIRA's eleven administrators have had law degrees." Jeremy K. Kessler, Book Review: The Struggle for Administrative Legitimacy (Reviewing Daniel R. Ernst, Tocqueville's Nightmare: The Administrative State Emerges in America 1900–1940 (Harvard, 2014)), 129 Harv. L. Rev. 718, 760 (2016) (quoting from page 144 of Ernst's book).

[1265] Caplan, *supra* note 1262, at 44.

consequences of rules, regulations, and policies with attention to the linkages between particular means and ends."[1266] Still, Sunstein has made it his life's work to explain how the basic assumption of Posnerian[1267] law and economics, that people are rational wealth-maximizers, is at least partially incorrect, since people, in Sunstein's view, often make choices that undercut their own well-being.

At some level, perhaps, there is no denying that Sunstein is correct. One of the clearest indications that this is so is given by Sunstein in his extremely accessible little e-book, *How to Humble a Wingnut and Other Lessons from Behavioral Economics*,[1268] a collection of some of his essays for *Bloomberg View*. Sunstein notes:

> If you take the average couple, and ask each member what percentage of the household work they do, the total number is very likely to be well over 100 ("self-serving bias"). About 90 percent of drivers believe themselves to be better than the average driver ("optimistic bias"). If you inform people that a product is 90 percent fat-free, they are a lot more likely to purchase it than if you [inform them] that it is 10 percent fat ("framing"). If you ask people whether certain events (a tornado, a hurricane, a terrorist attack) are likely, they might well be mistaken, because they will ask whether these kinds of events readily [come] to mind ("availability bias").[1269]

Given the facts that people can misperceive reality because of "self-serving bias," "optimistic bias," "framing," "availability bias," or other lapses in strict rationality, as

---

[1266] *Id.*, at 43.

[1267] On Posner, see Chapter 15, *supra*.

[1268] Cass R. Sunstein, How to Humble a Wingnut and Other Lessons From Behavioral Economics (U.Chicago, 2014).

[1269] *Id.*, at 1.

behavioral economics teaches, then, it would seem to be appropriate to have some means of correcting for these lapses in rationality. Accordingly, for Sunstein, it is important to have a regulatory state that can, to use one of his favorite concepts, "nudge" people into making correct choices.[1270] Cass Sunstein, in short, is thus in the business of saving the American people from themselves.

Like his former colleague Barack Obama, Professor Sunstein seems to start from the position that it is the obligation of government to act to enrich our lives, rather than the task of government simply to be a night watchman to enforce the working of the free market. As a recent piece on Sunstein by Lincoln Caplan, an important legal journalist and a member of the New York Times editorial board, observed, Sunstein is still working from a paradigm forged in the New Deal. Caplan quoted Sunstein, who observed that "New Deal regulation rested on the conviction that the common-law system 'reflected anachronistic, inefficient, and unjust principles of laissez-faire' and was inadequate 'because it was economically disastrous, insulated established property rights from democratic control, failed to protect the disadvantaged, and disabled the states and the national government from revitalizing or stabilizing the economy.' "[1271] In other words, the common law (or the judges who made it) were acting irrationally. The New Deal, for Sunstein, was an effort to correct that irrationality. As Caplan concluded regarding Sunstein's view of what had happened with the New Deal, and in words striking for their acceptance of the notion of "popular

---

[1270] As Caplan observes, explaining the basis for Sunstein's beliefs, "In recent decades, behavioral economists have shown that, out of impulse, impatience, or ignorance, people often make choices that are not the best or even good for them: we are not the rational self-interest maximizers that conventional economists have long assumed." Caplan, *supra* note 1262, at 44.

[1271] *Id.*, at 49.

constitutionalism,"[1272] "The New Deal transformed the system of federalism by transferring power from the states to the federal government. It redefined individual rights, from 'rights to be free from government intrusion' to 'government protection against the multiple hazards of industrialized society.' The result was 'a dramatic change in the fabric of the national government. . . . ' "[1273]

Sunstein, an undeniably brilliant intellectual theoretician, clearly believes that the United States government ought to be used broadly to increase the welfare of its citizens, even, or perhaps *especially*, when those individuals do not realize what is in their own best interests, and need a bit of coercion, or, as Sunstein would more gently describe it, a "nudge." As the author of another admiring profile of Sunstein explained:

> In "Nudge,"[1274] a popular book that [Sunstein] wrote with the influential behavioral economist Richard Thaler, Sunstein elaborated a philosophy called "libertarian paternalism." Conservative economists have long stressed that because people are rational, the best way for government to serve the public is to guarantee a fair market and to otherwise get out of the way. But in the real world, Sunstein and Thaler argue, people are subject to all sorts of biases and quirks. They also argue that this human quality, which some would call irrationality, can be predicted and—this is the controversial part—that if the social environment

---

[1272] On "popular constitutionalism," the notion that acts and understandings of the American people can effectively amend the United States Constitution outside of the Article V procedures, see generally Chapter 16, *supra*.

[1273] Caplan, *supra* note 1262, at 49.

[1274] Richard H. Thaler and Cass R. Sunstein, Nudge: Improving Decisions About Health, Wealth, and Happiness (Yale, 2008; Revised and Expanded edition, Penguin books, 2009).

can be changed, people might be nudged into more rational behavior.[1275]

"Libertarian Paternalism," if not clearly oxymoronic, if adopted as a governing philosophy, raises the same kind of questions as do other forms of paternalism. It is difficult to draw a line where Paternalism ends and tyranny or totalitarianism begins, and, no doubt this is why Conservative icon Glen Beck called Sunstein "the most dangerous guy out there."[1276]

Like many other contemporary academics on the left and right, Sunstein purportedly writes from a position of Olympian detachment, but some of his work can also be seen to be clearly politically partisan, making it a bit easier to understand why some conservatives are disturbed by Sunstein's views. Sunstein has been a prominent witness called before Congress by Democrats to testify, for example, against the impeachment of President Clinton,[1277] and on matters of "judicial ideology."[1278] Sunstein was one of three liberal or "progressive" legal theorists (the other two were Harvard Law Professor Laurence Tribe and lawyer Marsha Greenberger (founder and co-President of the National Women's Law Center)) who helped Democrats, in 2001, argue against Bush nominees to the lower federal bench.[1279]

[1275] Wells, *supra* note 1263.

[1276] Quoted by Wells, *supra* note 1263.

[1277] For Sunstein's testimony arguing that President Clinton should not have been impeached because his misconduct did not amount to the sort of high public wrongs that the Framers had in mind, see Testimony of Cass R. Sunstein, Background and History of Impeachment: Hearing Before the Subcommittee on the Constitution of the Committee on the Judiciary House of Representatives One Hundred Fifth Congress Second Session 81–91(November 9, 1998) (Serial No. 63).

[1278] See note 1280, *infra*, and see the discussion earlier in Chapter 20, text accompanying note 1199.

[1279] See, e.g., Byron York, Back to Bork?: A New Strategy of Demanding Nominees' Views on Judicial Issues Ensures That the Next Supreme Court

The three together influenced the powerful New York Democrat, Senator Charles Schumer, who held Senate hearings in 2001,[1280] to argue that it was improper for President Bush to nominate only candidates for judgeships who professed "conservative" judicial ideology. What was needed, Sunstein, Tribe, and Greenberger argued, was a "balance" of judicial ideologies, so that the body of federal judges would not be dominated by any particular ideological view. Some conservatives (I was one) testified against that notion, on the theory that there are not divergent "judicial ideologies," but only one acceptable perspective for judges— to follow the existing legal rules[1281]—but the notion of condemning Bush appointees for their "judicial ideology," was ingenious and had great popular appeal, at least among Democrats.

Sunstein, then, is not only a creative academic thinker, but a subtle political operative. As an advisor to President Obama, and a highly visible law professor, Sunstein might

---

Nomination Battle Will Be Ugly, The Atlantic Monthly, Mar. 2003, at 30, 30– 35. York wrote:

> Schumer invited three prominent liberal lawyers—Laurence Tribe, of Harvard Law School; Cass Sunstein, of the University of Chicago; and Marcia Greenberger, of the National Women's Law Center—to testify at the [2001 Senate] hearing. (Two months earlier the same three had appeared at a Democratic retreat and reportedly urged lawmakers to take an aggressive stance against Bush's judicial nominees.) Only a more assertive and openly ideological Judiciary Committee, they told the subcommittee, could stop the White House from packing the courts with doctrinaire conservatives. Democrats simply had to be tougher on Bush nominees.

Id.

[1280] See generally Judicial Nomination and Confirmation Process: Hearings Before the Subcomm. on Administrative Oversight and the Courts of the S. Comm. on the Judiciary, 107th Cong. 1 (2001).

[1281] The notion, that is, propounded by Blackstone, that it was the job of the judge to follow the rules previously laid down, and not to invent new ones. On Blackstone, see Chapter 1, *supra*. In fairness, of course, it would be the belief of Sunstein, and other progressives, that common law judges who purported to follow Blackstone were in error as to the effect of the rules they were following or, perhaps, formulating.

be viewed as a sort of Felix Frankfurter for the early twenty-first century.[1282] His work reveals the cutting edge of current progressive regulatory and constitutional theory, and to a degree, the thinking of the mandarins in one of our great political parties. Sunstein's most interesting star turn (with, perhaps, the exception of his service in the Obama administration as the Administrator of OIRA) was his testimony, referred to earlier,[1283] as a witness in the Clinton impeachment hearings. Sunstein sought to condemn those who tried to impeach and remove the President (all Republicans) because he believed that what Clinton had done—lying to a grand jury investigating his purported misconduct with his White House intern Monica Lewinsky and other women—was not related to his duties as President, and thus could not furnish an excuse to remove him from his office. Impeachment, Sunstein argued, should be reserved for abuses of governmental power which demonstrated a misuse of exclusively Presidential authority, such as, for example, covertly authorizing the use of force in Central America (a slap at the Republican President Reagan), or abusing the internal revenue service to punish one's political enemies (a slap at Republican President Nixon, although a criticism that Sunstein may not have anticipated could be eventually used against his former University of Chicago Law School colleague Barack Obama).

To allow impeachment and removal to move forward on the Republican charges that President Clinton had failed to carry out his duties "to take care that the law be faithfully executed," in a sexual harassment case, Sunstein appeared to believe, while it might merit later civil or criminal proceedings (which Sunstein argued should only take place after the President left office), should not be grounds for

[1282] On Frankfurter, see Chapter 9, *supra.*
[1283] Note 1277, *supra.*

impeachment. To seek to remove the President for what to Sunstein (and other analysts called by the Democrats such as Harvard History Professor Arthur Schlesinger, Jr.) seemed to regard as trivial misconduct, would risk damaging our carefully calibrated system of separation of powers, or the right of the people to choose their President through frequent elections.[1284]

Sunstein's positions on the law and government are carefully thought out, and are advanced with undoubtedly a good faith belief that their implementation would broadly benefit the whole society, but it seems more than a coincidence that in these two very important hearings, on judicial ideology and presidential impeachment, he was called as a witness by Democrats, and eloquently defended them while disparaging Republicans. Sunstein writes as if the democracy he favors begins with a lower case "d," but an analysis of his public persona might well belie this. Still, Caplan's sympathetic profile of Sunstein presents him as an objective proponent of popular sovereignty. As Caplan puts

---

[1284] Sunstein's testimony on President Clinton's impeachability appears in edited and annotated form as Cass R. Sunstein, Impeachment and Stability, 67 Geo. Wash. L. Rev. 699 (1999). Schlesinger's testimony was summarized in an excerpt quoted from his written submission at the hearings:

> The question we confront today is whether it is a good idea to lower the bar to impeachment. The charges levied against the President by the Independent Counsel plainly do not rise to the level of treason and bribery. They do not apply to acts committed by a President in his role of public official. They arise from instances of private misbehavior. All the Independent Counsel's charges [those gathered by former judge Kenneth Starr] thus far derive entirely from a President's lies about his own sex life. His attempts to hide personal misbehavior are certainly disgraceful; but if they are to be deemed impeachable, then we reject the standards laid down by the Framers in the Constitution and trivialize the process of impeachment.

Excerpted in the Minority Report on the impeachment hearings, January 8, 1999, available at https://www.gpo.gov/fdsys/pkg/GPO–CDOC–106sdoc3/html/GPO–CDOC–106sdoc3–18.htm (accessed 23 March 2016). For further rumination on the impeachment of President Clinton, see, e.g., his testimony regarding the meaning of the word "is," related in note 1322, *infra*.

it, Sunstein "argued that the justices of the Supreme Court should resolve questions before them as narrowly as possible, to encourage elected officials to deliberate on divisive issues and test their answers before the voters."[1285] But it's not so clear that Sunstein's philosophy of "judicial minimalism," which Caplan appears to laud, is completely even-handed.

Or at least we might make this criticism with some of Sunstein's writing. For example, in 2005, Sunstein published the far from neutrally-titled book *Radicals in Robes: Why Extreme Right-Wing Courts Are Wrong for America*.[1286] As I indicated in a non-neutral review of that book, while it did contain some "thoughtful jurisprudential analysis," its thrust was that "United States Supreme Court Justices Clarence Thomas and Antonin Scalia,[1287] and others like them on the lower courts, represent a threat to the American republic." These two, and others like them, for Sunstein, were "radicals" and should be consigned to the "extreme right wing." It is, however, quite possible to view Thomas, Scalia, and others like them as "engaged in what we might describe as traditionally conservative jurisprudence."[1288] Even in our time, this is hardly radical. A "conservative" or a "traditionalist" would then disagree with the disparaging manner in which Sunstein labels originalists such as Thomas or Scalia, justices who seek to interpret the Constitution in a manner that is faithful to the aims of the Constitution's Framers as they were understood at the time of the ratification of the Constitution or its

---

[1285] Caplan, *supra* note 1262, at 49.

[1286] Cass R. Sunstein, Radicals in Robes: Why Extreme Right-Wing Courts Are Wrong for America (Basic Books, 2005).

[1287] On Scalia, see Chapter 20, *supra.*

[1288] The quotes in this paragraph are taken from Stephen B. Presser, Was Ann Coulter Right? Some Realism About "Minimalism," 5 Ave Maria Law Review 23, 26 (2007).

amendments, as "fundamentalists."[1289] In so doing, apparently Sunstein sought, in his 2005 book, to imply that constitutional "fundamentalism" suffers from the "the same kind of mindless zealotry as those religious fundamentalists who insist on a rigid reading of the Koran or the Bible according to its original, literal understanding."[1290] If by this label Sunstein sought to "lump Justices Scalia and Thomas in with Osama bin Laden or Jerry Falwell," as I suspect he intended, this was not the move "of an entirely objective analyst."[1291]

To be fair to Caplan (and to Sunstein), Caplan notes that Sunstein recognizes that "Democracy's constitution is not tradition's constitution," and that "A central purpose of a constitution, and of a deliberative democracy, is to subject longstanding practices to critical scrutiny," as, Caplan quite properly notes, Sunstein does.[1292] But what if the central purpose of a Constitution is to preserve the rule of law, and that, in fact, *is* our tradition, as Scalia, Thomas and others have urged? What if a Constitution has the very purpose of preserving the republic, but limiting the operation of democracy? It appears that "Sunstein . . . is clearly an advocate of greater equality. Twelve years ago he published a book praising President Roosevelt's 1944 State of the Union address, in which FDR called for a radically redistributive bill of rights."[1293] What if what Sunstein appears to embrace as "democracy," is in fact simply the

---

[1289] Sunstein, Radicals in Robes, *supra* note 1286, at 26.

[1290] Presser, *supra* note 1288, at 33.

[1291] *Id.*, at 34.

[1292] Caplan, *supra* note 1262, at 49. It's unlikely that by use of the terms "critical scrutiny" Caplan had in mind the Critical Legal Studies theorists discussed in Chapter 14, but it is a nice question whether Sunstein might well share some of their attitude.

[1293] Michael Walzer, "Is the Right Choice a Good Bargain?", 62 The New York Review of Books 23, 25 (March 5, 2015), citing Cass Sunstein, The Second Bill of Rights: FDR's Unfinished Revolution and Why We Need It More Than Ever (Basic Books, 2004).

redistributive   policies   now   favored   by   progressive
Democrats, and disparaged by conservative Republicans?

To be fair to Sunstein, however, if he's a paternalist and
a redistributionist, he does believe that he is also a
libertarian. This is evident in perhaps the most concise and
accessible summary of Sunstein's thought, set out in his
"Why, Nudge?," the highly prestigious Storrs lectures, that
he delivered at the Yale Law School in 2013.[1294] In the
introduction to those lectures he makes the point that much
of our governing philosophy, over the years, has been based
on the "harm principle" of John Stuart Mill, set forth in 1851
in *On Liberty*,[1295] to the effect that individuals ought to be
free to order their own lives, and that the state should only
be able to intervene in order to protect individuals from each
other, and, in particular, the state was never justified in
intervening to protect individuals from themselves.

But what if, Sunstein, asks, in those lectures,
individuals don't really know what is best for them? What
if the insights of modern behavioral economics, that suggest
that aggregates of individuals simply are not capable in the
modern world of adequately evaluating information, are
correct? More disturbing, what if market forces drive
corporations and others to take advantage of this inability
of people to know what is best for themselves, and thus
enmesh   ordinary   citizens   in   harmful   financial
arrangements they cannot afford, or sell them consumer
products that they don't really need? Shouldn't the
government step in in order to promote better choices on the
part of its citizens, to "nudge" them, in Sunstein's felicitous
phrasing, to do the right thing for themselves?

[1294] Cass R. Sunstein, Why Nudge?: The Politics of Libertarian
Paternalism (Yale, 2014).

[1295] See, e.g., John Stuart Mill: 'On Liberty' and Other Writings
(Cambridge Texts in the History of Political Thought) (Cambridge, 1989,
Stefan Collini, Editor).

I don't pretend to be in a position fully to evaluate behavioral economics, but as Sunstein himself appears to recognize, the idea of the government knowing best puts us at risk of threatening "individual dignity and endanger[ing] liberty,"[1296] if not encouraging totalitarianism. Sunstein's theories come close to providing a justification for abolishing large swathes of the free market, and establishing essentially a centralized command and control economy, run by the federal government. This, of course, was the philosophy behind the Patient Protection and Affordable Care Act (PPACA or "Obamacare"), which, in effect, commandeered 1/6 of the national economy, that devoted to the provision of health care.

In this light, it is not difficult to see why Glenn Beck might mark out Sunstein as the most dangerous person out there. This law professor—Sunstein—Beck and others like him could argue, has been putting forth "a blueprint for a leviathan state," one that could slowly or rapidly erode the choices available to its citizens. Just as the PPACA gutted the 10th amendment, if law professors like Sunstein ran the country, it's not at all clear what would be left of the notion of limited federal government, or limited government at all. To Sunstein's credit he is not without some understanding of this problem,[1297] and while his latest efforts do endorse the paternalism of the federal government, it is what he believes to be an enlightened paternalism. For Sunstein his paternalism is one that does not do away with liberty, and, he seems to think, one that by eliminating some harmful choices, will actually enhance the value of those that remain, so that what we will have, in his words, is

---

[1296] Sunstein, "Why Nudge?," *supra* note 1294, at 124.

[1297] See generally for a demonstration that Sunstein is sensitive to the problem of deprivation of liberty, Why Nudge?, *supra* note 1294, and see also Cass R. Sunstein, Conspiracy Theories and Other Dangerous Ideas (Simon & Schuster, 2014) (particularly the introduction, where Sunstein explains how, in his opinion, Glenn Beck gets it wrong).

"libertarian paternalism." It sounds not so horrible, but drawing a line between libertarian paternalism and totalitarianism may not be easy.

More, there is something odious about a government that dictates particular choices, and deprives its citizens of the free will to make mistakes. Many years ago Learned Hand, railing against the Warren Court, protested the idea of judges making social policy for the polity, and taking policy-making away from the voters and their elected representatives. Hand explained that he knew his individual vote may have not counted for much, but living in a country where he at least had the opportunity formally to play his share in participating in the rule of laws, not men, was much better than to be governed by Nine Platonic Guardians on the Supreme Court.[1298] Sunstein is offering something similar to those Nine Platonic Guardians (and, indeed, he has strongly defended the Supreme Court's judicial law-making), although his Ephors may be working in the Office of Information and Regulatory Affairs and the other parts of the Executive Branch rather than in the judiciary.

What would be lost with a system like Sunstein's was made clear by the republication, in 2015, of a manifesto drafted by the late M. Stanton Evans,[1299] a brilliant

---

[1298] "For myself," wrote Hand, "it would be most irksome to be ruled by a bevy of Platonic Guardians, even if I knew how to choose them, which I assuredly do not. If they were in charge, I should miss the stimulus of living in a society where I have, at least theoretically, some part in the direction of public affairs. Of course, I know how illusory would be the belief that my vote determined anything; but nevertheless when I go to the polls I have a satisfaction in the sense that we are all engaged in a common venture." Learned Hand, The Bill of Rights 73–74 (Harvard, 1958).

[1299] For the best book-length statement of M. Stanton Evans's thought see his, The Theme Is Freedom: Religion, Politics, and the American Tradition (Regnery, 1994). M. Stanton Evans might also be thought of as a disciple of the profoundly influential conservative thinker, Russell Kirk. For the book that launched Kirk, see Russell Kirk, The Conservative Mind: From Burke to Eliot

conservative and an ally of William F. Buckley Jr., the "Sharon Statement," of September 11, 1960, written at the home of Mr. Buckley by Evans.[1300] Some selective quotes from that manifesto are instructive. The statement asserted "That foremost among the transcendent values is the individual's use of his God-given free will, whence derives his right to be free from the restrictions of arbitrary force. . . ." The Sharon Statement went on to observe that "[t]he purpose of government" was to protect political and economic freedom, and that "when government ventures beyond these rightful functions, it accumulates power, which tends to diminish order and liberty," that the Constitution's reservation of "primacy to the several states, or to the people,"[1301] must be maintained in order to check the federal government, and that "the market economy, allocating resources by the free play of supply and demand, is the single economic system compatible with the requirements of personal freedom and constitutional government, and that it is at the same time the most productive supplier of human needs. . . ." And, finally, that "when government interferes with the work of the market economy it tends to reduce the moral and physical strength of the nation; that when it takes from one man to bestow on another, it diminishes the incentive of the first, the integrity of the second, and the moral autonomy of both."[1302] If the

---

(7th ed. Regnery, 2001), and for a brilliant analysis of Kirk, see Gerald J. Russello, The Postmodern Imagination of Russell Kirk (Missouri, 2007).

[1300] Reprinted in The Wall Street Journal, "Notable & Quotable: M. Stanton Evans," The Wall Street Journal, Thursday, March 5, 2015, page A13.

[1301] Referring here to the 10th Amendment's text that "The powers not delegated to the United States by the Constitution, nor prohibited by it to the States, are reserved to the States respectively, or to the people." This is often taken as the central statement of our belief in "Federalism," the notion that the Federal government is one of limited and enumerated powers, and that other governmental powers are appropriately exercised by the state and local governments, those closest to the American people themselves.

[1302] See generally the Sharon Statement, reprinted in the Wall Street Journal, *supra* note 1300. The Sharon Statement is also available on the

Sharon Statement is right, of course, the behavioral economists and Cass Sunstein are very sadly and dangerously wrong, and perhaps Glenn Beck has a point.

It is undeniable that Sunstein is brilliant, but he is, perhaps, rather less than objective, as his work with Senator Schumer and his Clinton Impeachment testimony referred to earlier both suggest. As also suggested earlier, Sunstein appears to believe that Justices like Scalia and Thomas can properly be described as "right-wing radicals" in robes, bent on imposing repressive policies on the American people. Sunstein disparages their "fundamentalism," but when he does so, he, like many members of the current legal academy, is really disparaging the notion that judges can interpret the Constitution "according to the law." For Sunstein, apparently, "[t]his claim is at once correct and ludicrously unhelpful, in a way a sham."[1303] But if Sunstein is correct here, then the rule of law itself must be a sham. This is difficult to believe, given that the rule of law, is, after all, the foundation of American republican government itself.[1304] Perhaps then, it is Sunstein's jurisprudence which seems to present too easy an opportunity for judicial lawmaking and license, as it has done for the Justices of which he seems the most fond, Justices O'Connor and Kennedy, whom Sunstein labels, curiously, judicial "minimalists."[1305] Could it be that the

---

Heritage Foundation's website, http://www.heritage.org/initiatives/first-principles/primary-sources/the-sharon-statement (accessed 23 March 2016).

[1303] See, for example, Sunstein, Radicals in Robes, *supra* note 1286, at 23, where Sunstein observes that both President Bush and Senator John Kerry (D–Mass.), the 2004 Democratic presidential nominee, indicated that they favored judges who would interpret the Constitution "according to the law." Sunstein indicates that "[t]his claim is at once correct and ludicrously unhelpful, in a way a sham." *Id.*

[1304] See, e.g., John Phillip Reid, Rule of Law: The Jurisprudence of Liberty in the Seventeenth and Eighteenth Centuries 7 (2004).

[1305] See generally Sunstein, Radical in Robes, *supra* note 1286, at 31, 92–99 (on Justice Kennedy) and 29–30, 146–50 (on Justice O'Connor).

insights of behavioral science teach us that this tells us more about Sunstein's beliefs than these judges'? And what about the beliefs of Sunstein's former colleague at the University of Chicago, Barack Obama?

CHAPTER 23

THE LAW PROFESSOR
AS PRESIDENT

LATE TWENTIETH,
EARLY TWENTY-FIRST CENTURY

Barack Obama
(Chicago)

■ ■ ■

Barack Obama (b. 1961)
Official White House photo by Pete Souza, 2012.

What happens when a Harvard Law School-trained law professor becomes President? Other university professors have achieved that post (Woodrow Wilson comes to mind[1306]), but no one who actually had experience teaching

---

[1306] Theresa M, Beiner, The Con Law Professor with Judicial Appointment Power, 14 J.App.Prac. & Process 1, n.2 (2013). According to Professor Beiner, Wilson "was also trained as an attorney and practiced law briefly." He taught political science at Princeton, but he did develop a "pre-law program" there and "unsuccessfully lobbied for the start of a law school" at Princeton. Wilson also lectured at New York Law School, perhaps qualifying him as a law professor. *Ibid.*

at a great national law school (this may be less than charitable—both William Jefferson Clinton, and his spouse, Hillary Rodham Clinton, taught for a time (1973–76) at the law school of the University of Arkansas).[1307] It is true that Obama did not have a tenure-track position at Chicago, but following his graduation from Harvard Law School, where he had served as the first African-American President of the Harvard Law Review (and where he was a research assistant for Laurence Tribe),[1308] several law schools did seek to recruit him on the tenure track, Northwestern included.

Does it make sense, as I do here, to regard Barack Obama as a quintessential American law professor? Addressing this question, the New Yorker's perceptive legal commentator, Jeffrey Toobin, observes that Mr. Obama "taught classes once a week while practicing law, and, later, while serving in the Illinois state senate, in Springfield." Toobin proceeds with a nice turn of phrase to observe, however, that "When it comes to the law, Obama may never have been a full professor, but he remains fully

---

[1307] Interesting Facts about the Billgrimage: Tracing Bill Clinton's Steps through Arkansas, http://www.arkansas.com/things-to-do/arts/clinton-library/clinton-sites.aspx (accessed 16 January 2016). For Ted Cruz's brief stint as a law professor, at the University of Texas from 2004–2009, see "What it's like to have Ted Cruz as a law Professor," as told to Marissa Miller, from the Cosmopolitan Magazine web site, April 13, 2016, http://www.cosmopolitan.com/politics/news/a56785/ted-cruz-law-professor/ (accessed 15 April 2016).

[1308] Tribe was, at the time, Harvard's best-known professor of Constitutional law, and as we have already seen, Tribe had powerful connections to the Democrats. See, e.g., note 1279 and accompanying text, *supra*. Tribe was reported to have described Obama, whom he apparently shielded from the most mundane research assistant tasks, and instead retained to "exchange lofty ideas about the relationship between law and society," his "most amazing research assistant." Justin Driver, Obama's Law: A New Argument about the President's Legal Philosophy, The New Republic, June 9, 2011. This was high praise indeed, given that Tribe, as one of Harvard's pre-eminent scholars, would have been able to pick the *crème de la crème* of Harvard Law Students as his research assistants.

professorial."[1309] Indeed, Barack Obama might well have become one of the most prominent legal academics in the country, given that he clearly possesses the requisite intelligence and drive. And yet, unlike virtually all of the law professors profiled here, Mr. Obama has given us no scholarly writings on the law, and, except from the inferences to be drawn from his acts as a politician, little scholarly insight into what he thinks about law and legal institutions. Nevertheless, Mr. Obama's biographical writings, and his actions as a Senator and President fully reveal his thoughts about the nature of the law, and, in particular, Constitutional Law.

He chose to go to teach at the University of Chicago's law school, and accept a lectureship, and, from there, launched the political career that eventually carried him into the White House. Still, while he did spend a fair amount of time teaching at the University of Chicago, he may have been something less than a full-time engaged member of the faculty. He was not much involved in the internal politics of the school, or the vigorous give-and-take between the legal scholars that is the mainstay of that law school. At the same time he was a teacher there, he "was working two other jobs . . . in the State Senate and at a civil rights law firm."[1310] Still, he was a lecturer at Chicago for twelve years, and taught a course called "Constitutional Law III, which included equal protection and substantive due process. He also taught a course called Racism and the Law and a course that addressed voting rights."[1311] Obama eventually attained the rank of "Senior Lecturer," which,

---

[1309] Jeffrey Toobin, Annals of Law: The Obama Brief: The President considers his judicial Legacy, The New Yorker, October 27, 2014, at 26.

[1310] Jodi Kantor, Teaching Law, Testing Ideas, Obama Stood Slightly Apart, The New York Times, July 30, 2008., page A1. Available on the web at http://www.nytimes.com/2008/07/30/us/politics/30law.html?_r=0 (accessed 24 March 2016).

[1311] Beiner, *supra* note 1306, at 2.

while it did not carry with it tenure, was still a mark of accomplishment and respect.[1312]

It is clear, though, that Barack Obama may not have been a typical law professor at the University of Chicago school of law. "At a school where economic analysis was all the rage, he taught rights, race and gender. Other faculty members dreamed of tenured positions; he turned them down. While most colleagues published by the pound, he never completed a single work of legal scholarship."[1313] Even so, it is certainly fair to suggest that while at Chicago, he did learn to think like a law professor and he was a popular teacher. "As his reputation for frank, exciting discussion spread, enrollment in his classes swelled. Most scores on his teaching evaluations were positive to superlative."[1314] As hinted earlier, it appears that Obama's attitude toward the Constitution and also toward judicial appointments was profoundly influenced by his colleague at Chicago, his "intellectual kindred spirit, Cass Sunstein."[1315]

Along with Sunstein's influence, it bears remembering that Obama entered Harvard Law School in the fall of 1988, at a period when Critical Legal Studies was at its zenith, and when some of its most prominent practitioners, were on the Harvard faculty.[1316] It certainly seems possible, if not likely, that the malleability of law stressed by that intellectual movement had an influence on Obama, as did his work with the "living constitution" theorist Laurence

[1312] According to a piece in the New York Times on Obama's time at Chicago, the title of Senior lecturer to which Obama was eventually promoted was, when he was there, "a title otherwise carried only by a few federal judges." Kantor, *supra* note 1310.

[1313] Kantor, *supra* note 1310.

[1314] *Ibid.*

[1315] Beiner, *supra* note 1306, at 13. See also Driver, *supra* note 1308, "[A]ssessing how Obama approaches the law as President requires comprehending the legal views of his close friend from the University of Chicago: Cass Sunstein." For Sunstein, see Chapter 22, *supra.*

[1316] See generally Chapter 14, *supra.*

Tribe. It is also more than a coincidence that his hugely popular autobiographies (that helped him become a prominent politician) read like the sort of "story-telling" favored by Critical Race Theorists, such as Patricia Williams.[1317]

Among the President's political moves that suggest a relatively radical view of the law are his occasionally expressed penchant for redistribution, his ability to choose what parts of what laws he will seek to enforce, his tendency, in that effort, for suspending deadlines or exempting particular businesses or persons from general rules of the PPACA (perhaps putting a spin on his constitutional duties to "take care" that all the law be faithfully executed), or his bypassing of Congress in implementing immigration policy (as he did following the failure of the DREAM Act to be adopted legislatively).[1318]

[1317] See Chapter 21, *supra*.

[1318] The DREAM Act was legislation that would have made it easier for undocumented families with children to stay as legal residents in the United States. The President's immigration directives, in effect, accomplished this without legislation. His actions are currently being tested in Court, with, perhaps, some resolution expected late in the current (October 2015) Supreme Court term, although given the current eight-member status of the Court a tie vote may prevent definitive decision on the point. [This was, essentially what occurred, after this part of the text was drafted. See generally, United States v. Texas, 579 U.S. ___ (2016). An evenly divided Court issued a *per-curiam* opinion effectively affirming the Court of Appeals decision which had overruled the President's action, but on narrow, non-Constitutional grounds. The Constitutional issues remained unresolved.] For a book-length polemic arguing that all of these acts and more amount to an abandonment of President Obama's Constitutional duties, see David E. Bernstein, Lawless: The Obama Administration's Unprecedented Assault on the Constitution and the Rule of Law (Encounter Books, 2015). For a similar suggestion that President Obama is a powerful executive, increasing central power and, indeed, virtually becoming a "once and future King," see Ronald Rotunda, Book Review [of F.H. Buckley, The Once and Future King: The Rise of Crown Government in America (Encounter Books, 2014)], 65 J.Leg. Educ. 434 (2015). But see, for the argument that in the modern world a powerful American executive is inevitable, and that other restraints on such an executive are more important than law, Eric A. Posner and Adrian Vermeule, The Executive Unbound: After the Madisonian Republic (Oxford, 2011).

Similarly straying from an orthodox conception of the rule of law was Mr. Obama's willingness to make "recess" appointments when Congress has failed to declare itself in "recess" (a move unanimously rejected by the Supreme Court).[1319] Surely this flexibility, this sense that the strict legal rules need not be followed is influenced by the work of not only the Crits, but also scholars such as Bruce Ackerman and Akhil Amar, who presume that Constitutional change and meaning can be profoundly shaped by popular or political struggle.[1320]

More troubling, the President's critics have sometimes accused him of having no positions he will adhere to, and to being nothing but a creature of politics. The President who promised that his administration would be devoted to the rule of law and who promised as well that his administration would be the most transparent yet to serve, does not appear to have been vindicated by his

---

[1319] The President's track record before the United States Supreme Court is not particularly good. For a disparaging commentary on the President's "five biggest legal losses" of the year 2014, see Damon Root, 2014 Was a Lousy Year for Obama at the Supreme Court, Reason.com, Dec. 30, 2014, available at http://reason.com/blog/2014/12/30/2014–was-a-lousy-year-for-obama-at-the-s (accessed 12/31/2014) (Reviewing a 9–0 defeat in Bond v. United States (rejecting the Obama administration's 'boundless' interpretation of the federal chemical weapons law), a 9–0 defeat in Riley v. California (rejecting the Justice Department's contention that the police were not required to obtain a warrant before searching the cell phones of arrested individuals), a 9–0 defeat in NLRB v. Canning (holding, against the contention of the President, that the President's recess appointments power could not be exercised when the Senate determined it was not in recess), a 5–4 defeat in Burwell v. Hobby Lobby Stores, Inc. (rejecting the Administration's contention that pursuant to the Patient Protection and Affordable Care Act a closely held corporation could be compelled to provide abortifacient drugs), and a defeat in preventing the Court from granting *certiorari* in the case of *King v. Burwell* (which had the potential seriously to undermine the Patient Protection and Affordable Care Act, by determining that the word "state" in the statute referred only to the fifty states and not the federal government. That potential was not realized, as the Supreme Court eventually upheld the Obama administration's view by a 5 to 4 vote. King v. Burwell, 576 U.S. ___ (2015).).

[1320] See Chapter 16, *supra*.

Administration's practices.[1321] Those who know Barack Obama best do not appear to question his sincerity or his good faith, but what if the President's perspective was formed by a legal academic culture that believes that all law is politics, and that reality is almost endlessly mentally malleable, one in which, as former University of Arkansas law professor, William Jefferson Clinton, once remarked, "It depends on what the meaning of 'is' is."[1322] And, if this is the case, what is the future in the country and in the legal academy, for the position that there is such a thing as a clear and certain Rule of Law?

One opportunity for examining President Obama's thinking about the law is offered by what he wrote in his

---

[1321] See generally, Bernstein, *supra* note 1318.

[1322] That extraordinary statement was made in the course of the equally extraordinary investigation by Special Prosecutor Kenneth Starr, who, charged by the Attorney General with investigating whether the President had committed any impeachable offenses, found himself examining whether the President had lied, in the course of defending himself against sexual harassment (actually charges of interfering with civil rights and tortious infliction of mental distress) in the suit brought by Paula Jones, a former Arkansas state employee, at a time when Mr. Clinton was Arkansas Governor. In the course of that lawsuit, Ms. Jones's attorneys sought to demonstrate that the President had a pattern of amorous affairs, rewarding those who complied with his desires, and punishing those who did not. Among the questions put to the President in that grand jury proceeding was whether or not he was sexually involved with Monica Lewinsky, and, as he sat in the grand jury proceeding, by himself in a chair, he could, of course, have truthfully testified that he was not sexually involved with anyone, given that he was, at that time, alone on that piece of furniture. Hence the phrase, "it depends on what the meaning of 'is' is." If the verb referred only to the present moment, he was, of course, not involved with anyone, but if "is" meant at any time in the recent past, its meaning would, of course have different implications. See generally Kenneth Starr, The Starr Report: The Official Report of the Independent Counsel's Investigation of the President (Forum, An Imprint of Prima Publishing, Edition, 1998). (footnote 1,128: "It depends on what the meaning of the word 'is' is. If the—if he—if 'is' means is and never has been, that is not— that is one thing. If it means there is none, that was a completely true statement. . . . Now, if someone had asked me on that day, are you having any kind of sexual relations with Ms. Lewinsky, that is, asked me a question in the present tense, I would have said no. And it would have been completely true.") That sort of "lawyerly" hair-splitting is, of course, what gives lawyers a bad name.

second book, the quite passionate and appealing, *The Audacity of Hope: Thoughts on Reclaiming the American Dream* (2006).[1323] This was, no doubt, something of a standard campaign autobiography, prepared as the then Senator from Illinois was contemplating his campaign for the Presidency. Such tomes are written (often with the aid of a ghostwriter, although none is acknowledged or even hinted at in this book, leading one to believe that the soon-to-be-President was using his own words) usually to appeal to as broad a section of the electorate as possible. Thus such works tend to adopt a middle-of-the-road tone, and this is not completely absent from this book, but, still, reading carefully, the President's view of the law, and his conception of what it is that a law professor does, emerges without compromise and with some clarity. This conception is not particularly middle-of-the-road except, perhaps, for the road currently travelled by most American law professors, especially those at elite institutions.

The charge of thinking like a law professor, leveled by Secretary Panetta,[1324] does not appear to be an unfair one, when one reads the then Senator Obama's words on what he enjoyed about his years teaching law at the University of Chicago:

> I loved the law school classroom: the stripped-down nature of it, the high-wire act of standing in front of a room at the beginning of each class with just blackboard and chalk, the students taking measure of me, some intent or apprehensive, others demonstrative in their boredom, the tension broken by my first question—"What's this case about?"—and the hands tentatively rising, the initial responses and me pushing back against

---

[1323] Barack Obama, The Audacity of Hope: Thoughts on Reclaiming the American Dream (Crown, 2006).

[1324] Note 1, *supra*.

whatever arguments surfaced, until slowly the bare words were peeled back and what had appeared dry and lifeless just a few minutes before suddenly came alive, and my students' eyes stirred, the text becoming for them a part not just of the past but of their present and their future.

Sometimes I imagined my work to be not so different from the work of the theology professors who taught across campus—for, as I suspect was true for those teaching Scripture, I found that my students often felt they knew the Constitution without having really read it. They were accustomed to plucking out phrases that they'd heard and using them to bolster their immediate arguments, or ignoring passages that seemed to contradict their views.[1325]

These words do contain some elusive thoughts—what does it mean to suggest that the work of a law professor is like that of a theology professor?—but Obama proceeds to explain that the real joy of teaching law was revealing to his students the simplicity of the core documents of our legal tradition, and the clear values that were revealed in those documents. Precisely what those values were is not spelled out by the then Senator with great precision, but what seems most striking is that while to him those values are obvious, it is not at all clear that for Professor Obama their content, at any given time in history, has any fixed meaning. Indeed, in an even more telling passage on the nature of law itself, Mr. Obama writes:

[I]n the end laws are just words on a page— words that are sometimes malleable, opaque, as dependent on context and trust as they are in a story or poem or promise to someone, words whose

---

[1325] Obama, *supra* note 1323, at 101–102.

meanings are subject to erosion, sometimes collapsing in the blink of an eye.[1326]

This view of the law, consistent certainly with the professors of critical legal studies or critical race theory, in its assertion of the malleability of the text and the instrumental use of law to achieve particular ends by those in power, is some distance from the view of a Blackstone[1327] or Story,[1328] who saw, respectively, the English Common Law and the United States Constitution as a repository of eternal and unvarying truths. It is also far from the view of a Scalia, who always manifested a view that there was an objective meaning to the words of the Constitution which could be ascertained by examining the contemporary understanding of those who framed and ratified it.[1329]

The soon-to-be President Obama's view of the Constitution comes into even sharper focus when he quite nicely limns the two competing theories dominant in the two political parties these days, and clearly indicates his favoring of one over the other. In his book's chapter on "Our Constitution,"[1330] Senator Obama first disparages the notion expressed by a colleague of his in the Illinois legislature, who maintained that "judges would do whatever they wanted to anyway," because "It's all politics, and right now we've [meaning the Republicans] got the votes." To give the future President his due, he does struggle in this chapter to suggest a coherent content to Constitutional law, and to try to make clear that Constitutional Law is something more than mere political

---

[1326] *Id.*, at 92.

[1327] See Chapter 1, *supra.*

[1328] See Chapter 2, *supra.*

[1329] See Chapter 20, *supra.*

[1330] Obama, *supra* note 1323, Chapter Three.

whim, something more than the fickle desires of those who wield the levers of power.

Evaluating the work of other Constitutional scholars who have sought to attach a fixed meaning to the Constitution (and, at the same time limning the current difference between our leading political parties, as already explained) Obama makes reference by name to the theory of Constitutional interpretation held by Antonin Scalia,[1331] which Mr. Obama calls "the strict constructionists' reverence for the Founders," the tendency "to assume our democracy should be treated as fixed and unwavering: the fundamentalist faith that if the original understanding of the Constitution is followed without question or deviation, and if we remain true to the rules that the Founders set forth, as they intended, then we will be rewarded and all good will flow."[1332]

While he professes some sympathy for this view, the future President clearly rejects it in favor of a different approach to the Constitution held by

> Others, like Justice [Stephen] Breyer, [who] don't dispute that the original meaning of constitutional provisions matters. But they insist that sometimes the original understanding can take you only so far—that on the truly hard cases, the truly big arguments, we have to take context, history, and the practical outcomes of a decision into account. According to this view the Founding fathers and original ratifiers have told us *how* to think but are no longer around to tell us *what* to

---

[1331] See Chapter 20, *supra*.

[1332] Obama, *supra* note 1323, at 107. Note the use of the word "fundamentalist," echoing Mr. Obama's friend, Cass Sunstein. See notes 1286–91, *supra* and accompanying text.

think. We are on our own, and have only our own
reason and our judgment to rely on.[1333]

The future President leaves us in no doubt where he
stands. "Ultimately, though, I have to side with Justice
Breyer's view of the Constitution—that it is not a static but
rather a living document, and must be read in the context
of an ever-changing world."[1334] If Justice Scalia was correct,
in his blast against the "living Constitution" view in a book
published a few years after Obama's,[1335] this quicksilver
notion of the Constitution is anything but the rule of law,
and is, simply, a license for courts—or perhaps Presidents—
to make of the Constitution virtually anything they wish.
The future President's suggestion that meaning can be
altered if you take "context, history, and practical outcomes"
into consideration opens discretion up considerably, if not
totally.

To anyone who paid attention to what candidate
Obama had written about his view of law, it should have
come as no surprise that, as President, he would not feel
bound by its dictates, or at least that he would not feel
constrained by conservative interpretations of the United
States Constitution. Perhaps the outstanding example, as
President, of Mr. Obama's malleable Constitution is what
he did following the profound "shellacking" Democrats
received in the 2014 elections,[1336] his wholesale rewriting of

---

[1333] Obama, *supra* note 1323, at 106–107.

[1334] *Id.*, at 107.

[1335] See generally Antonin Scalia and Bryan A. Garner, Reading Law: The
Interpretation of Legal Texts 403–410, and *passim* (West Publishing, 2012).
Scalia's and Garner's view on this point is summed up on page 410, "[T]he
notion that the advocates of the Living Constitution want to bring us flexibility
and openness to change is a fraud and a delusion." For a penetrating study
demonstrating that the notion of a "living constitution" betrays the moral
understanding of the framers, see Gary L. McDowell, The Language of Law
and the Foundations of American Constitutionalism (Cambridge, 2010).

[1336] The President himself used the word "shellacking" to describe the
defeat Democrats suffered in the 2010 midterms. While what happened in

American immigration law. In what appears to have been an attempt to shore up the Democratic party's base by strengthening his appeal to the Hispanic community, the President announced that he would no longer permit his Justice Department to deport undocumented foreign nationals whose children, usually by having been born in this country, had been granted citizenship. This measure had the effect of granting amnesty to millions of people, and the President further announced measures that would give these millions social security numbers, and put them on the path to citizenship.[1337]

The justification of this measure was what the President's men called "Prosecutorial Discretion," the ability of prosecutors to choose how to implement the criminal law in individual cases, since prosecutorial resources are always limited, and it is impossible to bring to justice every criminal miscreant. A wholesale abandonment of the dictates of the law regarding immigration looks a bit different from what prosecutors have traditionally done in the case of particular individuals, however, and it is no surprise that the President's critics branded his actions as lawless. As Charles Hurt, writing in the conservative Washington Times, put it, addressing the President himself, "You have taken the Presidency and made a mockery of this nation's cherished system of checks and balances." Mr. Hurt asked, ironically, "And this guy

---

2014 also might be described as a similar "shellacking," at that time the President would only concede that the Republicans "had a good night." See generally Colin Campbell, Obama Says Republican Wave Won't Stop Him From Taking Action On Immigration, Business Insider: Politics, Nov. 5, 2014, available on the web at http://www.businessinsider.com/president-obama-reacts-to-midterms–2014–11 (accessed 24 March 2016).

[1337] See, e.g., Karen Tumulty, Illegal immigrants could receive Social Security, Medicare under Obama action, The Washington Post, November 25, 2014, available on the web, at https://www.washingtonpost.com/politics/illegal-immigrants-could-receive-social-security-medicare-under-obama-action/2014/11/25/571caefe–74d4–11e4–bd1b–03009bd3e984_story.html (accessed 24 March 2016).

went to Harvard Law School? Harvard should strip him of his degree. Or maybe recall him for further remedial instruction on how the whole constitution works." What Mr. Hurt didn't seem to acknowledge, of course, was that it was at Harvard that Mr. Obama learned what he showed was the plasticity of the Constitution.[1338]

And, indeed, it may not be just the plasticity of the Constitution that Mr. Obama learned at Harvard, or somewhere else. In his view of the world, everything may be malleable, and changeable if a former law professor can invoke the appropriate rhetoric to point out situations which are self-evident to him, but perhaps not to everyone else.[1339] One sharp critic of the President's foreign policy, which policy this critic argued was not grounded in reality, ascribed this purported error of the President to Obama's ideology, and, in particular, his belief that "History is on our side, and the arc of history bends toward justice." In this view, that critic, Bret Stephens, of the Wall Street journal, suggested, the President probably believes that America can pull back as a world power, and let good events unfold on their own. With more than a little condescension, Stephens wrote that "It's easy to accept this view of life if you owe your accelerated good fortune to a superficial charm and understanding of the way the world works. It's also easier to lecture than to learn, to preach than to act."[1340] Was Stephens, like Panetta, suggesting that thinking like a law professor is not good for a President? This trope appears to be becoming increasingly popular as

---

[1338] Charles Hurt, Welcome to lawless Obama's America, hombres! The Washington Times, Tuesday, December 16, 2014, available at http://www.washingtontimes.com/news/2014/dec/16/charles-hurt-welcome-to-lawless-obamas-america-hom/?page=all (accessed December 18, 2014).

[1339] Again this seems to be the thrust of Secretary Panetta's criticism of the President. See note 1, *supra*.

[1340] Bret Stephens Global View: An Unteachable President, The Wall Street Journal, September 29, 2015, page A11.

Obama nears the end of his term. The conservative commentator Charles Krauthammer, for example, claimed, in light of the President's foreign policy, that he was "a man living in a faculty-lounge fantasy world."[1341]

Returning however, to our principal concern, law professors and their view of the law, in the first opinion on the Constitutionality of the President's executive grant of amnesty for the undocumented parents, United States District judge Arthur Schwab, declaring the President's actions untenable, wrote that "President Obama's unilateral legislative action violates the separation of powers provided for in the United States Constitution as well as the Take Care Clause, and, therefore, is unconstitutional."[1342] Judge Schwab recognized that prosecutors had discretion in individual cases, but that did not justify the President exempting millions of undocumented aliens from the law, which, in Judge Schwab's view, was an act of legislation rather than an act of discretion. Mr. Hurt observed that the United States Supreme Court had already unanimously ruled "some 13 times," that "Mr. Obama had overstepped his authority, misread the law, misunderstood basic constitutional concepts or was otherwise out of order."[1343] District Judge Schwab's opinion, of course, was not the last word on the President's actions with regard to immigration, and, at this writing the case, United States v. Texas, is before the

---

[1341] Charles Krauthammer, Obama's Syria Debacle, The Washington Post, October 1, 2015, available on line at https://www.washingtonpost.com/opinions/obamas-world-falls-apart/2015/10/01/50c2a7d6–686f–11e5–8325–a4 2b5a459b1e_story.html (accessed October 2, 2015).

[1342] U.S. v. Juarez-Escobar, Case 2:14–cr–00180–AJS, issued 12/16/2014 (U.S.D.C. WDPA), slip op., at 22. The "Take Care Clause" of the United States Constitution is Article II, Section 3, clause 5, which provides that the President, "shall take Care that the Laws be faithfully executed."

[1343] Hurt, *supra* note 1338.

United States Supreme Court, with a decision expected in June, 2016.[1344]

With the recent passing of Justice Scalia, the Court is now evenly divided between four "living constitution" advocates like the President (Breyer, Ginsburg, Sotomayor, and Kagan) and four who are at least perceived as generally conservative (Roberts, Kennedy, Alito, and Thomas). Still, the "swing justices," now Kennedy and Roberts, who are somewhat unpredictable, for all practical purposes decide which way the Court will move. Whether President Obama, the former law professor, will see his view of the Constitution prevail is now uncertain. One seeking to figure out the meaning of the Constitution is in the same position as we were a few years ago, when the Court was equally divided between strict constructionist conservatives and "living constitution" liberals, and the deciding vote, with no theoretical consistency to it, was cast by the then key "swing Justice" Sandra Day O'Connor. At that time, echoing a view expressed by some conservative Constitutional scholars, most prominently Justice Scalia,[1345] that "The Only Good Constitution is a Dead Constitution," one wag sadly remarked that the Constitution means whatever Sandra Day O'Connor thinks it means "on any given Monday."[1346] Let's begin our Conclusion with some consideration of Justice O'Connor.

[1344] For the temporary disposition of the issue see note 1318, *supra.* A future case will probably be needed, when the Court returns to its full complement of nine Justices, for a final determination of whether or not the President acted unconstitutionally.

[1345] See Chapter 20, *supra.*

[1346] For the attribution of this statement to the conservative pundit Charles Krauthammer, see, e.g., Jonah Goldberg, The Only Good Constitution is a Dead Constitution, Townhall.com, July 9, 2003 http://townhall.com/columnists/jonahgoldberg/2003/07/09/the_only_good_constitution_is_a_dead_constitution/page/full (accessed 5 February 2016). ("As Charles Krauthammer put it recently, 'The Constitution is whatever Justice Sandra Day O'Connor says it is. On any given Monday.' ")

CHAPTER 24

CONCLUSION

■ ■ ■

Sandra Day O'Connor (b. 1930)
Associate Justice of the United States Supreme Court (1981–2006).
Photograph by Dane Penland.
Collection of the Supreme Court of the United States.

Retired Supreme Court Justice Sandra Day O'Connor recently protested what she called "an alarming degree of public ignorance" about the most basic facts of American governance.[1347] It might be even more alarming that the

---

[1347] Katie Terhune, Retired Justice Sandra Day O'Connor, in Boise, laments 'alarming degree of public ignorance' Idaho Statesman, September 6, 2013, http://www.mcclatchydc.com/2013/09/06/201376/retired-justice-sandra-day-oconnor.html (accessed November 1, 2014). The retired Justice observed that "Two-thirds of Americans cannot name a single Supreme Court justice," that only "About one-third can name the three branches of government., "and further that "Less than one-third of eighth-graders can identify the historical purpose of the Declaration of Independence, and it's right there in the name. . . ." Justice O'Connor's importance as a former "swing justice" should be evident by now. She appears on the dust jacket of this book among the gallery of Law Professors, and that appearance is justified by the additional fact that since her retirement as a Justice, she "teaches a two-week course called 'The Supreme Court' at the University of Arizona's James E. Rogers College of Law every spring semester." Wikipedia entry for "Sandra Day O'Connor."

American public is even less informed about how those who administer their government are taught. Legal education is widely understood to be deficient (it has yet, for example, really to come to terms with the information revolution and the new reliance of lawyers on digital data and the internet),[1348] and it is likely that the next few decades will see major transformation in the manner in which law schools operate. This book, by examining what law professors have written and taught, has sought to be of help in this process, so that it ought to be of interest both to those in legal education and those, outside of the legal academy, who wonder why American law now seems so unstable.[1349]

If there is a single over-arching theme from the progression of legal education from Blackstone to Barack Obama, it is that at least since the last half of the twentieth century and into the twenty-first, there is a profound dominance of a legal philosophy that repudiated earlier notions. At first there was "legal sociology" and "legal realism," and, then, later, the related developments of "critical legal studies," "feminism," and "critical race theory." This dominance of these schools of legal thought led to a legal pedagogy in the great American law schools which abandoned the Blackstonian notion that the law could be a clear, certain, and binding constraint on judges, and a rejection of the Blackstonian view that the law contained universal principles, principles of morality which were dictated by the Deity. Instead, a majority of the American legal academy all but concluded that law was little different

---

https://en.wikipedia.org/wiki/Sandra_Day_O%27Connor#Activities_and_mem berships (accessed 6 October 2016).

[1348] See, e.g., John O. McGinnis, Accelerating Democracy: Transforming Governance Through Technology (Princeton, 2015).

[1349] For a similar effort at recapturing the meaning of the American Constitutional system, see the recent volume on Constitutional Law, Michael Stokes Paulsen and Luke Paulsen, The Constitution: An Introduction (Basic Books, 2015).

from politics. For most American Law Professors, inspired perhaps by the Warren Court, and realizing the discretion that the American common law system and its analogues in Constitutional Law actually gave to judges, and idolizing as they did the creative jurist, the job of American law as administered in the courts was seen to be the redistribution of American wealth and power in order to reverse decades of discrimination against minorities and women, gays and other formerly disadvantaged groups. This is not to say that this movement did not result in the redress of some longstanding grievances, or that it did not, in some way promote some ideals of justice.

Still, for most of the American public, which somehow maintains belief in the notion that there ought to be reliable content to the law, and that our judges and politicians ought to be bound by it just as are ordinary citizens, this now-prevailing academic view of the law is puzzling, to say the least. It is a nice question whether the pursuit of "justice" through arbitrary means is not a betrayal of our deepest ideals, and the lingering disturbance of this question troubles many of us, even in the academy. Thus, another lesson contained in these pages is that even though the legal realists and their latter-day allies are dominant in the academy, there has always been a rearguard action fought by the champions of the rule of law, such as Wechsler,[1350] Carrington,[1351] and Scalia.[1352] Surely it is beginning to dawn on both the academy and the public that the result of all of this in the early twenty-first century is political turmoil over the role of judges, and an instability in the legal system that threatens basic American civic concepts such as that ours is a government of laws, not of men.

[1350] Chapter 11, *supra*.

[1351] Chapter 19, *supra*.

[1352] Chapter 20, *supra*.

The absolute Blackstonian version of the rule of law and, indeed of a government of laws not of men, it must be recognized, may be unattainable ideals in the real world, but if that is true, then we have strayed far indeed from the world of the framers and our heritage of the English common law.[1353] If the law is about nothing but implementing political preferences, about redistributing resources to currently favored groups, it will have ceased to be a noble profession preserving order, stability, deference, certainty and predictability, and it will become, as Thrasymachus cynically believed, only the tool of those in power.[1354] This is, however, not inevitable. By the end of the twentieth century a counter revolution had set in some quarters of the academy. Students at the elite bastions of Yale, Harvard, Michigan and other law schools cooperated in the formation of the Federalist Society for Law and Public Policy Studies, a group actually borrowing its name from the framers of the Constitution, and using a profile of Madison himself as their symbol. Probably the two most important beliefs of this group, which united what became the many thousands of law school and practicing lawyer members of the Federalist Society, were the ideas that judges should not legislate ("separation of powers") and that the Constitution's scheme of limited government and dual sovereignty ("federalism") should be preserved. This was also the view, of course, most famously articulated by the late Justice Antonin Scalia, the "rock star" of One First

---

[1353] On this heritage of the Common law see *supra* Chapter 1 on Blackstone, and Chapters 2 and 3, *supra*, on Wilson and Story.

[1354] Thrasymachus, a fifth-century BCE Athenian philosopher, appears in Book One of Plato's Republic, and makes the statement that "Justice is nothing but the advantage of the stronger." (Plato, Republic, Chapter One, 338c). Thrasymachus is presented as a foil for the central claim in the Republic, that, indeed, there is content to the concept and the ideal of justice, and that it is more than simply the will of those in power. On Thrasymachus, see, e.g., the entry for "Thrasymachus," in the Internet Encyclopedia of Philosophy, available on the web at http://www.iep.utm.edu/thrasymachus/ (accessed 25 March 2016).

Street, whose example was a powerful one for the Federalist Society.[1355]

As the outpouring of praise for Scalia following his death early in 2016 made clear, there are, then, those who still believe, after all, that the rule of law should govern and that justice should be administered blindly without regard to the identity or characteristics of citizens. This remains the belief that serves as the foundation of Constitutional government, and the inspiration behind the drafting of our Federal Constitution.[1356]

[1355] See Chapter 20, *supra*. On the formation and influence of the Federalist Society, see, in addition to note 1214 *supra* and accompanying text, e.g., Amanda Hollis-Brusky, Ideas with Consequences: The Federalist Society and the Conservative Counter-Revolution (Oxford, 2015). It should probably also be said that most, if not all, of the members of the Federalist Society would share some of the beliefs articulated in the Sharon Statement, *supra* notes 1300–1302, and accompanying text, and, in particular, the idea that governments are formed to preserve the liberties of the people, and not to endanger those liberties by unduly dictating how the lives of their people are to be lived. For a fine study of what the framers' original conception of federalism was, and how it was conceived as a means of protecting individuals, see Michael S. Greve, The Upside-Down Constitution (Harvard, 2012). For a somewhat similar, equally important study of how, beginning with the progressives in the early twentieth century, our constitutional structure and morality were undermined, see Bruce P. Frohnen and George W. Carey, Constitutional Morality and the Rise of Quasi-Law (Harvard, 2016).

[1356] See generally, Gordon S. Wood, The Creation of the American Republic, 1776–1787 (University of North Carolina Press, 1969) (Explaining the dissatisfaction with the arbitrary acts of the state legislatures in the post-revolutionary period as the cause of the framing and ratification of the federal Constitution). For a somewhat different take on the Founding, with a careful analysis of the framers of the Articles of Confederation, see William J. Watkins, Jr., Crossroads for Liberty: Recovering the Anti-Federalist Values of America's First Constitution (Independent Institute, 2016).

**Justitia Blindfolded and Holding
Balance Scales and a Sword**
Court of Final Appeal, Hong Kong.
Wikimedia commons.

Lady Justice may no longer be wearing her blindfold, as President Obama's increasing use of executive orders and memoranda to get around Congressional inaction demonstrated. This had been occurring for some time, as for example, illustrated by the President's decision (perhaps to appease part of his base) to suspend federal enforcement of the law prohibiting the sale of cannabis, to permit the states of Colorado, Alaska, Oregon and Washington to authorize (and tax) sales of the drug.[1357] Then, as already indicated in the preceding chapter, following the midterm elections in 2014, in which his political opponents scored a significant victory through running against his policies, the President proceeded, by executive order, to suspend the enforcement of the immigration laws, in order to grant amnesty in all but name to millions of undocumented aliens in the country. It was hard to view this action as anything other than a clear effort, in the face of partisan opposition, to exercise Thrasymachian power in a manner that seemed to fly in the

---

[1357] See generally, David B. Rivkin Jr. and Elizabeth Price Foley, Federal Antidrug Law Goes Up in Smoke: Irate about harmful spillover from Colorado's marijuana legalization, two neighboring states sue to overturn it, The Wall Street Journal, December 28, 2014, available at http://www.wsj.com/articles/david-b-rivkin-jr-and-elizabeth-price-foley-federal-antidrug-law-goes-up-in-smoke–1419810742 (accessed December 28, 2014).

face of the President's Constitutional obligation to take care that the laws be faithfully executed. A gaggle of law professors argued that the President was well within his Constitutionally-granted powers, although several years earlier, President Obama had clearly stated his belief that he, as President, was without the authority single-handedly to suspend the immigration laws.

The President's advisors pointed to what they regarded as similar behavior on the part of Presidents George H.W. Bush and Ronald Reagan, who did, in fact, announce that they would not be deporting thousands, if not millions, of undocumented residents, but they did so, they maintained, in pursuance of Congressional policy that had clearly indicated their actions in exercising prosecutorial discretion were in keeping with the wishes of the legislative branch.[1358] President Obama, by contrast, made clear that his action was taken because he believed Congress had failed to act, and the President's critics in Congress proclaimed that his actions smacked more of those of a Caesar or a caudillo. A cynical observer could conclude that the President had decided that satisfying the Hispanic base that had been faithful to the Democrats, was more important than preserving the Constitutional principles of faithful execution of the laws by the executive and the reservation of law-making powers to the legislature. The President's actions were praised by his ideological cohort in the academy, most notably Bruce Ackerman, whose flexible construction of Article V has already been observed.[1359]

[1358] On this point see, e.g., Robert Farley, Obama's Actions 'Same' as Past Presidents? FactCheck.Org (November 21, 2014, updated November 24, 2014), available on the web at http://www.factcheck.org/2014/11/obamas-actions-same-as-past-presidents/ (accessed 25 March 2016).

[1359] On Ackerman's views on the Constitution see Chapter 16, *supra*. For Ackerman's defense of the President's actions on immigration, see, e.g., Bruce Ackerman, Like the Emancipation Proclamation, Obama's order forces democracy, Los Angeles Times, November 21, 2014, available on the web at

There was, from the legal professoriate, scant defense of the Constitution, and, in general, approval of the President's actions. In the early twenty-first century, the law professoriate, perhaps, had become as highly politicized as the law itself.

Elizabeth Warren (b. 1949)
Photograph by Warren Farewell.
Courtesy Harvard Law School.

Perhaps the most notable sign of this was the possible candidacy for President of another former Harvard law professor, Elizabeth Warren, the senior senator from Massachusetts, who, while denying she was running (and, to be fair, she eventually did not), proceeded to publish the requisite campaign autobiography, in April 2014, an intriguing tome called "A Fighting Chance."[1360] The book tells the story of Warren's career as a law professor and consumer crusader, practicing the exceptionally esoteric legal academic specialty of bankruptcy law. In her 2012 campaign for the Senate, perhaps riding on the coattails of the then popular President Obama (in Massachusetts, at least), Professor Warren even outdid former Senator Obama in claiming that American corporations and American businesses didn't deserve the tax breaks or the other

---

http://www.latimes.com/opinion/op-ed/la-oe-ackerman-obama-immigration–20141123–story.html (accessed 25 March 2016).

[1360] Elizabeth Warren, A Fighting Chance (Metropolitan Books, 2014).

favorable treatments traditionally accorded them by American law. Her most famous utterance on this point, before she became a Senate candidate, but at a time when a future in politics may have been increasingly attractive to her, was her statement that

> I hear all this, you know, 'Well, this is class warfare, this is whatever.' No. There is nobody in this country who got rich on his own—nobody. You built a factory out there? Good for you. But I want to be clear. You moved your goods to market on the roads the rest of us paid for. You hired workers the rest of us paid to educate. You were safe in your factory because of police-forces and fire-forces that the rest of us paid for. You didn't have to worry that marauding bands would come and seize everything at your factory—and hire someone to protect against this—because of the work the rest of us did. Now look, you built a factory and it turned into something terrific, or a great idea. God bless—keep a big hunk of it. But part of the underlying social contract is, you take a hunk of that and pay forward for the next kid who comes along.[1361]

[1361] Transcript of Warren's remarks available at http://www.theblaze.com/ stories/2011/09/21/elizabeth-warren-on-class-warfare-there-is-nobody-in-this-country-who-got-rich-on-his-own/ (accessed December 28. 2014). President Obama appears to have picked up on this meme when he remarked, on July 23, 2012, in a campaign speech in Roanoke, Virginia, "There are a lot of wealthy, successful Americans who agree with me—because they want to give something back. They know they didn't—look, if you've been successful, you didn't get there on your own. . . . If you were successful, somebody along the line gave you some help. There was a great teacher somewhere in your life. Somebody helped to create this unbelievable American system that we have that allowed you to thrive. Somebody invested in roads and bridges. If you've got a business—you didn't build that. Somebody else made that happen." The President's remarks are available at http://www.c-span.org/video/?307056– 2/president-obama-campaign-rally-roanoke (accessed December 28. 2014).

"A Fighting Chance" develops this theme, making clear the then possible candidate Warren's views that the middle class in America is being crushed by corporate malefactors, particularly banks, whose recent deregulation (according to Senator Warren) has left them free rapaciously to raise interest rates, bamboozle consumers, and lure people into deeper and deeper debt, while at the same time rewriting bankruptcy laws to prevent ordinary Americans from ever escaping the clutches of high finance. Warren makes clear her belief that bankruptcy laws ought to allow Americans to walk away from their debts more easily, since, for her, those who might seek to declare bankruptcy find themselves inadvertently in that condition because of unanticipated financial reverses caused by catastrophic illness, unpredictable financial downturns, or unscrupulous lending practices by those wrongly dangling credit cards in front of unwary consumers. Warren appears to have nothing but contempt for those such as former Bankruptcy Commission member Judge Edith Jones, or, indeed, credit card companies, who took the position that adults ought to be able to manage their own debts, and assume the responsibility for paying off the obligations they accrue.[1362]

For Warren, as perhaps for Obama, business is out simply for profit, and compassion and human needs are sacrificed on an economic altar.[1363] Former Governor Mitt

---

[1362] On Warren's disagreement with the views of Judge Jones, Orrin Hatch, and others, see, in addition to the discussion in A Fighting Chance, *supra* note 1360, Elizabeth Warren, The Over-Consumption Myth and Other Tales of Economics, Law and Morality, available on the web at http://openscholarship.wustl.edu/law_lawreview/vol82/iss4/8 (accessed 25 March 2016). For Judge Jones's views, see, e.g., Edith H. Jones and Todd J. Zywicki, It's Time for Means-Testing, 1999 BYU L. Rev. 177.

[1363] Senator Warren has consistently made clear her belief that the system in Washington is rigged in favor of the banks and corporations and against ordinary Americans and consumers, and that Republicans and lobbyists are in the pocket of the corporate miscreants. See, e.g., her fiery speech at Netroots Nation, on July 18, 2014, where she stated:

Romney's insight that "corporations are people too" seems to have eluded them. Indeed, Elizabeth Warren attacked this notion full-frontally. Said she, before the Democrats' Convention, in 2012:

> No, Governor Romney, corporations are not people. People have hearts, they have kids, they get jobs, they get sick, they cry, they dance. They live, they love, and they die. And that matters. That matters because we don't run this country for

---

But it isn't just the big banks. Look at the choices the federal government makes right now. Our college kids are getting crushed by student loan debt. We need to rebuild our roads and bridges and upgrade our power grids. We need more investment in medical research and scientific research. But instead of building a future, this country is bleeding billions of dollars in tax loopholes and subsidies that go to the rich and powerful corporations. Billion dollar companies take advantage of every benefit they can squeeze out of the American government. And then they put together sleazy deals with foreign countries so [that] they can renounce their American citizenship and pay no taxes.

Billionaires pay taxes at lower rates than their secretaries. How does this happen? It happens because they all have lobbyists—lobbyists and Republican friends in Congress. Lobbyists and Republicans to protect every loophole and every privilege. The game is rigged and it isn't right. It is not fair.

Steven Rosenfeld, Progressive Values Are America's Values, Sen. Elizabeth Warren Tells Netroots Nation In Keynote Speech, available at http://www.alternet.org/activism/progressive-values-are-americas-values-sen-elizabeth-warren-tells-netroots-nation-keynote?paging=off&current_page=1#bookmark (accessed January 5, 2015). Or, as Senator Warren put it as starkly in a 2014 speech on the Senate Floor:

Washington already works really well for the billionaires and big corporations and the lawyers and lobbyists. But what about the families who lost their homes or their jobs or their retirement savings the last time [Citibank] bet big on derivatives and lost? What about the families who are living paycheck to paycheck and saw their tax dollars go to bail Citi out just six years ago? We were sent here to fight for those families, and it's time—it's past time—for Washington to start working for them.

Remarks by Senator Warren on Citigroup and its Bailout Provision, delivered Dec. 12. 2014, and available at Senator Warren's official website, http://www.warren.senate.gov/?p=press_release&id=686 (accessed January 5, 2014).

corporations, we run it for people. And that's why
we need Barack Obama.[1364]

The truth, however, is a bit more complex. Corporations
are not actually living breathing people, of course, but those
whom they serve, those whom they employ, and those who
operate and invest in them are all flesh and blood human
beings. Millions of members of the middle class own shares
in banks, credit card companies, and manufacturing
concerns, and those Americans of all classes who do not
invest directly in American corporations with shares in
brokerage accounts, most likely still have a stake in them
either because of direct or indirect ownership of mutual
funds, IRA's, or union pension funds, or because they
benefit from institutions with investment portfolios, such as
colleges and universities. Thus, when the President or
Senator Warren seek icily to reify corporations and ignore
financial realities in the service of redistributionist goals
they are either deceiving us or themselves. Elizabeth
Warren and men and women like her (for example Bernie
Sanders in the primary election cycle just ended) may or
may not ultimately succeed in selling themselves to
Americans as a bona-fide populists, although there are
those who question Senator Warren's credentials in this
regard.[1365] Nevertheless, what is striking about Warren's

[1364] Transcript of Elizabeth Warren's Democratic Convention Speech,
September 5, 2012, available on the web at http://abcnews.go.com/Politics/
OTUS/transcript-elizabeth-warrens-democratic-convention-speech/story?id=
17164726&singlePage=true (accessed January 5, 2015).

[1365] See, e.g., Salena Zito, Elizabeth Warren is no Populist, http://triblive.
com/opinion/salena/7449933–74/populist-populism-political#axzz3NFImoQfs
(From the Pittsburgh Tribune Review, accessed 28 December 2014), where it
is said that "Being anti-Big Business, which is Warren's thing, is not the core
of populism, although it can be a component. But it is the core of progressive
economics, which is socialism," and also that "Populism is an ideology extolling
the virtues of the people against the depravities of elites—such as Harvard
Law professors like Warren, according to Baylor University political science
professor Curt Nichols. Her 'well-established Harvard faculty progressivism
fits oddly with the classic left-of-center populism she is . . . attempting to
espouse,' said Nichols, an expert on populist movements."

rhetoric, at least, is Warren's bald assertions of the malevolence of the bankers and the goodness of the would-be bankrupts. And now we come to the relevance of this consideration of this final Harvard Law Professor to be examined here. Could there be something in the world of the law professor that leads one to see things in such Manichean stark black and white terms,[1366] and that breeds an almost unfathomable arrogance regarding the correctness of one's own political prejudices?

The challenge of our time is not just to the rule of law, but also to the freedoms that Americans have usually taken for granted but which are now under attack from, among others, law professors. In a powerful recent op-ed piece one commentator lamented the increasing restrictions on speech from the so-called "heckler's veto," pursuant to which protesting groups silence unfavored speakers, particularly on college campuses. Such silencing flows from the hecklers' concept of "political correctness," or from currently popular anti-hate-speech movements, which seek to ban any commentary that might offend previously discriminated-against groups. A similarly alarming development is to be found in international bodies or nations which seek to silence religious and other critics. Taking all of this into account, a prominent American civil rights attorney pointed his finger at the legal academy. Said Barry A. Fisher, "Law professors have concocted influential concepts like 'outsider jurisprudence,' 'critical race theory,' 'critical feminist theory' and 'storytelling' theory to define

---

[1366] See, e.g., for Warren's starkly contrasting Republicans and Conservatives on the one hand, and her and her fellow Democrats on the other:

Let's talk about this fight. This is a fight over economics, a fight over privilege, a fight over power. But deep down it is a fight over values. Conservatives and their powerful friends will continue to be guided by their internal motto, 'I've got mine. The rest of you are on your own.' Well, we're guided by principle, and it's a pretty simple idea. We all do better when we work together and invest in building a future.

Netroots Nation, Keynote Speech, *supra* note 1363.

some kinds of politically incorrect speech as not speech at all, but 'mechanisms of subordination.' "[1367] Through the guise of eliminating "subordination," then, cherished liberties can be lost.

We have seen, in the course of these chapters, how a group of men and women from a variety of backgrounds, classes, and educational institutions, working as law professors, both fought for and sought to undermine or radically alter our most basic constitutional and political beliefs. Indeed, there appears to be a temptation in the law professoriat habitually to live in an alternate reality. And this is not an exclusively recent phenomenon. A.N. Hirsch, in his biography of Felix Frankfurter, quotes Holmes himself as advising Frankfurter against joining the academy.[1368] "Holmes wrote that 'academic life is but half-life—it is withdrawal from the fight in order to utter smart things that cost you nothing except the thinking them from a cloister."[1369]

But this is not the way things ought to be in the academy, and there are some law professors, as we have seen, Frankfurter among them, who understood that the law and the Constitution needed to be preserved and enhanced in order for democracy to flourish in this country. For Frankfurter, one of his responsibilities was to "be in politics—with the emphasis on sustained thinking along the very questions of public affairs that have the greatest appeal to me."[1370] Frankfurter believed that it was the law professors' task to keep the Justices faithful to the Constitution. He wrote to one of his disciples, the great Yale

---

[1367] Barry A. Fisher, Free Speech's Shrinking Circle of Friends, The Wall Street Journal, Tuesday, December 30, 2014, at A11. On Critical Race Theory see generally Chapter 21, *supra*.

[1368] For Frankfurter, see Chapter 9, *supra*, and for Holmes, see Chapter 5, *supra*.

[1369] Hirsh, *supra* note 493, at 39.

[1370] *Ibid*, quoting Felix Frankfurter to Henry L. Stimson, July 7, 1913.

Law Professor Alexander Bickel that "You law professors really should sharpen your pens so that there is no mistaking as to what the trouble is and where the blame lies. I can give you proof that if you would speak out, you would get under [the Justices'] skins."[1371] Still, at the present time, the legal academy may have lost touch with the needs of the polity, especially if one believes, as some of us always have, that one of those needs is adherence to the rule of law itself.

As noted here, many American law professors—Akhil Amar[1372] and Cass Sunstein[1373] might be taken as two representative examples, have concocted elaborate systems and elaborate justifications for straying from the strict rule of law to implement what they believe to be the necessary remedies for the problems of our times. Barack Obama's view of the malleability of the law is similar, as his critics have argued.[1374] All of this, perhaps, in the manner in which it justifies moving beyond the objective meaning of the Constitution and laws, is somewhat reminiscent of what the great Victorian novelist, Anthony Trollope, had to say about what he was trying to portray in the character of August Melmotte, his unscrupulous financier, in his most fully realized novel, *The Way We Live Now*.[1375] Wrote Trollope in his autobiography:

> [A] certain class of dishonesty, dishonesty magnificent in its proportions, and climbing into high places, has become at the same time so rampant and so splendid that there seems to be reason for fearing that men and women will be

---

[1371] Felix Frankfurter to Alexander Bickel, March 18, 1963, quoted in Hirsch, *supra* note 493, at 183.

[1372] See Chapter 16, *supra*.

[1373] See Chapter 22, *supra*.

[1374] See Chapter 23, *supra*.

[1375] Anthony Trollope, The Way We Live Now (Chapman and Hall, 1875).

taught to feel that dishonesty, if it can become splendid, will cease to be abominable. If dishonesty can live in a gorgeous palace with pictures on all its walls, and gems in all its cupboards, with marble and ivory in all its corners, and can give Apician[1376] dinners, and get into Parliament, and deal in millions, then dishonesty is not disgraceful, and the man dishonest after such a fashion is not a low scoundrel.[1377]

The elegant and elaborate theories of contemporary American law professors that justify departures from prior precedents or implement new versions of constitutional meaning, are similarly splendid, but similarly dishonest. If the rule of law in this country means anything, it is that it cannot be set aside without endangering everything on which popular sovereignty as expressed in our Constitution and laws ultimately stands.

The legal philosopher John Finnis, now a law professor at Notre Dame and at Oxford, recently called for action to restrain what he, too, saw to be an alarming trend on the part of the Courts in many nations to engage in legislation rather than adjudication. He concluded that

> [W]e all, lawyers and non-lawyers alike, should be aware how much work we indispensably need the courts and their judges to do . . . so that in fidelity to real law applied to proven or admitted facts, they even-handedly restrain those individuals and groups who wield any of the many,

---

[1376] This is a reference to Apicius, a Roman voluptuary who lived about 90 BCE and was famous for his lavish entertainments.

[1377] Anthony Trollope, Autobiography, in Anthony Trollope: Complete Collection of Works with analysis and historical background (Annotated and Illustrated) (Annotated Classics) (Kindle Locations 20014–20018). For a modern scholar's suggestion that literature could profitably be analyzed from a free-market perspective see Allen Mendenhall, Literature and Liberty: Essays in Libertarian Literary Criticism (Lexington Books, 2014).

many kinds of private or public power—including the power of media pressure, groupthink and ostracism—to keep them within the specific bounds and measures of our genuinely established law's settled commitments, and to compensate those who have been unlawfully wronged.[1378]

In other words, Finnis, in clear and simple language, was calling for a return to the rule of law, as the only security to person and property from the acts of arbitrary power.

It is encouraging that other members of the legal academy are beginning increasingly to understand the need for a return to what some have called "First Principles."[1379] Steven Smith, long one of our more astute Constitutional commentators, recently noted the fact that what we have now is not the Constitution envisioned by our framers, because of judicial license and popular acquiescence in law making by unelected administrative agencies. As Professor Smith put it, articulating a major theme of this book, "For decades now, the whole project of constitutional law, in the profession and the legal academy, has centrally consisted of providing legitimation for the administrative state and for an active judicial implementation of a progressive political agenda."[1380] In that piece Professor Smith reiterated an earlier statement that "it would be a harsh penance, worthy

---

[1378] John Finnis, Judicial Power: Past, Present, and Future, a talk given at Gray's Inn Hall 20 October 2015, published as Oxford Legal Studies Research Paper No. 2/2016 Notre Dame Law School Legal Studies Research Paper No. 1604, and available on the web at SSRN-id2710880(1).pdf (accessed 25 March 2016), at 27.

[1379] See, e.g., Scott Douglas Gerber, First Principles: The Jurisprudence of Clarence Thomas (NYU Press, 1998).

[1380] Steven D. Smith, "Constitution Day: 'The Image of Liberty,'" Research Paper No. 15–196, page 8, September 2015, University of San Diego School of Law Research Paper Series, available at http://ssrn.com/abstract= 2667088 (accessed October 7. 2015). For a penetrating book length study of our current "Administrative State," see Philip Hamberger, Is Administrative Law Unlawful? (U.Chicago Press, 2014) (Professor Hamberger answers the question he poses in the affirmative).

if not of hell at least of purgatory to be sentenced to sit in a comfortable air-conditioned office perpetually reading opinions by Justice O'Connor or Justice Kennedy."[1381] Those two, of course, as indicated earlier, are the most notable "swing" justices of the late twentieth and early twenty-first Centuries, whose opinions often seemed, to many of us, bereft of actual grounding in the Constitution. But whether or not the Supreme Court grounds its opinions in the Constitution, there is some risk to the American polity if it surrenders completely to the law professors and lawyers.

In a thoughtful essay on our current administrative state, Professor Jeremy Kessler warns that "[T]he rule of lawyers still reigns, embedding both executive action and public reaction in a legalistic discourse that continues to limit and legitimate American public policy."[1382] But those who promulgated and succeeded in having ratified the Constitution in 1787 realized that only the virtue of the American people could preserve republican government in this country. This has not changed in two and one quarter centuries, and it is perhaps time now, as John Finnis hints, for the American people themselves to save us from the politicians and the professors. Surely the political ferment leading up to the Presidential elections of 2016, with the rise of anti-Establishment candidates in both parties, indicates a widespread perception that something has gone wrong with the operation of our Constitutional system, which to many Americans now seems rigged to favor the federal leviathan and those who benefit from its operations, many of whom occupy positions in the elite academy, and many of whom are or have been law professors. Many of these professors, as we have seen, have understood,

---

[1381] Smith, *supra* note 1380, at 9.

[1382] Jeremy K. Kessler, Book Review: The Struggle for Administrative Legitimacy (Reviewing Daniel R. Ernst, Tocqueville's Nightmare: The Administrative State Emerges in America 1900–1940 (Harvard, 2014)), 129 Harv. L. Rev. 718, 761 (2016).

articulated and imagined an American law that is now a danger to the legal and Constitutional foundations on which our republic rests. A real exercise of popular sovereignty, not through "popular constitutionalism,"[1383] but rather through the election of officials committed to restoring the rule of law, or even the most noble exercise of popular sovereignty, another Constitutional Convention, might now be necessary.[1384]

[1383] On popular constitutionalism see Chapter 16, *supra.*

[1384] For a suggestion of what such a Constitutional Convention might look like, see, e.g., Thomas E. Brennan, The Article V Amendatory Constitutional Convention: Keeping the Republic in the Twenty-First Century (Lexington Books, 2014).

INDEX

References are to Pages